MEDITERRANEAN
BY CRUISE SHIP

DOCUMENTATION

Passenger Name _____

Ship Name _____

Captain's Signature_____

Date of Voyage _____

Cabin Number _____

MEDITERRANEAN
By Cruise Ship

THE COMPLETE GUIDE TO MEDITERRANEAN CRUISING

ANNE VIPOND

THIRD EDITION

*YOUR PORTHOLE
COMPANION*

TM

**OCEAN
CRUISE
GUIDES**

Vancouver, Canada   Point Roberts, USA

Published by: Ocean Cruise Guides Ltd.
Canada   USA
325 English Bluff Road   PO Box 2041
Delta, BC V4M 2M9   Pt. Roberts, WA 98281-2041
Phone: (604) 948-0594 Email: info@oceancruiseguides.com
Third Edition. **Visit our web site: www.oceancruiseguides.com**
Editors: Anne Vipond, Mel-Lynda Andersen, Liz Cochien, Debbie Parker (UK), Karen Stevens, Stephen York (UK), William Kelly
Contributing Editors: Michael DeFreitas, Martin Gerretsen, Harvey Strydhorst
Cover Artwork by Alan H. Nakano.
Cover Design by Ocean Cruise Guides.
Cartography: Reid Jopson, Doug Quiring, Cartesia – USA, OCG.
Design: Ocean Cruise Guides
Printed in Canada.
Publisher: William Kelly
National Library of Canada Cataloguing in Publication Data

Vipond, Anne, 1957-
  Mediterranean by cruise ship : the complete guide to Mediterranean cruising / Anne Vipond. -- 3rd ed.

Includes index.
"Your porthole companion".
ISBN 0-9688389-3-6

1. Cruise ships--Mediterranean Region--Guidebooks.
2. Mediterranean Region--Guidebooks. I. Title.

D973.V56 2004   910'.91822   C2004-901489-7

CONTENTS

Santorini

PART TWO

THE VOYAGE & THE PORTS

Villefranche

Back in the mists of antiquity, the Mediterranean was the centre of the known world. Even after the seafaring Phoenicians ventured beyond the Pillars of Hercules, the Mediterranean remained the cradle of Western civilization. Empires rose and fell along its shores, and over the millennia much blood was spilled into Homer's wine-dark sea as various nations battled one another for world supremacy. Great armies marched up and down its coastal plains, and fleets of war ships sailed across its waters.

Today, as the birthplace of Western civilization, the Mediterranean offers cruise passengers a rich variety of destinations spanning 5,000 years of human history. Nowhere else in the world is there such a concentration of architectural wonders and artistic masterpieces. Cities of past glory now disarm visitors not only with their ancient ruins and Renaissance palaces, but with their waterfront promenades, outdoor cafes and chic boutiques. Baroque churches face fountain-filled squares, medieval castles overlook golden beaches, and subtropical flowers flourish in a mild climate and sensuous setting that has long appealed to poets, painters and romantics. The Mediterranean is a storied sea, and its layers of history and human drama inspire a passion for living. This intensity extends to affairs of the heart, with many a star-crossed romance unfolding beneath the Med's sunny skies.

Mark Twain described his Mediterranean cruise, which he took on board a steamer from New York in 1867, as "a picnic on a gigantic scale." By then the fashionable 'grand tour' of Europe was so popular with British and American travellers that members of the wealthy class began seeking ever more exclusive modes of travel in the form of Pullman rail cars, stately hotels and lavish ocean liners. Today we can all embark on a grand tour of the Mediterranean, where an expanding fleet of modern cruise ships now carries passengers from port to port in unsurpassed luxury and comfort.

A Mediterranean cruise is a heady mix of high culture and hedonism, an opportunity to indulge in sybaritic pleasures while enriching the mind with art and learning. As the world embarks upon a new millennium, the need to look back and understand where we came from is more compelling than ever. Cruising the Mediterranean Sea is an ideal way to revisit the past while thoroughly enjoying the here and now.

A cruise ship lies at anchor off Sorrento on Italy's south coast.

Porch of the Caryatids at the Acropolis in Athens.

Fine dining and quiet moments at the ship's rail are part of the timeless appeal of a cruise holiday.

Amalfi coast

PART I

GENERAL INFORMATION

CHOOSING YOUR CRUISE

The Mediterranean Sea, bordered by three continents and over a dozen countries, offers an extraordinary diversity of cruise destinations, with ports of call ranging from grand cities to idyllic islands. Ships plying the Mediterranean are as diverse as their destinations, and some of the newest and largest premium ships are currently offering Mediterranean cruises, along with a host of small luxury ships. (For more detail, please refer to the cruise line glossary at the back of this book.) The length of a Mediterranean cruise can vary, usually ranging from one to two weeks, and both loop cruises (which terminate at their port of departure) and line cruises (which depart one port and terminate at another) are available. The ships dock at the large ports, but often anchor and tender passengers ashore at smaller ports, such as those along the Riviera or among the Greek Islands.

Each spring, following a winter in the Caribbean, cruise ships begin arriving in the Mediterranean. Their transatlantic crossings often include stops at the Madeira and Canary Islands, as well as Morocco and Lisbon, before entering the Mediterranean Sea. Western Mediterranean ports of call include Gibraltar, Malaga and the Balearic Islands of Majorca and Minorca, with Barcelona a popular base port. The French ports of Marseille, Nice and others along the Côte D'Azur are also featured in western itineraries, as are the Italian islands of Sardinia and Sicily. The 'boot' of Italy lies in the middle of the Mediterranean and its famous ports are included in both western and eastern cruises. The Italian Riviera, Livorno (Florence's seaport),

Civitavecchia (Rome's seaport) and Naples are all popular stops, as of course is Venice, where ships often dock overnight so that passengers can fully enjoy this enchanting city.

Greece's mainland ports and far-flung islands are highlighted in eastern cruises, as are the intriguing Turkish destinations of Istanbul and ancient Ephesus. An eastern cruise might also include the Black Sea and Egypt's seaports of Alexandria and Port Said, both providing access to Cairo and the Great Pyramids.

Santorini is one of numerous Greek Islands visited by cruise ships.

Approaching Venice by ship is one of life's most memorable travel experiences.

The easiest way to choose a Mediterranean cruise is to visit a travel agent who specializes in cruises. Look for an agency displaying the CLIA logo, indicating its agents have received training from the Cruise Lines International Association. The cruise lines strongly encourage their customers to book through a travel agent with CLIA accreditation, and these qualified agents are usually a very good source of information, with personal knowledge of many ships. They are able to provide pertinent detail regarding on-board atmosphere, cabin selection and pricing. Supplied with the relevant information, i.e. which countries or specific destinations you would like to visit, the length of cruise you wish to take, and the type of onboard atmosphere you are seeking, a travel agent can recommend suitable itineraries and ships.

The cruise lines' websites and brochures are another good source of information regarding itineraries and the onboard atmosphere offered on their ships. Flights can be booked through the cruise company, these air/sea arrangements including ground transportation between airport and pier, along with baggage handling. Hotel packages are also available through the cruise lines, enabling passengers to spend an extra day or two in port before boarding their ship or after disembarking at the end of a cruise, and these packages include transfers between airport, hotel and pier.

Spring and fall are considered the best months for cruising the Med, although some ships remain there throughout the summer. The bulk of the fleet heads to Europe's northern waters for July and August, returning to the Med in September after the peak tourist season has ended but the weather is still warm and sunny. Mid-summer temperatures in southern Italy and parts of Greece can climb into the 90s, and cities such as Athens and Rome tend to be hot and crowded in July and August. On the other hand, coastal resorts such as the Balearic Islands and the French and Italian Riviera all offer ideal beach weather at the height of summer.

SHORE EXCURSIONS

The cruise lines offer organized shore excursions for the convenience of their passengers, and these are described in a booklet that is enclosed with your cruise tickets, as well as at on-board presentations given by the ship's shore excursion manager. With several cruise lines, the offered shore excursions can also be previewed on their websites, with the option of pre-booking your shore excursions on-line. Regardless of whether you book an excursion before or during your cruise, the charge for such excursions varies, depending on its length (half day / full day) and the activities involved. Most shore excursions are fairly priced and the local tour operators used are reliable and monitored by the cruise companies, with the added advantage that the ship will wait for any of its overdue excursions.

However, independent-minded passengers need not feel that pre-booked shore excursions are their only option when exploring various ports of call. If the ship docks right beside a town or city centre, a person can simply set off on foot to do some sightseeing and shopping. If the town centre is a few miles from the port, the cruise lines often offer a shuttle service. In some instances, such as Rome and Florence, where the city is an hour or more away from its seaport, your options include taking a train or hiring a taxi. Passengers who like the idea of exploring these cities on their own but wish to avoid any anxiety about getting back to the ship on time, may want to consider a ship-organized excursion that provides transportation to and from the city centre but leaves you to see the sights on your own before reboarding the coach at a pre-appointed time for the ride back to the ship.

Train travel in Europe is very efficient and is a convenient way to see a port's nearby attractions. The ship's shore excursion manager will likely have a current schedule, which is also posted at the local train station. Double-check the schedule at the other end before leaving the station to take in the local sights. Although the trains generally run on sched-

Local attractions can often be reached on foot, such as those on the Greek island of Patmos.

Rented scooters are often a good way to get around at the small ports of call. (Right) Touring a Greek isle by motor scooter.

ule, it's best not to plan your return train ride too close to the ship's time of departure, just in case there's an unforeseen delay. Local currency is needed to purchase a ticket. There are two classes of tickets, with first class being more expensive but allowing you to ride in slightly better cars. (A rail pass is another option for passengers planning an extended stay in Europe before or after their cruise; for details, see page 19). The local buses are often a good way to cover short distances, but are not recommended for longer trips, as they make frequent stops and are not always as reliable as trains for keeping to their schedules. Bus tickets are usually sold at local newsstands.

Taxis may seem expensive, but if you're splitting the fare with a few other people it can often be more economical than a ship-organized excursion. Keep in mind that some taxi drivers make better 'guides' than others, and be sure to agree on the fare before getting into the taxi. To avoid possible miscommunication due to a language barrier, it's a good idea to write on a piece of paper the exact amount both parties have agreed upon and show it to the driver to be certain he understands what you are willing to pay at the end of the trip. Don't hesitate to bargain with a few drivers before making your decision, and remember that a tip is certainly warranted if the driver proves to be pleasant and helpful. If you hail a taxi in a large city, the driver will simply charge you the metered fare.

Renting a car or motor scooter is often a good way to explore an island destination, but it's not recommended when visiting large cities where traffic can be extremely congested and fast-paced. Boat travel is another option in some ports such as Venice, where large boats serve as local buses, and taxis come in the form of motor boats. At Naples, ferries and hydrofoils transport visitors to the nearby isle of Capri, and at small ports on the Italian Riviera and the Greek Islands, boat transport is often the best way to see the area's sights.

Sightseeing in car-free Venice is done by boat and on foot.

Full-day shore excursions organized by the cruise lines are usually a combination of driving tour, guided walking tour and lunch at a local restaurant, with an interlude for shopping. The tour guides are local people providing narration of the sights and answering any questions you might have. When joining a ship-organized excursion, the decision to tip your guide or driver is personal and if you like the service, a tip of US$1 per person for a half-day tour and $2 per person for a full-day tour is standard.

The local sights to be seen on Mediterranean shore excursions include ancient ruins, medieval fortresses and Renaissance palaces. There is often a fair amount of walking involved, especially at the ruins where stone steps and uneven grades are common. In medieval towns and city quarters, where the roads are too narrow for vehicles, on foot is often the only way to explore the winding cobblestone streets.

PRE- AND POST-CRUISE STAYS

If time allows, fly to your port of embarkation at least a day before the cruise begins, thus avoiding the stress of making same-day travel connections. Better yet, stay two or three nights at your embarkation port to recover from jet lag, relax and have time to enjoy the local sights. Lisbon, Barcelona, Nice, Genoa, Rome (seaport: Civitavecchia), Venice, Athens (seaport: Pireaus), and Istanbul are all used as base ports for Mediterranean cruises. Thus, you could, for example, fly to Athens and spend a few days visiting the Acropolis and other famous sites before embarking on an eastern Mediterranean cruise that terminates in, for instance, Rome – where you could spend a few days exploring and enjoying the city before flying home.

Be sure to book your accommodations ahead of time, either through your travel agent or as part of a pre- or post-cruise package offered by the cruise line, the latter guaranteeing a level of accommodation on par with the ship and including transfers between pier and hotel. Reservations are critical in the major cities, and a travel agent will be able to get you the best rate. Let your agent know your priorities in terms of location. For instance, visitors to Barcelona can stay at a hotel in the heart of the historic Gothic quarter, or they can opt to stay in the city's main shopping district at one of numerous hotels located north of Placa de Catalunya.

Accommodations range from spartan to luxurious, and the hotel packages offered by the premium cruise lines usually utilize 4-star hotels, ensuring their clients a consistency of comfort and service. Once you have checked into your hotel, remember that the concierge and front desk staff offer a wealth of information for foreign visitors. They can direct you to the best shops and restaurants, and will usually provide miscellaneous services upon request, such as obtaining information on local tours or calling a taxi and confirming the destination and fare with your driver. If you're part of an organized cruise-tour, an experienced guide employed by the cruise line will be available to answer any questions (see next section on Land Tours).

If you're travelling with friends, other pre- and post-cruise options include weekly rentals of an apartment or townhouse. In Venice, for instance, a group of eight could rent for a week a palazzetto within walking distance of St. Mark's Square for about US$3000.

A water taxi pulls up to the entrance of the four-star Luna Baglioni hotel in Venice.

LAND TOURS

A cruise is a perfect opportunity to combine a vacation at sea with a land-based holiday, and a fully escorted cruisetour is an ideal way to see more of a European country. The tours offered by the cruise lines are a seamless form of travel, for the cruise companies maintain the same level of service on land as at sea, with well-planned itineraries, first-class hotel accommodations and professional tour direction. Hotels are centrally located, within walking distance of major attractions and shopping streets, and several hosted meals are often part of the package, while plenty of free time allows clients to do a bit of independent sightseeing, leisurely shopping or lingering in a sidewalk cafe. The group travels by comfortable motor coach or high-speed train, and the tour guides employed by the cruise companies are well-educated and highly qualified to introduce visitors to the history, culture and cuisine of the country they are visiting. All tours must be booked at the same time as the cruise, as part of a cruisetour package.

Italy is well covered by cruisetours, including six- and seven-night trips between Venice and Rome that take in several cities and towns of northern Italy as well as the hilltop towns of Tuscany and Umbria (see Chapter 4, Northern Italy, pages 206 and 207). Spain's interior is covered by land tours combined with cruises out of Barcelona, with Seville, Madrid and Toledo included in five-night itineraries. And Portugal's seaside villlages and summer palaces are featured in three-night cruisetours out of Lisbon.

If you plan to embark on an independent tour outside the major cities, your options include renting a car or purchasing a rail pass. If

Spain's ancient city of Toledo, overlooking a gorge of the Tagus River, is filled with famous landmarks.

you cherish total independence and the freedom to hop from village to village, stopping on a whim to admire a valley view or coastal lookout, then renting a car is probably for you. When reserving a car, confirm a number of details, such as whether the 'all-inclusive' rate includes taxes, drop-off charges and unlimited kilometres. European cars are generally smaller than North American models, with a 'compact' comfortably holding two people and two pieces of luggage; the next size up is usually worth the extra cost. Standard-shift transmissions are popular in Europe, but automatics are available in larger cars at higher rates. If you plan to use a credit card for insurance, ask for a copy of the policy's coverage; theft protection insurance is also required in some countries.

Rail travel is another option for independent travel in Europe. It is efficient and comfortable, and is a relaxing way to see the countryside as you settle into your window seat and watch the scenery slide by. An extensive rail system connects countries, cities, towns and villages, and most train stations are centrally located – whether in a resort town or a large city – so your hotel will likely be just a short taxi ride away.

In 1958, Western Europe's railroads developed the idea of an easy-to-use, multi-country, pre-paid ticket for unlimited mileage use, and that concept evolved into the popular Eurailpass, which now comes in a variety of forms. The range of passes offered by Rail Europe is exhaustive, including the EurailDrive Pass with which a person can combine four days of unlimited train travel with two days of car rental through Avis or Hertz. The flexible Eurorail Select pass has replaced the Europass and provides unlimited first-class train travel within a two-month period for lengths of five, six, eight, 10 or 15 days, and is valid

High speed trains pull into the Atocha Station in Madrid.

Train travel in Europe is an efficient and relaxing way to get around. (Above and left) Nice's train station.

in three, four or five bordering countries, depending on the specific pass purchased. To obtain more information about Rail Europe's selection of passes, visit the company's website at www.raileurope.com. All passes must be purchased before you leave for Europe, and reservations are required for some trains. Porters and luggage carts are not always available, so you must be prepared to handle your own baggage if travelling by train.

Accommodations should be reserved in advance when travelling by train, while car travel affords a bit more flexibility. Each country offers unique and varied accommodations, and it's best to do some research ahead of time. Places to stay in Portugal include *pousadas* (stately castles), which are palaces and private manor houses that have been converted into hotels. In Spain, many of the *paradores* (state-operated tourist hotels) are housed in castles, palaces, monasteries and convents that have been refurbished into three- and four-star hotels. France offers everything from grand hotels to family-run country inns serving regional cuisine. And in Italy, an umbrella organization called Agriturismo ('farm stays') provides information on an extensive network of rural bed-and-breakfast inns. Located on quiet counry roads, with views of valley fields and vineyards, these Italian B&B's are housed in country estates and quaint farmhouses.

There are hundreds of monasteries and convents throughout Europe, many of which welcome overnight visitors who enjoy the spartan but clean accommodations and the warm hospitality. Villa rentals are also popular with people travelling as a small group, and properties are available in Greece, France, Spain and Portugal, as well as Italy. There are numerous websites providing information on villa rentals. Those that include details and photos of each property, and that allow travellers to book directly with a villa owner, are your best bet. Each country's official tourism department is another source of helpful information regarding local accommodations, as is your travel agent.

(Right) Ritz Hotel, Madrid.
(Below) Spain's celebrated
Benedictine monastery on
Montserrat mountain near
Barcelona.

SPAIN & PORTUGAL

An 18th-century Portuguese palace at Queluz, near Lisbon.

Gothic cathedral in Palma, Majorca.

Plaza del Ayuntamiento, Valencia.

A whitewashed village on Gran Canaria island.

Cala Galdana, Minorca.

Arc del Triomf, Barcelona.

FRANCE

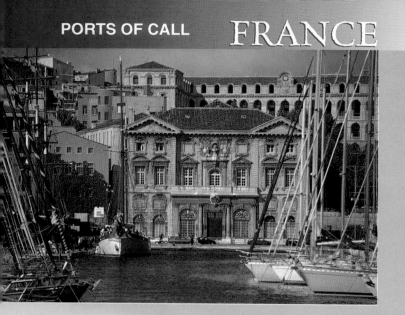

Vieux Port, Marseille.

Villefranche on the French Riviera.

Monaco (above)

A sidewalk cafe in Aix-en-Provence.

Flowers and fountains in Place Massena, Nice.

The ornate exterior of Monte Carlo's famous casino complex.

ITALY

Portofino, on the Italian Riviera.

A lone gondola crosses the Canale della Giudecca of Venice.

The tower that made Pisa famous.

Piazza Navona, Rome.

Mount Vesuvius looms above the Bay of Naples.

The view from Taormina, Sicily.

Ponte Vecchio on the Arno River, Florence.

The Parthenon stands atop the Acropolis in Athens.

A quiet street in Plaka, Athens.

A hidden square in the charming village of Chora, Patmos.

Lovely gardens lie outside the Grand Master's Palace in Old Rhodes.

A cruise ship anchors off the enchanting island of Santorini.

A local fisherman at Navplion on the Peloponnese peninsula.

TURKEY

The beautiful Hagia Sophia (above), Istanbul.

Observation Tower of Topkapi Palace (above). Istanbul's famous Grande Rue de Pera (left) is now Istiklal Caddesi.

Detail from the kaftan of Mehmet II.

Dolmabahçe Palace, Istanbul

The Library of Celsus at Ephesus.

A vendor with fresh simit – a sesame-coated bread ring – near Mermerlie Beach, Antalya.

The skyline of Antalya with its famous Grooved Minaret in the distance

DOCUMENTATION

Several weeks before your departure date, you will no doubt receive all pertinent documentation for your trip, including your cruise ticket, airline ticket (if applicable), luggage tags, a customs and immigration form, and information regarding your cruise. All of this documentation should be read carefully, the forms filled in, and a detailed itinerary left with a friend or family member in case someone needs to contact you while you're away. Be sure to include the name of your ship, its phone number and the applicable ocean code, as well as your cabin number – all of which will be included in your cruise documents. With this information, a person can call the international telephone operator and place a satellite call to your ship in an emergency.

A valid passport is required for travel to all countries bordering the Mediterranean. As a precaution, you should photocopy the identification page of your passport, along with your driver's licence and any credit cards you will be taking on your trip. Keep one copy of this photocopied information with you, separate from your passport and wallet, and leave another copy at home. A few countries in the Mediterranean region, such as Egypt, also require an entry visa, and your travel agent can advise you beforehand of any visa requirements your cruise might entail. With regard to travel insurance, a comprehensive policy can be bought when you book your cruise – one that covers trip cancellation, delayed departure, medical expenses, personal accident and liability, lost baggage and money, and legal expenses.

CURRENCY

When travelling abroad, it's best to take various forms of currency – cash, credit cards, bank cards and travellers cheques. If you're staying in a foreign city for a few days before or after your cruise, obtain some petty cash in that country's currency to cover taxi fares and other incidentals. Major credit cards are accepted by most hotels and restaurants, and ATM machines are widespread in larger cities.

Once you're aboard your ship, travellers cheques can be cashed at the purser's office and it's sometimes possible to obtain cash advances from credit cards. Most ships also have a currency exchange facility on board, offering a competitive rate on foreign currencies, so that passengers needn't spend time at each port of call exchanging funds into local currency. The rates offered by local currency exchange offices can vary and some will charge a higher commission on Sundays. The euro is now the official currency in member nations of the European Economic Community, making money transactions much simpler for cruise passengers visiting Greece, Italy, France, Spain and Portugal. The approximate rate of exchange is one euro costing $1.20 US and $1.60 CDN.

For major purchases or expenses, a credit card is recommended (rather than carrying large amounts of cash) and although a currency conversion fee is charged (usually 2 or 3%), the difference in service charges between using a credit card or withdrawing cash in the local currency from an ATM is not substantial. It's best to carry several credit cards, and married couples should arrange for at least one set of separate cards (without joint signing privileges) in case one spouse loses his or her wallet and all of the couple's joint cards have to be cancelled. It's also wise to take along a handful of small US bills and euros to cover possible tips for guides and other sundries when ashore.

HEALTH PRECAUTIONS

Vaccinations are not compulsory for a Mediterranean cruise, but you may want to consult your doctor in this regard. All ships have a fully equipped medical centre with a doctor and nurses. Passengers needing medical attention are billed at private rates which are added to their shipboard account. This invoice can be submitted to your insurance company upon your return home. You may already have supplementary health insurance through a credit card, automobile club policy or employment health plan, but you should check these carefully. Whatever policy you choose for your trip, carry details of it with you and documents showing that you are covered by a plan.

The overall standards of cleanliness on board cruise ships are extremely high, yet contagious viruses that are spread by person-to-person contact (such as the Norwalk-like stomach virus, which is a brief but severe gastrointestinal illness) do occasionally plague a small percentage of passengers. To avoid contracting such a virus, practise frequent, thorough handwashing with warm, soapy water.

Motion sickness is not a widespread or prolonged problem for most passengers, but for those who are susceptible, a number of remedies are available. One is a special wrist band, the balls of which rest on an acupressure point. These 'sea bands' are available at most drug stores. Another option is to chew meclizine tablets (usually available at the ship's infirmary) or take Dramamine, an over-the-counter antihistamine. It's best to take these pills ahead of time, before you feel too nauseous, and they may make you drowsy. Fresh air is one of the best antidotes, so stepping out on deck is often all that's needed to counter any queasiness. Other simple remedies include sipping ginger ale, nibbling dry crackers and an apple, or lying down.

To avoid traveller's diarrhea, it's best to drink bottled water when ashore, but don't worry about drinking the wine. Recent studies have shown that a glass of wine – either red or white – is a good way to fend off traveller's diarrhea. Wine contains a mild disinfectant that quickly destroys a variety of bacteria that can cause stomach problems. Wine loses its antidiarrheal advantage over time, so don't rely on vintages over 10 years old to be effective.

WHAT TO PACK

Pack casual attire for daytime wear – both aboard the ship and in port. The weather will be generally dry and sunny, but spring and fall temperatures in the Mediterranean can vary from cool to hot, so pack

Visitors to monasteries must cover their shoulders and legs.

clothes that can be layered. Cool, loose cotton clothes are recommended for the summertime heat, as are sunglasses and a wide-brimmed hat. A comfortable pair of rubber-soled shoes is essential for walking along cobblestone streets, and a light sweater or jacket will fend off the air-conditioning in restaurants, museums and aboard motorcoaches. Some European ports, such as Venice, can be chilly in late October, so pack one warm sweater or jacket if you're travelling at this time of year.

The dress code for churches and monasteries dictates that legs and shoulders be covered, so keep this in mind when heading ashore – either wear slacks or carry a wrap that can be tied around your waist as an ankle-length cover-up before entering religious sites. In Muslim countries, conservative attire is recommended, and removal of shoes is mandatory before entering mosques.

Your evening wear should include something suitable for the two or three formal nights held on board most ships. Women wear gowns or cocktail dresses, and men favour suits. For informal evenings, the women wear dresses, skirts or slacks, and the men wear jackets with either a shirt and tie or an open-necked sports shirt.

Check with your travel agent regarding on-board facilities; for instance, most cabins will have a built-in hair dryer. Many ships have coin-operated laundrettes with ironing boards; those that don't usually provide laundry service at an extra charge. Steam pressing and dry cleaning are standard services on most ships, and it's easy to do hand washing in your cabin. Poolside towels are provided by the ship, as are beach towels – upon request – for taking ashore.

To save room in your suitcase, pack sample sizes of toothpaste and other toiletries, which can also be purchased on board the ship. If you wear prescription eyeglasses or contact lenses, consider packing a spare pair. Keep prescribed medication in original, labelled containers and carry a doctor's prescription for any controlled drug. Other items you may want to bring along are a small pair of binoculars and a pocket calculator for tabulating exchange rates. And be sure to keep all valuables, such as travellers cheques, camera and expensive jewellery, in your carry-on luggage, as well as all prescription medicine and documentation, such as your passport, tickets and a copy of your insurance policy. Last but not least, be sure to leave room in one of your suitcases for souvenirs.

LIFE ABOARD

Cabins – also called staterooms – vary in size, ranging from standard inside cabins to suites with a verandah. Whatever the size of your accommodation, it will be clean and comfortable. If your budget permits, an outside cabin is preferable for gauging the weather and orienting yourself at a new port. Your cabin storage space will include a closet for hanging dresses and suits, and drawers to hold your other clothes and miscellaneous items. Valuables can be left in your stateroom safe or in a safety deposit box at the front office, also called the purser's office.

A suite on a modern cruise ship.

Both casual and formal dining are offered on the large ships, with breakfast and lunch available in the buffet-style lido restaurant or at an open seating in the main dining room. Dinner is served at two sittings in the dining room and, when booking your cruise, you will be asked to indicate your preference for first or second sitting at dinner. Some people prefer the first sitting as it leaves an entire evening afterwards to enjoy the stage shows and other venues. On the other hand, the second sitting allows plenty of time, after a full day in port, to freshen up before dinner. Many ships also offer alternative dining – small specialty restaurants that require a reservation and for which there is usually a charge (about $25 per person). Room service is also available, free of charge, for all meals and in-between snacks.

EXTRA EXPENSES

There are few additional expenses once you board a cruise ship. All meals are included, as are stage shows, lectures, movies, exercise classes and other activities held in the ship's public areas. Personal services and shore excursions, however, are extra as are any alcoholic drinks you might order in a ship's lounge or with a meal in the dining room. Most ships are cashless societies in which passengers sign for incidental expenses, which are itemized on a final statement that is slipped under your cabin door during the last night of your cruise and settled at the front office by credit card or cash.

Although **tipping** is a cruising tradition, no passenger is obligated to give out tips at the end of a cruise. However, most passengers do tip because the service is usually worth rewarding. A general guideline for tipping is to give your cabin steward US$3.50 per passenger per day, your waiter the same amount, and your assistant waiter half that amount. Tips are handed out during the last evening of your cruise or can be charged to your shipboard account.

☎ PHONING AND EMAIILING HOME

Passengers can phone home from the ship, either at the ship's radio office or by placing a direct satellite telephone call. This is expensive, however, and unless the call is urgent you may want to wait and place your call from a land-based phone. Using a prepaid telephone card is an easy way to place long-distance calls while in port. Sold on board some ships, and available at local newsstands and tobacconists, these cards allow you to make international and domestic calls from any touch-tone phone. If you prefer to use a personal calling card, the various telephone access codes are usually provided by the cruise ship staff in a daily port information handout or in the respective chapters of this book. Refer to the map (below) to determine the time difference before placing a call. E-mail is another way to keep in touch and most ships now have internet cafes where passengers have access to on-line computers and are charged for their use on a per-minute basis. If you plan to send frequent e-mails while on your cruise, you may want to open a hotmail account upon embarkation.

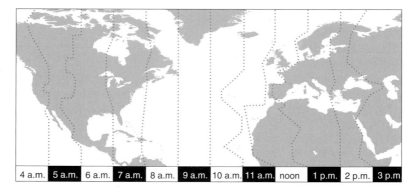

| 4 a.m. | 5 a.m. | 6 a.m. | 7 a.m. | 8 a.m. | 9 a.m. | 10 a.m. | 11 a.m. | noon | 1 p.m. | 2 p.m. | 3 p.m |

SECURITY

While security is not a major concern when on board the ship, you should take some precautions when venturing ashore. Property crime can occur anywhere, but tourists are especially vulnerable because they carry large amounts of money, as well as cameras and other valuables. Keep all credit cards and most of your cash securely stowed in an inside pocket of your clothes or shoulder bag, and keep a few small bills in a readily accessible pocket so you're not pulling out your wallet to pay for small impromptu purchases from street vendors.

Be aware of potential thieves. Many operate in pairs, with one creating a distraction, such as dropping a handful of coins, while the other lifts their victim's wallet. Don't wear expensive jewellery and don't wear a fanny pack because a professional pickpocket with surgical scissors can quickly snip the strap and lift your pack without you even noticing. A money belt or pouch concealed beneath your clothes is a much safer way to carry money. Leave your passport and other valuables in your cabin safe when going ashore.

One of the best lines of defence with potential thieves is to avoid advertising the fact that you're a tourist. Europeans tend to dress conservatively in the cities, favouring slacks, blazers and leather shoes, all in muted colours. Visitors wearing brightly coloured shorts and t-shirts, baseball caps and sneakers look like tourists and are thus easy targets for pickpockets. Situations requiring caution include any place where there are crowds of people, and at airports and train stations, where you should never turn your back on your luggage. When hiring a taxi, watch to make sure every piece of luggage is loaded into the trunk, and never leave valuables in a rented car.

HOLIDAY PHOTOS

If you are taking a new camera on your trip, shoot and develop a roll of film at home beforehand or, if digital, download the images to your computer to make sure the camera works properly and that you understand all of its features. Put fresh batteries in your camera and pack plenty of film. For automatic cameras, 200-ASA print film is your best choice for all-around lighting conditions, and this speed of film is less likely to be damaged by the powerful X-ray machines now used at airports. Exposed but undeveloped film should not be put in checked luggage but placed in a carry-on bag where it can withstand about five X-rays at walk-through security checkpoints before being damaged. Another option is to place your rolls of film in a see-through plastic bag and ask for a hand inspection, or have your film developed on board the ship. If you're using a digital camera, take an extra battery pack and be sure to have a total of at least 128 mb of flash card memory storage or a laptop computer to download your images.

SHOPPING

Most stores and upscale shops accept all major credit cards, but it's best to have local currency (in most cases the euro) for small and impromptu purchases. Value Added Tax is attached to most purchases in Europe, and North American visitors can obtain a refund by first requesting a refund form in the store where they make their purchase, then having it stamped by customs staff in the airport prior to departure. Refunds can be obtained on the spot or after you are home, by sending the form to the appropriate office. Check with your travel agent or local customs office before leaving home to determine your duty-free allowances.

The Mediterranean is rich in centuries-old craftsmanship, and memorable souvenirs include hand-painted ceramics, lustreware, terracotta pottery and decorative tiles. Hand-woven carpets, embroidered linens and delicate laceware are other traditional crafts, as is gold filigree jewellery. In the major cities and tourist resorts you will find boutiques selling high-fashion clothing, leather goods and jewellery.

The Mediterranean Sea, cobalt blue and robust, is a sea with a great past. Western history began along its shoreline and its well travelled waters have transported heroes, prophets and emperors to their appointments with destiny. For thousands of years, this inland sea has inspired hope and instilled fear in mariners, living up to Homer's description of being capricious and powerful, peaceful and calming.

For officers of a modern cruise ship, the Mediterranean does not present the same problems as it did to such legendary seafarers as Odysseus, and passengers cruising the Mediterranean can simply sit back and ponder the complex workings of a modern cruise ship. Where once a voyage could take many weeks from Alexandria to Rome, now it is only a matter of days. Yet, despite remarkable advancements in technology, many aspects of sea travel have remained the same throughout the centuries.

When mariners began venturing onto open seas, the complexities of a ship and its running gear prompted mariners to develop their own nomenclature. A colourful vocabulary, it has been adapted with lyrical precision to describe each task. As quoted in Smythe's Sailor's Word-Book, "How could the whereabouts of an aching tooth be better pointed out to an operative dentist than Jack's, 'Tis the aftermost grinder aloft, on the starboard quarter.'"

During the 15th century, when commerce with distant lands became increasingly profitable, trading countries began investing in improvements in ship design. This resulted in stronger, faster ships with better sailing characteristics. Chart making was also improved, as were navigational instruments, all of which resulted in Western influences spreading around the world. It is this legacy of discovery, combined with tales of daring and adventure, which has given shipboard travel an aura of romance and mystique.

Sea travel attained elegance in the late 19th century when grand transatlantic ocean liners were introduced. Opulent and breathtaking inside, graceful and inspiring to gaze upon from shore these ships generally featured a large raked bow, modest stern and creative finish to the funnel. Although some design aspects have changed, today's cruise ships are quite similar to those built in past decades.

While passengers enjoy the comforts and luxury provided them, the crew work around the clock to ensure a smooth, safe passage. It is from the bridge, located at the bow (or front) of the ship, that the officers use an array of computerized instrumen-

An example of today's advanced and beautiful new ships is the
Dawn Princess (77,000 tons), launched by Princess Cruises in 1997.

tation to assist with navigation and provide information for all ship
operations.

HOW SHIPS MOVE

Ships are pushed through the water with the turning of propellers, two
of which are usually used on cruise ships. A propeller is like a screw
threading its way through the sea, pushing water away from its pitched
blades. Props can be 15 to 20 feet in diameter on large cruise ships and
turn slowly at 100 to 150 revolutions per minute. It takes a lot of horse-
power – about 30,000 on a large ship – to make these propellers push a
ship along and almost all cruise ships use diesel engines to do the work.
It's the job of the chief engineer and his crew to keep these engines running efficiently.

In addition to propelling the ship, the engines generate electrical
power for the rest of the ship. Computer technology has transformed
the workings of a ship's engine room which, in addition to improving
engine efficiency, also gives more control and information to the crew
on the bridge. The bridge crew can tap into any amount of engine
power by moving small levers which adjust the angle (or pitch) of the
propeller blades which in turns alters the speed of the ship.

The amount of soot and smoke emitted from today's ships is a fraction of that produced by the early ocean liners. Up to the end of the
First World War, most ships used vast amounts of coal to heat large
boilers placed along the length of the lower part of the ship. As a result,
ocean liners of the past usually had two and sometimes three funnels to
dispel the exhaust. The *Titanic* had four with one being a false funnel.

After the Second World War, more efficient steam-turbine engines
replaced coal with diesel oil for generating power, usually requiring
just one funnel to collect and disperse the gases. Diesel engines on
modern ships transmit power either directly through a transmission,
which can result in some vibration felt throughout the ship, or by sup-
plying electricity to large motors that smoothly turn the prop shafts.
Steam-driven ships, a few of which are still in operation, also run very
smoothly.

To turn a ship, one or more rudders are used. When a ship is moving, the crew turns the helm, which is shaped like a steering wheel and

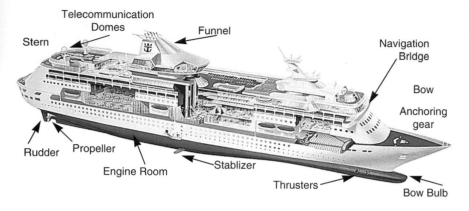

is connected to the rudder by a hydraulic arm. Turning a ship with a rudder can be compared to turning a canoe with a paddle. The person seated in the rear of a canoe can turn it to the left or right by dipping the paddle in the water and holding it at an angle.

A ship's underwater appendages and innovations help the crew in different ways. Most ships have stabilizers, which are small wings located near the middle of the ship about 10 feet below the water's surface. The angle of the wings is constantly adjusted to minimize any rolling motion of the ship. A symbol which looks like an upside-down question mark with two small circles inside is painted on the hull near the bow to indicate the location of the ship's bow thrusters. Thrusters have almost entirely replaced the use of tugboats for manoeuvring the ship sideways. The bow bulb reduces the bow wave, allowing a ship's hull to move more efficiently through the water, thus saving fuel.

SHIP SIZE -ROLE OF SERVICE STAFF

A ship's size is determined by measurements that result in a figure called tonnage. There are approximately 100 cubic feet to a measured ton. Cruise ships used to be called large if they exceeded 30,000 tons and, while that's still a big ship, most new ships are over 50,000 tons. Perhaps more important than a ship's size is the space ratio for its passengers. This can be determined by taking a ship's tonnage (usually noted in the cruise line brochure) and dividing it by passenger capacity. This ratio is usually between 20 and 40 – the higher the number, the more space per passenger. A ship with a high space ratio can carry many hundreds of passengers but not feel crowded.

At the stern of every ship, below its name, is the ship's country of registry. It may be surprising to note that your ship is registered in Monrovia, Liberia, Panama or the Bahamas. Certain countries grant registry to a cruise line's ships for a flat fee, without restrictions and onerous charges. Consequently, ships fly these 'flags of convenience' for tax reasons. Where a ship is registered has no bearing on the service and product on board.

The captain, chief engineer, and their officers and crew make up only a small portion of total staff on board a ship. The majority of employees, such as stewards and waiters, attend to the passengers. In charge of this service staff is the hotel manager (sometimes called the chief purser) who is second in rank only to the ship's captain. Reporting to the hotel manager are various managers in charge of departments ranging from galley staff to housekeeping staff. Most visible is the cruise director, who oversees the ship's entertainment and on-board events, and who usually has a background in show business.

Food is a very important issue on cruise ships and the quality and preparation of meals receives a great deal of attention. Quality control begins on the dock as various food managers inspect shipments before they are brought on board. Most ships also undergo voluntary inspections by local health authorities.

NAVIGATIONAL CHALLENGES OF THE MEDITERRANEAN

Although the Mediterranean is the world's largest inland sea at just under one million square miles, this body of water doesn't possess the characteristics of an open ocean, such as swell, and captains generally regard the Mediterranean as one of the safest and easiest cruise areas to navigate.

Thoroughly charted, the Mediterranean is surprisingly deep in places. Thirty miles west of Greece's Peloponnese Peninsula, along a major subduction zone, the depths plunge to over 15,000 feet. Conversely, sea depths become shallow at river mouths, where silt carried downstream and deposited on the river's delta can alter the course of tributaries and reduce water depths at harbour entrances.

The Mediterranean and its adjacent bodies of water have few strong currents but two passes of concern are the Straits of Messina, lying between Sicily and the 'toe' of Italy, and the Dardanelles, leading to the Sea of Marmara and Istanbul. In both cases, however, currents rarely exceed five knots, which modern ships can handle without difficulty.

The enclosed Mediterranean produces smaller waves than an open ocean, but there can on occasion be steep seas if the wind is strong. Although this normally doesn't present a problem for modern ships, it can be uncomfortable for passengers if the ship is sailing broadside to the direction of the waves. Strong winds and choppy waves can occur in the Sea of Crete, the Tyrrhenian Sea between the Straits of Messina and Naples, and the area between Barcelona and Marseille where ships cross the Gulf of Lions. At such times, the centre of the ship in an inside cabin can be the most comfortable spot.

Many harbours of the Mediterranean are man-made, and some are quite old with narrow entrances. The entrances to Marseille, Livorno and Civitavecchia for example, are very tight and require close attention from the crew. The entrance to the ship dock at Venice is also very narrow and the west side of the docking area is shallow, making manoeuvring for large ships very challenging.

Cataclysmic events, once thought to be caused by the actions of angry gods, have since been explained by scientific data and an understanding of seismic activity. Yet, rather than discredit ancient myths, the scientific evidence offered by modern geologists and oceanographers may prove that certain legendary events did in fact occur. Indeed, the earth did shake from time to time with deafening force, huge waves did wash ashore, and islands did rise from the sea.

Such phenomena is currently happening off the coast of Sicily, where a submerged volcanic island called Graham Bank is rising to the sea's surface due to seismic activity in the area. It last emerged in 1831 when its six-month appearance sparked a diplomatic debate among Britain, Spain and the Bourbon court of Sicily, all claiming ownership of the tiny island. This time around, in hopes of claiming this new territory for Italy the moment it reappears, Sicilian divers have planted a flag on the submerged rock, which lies about 20 feet below the surface and is located in between the coasts of Sicily and Tunisia.

Through radiocarbon dating of sediment cores, scientists can now explain phenomena from the distant past, such as the formation of the Black Sea. According to the evidence, in about 5500 BC a worldwide rise in sea levels caused the waters of the Mediterranean Sea to spill into the Bosporus strait and transform an existing freshwater lake into the Black Sea. This finding has prompted speculation that the subsequent flooding of shorelines and displacement of people may have been the basis for the story of Noah's ark in the Book of Genesis.

TECTONIC BEGINNINGS

The earth's crust – called the lithosphere – is broken into large plates bordered by volcanoes and centres of earthquake activity. The granitic continental plates were once joined together as a supercontinent which began to break apart about 200 million years ago. The Mediterranean, the world's largest inland sea, was originally a vast ocean stretching across half the globe. Its surrounding land masses emerged some 30 million years ago, during the Oligocene era, when collisions of the earth's crustal plates created mountain ranges and deep sea rifts, such as the Red Sea, which formed when Africa and Arabia split. The Mediterranean Sea marks the boundary of two major plates – the

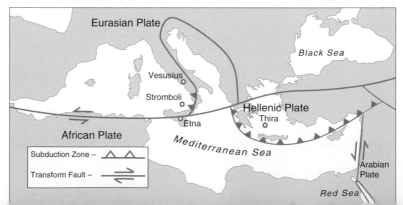

Eurasian Plate

Black Sea

Vesusius

Stromboli

Hellenic Plate

Thira

Etna

African Plate

Mediterranean Sea

Subduction Zone –

Transform Fault –

Arabian Plate

Red Sea

Eurasian and African. Much of this boundary – from the toe of Italy's 'boot' to the coast of Turkey – is a subduction zone. The world's most destructive earthquakes occur along such zones, where the leading edge of one plate is pushing beneath the edge of another. Transform faults – where the edges of two plates are sliding past one another – run along the Mediterranean's North African coastline and extend from Turkey to the Red Sea.

The biblical cities of Sodom and Gomorrah were quite likely destroyed not by 'fire and brimstone' but by earthquakes. In more recent times, an earthquake registering 6.3 on the Richter scale shook southern Turkey in June 1998, followed by two more in 1999, both in western Turkey, the latter registering a magnitude of 7.2. In February 2004, a 6.5-magnitude quake hit northern Morocco, its epicentre located beneath the sea bed near the Strait of Gibraltar. Italy has also been struck in recent years by earthquakes, including a series of quakes that battered central Italy in 1997. Increased seismic activity on Sicily in 2002 resulted in 200 small quakes which rattled the island's east side in the vicinity of Mount Etna, Europe's largest and most active volcano.

VOLCANIC ERUPTIONS

Volcanoes form around an aperture in the earth's crust, through which gases, lava (molten rock) and solid fragments are ejected. Any mountain that is cone-shaped can be considered a potentially active volcano. A volcano's crater is formed when the cone collapses during an eruption, with steam vents left covering the crater floor.

The Mediterranean's legendary volcanoes include the Greek island of Santorini (Thira), which is the site of an exploded volcano, its harbour a flooded crater. Italy's Lipari Islands (formerly the Aeolian Islands) comprise a volcanic island group which includes Lipari, an exporter of pumice; Vulcano, where the mythical fire god was once worshipped; and Stromboli, an active volcano with several craters for which the Strombolian form of volcanic eruption is named. This fairly mild type of eruption consists of a continuous discharge of viscous lava, emitted in recurring explosions, along with the ejection of incandescent material which produces luminous clouds. In December 2002,

Stromboli, one of Italy's Lipari Islands, is an active volcano.

after 20 years of relative quiet, Stromboli began erupting with unusual force, suggesting a new interaction between its magma and seawater. Residents of the tiny volcanic island had to evacuate when part of Stromboli's lava field slid down the steep slope of Sciara del Fuoco into the Tyrrhenian Sea, triggering a huge harbour wave.

Sicily's Mount Etna also has become increasingly active, erupting more than 60 times in the first six months of 2000. Huge 'bombs' of lava, 4.5 feet in diameter, have shot from Etna's main summit cone, followed by explosions of ash from the northern vent area and slow lava flows that pour from the volanco's youngest crater on its southeastern flank. Ash has fallen on nearby villages, and trenches have been dug to divert the flow of magma away from the town of Linguaglossa. In October 2002 a stream of lava destroyed some ski lift pylons as it flowed toward Piano Provenzana, a plateau used by visitors as a starting point for mountain hikes. Scientists surmise that Etna is evolving from a predictable 'hotspot-type' of volcano to a more violent 'island-arc' variety similar to those in the Hawaiian Islands.

Vesuvius, standing on the eastern shore of the Bay of Naples, is the only active volcano on the European mainland. Its cataclysmic eruption of 79 AD buried Pompeii, Herculaneum and Stabiae under cinders, ashes and mud. Vesuvius has frequently erupted since then, including three times in the 20th century, and scientists predict another catastrophic eruption. The height of the main cone is about 4,000 feet (1,200 metres) and is half encircled by the ridge of a second summit, Monte Somma, which is slightly lower and separated from the main cone by a valley. The lower slopes of Vesuvius are extremely fertile, where vineyards produce the famous Lachryma Christi wine.

A STORIED SEA

The strong local winds that blow across the Mediterranean Sea, such as the hot, dry sirocco from the south and the cold mistral from the north, were believed to be controlled by gods when ancient mariners plied these waters. Inspiring several myths were the winds, currents and whirlpools that plague the Strait of Messina, which lies between mainland Italy and the island of Sicily. The whirlpools in particular were attributed to the sea monster Scylla, who lived on the rocks on the mainland side of the strait, where she would seize and devour sailors. Odysseus passed through this strait in his wanderings, as did Jason and the Argonauts.

The enclosed Mediterranean is an almost tideless sea, and its currents are generally estuarine in nature. This two-way circulation is created by extensive evaporation of the surface waters, which become saltier and therefore heavier than waters at lower levels, causing the surface waters to sink to the bottom of the seabed and eventually flow out through the Straits of Gibraltar where less salty (and lighter) Atlantic water is flowing into the Mediterranean. During World War II, German submarines that were trapped by the Allied blockade of the

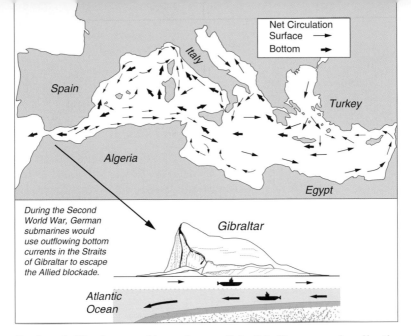

During the Second World War, German submarines would use outflowing bottom currents in the Straits of Gibraltar to escape the Allied blockade.

Straits of Gibraltar would sneak out of the Mediterranean by silently drifting seaward on these bottom currents.

The Mediterranean once supported a brilliant array of sponges, corals and fish species, and tales of dolphins rescuing people from drowning date back to Greek mythology. In recent decades, the sea has suffered from overfishing and pollution. When Jacques-Yves Cousteau, in the summer of 1943, slipped into the warm waters of a cove on the French Riviera to test the Aqualung he had developed with a French engineer, the Mediterranean teemed with life. By the early '70s, Cousteau was so concerned with the drastic decrease in marine life, he founded the Cousteau Society to spread his ardent advocacy of the seas.

Military exercises in the Mediterranean also pose a threat to the sea's marine life. When a dozen Cuvier's beaked whales beached themselves on the coast of the Kyparissiakos Gulf in May 1997, a Greek researcher suggested that a NATO test of Low Frequency Active Sonar – very loud, low-frequency sounds designed to detect quiet diesel and nuclear submarines – may have disoriented the whales. And when the corpses of 22 dolphins washed up on the south coast of France in March 1998, military naval operations were again suspect.

Another troubling trend, this one attributed to global warming and the accompanying rise in water temperature, is the growing number of tropical fish species now making the Mediterranean Sea their permanent home. They are arriving from the Red Sea and the Atlantic Ocean off Africa, and are thriving in part because the Mediterranean's indigenous species have been weakened by environmental stress.

When the ancient Greeks, using ropes and stone weights, began diving beneath the sea's surface in search of sponges and sunken treasure, they feared the mysterious creatures of the deep. Today we fear the threat of their extinction.

ANCIENT MARINERS

Since prehistoric times, shipping has determined human social development. Early civilizations formed along navigable rivers or on the coasts of warm seas, and the ideally situated Mediterranean became the cradle of maritime endeavour. As early as 3500 BC the Egyptians were sailing boats on the Nile, and by 2500 BC they were making tentative voyages into the Mediterranean Sea, tracing the coast by day and anchoring at night. Egypt was also the first Mediterranean nation to engage in shipbuilding. Early boats were made from bundles of papyrus reeds lashed together, their ends raised and bound, while those made of wood consisted of planks 'sewn' together with ropes. The larger boats were multi-oared and rigged with a steering oar. Over time, the Egyptians became skilled shipwrights, adept at dovetailing and scarfing hundreds of small timbers together, for there were no tall trees in Egypt from which to cut long planks.

Travelling the Nile by boat was an integral aspect of Egyptian life. Boats were carried north with the downstream current, and those that were southbound would raise their linen sails and ride the prevailing northerly wind back up the river. This mode of travel was so ingrained in the Egyptian psyche, that the hieroglyph for 'travelling north' was a boat with its sails down and the hieroglyph for 'travelling south' was a boat under sail. Boat travel was also an important religious metaphor, with the sun god Ra travelling through the sky in a solar bark. These barks played an important role in the Egyptian funerary cult, providing

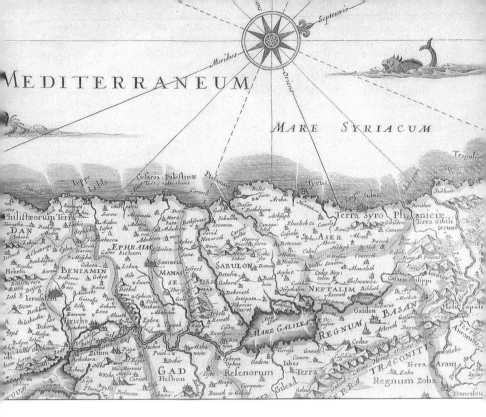

the deceased pharaoh with a vessel for divine travel. The solar bark excavated beside the Great Pyramid of Cheops is the earliest known example of such a boat, its narrow hull with high, tapered ends extending to 142 feet (43 m) in length. Ceremonial boats were also used to carry statues of the gods between temples.

While the Egyptians were sailing along the shores of the eastern Mediterranean, another ancient civilization was flourishing on the island of Crete. The seat of Minoan culture, Crete's seafaring people had mercantile contact with both Egypt and the Mycenaean cities of mainland Greece. By 1600 BC the Minoans were battling the Mycenaeans for maritime control of the Aegean Sea. Then several earthquakes struck Crete and, by 1400 BC, the centre of Aegean culture had shifted from Crete to the mainland.

The maritime commerce that had once been controlled by the Aegeans fell to the Phoenicians who, by 1250 BC, were well established as the primary navigators and traders of the Mediterranean world. The Phoenicians were a Semitic people, a seafaring branch of the Canaanites of northern Palestine, and they lived on the shores of the eastern Mediterranean. Their territory corresponded roughly with that of present-day Lebanon, and their main city-states were Tyre and Sidon. When Egyptian power waned in the 12th century BC, Phoenician mariners began to dominate the entire Mediterranean. They sailed to the edges of the known world, and eventually ventured beyond the Pillars of Hercules at the western entrance to the Mediterranean, travelling north to England in search of tin, and south along the coast of Africa, possibly completing a circumnavigation of the continent in the 7th century BC. The Phoenicians established numerous colonies along the shores of the Mediterranean, including Carthage on the north coast of Africa, which eventually became a powerful city-state and rival of imperial Rome.

NAVIGATION & CHARTMAKING

Mediterranean is a Latin word meaning 'sea in the midst of lands', and strong local winds blow across this inland sea. The early sailors used these winds as a means of navigation when sailing across the sea from one port to another. Greek mariners, when out of sight of land, used four winds to determine their position. The Boreas blew from the north, the Euros from the east, the Notos from the south and the Zephuros from the west. Each wind was identified in relation to the sun's bearing or, at night, by the star Polaris. Other telltale signs were the wind's temperature and moisture content. As longer voyages were taken, four more winds, indicating the directions of northeast, southeast, southwest and northwest, were added to the wind-rose, which was the compass of ancient mariners. Over time the system was expanded until eventually there were 32 winds, representing the 32 points of the wind-rose.

The first pilot books were written about 500 BC. The mouth of the Nile was a starting point, from which the pilot would guide mariners, in a clockwise direction, from port to port. Tides, which are minimal in the Mediterranean, were believed to be controlled by sea monsters until a Greek navigator and astronomer named Pytheas, who lived in Massilia

Rhodes, an important trading port as early as 400 BC, was used by ancient cartographers as a central reference point on their maps.

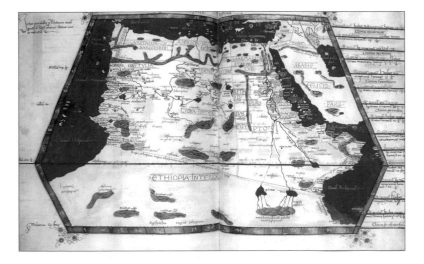

The above map of North Africa was drafted in the 2nd century AD
by the great cartographer Claudius Ptolemaeus (Ptolemy).

(modern Marseilles) during the 4th century BC, discovered that the tides were connected with the moon. Pytheas also embarked, from Cadiz, on a famous voyage along the Atlantic coast to the British Isles.

As early as the 6th century BC, the Greek philosopher Pythagoras realized that the earth was spherical. Eratosthenes, keeper of Alexandria's great library in the 3rd century BC, expanded on Pythagoras's theory and devised a method for measuring the earth's circumference which incorporated existing surveys of the Nile river valley. He then constructed a map of the known world using parallels and meridians that passed through important places such as Rhodes, then the maritime centre of the known world, and the Pillars of Hercules, which marked the western end of the Mediterranean.

In the 1st century AD, Marinus of Tyre created the first charts for seamen, with Rhodes remaining the primary meridian and parallel. But it was Ptolemy (85-160 AD), perhaps the greatest cartographer of all, who first projected part of the spherical earth's surface onto a plane surface. A Greek born in Egypt, Ptolemy spent most of his life in Alexandria where he studied mathematics and astronomy. He wrote many works, the most famous of which was his *Geography* or *Geographica*, compiled into eight books and containing an atlas of the known world. This great work was lost with the fall of the Roman Empire, but it resurfaced in 1400 in Constantinople (now Istanbul). A century later, in Italy, Ptolemy's *Geography* was translated into Latin and, with the development of printing allowing for its wide distribution, the work became the basis for mapping new discoveries throughout the 15th and 16th centuries.

SHIP DESIGN

In the beginning, small merchant ships plied the waters between Phoenicia, Egypt and Greece, carrying such luxury items as spices, perfumes and fine pottery for trade. Large stones or baskets filled with stones were used as anchors, but as ships grew larger, iron hooks were designed to dig into the sea bed. When the Phoenician sailors began making longer voyages, they built larger ships which carried, in addition to oars, a square sail for running before the wind.

The Romans, skilled engineers who both imitated and improved upon their neighbouring nations' ship designs, built larger and stronger ships for transporting military supplies and troops to outlying outposts of Rome's expanding empire. These broad, full-bodied ships could carry up to 400 tons of cargo, and were used for shipping grain and other foodstuffs from their colonies. They were propelled by sails and steered by two deep oars, one on each quarter.

An innovative application of nautical know-how was used by the Romans during construction of the Colosseum in the 1st century AD, when a retractable sailcloth was rigged as a sun shade for spectators. The sailors living in a camp nearby were adept at handling the wooden pulleys and ropes used to furl this cloth roof in heavy rains and winds, then unfurl it in fair weather.

Merchant ships, designed to carry cargo, were often accompanied by galleys for protection. War galleys were long, narrow vessels designed for speed and rowed by slaves and prisoners of war who were chained to benches. A beak or metal point was fixed on the bow and was used for ramming enemy vessels with the intent of piercing their hulls and sinking them. The crew of ancient warships used catapults for firing missiles and incendiaries such as Greek Fire, which was a flammable substance of sulphur, naphtha and quicklime.

Ancient galleys of the Mediterranean were rigged with a square sail for running before the wind.

Attached to the ship's beak was a figurehead. Associated with a sea deity for protection, this figure had eyes enabling the ship to 'see' its way swiftly across the water. The Egyptians mounted figures of various holy birds on the prows of their ships; the Phoenicians used a horse's head; the Greeks favoured a boar's head; and the Romans often used a centurion.

A number of superstitions and rituals still practised by modern mariners originated in ancient times. The tradition of breaking a bottle of champagne across a new ship's bow began as a cruel ritual during antiquity when a new galley had to 'taste blood' to be successful in battle. To this end, galleys were launched by rolling them across slaves tied to the keel blocks. Their bodies, when crushed, would splash blood against the ship's hull.

Galleys were eventually rigged as sailing vessels, and by the 15th century, the caravel – a three-masted sailing vessel with a roundish hull – was being used by the Portuguese and Spanish for ocean-going exploration. The galley continued to be used in the eastern Mediterranean until the 18th century. Traditional boats which are still in use include the felucca, a lateen-rigged sailing vessel once used in the Mediterranean and still seen on the Nile, as is the dahabeeyah, a large river vessel with high lateen sails.

The word dahabeeyah is Arabic for 'golden' and was orginally applied in reference to the gilded barges Egyptian rulers used for river processions and ceremonies of state. Cleopatra's barge was described by Shakespeare in *Antony and Cleopatra* as "a burnished throne" with a golden poop, silver oars and purple sails "so perfumed the winds were love-sick with them".

A felucca on the Nile (above).
Traditional beaks are still seen
on Venetian gondolas (below).

The Venetian bucentaur, from the Italian *buzino d'oro* (meaning 'golden bark'), was another sumptuously decorated vessel. The state galley of the doges (rulers of Venice), it was used in an annual symbolic ceremony called 'the wedding of the sea' which commemorated Venice's victory over the Dalmatian pirates in 1000 AD. Venice's most famous vessel is the gondola, which dates to at least the 11th century and is still used today as a popular mode of transport for tourists transiting the city's canals. Long, sleek and efficient, its hull shape embodies the principles of the wave line theory of modern shipbuilding. With a flat bottom and a high prow and stern, it is propelled by a single oarsman – called a gondolier – positioned near the stern. The bright metal beak at the bow, called a *ferro*, is shaped like the ancient *rostrum tridens*.

NAVAL BATTLES

The word 'navy' derives from *naves*, the Latin word for ships. The Mediterranean's early fleets set off on raiding or trading expeditions and were eventually organized for conquest and defence as naval supremacy became critical to an empire's survival. The first recorded naval battle was waged about 1200 BC, between the Egyptians and the Sea Peoples, who were displaced tribes of the eastern Mediterranean. The Egyptian pharaoh Merenptah recorded his great triumph on the wall of the temple of Amun at Karnak and on a victory stele in his funerary temple at Thebes.

When the Athenian navy destroyed a Persian fleet off the Aegean island of Salamis in 480 BC, this great naval victory established the maritime supremacy of Athens and ushered in the city-state's golden age under the leadership of Pericles. The port of Piraeus, linked to Athens by a fortified corridor called the Long Walls, became an important naval centre holding nearly 300 war galleys. Fifty years later, the rival city-state of Sparta, aided by the Persians, defeated the Athenian navy and tore down the Long Walls.

In the 3rd century BC, following its conquest of central and southern Italy, Rome began to look seaward. The North African city of Carthage ruled the western Mediterranean and Rome's designs on Sicily drew these two city-states into a conflict destined to determine the supremacy of one or the other. Rome emerged as victor and, as the new ruler of the Mediterranean, referred to it as *Mare Nostrum*, meaning 'Our Sea'.

Rome's first naval hero was Gaius Duillius, who led a fleet to victory in the Battle of Mylae in 260 BC, defeating the Carthaginian fleet off the northern coast of Sicily. Duillius carried boarding bridges and designed grappling irons which he used to bind his ships to those of the enemy. Thus aided, he captured fifty ships and was the first Roman to achieve victory over the naval power of Carthage. His great triumph was honoured in Rome with the raising of a column adorned with the beakheads of the captured vessels. Hailed as a hero, he was attended by a torchbearer and flute player whenever he walked the streets of Rome in the evening.

Centuries later, when Horatio Nelson resoundingly defeated a French fleet off the north coast of Egypt in the Battle of the Nile, he too was showered with accolades which included a peerage. Lady Hamilton, with whom he was falling in love, wrote to him that, "Your statue ought to be made of pure gold and placed in the middle of London." Nelson died a national hero at the Battle of Trafalgar in 1805 and was buried in a crypt of St. Paul's Cathedral, his coffin made of timber cut from the main mast of the French flagship that was destroyed in the Battle of the Nile.

Piracy & Plunder

The fall of the Roman Empire was followed by the rise of piracy, and throughout the Middle Ages pirates plagued the Mediterranean. Coastal trading ports were fortified with walls and bastions, and chains were drawn across harbour entrances during times of attack. Sacking and plundering coastal settlements was highly lucrative and became even more so when oared galleys were replaced with sailing ships, which greatly increased a pirate's range of operation.

The most famous pirates of the Mediterranean operated from the coast of north Africa. Many were displaced Moors of Spain who had been driven into exile in the 15th century by the Catholic forces of Ferdinand and Isabella. Bent on revenge against Christians in general and the Spanish in particular, they were called Barbary pirates for the Berber settlements from which they embarked on their raids. These notorious corsairs, who lived by plunder, operated out of Tripoli, Tunis and Algiers, all of which were military republics that broke free of Turkish rule in the mid-1600s.

The Barbary pirates specialized in the capture and sale of slaves, with some venturing as far away as Iceland. The most feared were the Barbarossa brothers, whose names struck terror in the hearts of Christians. From 1510 to 1545, they burned, pillaged and murdered in raids along the Spanish and Italian coasts. One brother was eventually killed by Spanish troops but the other retired with vast riches to a palace he had built at Constantinople.

Piracy's promise of easy money attracted European renegades to the Barbary ranks, including an Englishman named Verney, who was from a distinguished Buckinghamshire family, and a Fleming who took the Arabic name of Murad Reise. The latter led a raid on Baltimore, Ireland, during which the town was sacked and most of its residents seized as slaves to be sold at the slave market in Algiers. Despite numerous attempts to stamp out piracy in the Mediterranean, it wasn't completely eliminated until 1830 when a French fleet bombarded and captured the port of Algiers, the last stronghold of organized piracy.

ANCIENT EGYPT

The mysterious monuments, rituals and relics of ancient Egypt may seem strange and unconnected to modern life, but they have in fact influenced the art, culture and conceptions of subsequent civilizations, including our own. More than four thousand years ago, during the time of the Old Kingdom (2686-2181 BC), the Egyptians had devised a solar calendar based on a year of 365 days. They had also invented the sun dial, the water clock and various mathematical formulas, including one for calculating the area of a circle. Their knowledge of medicine was also remarkably advanced, for they had already developed an understanding of the circulatory system.

The chair, one of the oldest forms of furniture, dates from the Old Kingdom, as does taxation, which was based on a biennial census of farmers' produce. The world's first recorded labour strike occurred during the reign of Rameses III, in the 12th century BC, when royal tomb-workers from the village of Deir El-Medina on the Theban west bank staged protests in front of several mortuary temples.

Wages back then were paid in the form of food rations. Emmer-wheat, used for making stone-ground flour, and barley, used for brewing a thick, soup-like beer, were highly valued as staples of the Egyptian diet. The wealthier classes dined on meat, salted fish, lettuces and cucumbers, in addition to onions, which were widely available, and such fruits as dates, figs and pomegranates. The nobility also drank wine – both red and white – which was stored in stone

Hieroglyphs, proclaiming the pharaoh's names and titles, ran down an obelisk's four sides.

vessels inscribed with the same information that is currently displayed on modern wine labels, i.e., the vineyard, the variety of grape and the year of production. Noblemen and their families lived in villas with gardens, and kept house pets, including cats, monkeys and dogs.

We know all of this and more because the Egyptians invented one of the earliest forms of writing called hieroglyphics, meaning 'priestly carvings' in Greek. Hieroglyphs were pictorial symbols for words, sounds or syllables, and were carved and painted on the walls of temples and tombs to record funerary and religious texts. Over time hieroglyphs evolved into a form of cursive handwriting called hieratic, which was used primarily for administrative and literary texts.

Only a small minority of the population were literate in ancient times (possibly less than one per cent of the population), and professional scribes were members of an elite class, passing their skills from father to son, from one generation to the next. Using ink cakes and reed brushes wetted with water, they wrote on papyrus and other surfaces, and these hieratic writings preserved on ancient papyri have provided priceless data to Egyptologists. By the 5th century BC, hieratic script had been replaced by a simplified script called demotic, which often appeared beside Greek script. With the arrival of Christianity in Egypt came the Coptic language, written using a modified version of the Greek alphabet. Many of the Greek words have remained in common usage, such as pyramid (from the Greek word *pyramis*) and pharaoh (from a Greek word meaning 'great house').

The famous Rosetta Stone, found in 1799 by Napoleon's soldiers and now on display in the British Museum, is inscribed in three scripts and two languages: Egyptian hieroglyphs, Egyptian demotic script, and Greek. It was the Greek version of the Egyptian texts that helped scholars, after 20 years of study, decipher their meaning and begin to understand the far-reaching and complex legacy of ancient Egypt.

ANCIENT BELIEFS

Ancient Egyptians believed the world was shaped like a disk. In the centre lay the flat plains of Egypt, surrounded by a rim of mountainous foreign lands. Below were the deep waters of the underworld and above stretched the sky. Animals were the first to be worshipped in predynastic Egypt and sacred species included the cat, which was worshipped at Bubastis (northeast of modern Cairo), and the Apis bull, its principal sanctuary located at Memphis (to the south of modern Cairo). As civilization progressed, the deities were gradually humanized and portrayed in various forms, often half human/half animal. The major gods were supported by cults, their followers building and maintaining temples for worshipping a specific deity.

The dominant god of the Old Kingdom pantheon was Ra, the sun god. Ra's daily journey across the sky, from birth to death, was a fundamental theme in Egyptian religion. The first sun temple was built about 2600 BC at Heliopolis, its site now buried beneath a northwestern suburb of Cairo. Worship of Ra reached its peak during the Old Kingdom's 4th Dynasty when the Great Pyramids were built.

Osiris, god of the underworld and protector of all, symbolized the imperishability of life and was often depicted in mummy wrappings, wearing the crown of Upper Egypt and holding a crook and flail. According to a famous myth, Osiris was murdered by his brother Seth, god of chaos, then resurrected by his wife Isis who conceived a son with her deceased

Horus, the sky god.

husband. When their son Horus was born, he avenged his father's death by defeating Seth and banishing him to the desert where he ruled as god of chaos and evil. Horus, god of the sky, was often depicted with a hawk's head for his swift flight across the sky, and his battle with Seth represented the triumph of good over evil, of order over chaos.

The Osiris-Horus creation myth has parallels with Christianity's mystery of creation and the god-man Jesus, while the Egyptian image of the 'great mother' Isis suckling her son Horus, who is seated on her lap, is analogous with the Madonna and Child imagery found in Christian art. Another ancient Egyptian symbol later embodied in Christian art concerns the four sons of Horus, three of whom were depicted as animals, just as three of the four evangelists are symbolized as animals – Mark the lion, Luke the ox and John the eagle.

Amun, another important god, rose to prominence during the Middle Kingdom (2055-1650 BC) when the capital of Egypt moved from Memphis to Thebes, where Amun was worshipped as a local deity. Often depicted with a ram's head, Amun was combined with the sun-god Ra to become the powerful god Amun-Ra. The heretic pharaoh Akhenaten tried to suppress the cult of Amun and the cults of other deities by promoting the worship of a single god named Aten, but this was unpopular with the people and the pantheon of gods was soon restored under Tutankhamun. By the end of the New Kingdom (1550-1069 BC),

Amun, in the form of a ram, protects the pharaoh whose figure stands between the god's paws (above). Hathor, goddess of love, was often depicted with cow ears (below).

Cartouche with the name of the female pharaoh Hatshepsut.

the cult of Amun-Ra had gained such prestige its priests rivalled the pharaoh himself.

Other gods with temples dedicated to them included Hathor, the cow-earred goddess of love, and Sobek, the crocodile god. Ultimately, Egypt's pantheon of gods influenced both the Greeks and Romans, who adopted various Egyptian deities and fused them with their own gods. Isis the nature goddess, whose sanctuary on the island of Philae near Aswan survived until the 6th century AD, was widely worshipped throughout the Hellenistic world and the Roman empire, and she seriously rivalled both the traditional Roman gods and early Christianity.

The ancient Egyptians believed that the pharaohs descended from the gods, and the sun god Ra was considered the direct ancestor of the first pharaoh. The living pharaoh, whose role was to impose order and prevent chaos, was linked with the falcon-god Horus, while the deceased kings were associated with Osiris. Each pharaoh had five names – three of which stressed his role as a god – and each of these royal names were framed by a cartouche, a French term introduced by Napoleon's soldiers when they compared these elliptical outlines to the shape of a gun cartridge. A cartouche actually represented a length of knotted rope and symbolized encircling protection of the name. In ancient Egypt, a name was of great symbolic importance and a pharaoh who wanted to destroy the memory, and thus the very existence, of a previous ruler would order the deceased pharaoh's birth name chiselled off existing monuments and replaced with his own name.

The names of queens were also important. Nefer, a hieroglyphic sign meaning beautiful, good and happy, was used for several royal wives including Akenaten's wife Nefertiti ('the beautiful one is come'). Rameses II's principal wife was called Nefertari, to whom he dedicated a temple at Abu Simbel and on whose tomb he inscribed the words, 'Possessor of charm, sweetness and love.'

There were three types of queens in ancient Egypt. The 'great royal wife', second only to the king, was depicted alongside him in monuments, and one of her sons was usually named heir to the throne. The king's mother was also a queen and a prominent figure, while the king's many other wives were secondary queens who lived in the harem. Familial bliss did not always prevail, and during the reign of Rameses III, one of his secondary queens conspired with the other women in the harem to murder the pharaoh so her son could ascend the throne.

One of the few queens to actually rule Egypt was Hatshepsut. A daughter of Thutmose I, she became the wife of her half-brother Thutmose II and step-mother to his son and heir Thutmose III. The younger Thutmose was still a child

At Abu Simbel, figures of Rameses II flank his queen, Nefertari, outside her temple.

when his father died, so Hatshepsut was appointed temporary regent. She shrewdly had herself crowned king to extend her co-regency with the young pharaoh and thus block him from holding full power.

The king's chief minister, the vizier, also wielded considerable power within the royal court. In charge of most areas of government except for religious and military duties, the vizier was sometimes of royal blood but more often was a member of the non-royal elite. One of Egypt's most important viziers was Imhotep, a learned man and the architect of the first pyramid. Greatly respected during his lifetime,

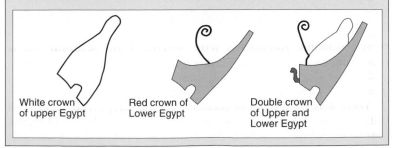

R O Y A L   R E G A L I A

Pharaohs always wore headgear of some sort, whether it was the simple *nemes* headcloth or the double crown of Upper and Lower Egypt, which combined the conical white crown of Upper Egypt with the chair-shaped red crown of Lower Egypt. The vulture and lotus flower were other symbols of Upper Egypt, while the cobra and papyrus flower symbolized Lower Egypt. The pharaoh was frequently shown holding a crook, which was a sceptre symbolizing government, and a flail, associated with Osiris, god of the afterlife.

White crown of upper Egypt

Red crown of Lower Egypt

Double crown of Upper and Lower Egypt

AFTERLIFE ESSENTIALS

The hereafter was paramount to the Ancient Egyptians, whose elaborate funerary rituals were devised to perpetuate the afterlife of the deceased. The corpse had to be preserved in order for its *ka*, a vital life force that could not exist without the body, to journey to the underworld and there reunite with its *ba*, similar to our concept of personality. Once this reunion took place, the deceased was transformed into an *akh*, one of the 'blessed dead'.

The 70-day mummification process began with the removal of vital organs and their placement in canopic jars. The body fluids were drained and all cavities were stuffed with linen before the corpse was wrapped. As a final protection, elaborate tombs were built to protect the corpse and its funerary equipment, including a copy of the Book of the Dead. This document contained instructions on how to safely journey to the kingdom of the dead and it provided a code of conduct for appearing before Osiris, king of the dead, who judged the *ka* upon arrival. If deemed a sinner by Osiris, the deceased was torn apart by executioners; if the *ka* was judged favourably, he was allowed into the fields of Yaru, a heavenly paradise where he could use the furniture and other items placed in his tomb. Especially useful were the small statuettes, called ushabtis, which served as the deceased's substitutes when summoned to work in the grain fields or perform menial tasks for Osiris.

Imhotep later became one of ancient Egypt's few non-royal individuals to be deified – as a god of wisdom, writing and medicine.

Another vizier of note, but for much different reasons, was Ay (pronounced 'I') who served as regent while the boy king Tutankhamun grew up. A recent theory has been put forward, based on court inscriptions and a fracture found at the back of the pharaoh's skull, that Ay not only murdered the young king, he also killed a Hittite prince who was

Rameses II's many building projects included those at Abu Simbel and Karnak (below).

supposed to marry Tut's widow, then proceeded to marry her himself, only to then have her murdered. Ay also usurped a tomb in the Valley of the Kings that had likely been intended for Tutankhamun, who was placed in a smaller tomb.

The pharaoh who succeeded Ay was a general named Horemheb, and he in turn was succeeded by another military officer who had risen to the rank of vizier. His name was Rameses and his reign marked the beginning of the New Kingdom's 'Ramesside' period that is best known for the remarkable reign of Rameses II. A grandson of Rameses I, he ruled Egypt for 63 years, sired at least 90 children, and built more monuments, temples and statuary than any other pharaoh in the history of Egypt. A great warrior, he led a huge army of 20,000 men into Syria where his victory over the Hittite forces at the Battle of Kadesh is repeatedly celebrated on the walls of his major temples.

Egyptian art often depicted the pharaoh smiting the enemy or leading a charge in his horse-drawn chariot, and Rameses II introduced a new style of art by having his name carved very deeply into the stone, instead of using reliefs that could be chiselled off. He did this so that subsequent pharaohs couldn't erase his name from monuments, as he had done to previous rulers. When Rameses finally died in his 70s, he had been predeceased by twelve of his sons and was succeeded by his 13th son, Merenptah.

THE PHOENICIANS

The Phoenicians traded with the Egyptians as early as 2800 BC. Large cedars grew in their homeland and this source of wood, which was in short supply in Egypt, was of great value to the ancient Egyptians. Skilled artisans, the Phoenicians also traded with the Greeks and were known for their textiles, especially a purple-coloured cloth they made using dye from shellfish. The Greek word for purple – *phoenicia* – became the name by which their territory was known. The Phoenicians were also accomplished architects, their cities built to withstand attacks, but their greatest contribution to western civilization was their development of a standardized phonetic alphabet which served as a basis for the Greek alphabet and became a key factor in the development of Greek literature. In the 6th century BC, Phoenicia fell under the influence of the Persian Empire and, with the rise of Greek maritime power, Phoenician cities began to fade in importance. The last traces of Phoenician civilization were eventually absorbed by Hellenistic culture.

ANCIENT GREECE

A recurring theme throughout the history of ancient Greece is the seaborne search for fertile lands. Facing chronic food shortages at home, the people of ancient Greece frequently cast their fate to the wind and set off across the Mediterranean Sea to seek a better life on distant shores. The mountains that isolated mainland Greece's city-states from one another were once an abundant source of timber, their slopes covered with forests of oak, pine and fir from which the early shipwrights built sturdy vessels for seagoing trade and migration. Between the 8th and 6th centuries BC, Greek civilization spread eastward to the shores of the Black Sea and west to the coast of southern Spain. The coastlines of France, North Africa, Sicily and southern Italy (*Magna Graecia*) were all colonized by Greek emigrants, and this period of mass migration marked the greatest geographical extent of Greek civilization.

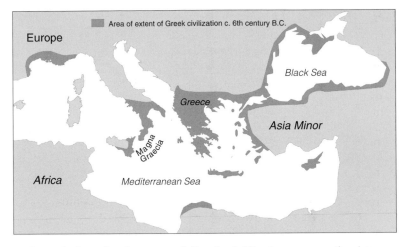

Long before development of Greek civilization proper, the Aegean Islands were inhabited by a primitive Stone Age people who can be traced as far back as 4000 BC. Over time, they evolved into a Bronze Age civilization which gave rise to three main cultures: the Cycladic on the islands of the same name, the Minoan on the island of Crete, and the Mycenaean (also called Helladic) on the Peloponnese peninsula. The Minoans were skilled sailors who engaged in seagoing commerce. Although influenced by the advanced civilization of Egypt, which was located only 400 miles away, the culture they created was distinct. They built palace cities of multi-storied pavilions set amid gardens and pools, and their wall art was fluid and dynamic, with marine life and other scenes of nature portrayed in a joyful, vibrant style. The bull was a sacred animal, and frescoes often depicted a popular ritual in which young Minoans would vault over the back of a leaping bull.

Minoan culture eventually dominated the Aegean, and from 1600 to 1400 BC both the Minoan and Mycenaean civilizations flourished. There were stark differences in the two cultures, with the Minoans on Crete building no fortifications, in contrast to those erected on the mainland by the warrior Mycenaeans, whose mas-

A Minoan mural at the Palace of Knossos, Crete.

ANCIENT GREECE

sive hilltop fortresses at Mycenae and Tiryns were regarded by later Greeks as the work of the Cyclopes, those mythical one-eyed giants who were strong enough to move the huge stone blocks into place. After several devastating earthquakes struck Crete, the centre of Aegean civilization shifted to Mycenae on the mainland, where it was eventually absorbed by waves of invasions from the north.

About 1400 BC, the first of these northern war-like tribes of the Aryan race began invading Greece, sweeping southward onto the Peloponnese peninsula. The first to arrive were the Ionians and Aeolians, followed in 1100 BC by the Dorians, who pushed their way south to the Peloponnesus where they established their chief cities, Sparta and Corinth. The Dorians, who subjected and enslaved the con-quered population, were responsible for a cultural decline in Greece. The Ionians fled the Peloponnesus and eventually migrated to the coast of Asia Minor where they settled the islands of Chios and Samos, and established the great cities of Ephesus, Miletus and Phocaea. The Dorians later migrated to Asia Minor as well, establishing themselves south of the Ionians in Doris and on the islands of Rhodes and Cos. The Aeolians settled north of the Ionians, colonizing the island of Lesbos.

As Greek civilization spread seaward across the Aegean Sea to the shores of modern Turkey, its mainland harbours and close-lying islands were linked by mariners, resulting in the development of a homoge-neous culture. Calling themselves Hellenes (the name of one of the

Ancient Corinth was one of the oldest and most powerful of the Greek city-states.

original tribes), the Aeolians, Dorians and Ionians shared a growing racial pride. The Dorians and Ionians, the two foremost branches of the Hellenes, developed a rivalry, with each branch claiming to be more purely Hellenic than the other. The Hellenes' mythology became the basis for an intricate religion with a pantheon of immortal gods and legendary heroes. One of the most famous of the Greek heroes was Odysseus, the archetypal Greek sailor whose maritime adventures inspired a great seafaring civilization.

Odysseus was a hero of the Trojan War, a 10-year battle between the Greeks and the Trojans, who once inhabited Asia Minor (modern Turkey) at the mouth of the Hellespont Strait (Dardanelles). The Trojan War likely occurred around 1200 BC when invading Greeks may have sought control of trade through the Dardanelles. In mythological terms, the war began after the Trojan prince Paris abducted Helen, wife of Menelaus of Sparta. Menelaus persuaded his brother Agamemnon to lead an army against Troy, and troop ships were gathered by Achilles, Odysseus and other Greek heroes. After nine years spent ravaging Troy's surrounding cities, the Greeks finally defeated the fortified city of Troy with a cunning plan. After building a hollow wooden horse outside Troy's walls, the Greeks boarded their ships and pretended to sail for home. One Greek soldier remained, and persuaded the Trojans to bring the horse within the city walls. When night fell, the Greek ships returned and some soldiers who were hiding inside the horse opened the city gates.

The Trojan War is the subject of Homer's epic poem the *Iliad*, and Odysseus's struggle to return home to Ithaca after the fall of Troy is the basis of the *Odyssey*. These poems rank among the finest literature ever written, and were likely repeated by word of mouth in Homer's day. The great poet himself is shrouded in myth. His birthplace is not known for certain but was most likely the island of Chios or Smyrna in Asia Minor. He lived sometime before 700 BC, and he may have been blind. The period of which he wrote is now referred to as the Homeric Age.

While ancient Greece displayed cultural homogeneity, it did not comprise a single political entity; rather, it consisted of small economic and political units called city-states, with each encompassing a city and its surrounding territory. The Greek city-states often quarrelled and waged war against one another, but they shared a sense of unity based on their Hellenic culture and religion, which encompassed a vast set of myths and legends. The sanctuary of Delphi became a national shrine and national festivals included the important Olympian games, with the Greeks dating their own historical reckoning from the first Olympiad held in 776 BC.

THE GODS OF OLYMPUS

The Greek gods dwelt on Mount Olympus and the Olympian games, held every four years, were in honour of Zeus, the sky god. Zeus was supreme lord of the heavens and earth, and head of the divine family of gods and goddesses. The deities exercised supernatural powers but these were curbed by fate, which the early Greeks defined as the relentless force of destiny. The gods were immortal and physically larger than their human counterparts but they behaved, in many respects, just like people: they squabbled amongst themselves, betrayed one another and took delight in their mortal loves. Their meddling in human affairs was seen as divine intervention and their ability to see the future was relayed through oracles. Each Greek city-state adopted one or more gods as protective guardians, and these civic deities were honoured with temples, statues and religious festivals.

The 12 Olympian gods, who succeeded the Titans as rulers of the universe, were a collection of deities adopted from various cultures that had influenced Hellenic Greece, including Egypt and Asia. Zeus, a god of the invading Aryan tribes, shared his dominion with his two brothers, Hades (lord of the underworld) and Poseidon (lord of the waters). Zeus was married to Hera, an Aegean fertility goddess, but it was a match fraught with tension. The divine children of Zeus, begat by various lovers, were Ares, Hermes, Apollo, Hephaestus, Athena, Aphrodite and Artemis.

Poseidon, god of the sea, was often violent and vengeful.

Apollo and his twin sister Artemis, goddess of the moon, were born on the Cycladic island of Delos, where their mother Leto had fled to escape the jealous anger of Zeus's wife, Hera. Apollo, the sun god, was one of most versatile of the Olympian gods. In addition to being the god of youth, manly beauty, music and song, he was also the god of prophecy with a famous oracle at Delphi.

Athena, originally a Mycenaean deity, was the goddess of wisdom, war and the liberal arts, as well as the mythological patroness of shipbuilding. She aided the Argonauts in their voyage to the Black Sea in search of the Golden Fleece, and she favoured the Greeks during the Trojan war, mainly because the Trojan prince Paris awarded the prize for beauty to her rival Aphrodite, goddess of love and beauty, who sprang from the foam of the sea. The 12th Olympian was Zeus's sister Hestia, who resigned her place to Dionysus, god of fertility and wine.

Hercules was famous for his strength and courage.

Athena was one of the Olympian gods.

The Greek heroes descended from the gods, and one of the most famous was Hercules (Herakles), who performed great feats and was the only mortal ever to ascend Mount Olympus. The son of Zeus and the princess Alcmene, Hercules was hated by Hera, who sent serpents to his cradle, which he strangled. She later drove him mad, causing him to kill his wife and children in a moment of insanity. Afterwards, as an atonement for his crime, Hercules undertook 12 mighty labours (feats of strength) while at the royal court in Tiryns.

The religious importance of the Olympian gods began to decline in the 6th century BC. As Greek philosophers sought a more intellectual approach to humanity's relationship with nature, their philosophical inquiries led to the rationalization of myths and the eventual destruction of the Olympian pantheon.

THE GREEK CITY-STATE

During pre-Hellenic times, the chiefs of invading tribes became kings of their conquered territories. Then, from 800 to 650 BC, monarchies were replaced by oligarchies as aristocrats began acquiring land, a measure of wealth and power. The introduction of coined money, by the Phoenicians, hastened the development of a landless wealthy class and,

Horsemen from the north frieze of the Parthenon, Athens, built between 447 and 432 BC. (British Museum, London)

around 650 BC, these wealthy commoners, called tyrants, began overthrowing the Hellenic oligarchies. The title of tyrant meant a ruler had acquired political power illegally, not that it was abused. In fact, most tyrants were wise and popular rulers under whose leadership trade flourished and Hellenic culture flowered.

Between the 8th and 6th centuries, Athens and Sparta emerged as Greece's two dominant city-states, and each united its weaker neighbours into a confederacy under its control. The two city-states were a study in contrasts. Sparta was a militarized state that led by conquest and kept its subject states under strict control. Athens, on the other hand, united Attica through mutual and peaceful agreement. Athenian reforms, first introduced in 594 BC to grant citizenship to the lower classes, eventually led to the establishment, around 508 BC, of the first government based on democratic principles.

Meanwhile, in 546 BC the great Greek centres in Asia Minor had fallen to the Persians. When Ionia revolted in 499 BC, it was aided by Athens. The Persian king Darius I squashed the revolt in 493 BC, swearing revenge on Greece, and the following year he sent heralds to Greece demanding tokens of submission. All of the city-states complied except for Athens and Sparta, further enraging Darius whose fleet of ships, commanded by his son-in-law, was wrecked off Mt. Athos.

Darius prepared a second expedition that set sail in 490 BC. The Persian fleet delivered an army three times the size of Athen's, but it was defeated at a famous battle on the plain of Marathon near Athens and forced to withdraw. A third expedition, this time overseen by Darius's son Xerxes I, was launched by Persia in 481 BC. One of the largest armies in ancient history, it crossed the Hellespont Strait (Dardanelles) over a bridge of boats and marched southward into Athens where it burned the abandoned city, destroying the temple and statues atop the Acropolis. Meanwhile, the Persian fleet pursued the Greek fleet to Salamis, an island near Athens. In the ensuing battle, 400 Greek vessels under Themistocles defeated 1200 Persian vessels. Xerxes, who watched from a golden throne on a hill overlooking the harbour, fled to Asia.

The following year the Persian army was driven out of Attica and Athens' brilliant leadership catapulted the city-state into a position of Greek domination. This period, the apex of Classical Greece, is known as the Golden Age of Athens, for it was a period in world history that has exerted a profound influence over subsequent civilizations. The great statesman Pericles, who became head of the Athenian city-state in 460 BC, commissioned the famous sculptor Phidias to design and oversee the completion of the Parthenon and other architectural masterpieces. Art and culture thrived, and Greek drama reached its highest development with the tragic plays of Euripides and Sophocles.

Born in a suburb of Athens, Sophocles repeatedly won the city's annual dramatic contest and his surviving works include the masterpieces *Antigone*, *Oedipus Tyrannus* and *Oedipus at Colonus*. Sophocles introduced important innovations to Greek drama, increasing the number of actors from two to three, which reduced the influence of the chorus and allowed for more complicated action and characterization. He crafted his plays using a psychological and dramatic unity, rather than a central myth, and his characters humanized Greek drama, their struggles no longer controlled by the plays' themes of religion and morality.

Another famous playwright from this period was Aristophanes, whose comic satire later influenced Ben Jonson and Henry Fielding. Prominent citizens of Athens were often the targets of Aristophanes's biting wit and astute characterization. Among those he satirized were his fellow playwright Euripides and the philosopher Socrates.

THE GREEK PHILOSOPHERS

Philosophy, the search for wisdom, originated in ancient Greece, where the pursuit of knowledge for its own sake began with speculation about the underlying nature of the physical world. The first school of philosophy, founded near Ephesus in Asia Minor, took the initial radical step of applying a scientific rather than a mythological explanation to natural phenomena. Other schools of philosophy were subsequently founded, each contributing to a growing knowledge of natural science. Some philosophers were of questionable reputation, such as the Sophists who instructed the emerging merchant classes on how to achieve success in life, by offering lessons in public speaking, legal argument and general culture in return for large sums of money.

In contrast to the Sophists, defined by Aristotle as men "who make money by sham wisdom", was the great philosopher Socrates who

Philosophers such as Socrates would stroll the shady colonnades of ancient Athens.

refused to accept payment for his teachings, maintaining that he had no positive knowledge to offer except the awareness of the need for more knowledge. Born in Athens around 470 BC, the son of a sculptor and a mid-wife, Socrates received a regular elementary education in literature, music and gymnastics. He initially followed his father's craft and even served as an infantryman in several battles, but he spent most of his mature life strolling barefooted in the streets of Athens, engaging people in conversation. Socrates, who believed in provoking people to think for themselves, founded no school of philosophy and left no written records of his teachings, although these were preserved by his famous pupil Plato.

The teachings of Socrates, who was considered the wisest man in Greece, were based on self-control and self-knowledge. He inspired other philosophers with both his words ("How many things there are that I do not need") and his actions (wearing one garment in both summer and winter). His religious views were eventually declared blasphemous and he was charged in 399 BC with various offences, including corrupting the morals of the young. Plato defended Socrates at his trial by jury, but Socrates was condemned by a small majority. Although his friends planned his escape from prison, Socrates refused to break the law and, after spending his last day with friends, he calmly drank a cup of hemlock according to the customary procedure of execution.

Plato continued extolling his teacher's insights. An ethical and social idealist, Plato believed that the ideal state of a sound mind in a sound body required that the intellect control desires and passions, just as the ideal state of society requires that the wisest men rule the pleasure-seeking masses. One of Plato's students was Aristotle, whose father was a physician to the King of Macedonia. The king's grandson, who became Alexander the Great, was placed under the tutorship of Aristotle in 343 BC, who took charge of the young Alexander's education. Aristotle remained the single great authority of science and philosophy throughout the Middle Ages, laying the foundation for modern science with his accumulation of facts and observations. A prolific author, he wrote essays and books on many subjects including logic, metaphysics and politics.

THE DECLINE OF ATHENS

While Athens thrived both economically and artistically in the 5th century BC, its foreign policy proved its undoing. Sparta, ever envious of Athenian prosperity, led the Peloponnesian League in active opposition to Athens, a power struggle that lasted from 431 to 404 BC, when Sparta finally established its supremacy. The Athenians revolted a year later, followed by other city states, and each began individually to seek aid from their former enemy, Persia.

Alliances formed and fell, with Sparta eventually reaching a peace settlement with Persia in which the west coast of Asia Minor was ceded to the Persians and the Greek city-states were declared autonomous. But bickering and fighting continued among the city-states and Greece's internal strife eventually resulted in its northern neighbour, Macedon, slowly gaining military and political control of the Greek states under the leadership of Philip II. The Macedonian king was preparing for war with Persia when he was assassinated in 336 BC and succeeded by his 20-year-old son Alexander III, who quickly suppressed any Greek rebellion by razing Thebes as a warning to other city-states.

Alexander, as head of an allied Greek army, viewed himself as the champion of pan-Hellenism and in 334 BC, when he embarked on the greatest conquest of ancient times, overthrowing the Persian Empire and extending his empire into India, he also spread Hellenistic culture throughout the eastern Mediterranean, Near East and parts of Asia. While the city-states of Greece stagnated, their culture flourished elsewhere, most notably at Alexandria in Egypt. Founded by Alexander the Great in 332 BC, the city became a great centre of Hellenistic culture, its famous university and celebrated libraries perpetuating the art and learning of classical Greece.

THE ROMAN EMPIRE

The rise of Rome, from city-state to empire, is one of history's most gripping epics of war and conquest. Founded around 750 BC, Rome grew from a salt port on the River Tiber to a sizeable city governed by a republic. The leaders of the Roman Republic eventually embarked on a campaign of military expansion that marked the beginning of Rome's long march to empire. Moving southward across Italy to the shores of Sicily, they eventually came face to face with the imperial ambitions of Carthage, a city-state that controlled northwest Africa and the islands of the western Mediterranean. The two powers engaged in a titanic struggle called the Punic Wars, which unfolded in three distinct conflicts between 264 and 146 BC. During the Second Punic War, from 218 to 201 BC, the Carthaginian general Hannibal led a famous military expedition, transported by elephants, across the Alps into Italy where he was initially victorious against Rome. However, Carthage was ultimately defeated, and the weakened city was finally blockaded and razed by the Romans during the Third Punic War.

Rome's territorial gains continued expanding both eastward and westward. Julius Caesar, born into one of oldest patrician families in Rome about 100 BC, left his mark across Western Europe, from the Alps to the Atlantic. From 58 to 49 BC he fought in the Gallic Wars, by the end of which all of Gaul – the seed of modern France – had fallen under Roman control. Caesar also defeated the Britons in 54 BC, and his military campaigns established him as one of the greatest commanders of all time. His willingness to endure hardships and his personal attention to his troops (he was said to know all by name) earned him the devotion of his men. Caesar eventually became leader of the democratic (or popular) party and an adversary of the senate. Against their opposition, Caesar organized a coalition – the First Triumvirate – which consisted of Pompey, commander-in-chief of the army, Crassus, the wealthiest man in Rome, and Caesar, whose forceful personality kept the coalition intact despite an ongoing animosity between Pompey and Crassus.

Upon the death of Caesar's daughter Julia, who was married to Pompey, the principal personal tie between the two men was broken

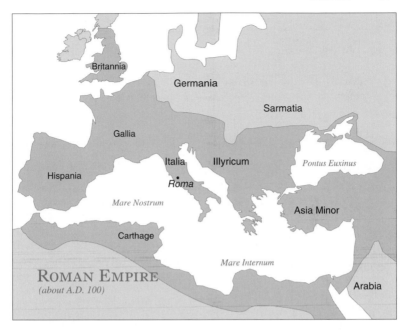

Britannia

Germania

Sarmatia

Gallia

Italia   Illyricum   *Pontus Euxinus*

Hispania

Roma

Mare Nostrum

Asia Minor

Carthage

Mare Internum

ROMAN EMPIRE
(about A.D. 100)

Arabia

and Pompey's jealousy of Caesar's military victories came to a head when Crassus died in 53 BC and the First Triumvirate ended. The senate feared Caesar, a military hero and champion of the people, and supported Pompey. In December, 50 BC, the senate demanded that Caesar relinquish his army. He responded that he would do so only if Pompey relinquished his. This enraged the senate which drew up a bill demanding the dismantlement of Caesar's army. Marc Antony and Cassius, who remained faithful to Caesar, vetoed the bill and were expelled from the senate. They joined Caesar, who mobilized his army and, upon declaring that "the die is cast", crossed the Rubicon to enter Italy and thus begin a civil war. His triumphant march to Rome caused the senate to flee.

Caesar pursued Pompey to Greece and, with a much smaller army, routed Pompey's fleet near Pharsalus. Pompey then fled to Egypt, again with Caesar in pursuit, and was killed there. At Alexandria, Caesar lived for a while with Cleopatra, establishing her firmly on the Egyptian throne. He then headed to Asia Minor, where an easy victory over the ancient country of Pontus prompted his famous words "Veni, vidi, vici" – I came, I saw, I conquered. When a triumphant Caesar returned to Rome in 47 BC, the great leader pardoned all his enemies, then set about improving the living conditions of the people. His dictatorial powers aroused widespread resentment, however, and Caesar was stabbed to death in the senate house on March 15, 44 BC.

Antony, who gave a famous funeral address in Caesar's honour, stirred the mob into anger and drove Caesar's conspirators from Rome. Antony then formed an alliance with Octavian, Caesar's grand-nephew

*Rome became a city of grandeur
as each succeeding emperor
after Augustus (shown here)
added his own monuments.*

and heir, who arranged a Second
Triumvirate consisting of himself,
Antony and Lepidus, which ruled
Rome for five years amid political
turmoil and the ongoing threat of
civil war. Antony, who had a
notorious reputation for riotous
living, met Cleopatra in 42 BC
and fell hopelessly in love. Five
years later, he settled with her in
Alexandria to pursue a life of pleasure. Back in Rome, the growing ill
will towards him culminated in the famous naval battle off Actium in
31 BC, at which Octavian's fleet, commanded by Agrippa, defeated the
less-manouevrable ships of Antony and Cleopatra. The two lovers fled
to Egypt where they committed suicide.

Octavian became the first emperor of Rome in 27 BC, receiving
from the senate the title Augustus. His rule began a long 200-year period of peace, during which an extensive system of roads was built, linking Rome with its most distant provinces. Remarkably durable, these
roads were generally built in four layers, the uppermost layer consisting
of a pavement of stones or pebbles set in concrete. The Appian Way
was one of the first of these great highways, many of which are, in part,
still used today.

Augustus also patronized the arts and letters, which were largely an imitation of Greek culture. Many of the Greek gods had been adopted by the Romans, who also became influenced by Greek mysteries – secret cults based on primitive fertility rites, including the worship of Isis, the nature goddess of ancient Egypt. The mysteries, which fulfilled an individual's desire for personal salvation, created a religious climate conducive to the eventual ascent of Christianity.

Meanwhile a line of notorious emperors left their mark on the Roman Empire. Tiberius, step-son of Augustus, was unpopular in Rome and spent his latter years ruling the empire by correspondence from Capri. Caligula, a cruel and insane tyrant, was eventually murdered. His successor, Claudius, found by soldiers hiding behind a palace curtain when Caligula was murdered, was hauled forth and proclaimed emperor. During his reign, Claudius had one of his wives killed and he himself was eventually poisoned by his wife Agrippina, who was a sister of Caligula and a niece of Claudius. Her son Nero, begat from a previous marriage, became emperor. Cruel and calculating, Nero eventually murdered his step-brother, his mother and his wife Octavia. When a fire destroyed half of Rome in 64 AD, Nero accused the Christians of starting it and thus began a barbarous persecution, with St. Peter and St. Paul among the many Christians killed. Nero rebuilt much of the city on the right bank of the Tiber, with broader streets and impressive buildings, but a series of revolts caused him to commit suicide in 68 and his memory was publicly execrated.

The death of Nero marked the end of the Julio-Claudian line. After a brief struggle, Vespasian became emperor, followed by his son Titus in

Constantine's arch was raised in 312 AD to commemorate a military victory making him the unchallenged ruler of Rome's west empire.

79 AD. A benevolent ruler, Titus completed the Colosseum and built a luxurious bath. He also lent aid to victims of the volcanic eruption of Vesuvius, which buried Pompeii and Herculaneum. Before becoming emperor, his military campaigns had included the capture and destruction of Jerusalem in 70 AD.

Several great emperors ruled during the 1st century AD. Trajan, born in Spain and the first non-Italian to head the empire, pushed its eastern borders past Mesopotamia. His successor Hadrian pulled Roman rule back to the Euphrates, and in Britain he built Hadrian's Wall to keep out the northern barbarians who were threatening Rome's developing province. Marcus Aurelius ruled during the Golden Age of the empire, from 161 to 180 AD. A humanitarian, he improved the living conditions of poor children and tried to curb the brutality at gladiatorial shows. He was also a man of letters, whose philosophy was based on Stoicism, a Greek school of philosophy which incorporated the Socratic ideals of virtue and self-sufficiency.

Roman law forms the basis of modern civil law, and the greatest figure in its development was the learned jurist Papinian. A close friend of the emperor Septimius Severus who ruled from 193 to 211, Papian was a stern moralist whose chief works became the foremost authority in legal decisions. Under Roman law, an important distinction was established between public law, in which the state is directly involved, and private law, which addresses disputes between individuals.

As the 2nd century drew to a close, the decline of the Roman Empire began. A series of emperors ruled in rapid succession during the 3rd century and, with the capture of the emperor Valerian by the Persians in 260, the empire fell into anarchy. Diocletian, named emperor by the army in 284, divided the empire into four political sections: two eastern and two western. In 330, Constantine I moved the empire's capital to Byzantium and renamed it Constantinople. He also granted universal religious tolerance, which allowed Christians to worship without fear of persecution.

The Roman empire became permanently divided into East and West after the death of Theodosius I in 395. As the Dark Ages descended on Europe, Rome's western empire soon foundered, and not until the 19th century did Italy recover from the fall of Rome. The eastern (Byzantine) empire, however, endured for a thousand years despite constant invasions, religious controversies and internal political strife.

Constantine the Great

MIDDLE AGES

The Middle Ages, between the fall of Rome and the beginning of the Renaissance, were once viewed as a thousand years of darkness. The designation of Dark Ages now refers strictly to the Early Middle Ages (c. 450-750), when the collapse of the West Roman Empire plunged western Europe into turmoil. Historians view the year 476, when emperor Romulus Augustulus abdicated, as the end of Rome.

The seeds of Rome's demise were sown by the emperor Constantine. Within 15 years of taking the reins of power, Constantine made two decisions, either of which alone would have changed the future of the world. The first was to embrace Christianity as the official religion of the Roman Empire and the second was to transfer the capital from Rome to the city of Byzantium, which became known as Constantinople.

Genoa, like other medieval seaports, was entered through fortified gates.

Constantine's disillusionment with Rome – its republican and pagan traditions matched with its inferior location – was confirmed on his second visit to the city in 326 AD. To him, the old city seemed decadent, tired and vulnerable. Constantine's vision was to create a New Rome where its citizens were Christian, its streets and public buildings clean and new, and its grandeur supreme in the world. In a period of just three years, he stripped cities throughout the empire of monuments, columns and artwork for his new capital, and in 330 he formally dedicated Constantinople to the God of the Christians.

Moving the capital east resulted quite quickly – and unexpectedly – in splitting the realm, and eventually led to a schism between the Roman (Catholic) church and the Eastern (Orthodox) church. While the Eastern (or Byzantine) Empire became a military, commercial and cultural power, focused on regaining territories from the Persians, the West Roman Empire suffered waves of Germanic invaders: Visigoths, Vandals, Franks, Ostrogoths and Lombards. The emperors of Constantinople tried to hold on to the empire's western province but their attention was soon directed at a new threat to their eastern frontiers, namely the rise of Islam.

Paganism & Christianity

The pagan rituals of ancient Rome were slowly assimilated into Christian festivals during the Middle Ages. Saint Valentine's Day, a feast day established by the Christians in memory of the martyrdom of the 3rd-century saint, was rooted in the Roman feast of Lupercalia. This ancient festival was held in honour of Faunus, a woodland deity (identified with the Greek Pan), who was attended by fauns (similar to the Greek satyrs), which were half man and half goat. In ancient Rome, two male youths dressed as goats (which embodied sexuality) would run around the city slapping people with strips of goat skin.

When this pagan holiday became christianized in medieval times, St. Valentine came to be associated with the union of lovers under conditions of duress. According to legend, the young priest Valentine, while imprisoned for his Christian beliefs, would pick violets that grew outside his cell window and write messages to his loved ones on the heart-shaped leaves, delivering them by dove. The modern 'valentine' appeared in England and America in the mid-19th century, establishing the popular custom of exchanging Valentine's Day cards each February 14th.

Also dating from the Middle Ages is the great Christian festival of Christmas (Christ's mass), which became a widely celebrated feast day in western Europe in the 4th century. December 25th was chosen as the date to celebrate the nativity of Jesus Christ, a date coinciding closely with winter solstice in the Northern hemisphere, which was traditionally a time of pagan rejoicing. Saint Nicholas, the patron of children and sailors in Greece, Sicily and other places, was a 4th-century bishop of Myra in Asia Minor, and the December 6th feast day of St. Nicholas eventually became a children's holiday in parts of Europe. Called Sint Nikolaas in Dutch, the saint was adopted by the English in colonial New York and transformed into Santa Claus, and the children's festival was moved to Christmas Day. In the mid-19th century, Christmas started to become secularized as a holiday of gift giving and good cheer.

With lightening speed this new religion, founded by the Arab prophet Muhammad in 622, spread outward from his birthplace of Mecca. By 732 the Arabs had swept across northern Africa into Spain, threatening to add southwestern France to their conquests. Called Saracens by the Christians (Moors in Spain), the Arabs closed the Mediterranean to outside commerce, thus isolating western Europe. Amid the political and social upheaval of western Europe, in which the Germanic and Roman cultures were assimilating, Christianity became a unifying force – despite an ongoing dispute between the pope in Rome and the patriarch in Constantinople, both of whom claimed leadership of Christendom.

In 800, Charlemagne, the Carolingian king of the Franks, was crowned emperor of the West by the pope in Rome, and this symbolic ceremony introduced a new concept: the interdependence of church and state. Such sharing of power did not exist in the Orthodox East, where the emperors embodied both spiritual and secular authority, regularly installing patriarchs of their choice. Charlemagne's splendid court was located not in Rome but in Aachen (now part of West Germany near the Belgian and Dutch borders), and the centre of civilization in western Europe shifted northward. The Mediterranean, once a great highway of commerce and cultural exchange, became a border zone dominated by the Arabs and the Byzantine Empire.

Feudalism, originating in the empire of Charlemagne, spread to neighbouring countries and provided protection from attack by plundering Germanic bands. An agricultural-based system of distributing wealth, feudalism was based on a hierarchy of king, nobility and peasantry. The nobles, who held land directly from the king, provided protection to the serfs who worked the land. Chivalry, a fusion of Christian and military concepts, grew out of feudalism and

The cross became the coat-of-arms of the Knights Hospitalers.

inspired the Crusades – an attempt by western Europeans to regain the Holy Land from the Muslims. Monastic orders of knights were sworn to uphold the Christian ideal, and tournaments were staged in which knights could prove their chivalric virtues.

The Holy Roman Empire, successor state to the empire of Charlemagne, was established in 936, but its emperors, who were initially elected by German princes and crowned by the pope, were constantly struggling to assert their control over a fragmented western Europe. The papacy, surrounded by corruption, was weakened in 1083 when Rome was sacked by the Normans. In 1305, Pole Clement V moved the papal court to Avignon, where it came under French control until its return to Rome in 1378.

Meanwhile, the Byzantine Empire had spiralled into a slow decline upon the death of one of its greatest emperors, Justinian, in 565 AD. Justinian's energy and determination were evidenced by his ambitious building and reform programs for Constantinople, and had also resulted in the recovery of most of Italy. Although the empire stayed more or less intact over the next four centuries, encompassing the area of present-day Turkey and beyond to the Danube, most of Greece and southern Italy, it was riven from within with political and religious intrigues. The Byzantine Empire nearly fell apart in the early 7th century, but was saved, and its borders actually expanded, thanks to the efforts of the great warrior and administrator Emperor Heraclius.

During a time when most of Europe was vulnerable and in chaos, the Byzantine Empire was a bulwark against waves of Arab attacks. Then, during the 11th and 12th centuries, as the Franks and Southern Italians grew in strength and the rift between the Catholic Latins and the Orthodox Byzantines grew, Constantinople found itself fighting on two fronts and becoming progressively weaker. In 1071, the Seljuk Turks finally broke into the Byzantine heartland of Antolia (Asia Minor) in a decisive battle at Manzikert. Although this led to the fall of most of the empire's Asian possessions, the death blow was administered not by the determined Turks, but by a 90-year-old man from Venice. His name was Enrico Dandolo who, as doge of Venice, led a fleet of Crusaders to take the fabled city of Constantinople – the largest and most splendid city of medieval Europe. In 1204, the Crusaders breached the seawalls of the city and Dandolo, who was blind, led his troops into the 'Queen of Cities' and stripped Constantinople of its wealth. It was a blow from which the Byzantines never recovered.

In the middle of the 14th century, a tribe broke away from the crumbling Seljuk Turk nation and became, under a series of strong leaders, the rapidly growing Ottoman Empire. In 1451, with the accession of Sultan Mehmet II, the city of Constantinople (all that remained of the Byzantine Empire) found itself surrounded. In preparation for the siege of the great city, Mehmet built the largest cannon the world had ever known, and in 1453, the Ottoman Turks broke through the great Theodosian land walls and seized Constantinople. The glorious capital of one of the world's longest-lasting empires had fallen, and the new Ottoman Empire now occupied the 'Queen of Cities'.

By the late Middle Ages, feudalism was firmly entrenched in France and southern Italy, but not in northern Italy, where the rise of the city state had begun in the 10th century. The two great Italian seaports of Venice and Genoa, distinct in character and constantly warring with each other, enjoyed a material prosperity based largely on trade with the Middle East. The Christian crusades generated additional wealth for these and other city states, and influential banking firms came to domi-

MONASTICISM & SCHOLASTICISM

Christian monasticism originated on the Egyptian deserts in the 3rd and 4th centuries AD. St. Anthony, an Egyptian recluse who gave away his large inheritance at the age of 20, founded the first monastic community when a colony of hermits grew up about him. During the Middle Ages, monastic orders became seats of learning and administration, and were strongly supported by Charlemagne and his heirs. Young children of nobility and gifted youngsters from the lower classes were often educated in monasteries and convents. Daily life in a monastic community emphasized prayer, scriptural reading and work. The Christian crusades, between the 11th and 13th centuries, led to the founding of such monastic orders as the Knights Hospitalers and the Knights Templars.

Religious orders also played a leading role in the expansion of universities and the development of scholasticism. When Arabic translations of Aristotle's teachings were rendered into Latin between 1120 and 1220, the impact on western scholars was immense. Using reason to deepen his understanding of religious beliefs, a Dominican named St. Thomas Aquinas became the leading figure in the scholastic movement to 'christianize Aristotle'.

nate Genoa and the powerful republic of Florence, where the prominent Medici family rose from bankers to dukes. Although guilds perpetuated the Christian and medieval spirit of collective wealth and regulated competition, the growth of cities and the ascent of the merchant class eventually brought about the demise of feudalism, marking the end of the Middle Ages and the dawn of the Renaissance.

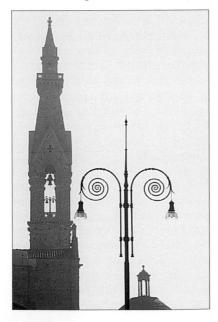

THE RENAISSANCE

Called the *rinascita* in Italian and the *renaissance* in French, this 'rebirth' of classical antiquity's arts and sciences not only produced an outpouring of creativity never before seen, it ultimately ushered in modern civilization. The Renaissance, which originated in Italy, did not begin with a single momentous event but began as an artistic and intellectual movement that gradually gained momentum and eventually spread across Western Europe to Great Britain, where humanist thought influenced the works of Ben Jonson and William Shakespeare.

The seeds of the Renaissance's flowering were planted during the late Middle Ages, when a rediscovery of Greek and Roman literature led to the eventual development of the humanist movement. The Italian poet Petrarch, who lived from 1304 to 1374, is considered the first modern poet and the father of humanism. By proclaiming pagan antiquity as the most enlightened stage of history, and the centuries that followed as a time of darkness, he set in motion the pursuit of learning based on a secular rather than a religious framework. This humanistic challenge to scholasticism advocated not a pre-Christian paganism but a reconciliation of classical antiquity's artistic and intellectual achievements with Christian beliefs.

The Renaissance began around 1400 in Florence, where local writers and artists cultivated an interest in the classical teachings of Greek scholars. By the mid-14th century, the triumph of an emerging capitalist class over the medieval guild merchants and artisans was marked by the rise of the Medici banking family. Politically powerful and generous patrons of the arts and letters, the Medicis founded a library and filled it with Greek and Roman manuscripts. When Constantinople fell to the Turks in 1453, Greek scholars fled to Italy with manuscripts documenting the civilizations of ancient Greece, further fuelling a thirst for knowledge and an active search for classical works. The bronze and marble sculptures excavated in Rome and other ancient sites, which had previously been treated as scrap metal or mortar, were now highly valued by collectors.

As medieval courtliness and codes of conduct gave way to a new era that focussed on expressiveness and emotionalism, the social status of the artist was elevated. Lorenzo de Medici's Florentine court became known as the Platonic Academy and prominent members of this circle included the artists Botticelli and Michelangelo. Stressing human values and capabilities, humanism's rejection of medieval religious authority climaxed in 1517 when the German cleric Martin Luther sparked the Protestant Reformation with his open attack on the doctrines of the wealthy and corrupt Catholic church. Condemning such practises as the sale of indulgences (pardons for sin), Luther believed that individuals could communicate directly with God and could seek salvation by reading the Bible, obtaining grace not through the sacraments (religious ceremonies conducted by priests) but through faith.

The growth of literacy, education and middle-class wealth provided a fertile environment for the new Protestant culture, which adopted an austere taste in Christian art, in contrast to the worldly opulence of Rome. Secular art was, however, patronized and new subject matters – landscapes, still lifes and scenes of daily life – formed part of the Renaissance taste in personal artwork, as did portraiture. Wealthy private collectors commissioned painters to decorate the walls, chests and other objects of their private palaces. The church, however, continued to be the foremost patron of the arts, and in the 16th century the centre of Italian art shifted from Florence to Rome, where the Vatican commissioned Michelangelo, Leonardo da Vinci and Raphael for various projects, resulting in some of the greatest masterpieces of Renaissance art. Venetian art also came into its full glory in the 16th century. The Venetian school was known for the superb colouring of its oil paintings, created by such masters as Bellini and Giorgione, and later succeeded by Titian, Veronese and Tintoretto.

The sciences were also advanced during the 16th century, aided by the rediscovery of Galen's physiological and anatomical studies and Ptolemy's *Geography*. Scientific thinkers began refining the theories of classical physics, with Copernicus proposing the heliocentric model of the solar system, and Galileo inventing an accurate telescope for viewing the heavens. Leonardo da Vinci, the consummate Renaissance man, studied anatomy and astronomy, his copious notes covering everything from the curved trajectory to metallurgical techniques. In his paintings, accurate depictions of the human form were based on his anatomical observations. Other sciences that were developed during the Renaissance included botany, zoology and astrology.

The scientific and intellectual achievements of the Renaissance, along with seaborne exploration and the discovery of new lands and cultures, fostered further learning in the 17th century. The rationalism of Descartes, the empiricism of Francis Bacon and John Locke, and the ground breaking achievements of Isaac Newton, widely considered the greatest scientist of all time, reflected an intensifying belief in natural law, universal order and human reason. The Renaissance also set the stage for an emerging middle class which originated with the merchants and craftsmen in medieval towns and which eventually spearheaded the revolutionary upheavals of the 18th century.

THE GRAND TOUR

The 18th century in Europe was called the Age of Enlightenment – an era marked by colonial expansion, scientific discoveries and mechanical inventions. The first geographical survey was undertaken in France, as was the first flight in a hot-air balloon. Captain James Cook and other explorers opened up new territories across vast expanses of the Pacific Ocean, while Wolfgang Amadeus Mozart entertained the courts of Europe with his musical genius. Rational and scientific approaches were now applied to all issues – whether social, economic, religious or political. Amid a stimulating atmosphere of skepticism and idealism, Christianity was questioned and classical teachings were scru-

A British tour group at Giza.

tinized. The French philosopher Voltaire even dared to declare that Plato "wrote better than he reasoned".

The most cataclysmic event of 18th-century Europe was the French Revolution, which began in 1789 and eventually affected the entire world as it tore down the medieval structures of Europe and made way for 19th-century liberalism and nationalism. France, not yet free of feudalism, was ripe for rebellion. The country was still ruled by two privileged classes, the nobility and the clergy, and a simmering resentment among the oppressed bourgeoisie and working classes led to widespread violence and anarchy. A Parisian mob's storming of the Bastille, a prison fortress, symbolized the revolt of the lower classes. In 1793, to the horror of other European monarchs, the king of France was beheaded, along with hundreds of aristocrats.

The army general Napoleon Bonaparte rose to dictatorial power in 1799 and had himself crowned emperor in 1804. Although the British navy defeated the French at Trafalgar in 1805, Napoleon soon controlled the European continent. The Holy Roman Empire dissolved in 1806, and Napoleon installed his brothers on the thrones of Europe. Napoleon was defeated by the allied forces of Britain, Prussia, Sweden and Austria in 1814 and exiled to the island of Elba off the coast of Italy, but he returned a year later, only to be defeated in the Waterloo Campaign and sent as a prisoner of war to the isolated British island of Saint Helena in the south Atlantic, where he died six years later. The French monarchy was restored, but unrest and rebellion continued, culminating in a bloody insurrection in 1848. The collapse of the French monarchy and the establishment of a new republic caused a chain reaction across Europe, spawning public demonstrations and a general cry for the overthrow of monarchies as an urban bourgeoisie called for constitutional, representative government.

Propelling this massive upheaval was the Industrial Revolution. Originating in England in the mid-1700s, it marked Europe's transition from an agricultural-based society to a modern industrialized society. The steam engine was invented in England in 1698 and by 1814 the steam locomotive was being used to power early rail travel, followed by the first steamship crossing of the Atlantic in 1819. Europe began rapidly industrializing, building roads and rail lines. A line from Marseille to Cannes was laid in 1863 and extended a year later to Nice, with Tsar Alexander II and his wife among the first to arrive by train in Nice. The railroad line was extended to Monaco a few years later, transforming the tiny principality into a gambling mecca, and by 1870 the rail line reached the Italian border. The railroad revolutionized travel, for people could now journey across the continent in a fraction of the time it had once taken. Leisure travel, formerly the reserve of the privileged wealthy, would soon become the domain of the masses.

Leisure travel to the Mediterranean originated with the grand tours of the British aristocracy. By the mid-18th century, it was commonplace for the young men of Britain's upper classes to embark on an educational tour of Europe to acquaint themselves with famous classical ruins and the Renaissance art of Rome and other Italian cities. Although politically fragmented and in a state of economic decline, Italy was still considered the heart of western culture. Britain had become the wealthiest nation in the world due to its colonial trade, but its privileged classes, who were schooled in Latin and the classics, felt isolated from the cultural riches of Europe. Thus, a Grand Tour was considered necessary for a person to become a fully educated member of elite society.

Italy, and the Mediterranean in general, also held a sensual allure. Escaping damp winters and the prevailing work ethic of the Protestant north, young Englishmen were understandably eager to sojourn in the sunny south of Europe where warm weather and uninhibited attitudes extended to the pleasures of the flesh.

Reaching the Grand Tour's 'must-sees' – namely Rome, Florence, Naples and Venice – entailed a lengthy and at times arduous journey by boat and stage-coach. Early tourists included James Boswell, who achieved fame with his *Account of Corsica* (1768), and Edward Gibbon, who claimed that a walk through the Forum's ruins inspired him to write *The History of the Decline and Fall of the Roman Empire*. Goethe, the German poet and scientist, was smitten with Naples and its bright colours and carefree mood. As there were no guidebooks for the early travellers, works by Vergil and other ancient classics were used as references.

The French Revolution and the Napoleonic Wars interrupted continental touring by the British, but these conflicts didn't stop Lord Byron from voyaging to the Mediterranean in 1809. Fresh from Cambridge, he sailed to Lisbon, then entered the Mediterranean Sea, stopping at Gibraltar, Sardinia and Malta before embarking on an overland tour of Greece and Turkey. The defeat of Napoleon at Waterloo in 1815 brought peace to the continent and one of the first postwar travellers to

Grand Canal, Venice

return was Lord Byron, who lived for three years in Venice before settling in Genoa. Other Romantic poets followed suit, including Keats,
who died in Rome, and Shelley, who drowned while sailing in the Bay
of Spezia on the Italian Riviera. Byron died of a fever in 1824, while
working for the the cause of Greek independence. The Romantic poets'
literary works spawned a fresh interest by the British in the antiquities
of continental Europe, and the first modern guidebooks appeared
around this time, with the Mediterranean homes of Byron joining the
lists of local attractions. William Thackery, Charles Dickens and Mark
Twain were among the popular writers given free passage on
steamships in exchange for writing a book about their travels. By the
end of the 19th century, the Americans were second only to the British
in terms of numbers touring the Mediterranean.

In 1841, an English cabinet maker named Thomas Cook organized
the first group excursion when he obtained reduced train fares for members of his temperance society, who were travelling to a regional meeting. His organizational skills soon led to a new concept – the guided
tour. These packaged holidays appealed to average Britons of modest
means who wanted to travel abroad and see the sights previously
enjoyed only by the wealthy, who would spend months, even years,
completing their grand tours.

As British and American tourists began travelling through Europe in
steadily increasing numbers, the wealthy elite sought ever more exclusive and exotic destinations. Egypt became a popular winter destination, with tourists arriving by steamer at Alexandria and spending a few
days in Cairo to view the pyramids before heading up the Nile aboard a
hired dahabeeyah, a river sailing craft. Cook's tours expanded into
Egypt as well, when regular steamer service was introduced in the early
1870s, and within a decade Cook's Nile fleet had grown to 40 vessels.

A Middle East grand tour wasn't complete without a pilgrimage to
the Holy Land, with tourists travelling by horseback across the desert
accompanied by an army of servants, including armed guards, who
would set up tents for sleeping each night. This was luxury camping,
with meals served in dining tents on white linen and fine china, and the
sleeping tents outfitted with iron bedsteads and clean sheets.

Luxury travel, in the form of Pullman rail cars, grand hotels and
palatial steamships, enabled the wealthy to isolate themselves from the
travelling masses. By the end of the industrial revolution, the 'high
bourgeoisie', consisting of rich industrialists and bankers, were distin-
guishing themselves from the 'petty bourgeoisie', which comprised
tradespeople and white-collar workers. The bourgeoisie's preoccupa-
tion with status and material gain had long been ridiculed, beginning in
the 17th century with witty satires by the French playwright Moliere,
who was himself the son of a merchant, but some of society's commen-
tators rose to the defence of working men and women, including Karl
Marx, who interpreted attacks on the upwardly mobile classes as an
effort to subdue the wage-earning proletariat.

*A group of 19th-century British tourists, organized by Thomas Cook,
pose for a photograph at the ruins of Pompeii.*

Archaeology, which originated in Renaissance Italy with the excavation of ancient Greek sculptures, was advanced in the 18th century by
the chance discovery of an ancient Roman resort called Herculaneum,
on the Bay of Naples, followed a few decades later by the unearthing of
Pompeii. Both places had been buried in ash when Mt. Vesuvius erupted in 79 AD, and their discovery triggered a new wave of interest in
antiquarian culture, with parties of fashionable ladies and gentlemen,
equipped with shovels and picnic baskets, digging for bronze and marble statuary to add to their collections. In 1764, the German classical
archaeologist Johann Winckelmann published a scholarly account of
the Naples discoveries – the first such report in the field of classical
antiquities.

Another movement, fostered during the Age of Enlightenment, was
the construction of art museums, galleries and academies, including the
famous British Museum, which was established in 1753 and began
occupying its present buildings in 1829. The Athenian monuments of
ancient Greece sparked public interest in England when Lord Elgin, the
British ambassador to Turkey (which at that time ruled Greece),
removed numerous marble sculptures from the Parthenon. Byron was
among those critical of Elgin, who defended his actions in a pamphlet
he wrote in 1820, claiming he wanted to protect the Greek sculptures
from destruction under Turkish rule. In any event, the 'Elgin marbles',
currently in the British Museum, stimulated a strong interest in ancient
Greece among the English Romantic poets and became the subject of a
poem by John Keats entitled 'On Seeing the Elgin Marbles'.

Egypt also became a source of historical interest when the Rosetta
Stone, a slab of black basalt engraved with hieroglyphics, was discovered at the mouth of the Nile by scientists accompanying Napoleon on

his Egyptian campaign of 1798. Deciphered a quarter of a century later by the French scholar Jean Francois Champollion, the Rosetta Stone's inscriptions provided the first key to understanding the language and lives of the ancient Egyptians. Scientific findings from Napoleon's Egyptian campaign were published in 21 volumes over a 20-year period, thus launching Europe's fascination with ancient Egypt.

Museums began indiscriminately collecting Egyptian antiquities, as dozens of explorers and collectors dug through the desert sands in search of treasures. Eventually a more systematic process was enforced following the British occupation of Egypt in 1882, with all excavated objects recorded and catalogued. Meanwhile, the Egyptian government had made diplomatic gifts of several New Kingdom obelisks, presenting France with one from the Luxor temple, which now stands in the Place de la Concorde in Paris, and sending one of Cleopatra's Needles to England where it was re-erected on the Thames Embankment.

Famous archaeological treasures were also discovered in the Aegean region in the latter half of the 19th century, most notably the discovery of the ruins of Troy by German archaeologist Heinrich Schliemann, a wealthy businessman and student of Homer who used the Homeric poems for reference when searching for ancient sites and identifying the unearthed objects. Schliemann also excavated the ruins of Mycenae, Ithaca and Tiryns. As the century drew to a close, the English archaeologist Arthur Evans began devoting his time to the excavation of the Minoan ruins on Crete.

By the end of the 19th century, advancements in science, mathematics and engineering had produced the diesel and turbine engines, the electric motor, the automobile, the light bulb and the camera. The invention of photography introduced a new medium to the visual arts, and helped fuel the growth of tourism, as people were increasingly exposed to photographic images of faraway lands and exotic cultures.

The opening of the Suez Canal in 1869, linking the Mediterranean to the Red Sea, transformed the Mediterranean from a vast seawater lake into a direct seaway between the Far East and Europe, making it one of the most strategically important areas in the world. The British built a great naval dockyard at Valletta, Malta, as a base for its British Mediterranean Fleet, and other maritime nations maintained fleets in the Mediterranean to protect their seagoing trade. The canal, which is level and has no locks, is about 100 miles (160 km) long. Its construction took 10 years and was supervised by the French engineer Ferdinand de Lesseps, who later faced bankruptcy and was convicted for misappropriating funds when attempting to build the Panama Canal.

MODERN MEDITERRANEAN

The 20th century began with optimism, preceded by a long era of relative peace. However, the decaying Ottoman Empire had left the Balkan territories susceptible to diplomatic intrigue among the European powers of Austria, Britain, Prussia, Russia and France. The imperialistic, territorial and economic rivalries of these countries, along with a rampant spirit of nationalism, all contributed to the outbreak of World War I. Called the Great War, it was the largest war the world had yet seen. Fought chiefly in the trenches of Europe, it spread to the Middle East where Britain stopped a Turkish drive on the Suez Canal, then proceeded to destroy the Ottoman Empire. The British soldier T.E. Lawrence (Lawrence of Arabia) became a leader in the Arab revolt against Turkish domination, and British field marshal Edmund Allenby invaded Palestine, taking Jerusalem in December 1917.

When the First World War ended on November 11, 1918, without a single decisive battle having been fought, at least 10 million people had been killed and 20 million wounded, with additional deaths from starvation and epidemics in the war's aftermath. The face of Europe had radically changed, and a general revulsion to the destruction and suffering of war was symbolized by the creation of the League of Nations. Still, a fervent nationalism soon resurfaced in several countries where the hardships of the Great Depression made the masses vulnerable to the promises of demagogues. In Italy, Benito Mussolini and his Fascists rose to power in 1922. Mussolini gradually turned his premiership into a dictatorship, then began his imperialist designs with the conquest of Ethiopia in 1935. Meanwhile, Adolf Hitler had risen to power in Germany in 1933, where he began rebuilding the German army in preparation for a war of conquest. Both he and Mussolini helped the fascist general Francisco Franco win the Spanish Civil War in 1939.

When Germany invaded Poland on September 1, 1939, the democratic governments of Britain and France declared war. Soon all of the Mediterranean region was pulled into the war, with the Axis powers (Germany, Japan and Italy) occupying North Africa, Greece and Yugoslavia. The German commander Rommel seemed about to take Cairo when British General Montgomery routed the German forces at Alamein in October 1941. Less than a week later, US troops landed in Algeria, helping to clinch an Allied victory in North Africa. Italy surrendered in September 1943, following Allied invasions of Sicily and southern Italy, but German resistance continued until Hitler's suicide in April 1945.

An Allied victory in the Pacific brought the war to an end in August 1945, but the devastation it wreaked remains horrifying to contemplate. Modern warfare had brought upon the world a barbarism of such scale that previous wars paled in comparison. The blanket bombing of cities and Germany's systematic attempt to exterminate entire racial groups had terrorized civilians as well as soldiers and caused millions to die.

In post-war Europe, a widespread aversion to the national rivalries that had provoked such bloodshed and destruction prompted the idea of a united Europe as a way to provide strength and security to the wartorn region and prevent further hostilities. The European Economic Community, formerly referred to as the Common Market, was established in 1957 as an economic and political confederation of European nations. Its original members included Great Britain, Germany, France and Italy, with Greece joining in 1981, followed by Spain and Portugal in 1986. A central banking system was provided by the 1992 Maastricht Treaty, and the gradual introduction of a common currency – the euro – was completed in 2002, the national currencies of 300 million Europeans replaced with 10 billion new bills and 50 billion new coins. Not since the 8th century, when Charlemagne circulated his own silver coinage throughout his empire, had Europe used a common currency. Its introduction has created the practice of 'rounding up' prices, thus making some things more expensive for locals. In Italy, for instance, people grumbled about the price of fruit and vegetables being affected by the introduction of the euro. When a cafe in a seaside town near Rome overcharged someone 23 euro cents for his cappuccino, this was too much to bear and a justice of the peace ordered the cafe to refund the price increase plus the plantiff's legal costs – a symbolic victory for Italians bemoaning the loss of the lira.

Joining the European Union has been a hotly debated issue for the citizens of Europe, in both its member and candidate nations. Fierce national rivalries remain, as do economic disparities. Italy's government, looking to reduce its debt before joining the European single currency, considered privatizing some of its famous museums and national monuments, and eventually granted five-year contracts to private companies to maintain and run the Colosseum in Rome and the ruins of Pompeii near Naples.

In 2004, the 15-member European Union admitted 10 new members, including Malta and Cypress, thus increasing the EU's population to more than 450 million. Additional candidate nations, including Croatia, will likely be allowed to join in the following three or four years. Meanwhile, after waiting nearly 40 years, the Muslim (but officially secular) nation of Turkey has been offered a calendar for entry talks, with EU leaders monitoring Turkey's reform progress.

Western Europe's societies have become increasingly diverse in recent decades, with several countries now containing substantial Muslim minorities. The accompanying cultural and religious tensions have resulted in immigration becoming a key election issue in countries such as Italy, where conservatives want to preserve the country's Christian roots. In France, a fiercely secular nation, the government has banned the wearing of ostentatious religious symbols by workers in the public sector and by students in public schools. The ban includes Jewish skullcaps and large Christian crosses, but it was the refusal of Muslim schoolgirls to remove their head scarves – perceived by many French citizens to be a symbol of militant Islam – that prompted the appointment of a presidential commission to address this controversial issue in a country containing the largest Muslim population of western Europe (about seven per cent of France's 60 million people).

According to scholars, Europe's fear of a Muslim invasion dates to medieval times, when Islam was poised to conquer Europe and three-

quarters of Spain was under Moorish (Muslim) rule. For most western-
ers, the year 1492 marks Christopher Columbus's famous voyage from
Spain to the New World, but for fundamentalist Islam this date marks
the end of a halcyon age of Muslim culture and the decline of Muslim
power when the Moors were driven from Spain by the Christian monarchs Ferdinand and Isabella. Shortly after bombs exploded on several
Madrid commuter trains in March 2004, the al-Qaida terrorist network
claimed responsibility and reiterated militant Islam's goal of reclaiming
its lost kingdom of Al-Andalus (Andalusia in southern Spain).

As Europe faces a new war, this time against terrorism, old scores
are still being settled. Efforts to regain the spoils of Holocaust plunder
have intensified, with several officially neutral countries accused of
selling vital supplies to the Nazis in exchange for gold stolen from Jews
and from the central banks of conquered countries. Much of this plundered gold was channelled through Swiss banks, which have agreed to
pay an estimated $1.25 billion in compensation to the tens of thousands
of Holocaust survivors who launched a class-action lawsuit. Art treasures seized during the war are another bone of contention, with governments and individuals pressuring museums to return plundered artwork. The question of rightful ownership is, of course, a contentious
issue, and one that existed long before WWII.

The Greek government has pleaded for decades with the British
Museum to return the marble sculptures taken from the Parthenon in
1802 by Lord Elgin, British ambassador to Greece when it was under
Turkish occupation. Meanwhile, Egypt has sought the return of the
Rosetta Stone and a fragment of the Sphinx's beard, both of which are
housed in the British Museum. But these attempts to repatriate cultural
property have clashed with the mandate of museums, which is to preserve artifacts that might otherwise have been lost or damaged.

Following the sensational discovery in 1922 of King Tutankhamun's
tomb by Howard Carter while under the employ of Lord Carnarvon, the
Egyptian government passed a law that strictly controls excavation and
allows the Egyptian Department of Antiquities to confiscate any findings of archaeological significance. Other countries have established
similar measures. In Greece, permits must be obtained from the government before a team of archaeologists can proceed with an excavation.

During construction of a new airport and highway outside Athens
prior to the 2004 Olympic Games, enough antiquities to fill 4,000
crates were unearthed by archaeologists. Another 30,000 ancient
objects were uncovered in a 10-year dig during construction of the
city's new subway system, and these artifacts, or their replicas, are now
on display at several of the subway stations. Construction projects in
Rome often face delays because almost any digging there leads to the
discovery of antiquities, bringing all work to a halt until study and/or
removal can be completed. The past is a constant companion to the peoples of the Mediterranean.

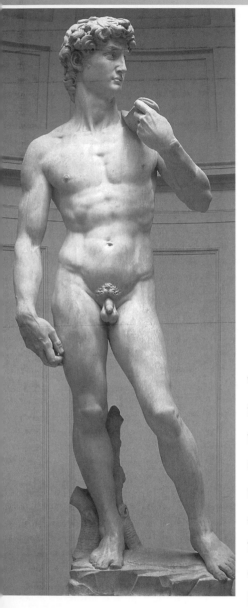

*Michelangelo's David
Galleria dell'Accademia,
Florence*

Western civilization's vast treasury of art and architecture began with the ancient Egyptians, whose megaprojects involved the construction of massive temple complexes. These colossal creations later inspired the Athenians of Classical Greece to transform the Acropolis into a showpiece of artistic and architectural perfection.

Bernini's colonnade
St. Peter's Square, Rome

architecture

architectu

cornice

frieze

architrave

Two thousand years later, when Renaissance artists looked for inspiration, they turned to the classical antiquities of Greece and Rome. In this section, we embark on a visual journey that covers nearly 5,000 years of artistic vision.

The glossary on the next two pages contains terminology used by artists and architects.

Corinthian capital

TALKING ART & ARCHITECTURE

arcade – a series of arches supported by piers or columns; called a 'blind arcade' when attached to a wall.

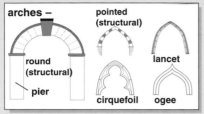

arches –
pointed (structural)
round (structural)
lancet
pier
cirquefoil
ogee

art categories – fine art is any painting, drawing or sculpture that is aesthetically beautiful. In free art, the object is purely ornamental. Decorative art adorns a useful object, such as a flower painted on a plate. The applied arts are functional and include the crafts of weaving, furniture-making, glassmaking and ceramics.

balustrade – railing supported by short pillars, called balusters.

basilica – in ancient Rome, a large rectangular building containing the law courts and serving as a public meeting place. Elements of the Roman basilica were later implemented in Christian churches. Differing from the longitudinal, basilica-plan church is the central-plan church (also called Greek-cross church) which has four arms of equal length.

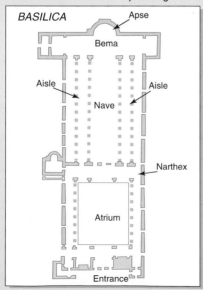

BASILICA
Apse
Bema
Aisle
Aisle
Nave
Narthex
Atrium
Entrance

campanile – bell tower, from the Italian word for bell, *campana*.

caryatid – a sculptured female figure serving as a structural support, used in Egyptian and Greek architecture. A celebrated example is the Porch of the Caryatids atop the Acropolis in Athens.

cathedral – church in which a bishop resides. Important medieval cathedrals include those of Florence, Pisa and Barcelona.

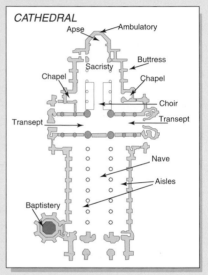

CATHEDRAL
Apse
Ambulatory
Buttress
Sacristy
Chapel
Chapel
Choir
Transept
Transept
Nave
Aisles
Baptistery

clerestory – an upper row of openings or windows that is higher than the rest of the structure. Implemented in certain Egyptian temples, this feature was later used in the great halls of Roman basilicas and became a characteristic element of Gothic churches.

colonnade – a row of columns supporting either an entablature or a series of arches.

fresco – the Italian word for 'fresh'; a technique of painting on wet plaster so that the paint becomes part of the wall.

frieze – a continuous band of painted or sculptured decoration.

gold leaf – gold beaten into very thin 'leaves' and applied to illuminated manuscripts and panel paintings.

hypostyle hall – an outer courtyard bordered with columns.

TALKING ART & ARCHITECTURE

icon – small panel painting of a sacred image, usually Christ, the Virgin Mary or a saint.

Iconoclasm – a movement in 8th and 9th century Byzantium to destroy all figurative religious images.

loggia – an open-air, covered arcade, either free-standing or running alongside a building.

lustreware – pottery finished with an overglaze containing copper and silver to create an iridescent effect. Initially used by Islamic potters, the technique was practised in Moorish Spain and later adopted by Josiah Wedgwood in 18th-century England.

majolica – a technique of decorating and glazing pottery that was highly developed in medieval Italy, beginning in the 11th century, and named for the island of Majorca where the craft was first introduced by Muslim artisans during the Arab conquest of the western Mediterranean.

minaret – a tall slender tower attached to a mosque from which a muezzin calls the faithful to prayer.

mosaic – decorative work in which surfaces are covered with small pieces of coloured materials, such as marble or glass, that are set in plaster or concrete.

orders of architecture – a system devised in Roman times to categorize architectural styles. The three main orders are Doric, Ionic and Corinthian. Tuscan is a simplified version of Doric, with unfluted columns. Composite combines Ionic and Corinthian. Colossal is any order with columns or pillars rising above one storey.

palazzo – stately residence or government building.

pantheon – temple dedicated to all the gods.

pediment – triangular area formed by a gabled roof. A feature of Greek temples, it later became a decorative motif as well, used chiefly over doors and windows.

peristyle hall – an inner court filled with columns

Pieta – representation of the Virgin grieving over the dead Christ lying in her lap.

pillar – general term for upright structural supports, including columns (which are cylindrical), piers (which are square or rectangular) and pilasters (which are piers that project from a wall surface and are generally decorative rather than structural).

plateresque – earliest phase of Spanish Renaissance art, combining Italian influences with Moorish and Gothic elements.

portal – a monumental door or gate.

portico – a columned porch.

relief – figures carved from a flat surface. High relief is deeply carved so that the figures are almost fully detached from their support. Bas-relief consists of low sculptures that barely protrude.

rose window – a large circular window of stained glass and ornamental stonework (tracery), frequently used in Gothic churches.

rustication – a masonry technique that creates a roughly textured surface by projecting blocks of stone beyond the mortar joints.

sarcophagus – large stone coffin, often ornamented.

stele – an upright stone slab bearing a carved illustration or inscription.

stoa – an ancient Greek portico, providing a sheltered promenade.

tempera – form of painting used before the development of oil painting, in which pigments were mixed with egg yolk and water.

terracotta – Italian word for 'baked earth'; a fired, unglazed clay of varying colour (depending on the type of clay), but often a shade of red. One of the oldest known building materials, it is used for pottery and architectural ornament.

treasury – miniature temple for storing votive gifts.

trompe-l'oeil – French for 'deceives the eye'; painting style that utilizes realism and perspective to create the illusion that what is depicted actually exists, i.e. a door or window painted on a wall.

EGYPTIAN ART

In ancient Egypt, where religion dominated all aspects of society, art and architecture served a religious purpose. Stone construction was limited to tombs and temples while people lived in mud-brick dwellings. Even royal palaces were made of mud-brick or wood, with stone used sparingly. A diverse range of stone types were found in the deserts on either side of the Nile valley, and by 2500 BC there were hundreds of quarries scattered across Egypt. Although slave labour was sometimes used to build royal funerary monuments, most work was carried out by free labourers who lived in villages near the building sites and were paid with simple rations.

The basic post-and-lintel system – later adopted by the Greeks – was used exclusively in building temples. Their general design consisted of a massive entrance gate (called a pylon) which opened onto an outer courtyard bordered with columns, which in turn led to an inner court filled with columns. The capitals of Egyptian columns often depicted the closed bud or open flower of the papyrus and lotus flowers, symbols of Lower and Upper Egypt.

The art of ancient Egypt changed little over the centuries, and features of the highly admired Old Kingdom art were imitated by subsequent dynasties. Subjects were portrayed in a formulaic manner so they would be easily recognized and fulfil their symbolic roles. There was an

emphasis on symmetry and separate components, with the human torso and an eye viewed frontally and the arms, legs and face shown in profile. Outer temple walls were decorated with shallow reliefs depicting the victorious pharaoh smiting the enemy, and those on inner walls depicted the pharaoh performing religious rituals. The colourful wall paintings inside royal tombs portrayed military, hunting and ceremonial scenes, along with domestic activities to be continued in the afterlife. Male figures were depicted with a darker skin tone than female figures, a practise introduced in 2580 BC and later adopted by, among others, the artists of the Renaissance.

Entrance to the temple of Horus at Edfu, Upper Egypt.

*Items of trade
are depicted on
the walls of the
temple of
Hatshepsut
(1473-1458 BC).*

Statues of pharaohs were usually huge, to represent their godlike stature, and often combined the human figure, which represented intelligence, with an animal, such as a lion or eagle, which represented strength or swiftness. A famous example is the Great Sphinx at Giza, with the head of a man and the body of a lion. Other colossal monuments included obelisks, which were often raised in pairs outside the entrances to temples. These tapering shafts of red granite, dedicated to the sun god, were covered with deeply incised hieroglyphs and terminated in a pyramidal top that was gilded to reflect the sun's rays. Obelisks became popular with other ancient cultures, and many of those erected in Egypt were later removed to imperial Rome. (For information on the pyramids of Egypt, please turn to Chapter 10.)

GREEK ART

Greek art was influenced both by monumental Egyptian art and by the more sensual art of Minoan Crete, which dates from about 2000 BC and brought an Oriental opulence to Greek art. Several periods preceded the great Classical Period, including the Geometric Period (1100 to 700 BC) which produced pottery painted with angular designs. The famous Dipylon vases from this period are named for the cemetery near Athens where they were found.

The Archaic Period (700 to 475 BC) reflected an Oriental influence, evidenced by its painted vases with motifs of fighting animals and winged monsters. Greek sculptors of this period, unlike Egyptian sculptors, began to free their human forms from the stone by carving spaces in between the legs and between the arms and torso, creating the first free-standing statues.

Minoan mural at Knossos, Crete.

The culmination of these artistic developments was reached in the Classical Period (475 to 323 BC) when Greek art reached its pinnacle of beauty and perfection. With an emphasis on physical beauty, classical Greek art idealized the human form. The marble decorations of the Parthenon included the east pediment's ensemble of deities watching the birth of Athena from the head of Zeus. Their relaxed and reclining forms reflect a complete ease of movement, both in the masculinity of Dionysus and in the flowing drapery of the three goddesses. These marble sculptures, removed by Lord Elgin between 1801 and 1803, are now on display in the British Museum.

The profound influence Classical Greek art would exert on later civilizations began in about 200 BC, during the Hellenistic age, when statues and paintings were first recognized as works of art to be appreciated for their own sake. During this period, the wealthy began decorating their homes with copies of the great works. Hellenistic sculptures were distinctly different from the Classical works in that they conveyed a more pronounced realism. Famous Hellenistic works include the Rhodian *Nike of Samothrace* (c. 200 BC) which portrays the outspread wings of the goddess lifted by a strong head wind as she stands at the prow of a ship.

Until the *Nike* was discovered in the last century, the most admired work of Hellenistic statuary had been *The Laocoön Group*, created in the 1st century BC by three Rhodian sculptors. This work depicts the horrible death of Laocoon and his two sons by a pair of sea serpents sent by Athena to punish the Trojan priest for trying to warn his people of the trick wooden horse. Found in a Roman vineyard in 1506, *The Laocoön Group* was admired by, among others, Michelangelo, who considered it the finest sculpture ever created.

Although the Minoans of Crete began constructing palace complexes some 4,000 years ago, it was on mainland Greece where the building of temples culminated in the zenith of Classical Greek architecture. Between 480 BC and 323 BC all of the major masterpieces were created, including the famous Parthenon. By then three columnar types had evolved, called Doric, Ionic and Corinthian. The Doric order originated on mainland Greece, while the Ionic order developed on the Aegean Islands and the coast of Asia Minor. The Corinthian capital was invented as an elaborate substitute for the Ionic order and was initially used only for interiors. The Greek orders of column consisted of a shaft composed of sections, called drums,

A replica of The Laocoön Group.

(Grand Master's Palace, Rhodes)

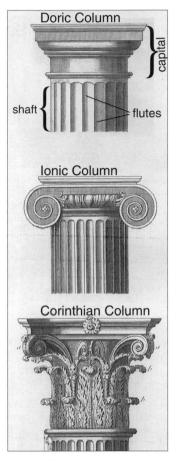

Doric Column

shaft

flutes

capital

Ionic Column

Corinthian Column

and a capital. A row of regularly spaced columns formed a colonnade that supported an entablature decorated with carved friezes. A triangular pediment atop the entablature held sculptures. The structure was built entirely of stone blocks that were carefully shaped and fitted together without mortar, although metal dowels were sometimes used. Shallow vertical grooves, called flutes, were carved the length of the column once it was erect.

The Parthenon, built atop the sacred Acropolis of Athens between 447 and 432 BC, was a Doric temple dedicated to the goddess Athena. Designed by the architect Ictinus, this columned structure was built using a white, fine-grained marble and is considered a perfect composition of grace and unity. Subtle adjustments were made to the colonnade's columns, and these deviations lend the structure an organic quality. For example, the columns all lean inward and their capitals are distorted to fit the architrave, which is slightly curved, so that the centre of the entablature is a bit higher than the ends. Another feature is that the corner columns are spaced more closely to their neighbouring columns than are the middle columns.

The Erechtheum, built on the Acropolis between 421 and 405 BC, is one of the finest examples of the Ionic order. The Monument of Lysicrates in Athens, built a century later, is the earliest known example of exterior Corinthian columns. Greek theatres, before the 4th century, consisted simply of stone benches or wooden bleachers placed on a natural slope. These basic seating arrangements evolved into concentric rows of seats built into the hillside, with regularly-spaced staircase aisles providing seating access. The front-row seats, made of luxurious marble, were reserved for eminent public figures.

Marble sculptures from the Parthenon's east pediment. (British Museum, London)

Tomb paintings, Tarquinia

The Etruscans settled in an area known as Tuscany between Florence and Rome in the 8th century BC, about the same time the Greeks were settling along the southern shores of Italy and Sicily. At their height of power in the 7th and 6th centuries, Etruscan cities rivalled Greece's city-states. The Etruscans ruled Rome for about a century, until the establishment of the Republic in 510 BC. They, like the Egyptians, created elaborate sculptures and wall paintings devoted to the afterlife, but Etruscan art also reflects a Greek influence, similar to that created during the Archaic Period.

ROMAN ART

The Romans were great builders and architectural engineers. They admired Greek models but Roman designs stressed power and boldness, in contrast to the Greek emphasis on harmony and beauty. By perfecting the use of brick and concrete, the Romans were able to use arches and vaults to create complex and spacious interiors with soaring roofs that could accommodate large numbers of people. The most famous example of their oustanding engineering is the Colosseum, with its miles of stairways and vaulted corridors.

The Romans created concrete by combining pozzuolana (a volcanic earth) with lime, broken stones, bricks and tuff (a rock formed by the consolidation of volcanic ashes). Easily made and extremely durable, this concrete was used in the vast construction projects undertaken to sustain Rome's growing empire, including the building of roads, aqueducts and bridges. Cities and towns were laid out according to a logical plan with an emphasis on drainage, water supply and zoning. The urban centre's focus was the forum, an open public square surrounded by public buildings which included temples, exchanges and basilicas (law

Vaults

Barrel   Cross   Ribbed

The ancient roads and buildings of Pompeii (above). A Roman fresco adorns the interior wall of a villa in Pompeii (opposite).

courts). Public baths, derived from Greek gymnasia, were built on an unprecedented scale and the Romans engaged in ritual bathing in hot, cold and steam baths. These baths also served as community centres with libraries, shops, shaded walks and open areas for poetry reading. A typical town house consisted of rooms arranged around a central atrium with an opening in the roof. Multistorey apartment buildings were also common in the larger cities, in contrast to the spacious country villas of the wealthy which contained central courtyard gardens.

The Roman amphitheatres, unlike their Greek prototypes, were free-standing and oval-shaped. The exposed concrete of Roman ruins, which makes them today look less appealing than those of Greece, would have been covered during ancient times by a facing of brick, stone, marble or smooth plaster. The Roman imperial practice of raising free-standing, commemorative columns may have originated from the Egyptian tradition of raising obelisks, but the triumphal arch was a purely Roman invention. Raised to honour an emperor or commemorate a military triumph, these monumental structures were built throughout the empire and would often span a road.

Roman roads were usually built in a straight line, regardless of obstacles, and consisted of four layers, the uppermost being a pavement of flat stones, concrete or pebbles set in mortar. Such roads still exist near Rome and elsewhere, as do some of the aqueducts. The bridge portion of aqueducts consisted of one to three tiers of arches, depending on the depth of the valley crossed. Nine aqueducts brought water to ancient Rome, three of which still supply the modern city, along with another one that was completed in 1585. Other aqueducts still exist in Italy and in France, where the famous Pont du Gard stands near Nimes.

Roman art was highly imitative and eclectic, reflecting the various cultures encompassed by its far-reaching empire. Pseudo-Egyptian statuary were popular and the low reliefs on Trajan's Column mirror the Egyptian illustrative tradition. However, it was the art and culture of Greece that thoroughly permeated Roman tastes. The Romans held Greek art and culture in such high esteem that original sculptures of every Greek period – Archaic, Classical and Hellenistic – were imported and copied by the thousands. Modifications were made to reflect the Roman emphasis on action and strength versus the contemplative nature inherent in Greek culture, and a distinct Roman style of portraiture developed which combined Greek idealism with Roman realism. The Italianate tradition of making death masks also led to the Roman style of portrait bust.

In about 200 AD, just as Roman art was fusing with Greek, the doctrines of Christianity, including denunciation of all pleasures of the flesh, shattered the synthesizing process. Eastern influences that had been introduced during the time of Constantine eventually developed into the stiff iconographic forms of the early Christian and Byzantine eras. Early Christian churches, inspired by imperial Rome, were basilican in design (an oblong interior divided into three or five aisles by rows of columns) and decorated with Byzantine-style mosaics.

The famous Portland Vase (1st century BC) was excavated near Rome in the 17th century. Made of dark blue glass overlaid with white cameo relief, the vase was widely copied, most notably in jasper ware by Josiah Wedgwood. It was eventually acquired by the Duke of Portland, who lent it to the British Museum. In 1845, a deranged museum visitor smashed the priceless vase to pieces, but it was skillfully restored and remains on display.

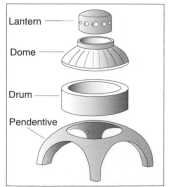

Renowned for its raised dome and golden mosaics, the impressive Hagia Sophia in Istanbul is considered the greatest monument of Byzantine art.

MEDIEVAL ART

Christian art initially declined in Europe following the fall of the Western Roman Empire in the 5th century, but continued to thrive in the Eastern Roman Empire where Byzantine art, especially mosaic decoration, flourished. Oriental influences combined with Hellenistic and Roman art forms to produce an ornate style exhibiting great pomp and dignity. Byzantine architects created a medieval masterpiece when they developed the pendentive to elevate the dome of Hagia Sophia (The Church of Holy Wisdom) in Constantinople. Built in the 6th century during the reign of Emperor Justinian I, the vaulted and domed Hagia Sophia was daring in design. With the brilliant use of piers, penditives and semi-domes to create an expansive interior, Hagia Sophia's architects successfully captured the splendour of the heavens.

Medieval cities, facing barbarian invasions and pirate attacks, were designed with security in mind and were protected by thick walls. The only open areas amid the narrow winding streets were municipal or church squares. Fortresses, castles, even monasteries were built for defence. The 9th century's Carolingian style, so named for the Frankish emperor Charlemagne, was followed by the Romanesque ('in the manner of the Roman') and its variants, such as Norman and Gothic. Local styles developed under the generic name

Interior view of Hagia Sophia, Istanbul, reveals its revolutionary dome and semi-dome design. Below: The Grand Master's Palace in Rhodes is an example of medieval military architecture.

Romanesque, but common features included the rounded arch and vault, as well as heavy walls and piers for structural support.

The **Gothic** style originated in France in about 1150 and flourished until 1450, especially in the cathedrals of northern Europe. Churches became airy and soaring, with pointed arches and vaults, slender piers and counterbalancing flying buttresses. Walls were thin and windows were large to allow a mystical and wondrous light to filter through their panes of stained glass. The sculpting of gargoyles in the form of beasts and grotesque human forms reached its peak in the Gothic period, after which the use of these ornate waterspouts was gradually replaced with lead drainpipes. In Italy the Gothic style of architecture was tempered by Romanesque proportions, and Spanish Gothic architecture was influenced by Moorish traditions.

All other visual art forms were dominated by architecture during the Gothic period, with sculpture and stained glass integrated into the churches. The exception was in Italy where medieval painting, long influenced by Byzantine art's use of mosaics and murals, took on a new and revolutionary form in the early 14th century with the works of Giotto di Bondone. A Florentine artist, he painted lifelike scenes with a three-dimensional reality and tactile quality, which prompted some to claim that painting had surpassed sculpture as an art form. The newly elevated status of painting was symbolized by Giotto's appointment in 1334 as head of the Florence Cathedral workshop, a position formerly held only by architects or sculptors. The artistic momentum generated by Giotto was, however, temporarily extinguished when an epidemic of the bubonic plague – called the Black Death – swept across Europe between 1347 and 1350, killing about one third of Europe's population.

Above: Clerestory of Barcelona's Gothic cathedral with 15th-century stained glass windows.
Opposite: Mosaics adorn St. Mark's in Venice.

Islamic Art

With the Muslim faith discouraging pictorial representation, Islamic art specializes in the decoration of surfaces with patterns that are abstract or geometrical, characterized by interlaced lines and brilliant colours. Calligraphy (Greek for 'beautiful writing') is highly esteemed and used by Muslims to decorate mosques, pottery, metalwork, and textiles, as well as books. The Islamic (Moorish) presence in western Europe during the Middle Ages was reflected in such decorative arts as tile work and lustreware.

Early mosques were simple in design, based on the floor plan of the Prophet Muhammad's house. As Islam spread, a variety of existing edifices were taken over and converted into mosques. The Muslim practise of whitewashing the walls of temples and churches when converting them into mosques often resulted in the preservation of the underlying frescoes. Domed mosques were not common until the Byzantine church of Hagia Sofia became a model for mosques following the Turkish conquest of Constantinople in 1453. One famous exception is the Dome of the Rock in Jerusalem, built in 691 AD, which follows an octagonal Byzantine plan and has a wooden dome. Elements of Islamic art were often incorporated in Romanesque, Gothic and Renaissance buildings.

RENAISSANCE ART

The Italian Renaissance, which began shortly after 1400 in Florence, ushered in a new and exciting age. Whereas medieval towns were built with moats, fortresses and city walls for protection from marauding bands, Renaissance cities were built with monumental views provided by wide avenues and long approaches to handsome buildings. New World discoveries contributed to the joy of expansion, but it was a revival of classical antiquity that formed the basis of Renaissance thought and art. The great masters studied the works of Plato and other Greek philosophers, embracing humanism and a belief in man's ability to understand the universe.

In architecture, the classical ideals of order, symmetry and unity were adopted. Rome's structural elements – arches, vaults and domes – were used in original combinations, with the dome symbolizing Renaissance man's pursuit of both learning and clarity. The great Florentine architect Brunelleschi, who made several trips to Rome to study classical buildings, incorporated the systematic use of perspective and proportion in his designs, which included the octagonal ribbed dome of the Florence cathedral. The famous sculptor Donatello accompanied Brunelleschi on one of his trips to Rome, and the classical influence is evident in such works as his bronze *David*. This statue is one of the earliest free-standing nude figures of the Renaissance, and it marked the end of a medieval interdependence of architecture and sculpture.

In painting, as in the other visual arts, the Renaissance artists sought perfection. Three staggered planes – foreground, middle distance and background – were used to achieve perspective depth, and the painting's figures were harmoniously arranged, their expressive gestures achieving a heightened emotional intensity. The ideal human figure measured seven times the height of the head, and male nudes were painted with golden brown skin in contrast to the pink rose skin of a female nude.

Leonardo da Vinci best personified the ideal 'Renaissance man' with his restless quest for beauty and truth, both in his paintings and in his scientific studies, which

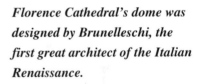

Florence Cathedral's dome was designed by Brunelleschi, the first great architect of the Italian Renaissance.

relied on a precise observation of the phenomena of nature. Leonardo was one of several supreme artists who generated the great works of the High Renaissance between 1495 and 1520. Others included Bramante, Michelangelo, Raphael and Titian. Bramante, an architect and painter,

Self portrait, Leonardo da Vinci.

designed the original plan for St. Peter's Basilica in Rome, influencing the appearance of many smaller churches. The paintings of Raphael were considered the Renaissance ideal of harmony and balance, and he was known for centuries as the 'divine'. The Venetian painter Titian, celebrated for his use of colour, was admired by Michelangelo who apparently said, "Only he alone deserves to be called a painter."

Although the Renaissance artist was liberated from medieval convention, with pagan symbols reappearing alongside symbols of the

the REDISCOVERY of LIGHT

Andrea del Verrocchio and
Leonardo da Vinci
Detail from: The Baptism of
Christ, c. 1470-75
Uffizi Gallery, Florence

Michelangelo
Holy Family, c. 1503-04
Uffizi Gallery, Florence

Titian
Venus of Urbino (1536)
Uffizi Gallery, Florence

Giovanni Bellini
Enthroned Madonna, with
Saints, 1505
San Zaccaria, Venice

Raphael
Madonna with the Goldfinch, c. 1507
Uffizi Gallery, Florence

Sandro Botticelli
The Birth of Venus, c. 1485
Uffizi Gallery, Florence

Christian faith, the challenge of reconciling rational thought with religious belief was personified in the tormented genius of Michelangelo. A master of the three major visual arts – sculpture, painting and architecture – he transcended conventions and traditions, and is considered the first truly modern artist. Michelangelo believed that his artistic genius was a divine inspiration, and when sculpting a piece of marble he sought to free its pre-existing figures from the stone.

On the heels of the High Renaissance came mannerism, a style in which scale and spatial relationships between figures were deliberately confused. Mannerism, lasting from about 1520 to 1600, originated in Italy as a reaction to the High Renaissance's equilibrium of form and proportion. While the term 'mannerism' was coined to describe the painting of this period, the characteristics of mannerist architecture included an artificial integration of elements and an emphasis on surface effect, especially through the use of encrusted decoration. Jacopo Sansovino's Library of St. Mark's in Venice is a classic example of this lavish use of sculptural encrustation.

The mannerist schools of painting produced some outstanding artists, including Tintoretto and Veronese, both of the Venetian school. The famous mannerist painter El Greco, born on the Greek island of Crete in 1541, was initially trained in the Byzantine tradition of iconography, but he later studied in Venice, then in Rome, absorbing the lessons of the Italian masters, before settling in Spain. In Mannerist nativity scenes, signs of poverty were erased from the manger and the newborn Christ child was transformed into a cherub-like one-year-old perched on the lap of a rosy-cheeked Madonna. This less reverent and more intimate attitude was also reflected in the artists' penchant for painting themselves and fellow artists into scenes – positioning themselves not modestly to one side, as had been the customary position for donors of religious pictures, but squarely in the centre of the canvas. The jubilant and joyous nature of mannerist art was criticized by austere theologians, but the last glorious outburst of Christian art was yet to come in the form of baroque, the dominant art of the 17th century.

The baroque Church of Sant'Agnese in Agone faces Bernini's Fountain of the Four Rivers in Piazza Navona, Rome.

BAROQUE

The baroque style harmoniously united painting, sculpture and architecture. The latter became fluid, like sculpture on a massive scale, with curving forms and undulating facades. Sculptures set within this elaborate architecture seem to spill from their niches or soar heavenward. Famous baroque works include those of the Italian sculptor and architect Bernini, who adorned Rome with his fountains, statues and other monuments, including the elliptical piazza in front of St. Peter's Basilica. Baroque painters used illusionist effects to create a deep sense of space, and its masters included Rembrandt, Rubens and van Dyck. In the late phases of baroque, the centre of the movement shifted from Italy to France, due largely to the patronage of Louis XIV.

Rome's Trevi Fountain, completed in 1762, is rococo in style.

As the vitality and force of baroque spilled into the 18th century, its final flowering became known as rococo. Originating in France and lasting from 1700 to 1750, the rococo style, with its light lines and exquisite refinement, was especially popular for interiors and the decorative arts. It was an unfettered style of excessive ornamentation and embellishment, with frescoes travelling across entire walls and ceilings, often multiplied in wall mirrors and reflected in polished parquet floors. In Venice, the painter Tiepolo won international fame with his frescoes in the doge's palace.

MODERN ART

The first of a series of overlapping movements and counter-movements began in the mid-18th century. These 'revival' movements were manifested mostly in architecture and began with neoclassicism, which was inspired by the discovery of the ancient Roman ruins of Herculaneum and Pompeii on the Bay of Naples. In tandem with the classical revival was the Gothic revival, which began to dominate after 1800, its largest monument being the Houses of Parliament in London. The final revival phases were the neo-Renaissance and neo-baroque, which dominated from 1850 to 1875 and lingered through the turn of the century. Neo-baroque buildings favoured a profusion of ornament, creating an excess

Pena Palace in Sintra, Portugal, is an exotic mix of architectural styles.

of opulence that appealed particularly to the newly rich and powerful of the Industrial Revolution. New materials and building techniques included the use of iron, which was used extensively in the construction of railroad stations, exhibitions halls and public libraries. The Eiffel Tower, erected at the entrance to the Paris World's Fair of 1889, became a famous symbol of 19th-century technology.

Art nouveau, a decorative arts movement lasting from the 1880s to World War I, was originally meant to produce art for the masses. As a reaction to the historical emphasis of mid-19th century art, this new style incorporated dreamlike forms which are best exemplified architecturally in the innovative designs of Antonio Gaudi, who lived and worked in Barcelona. Another turn-of-the-century style was associated with the Ecole des Beaux-Arts in Paris and became fashionable both in Europe and North America. Beaux-arts buildings were an eclectic mix of styles, often incorporating Greek, Roman and Egyptian elements.

Romanticism was another artistic movement that arose in the late 18th century. Inspired by ideals of the Enlightenment, the romantics revered nature and the individual's freedom to act naturally. As artists and intellectuals scrutinized classical thought and Christian beliefs, two conflicting views emerged: one supporting scientific and material progress, which was identified with the middle class; the other regarding the bourgeoisie as the enemy of culture. It was the second view that became the battle cry of modern artists, many of whom fervently challenged accepted perceptions of the world with the avant-garde, a term from French warfare meaning 'vanguard'.

After romanticism, most painters rejected traditional subjects taken from the Bible, the classics or the life of the courts, and turned instead to everyday scenes around them. No single movement has dominated modern western art for long periods of time since the 18th century, and there has been a speeding up of successive styles and ideas. The impressionist movement, originating in late-19th century France, rejected the romantics' emphasis on emotion and instead pursued objectivity when painting visual impressions, often directly from nature.

Following the impressionist movement, artists sought new inspiration in fresh landscapes. Fleeing the industrial north, Vincent van Gogh headed to the south of France to be 'near Africa', Paul Cezanne retreated to his native Provence, and Gauguin eventually left Europe for the tropical island paradise of Tahiti. Van Gogh's dark and sombre early paintings gave way to swirling brush strokes and intense yellows, greens and blues found in his later works, which represented the archetype of expressionism's emotional spontaneity in painting.

20th Century Art

Artists in the early 20th century, attempting to express an inner vision, intensified their search into the subconscious. The French painter Henri Matisse, considered one of the foremost artists of the modern period, began using strong primary colours while living in the Mediterranean village of Collioure, and he became a leader of Fauvism, a style that emphasized the use of vivid colour. Pablo Picasso, who played a leading role in most of the 20th-century art movements, created cubism's most significant work when he painted *Les Demoiselles d'Avignon* in 1907. Surrealism, an artistic and literary movement founded in Paris in 1924 and influenced by Freudian theories, used dream-inspired symbols. The paintings of Salvador Dali, who was born near Barcelona in 1904, combined dream imagery with near-photographic realism.

Umberto Primo Arcade, Naples (above). The facade of Chapelle St. Pierre, Villefranche, painted by avant-garde artist Jean Cocteau.

PRESERVING & RESTORING ART

Art museums take extraordinary precautions to preserve their priceless works, using climate control systems that filter dust and chemical pollutants from the air, and sensors that monitor temperature and humidity. Even the wrong kind of carpet, when walked on, can produce dust and lint that settles onto paintings. When Leonardo da Vinci's masterpiece *The Last Supper* was reopened to the public in Milan, visitors were required to pass through three antechambers designed to remove dust, dirt, car exhaust and other particles from their clothes. A bubble of clean air surrounds the restored painting, which covers most of one wall in the refectory of Santa Maria delle Grazie. The original painting was applied to a dry finished wall, rather than on wet plaster, and shortly after its completion it began to deteriorate.

Art restoration is as old as art itself, with early restorers using varnishes made of animal glue to temporarily brighten fresco paintings. When modern restorers cleaned Michelangelo's frescoes in the Sistine Chapel, their painstaking methods involved washing an area with deionized water and an organic solvent, then sponging ammonium carbonate onto the area through layers of absorbent paper, which were left in place for several minutes before being removed. Any loosened dirt was wiped away and the area given a final rinse with water.

Space age technology is also being applied to art restoration, with a NASA researcher developing a way to use corrosive, atomic oxygen to dissolve sticky soot left on paintings after a fire. Modern laser and microwave techniques were used to clean the marble sculptures that once adorned the Parthenon in Athens, a technique approved by Greece's Central Archaeological Council only after experts spent two years practising this method on other marbles. In Florence, a thorough cleaning of Michelangelo's statue *David* came to a halt when experts disagreed over the cleaning technique to be used.

When paintings travel to other museums, there is always the risk of damage, despite careful handling by white-gloved workers and the use of custom-designed metal cases fitted with high-density foam. Concerns include potential damage from jet engine vibrations, which can gradually shiver paint from a fragile canvas, and sudden decreases in humidity, which can cause a canvas to shrink and possibly crack.

Preserving outdoor monuments is another challenge. In Egypt, the restoration of the Great Sphinx took 10 years to complete, with 12,244 white limestone blocks needed to repair this colossal sculpture. The ancient marble monuments of Greece and Rome have long been threatened by air pollution, as well as microorganisms like algae, lichens and fungi, which discolour surfaces and burrow beneath the surface. Ongoing restoration work on the Athenian Acropolis is estimated to take several more decades to complete and cost millions of dollars. Scaffolding is a fact of life in Europe, where restoration work by skilled marble masons is time-consuming and extremely costly.

Gardens have been cultivated since antiquity. The ancient Egyptians built walled gardens centred around a pool stocked with ornamental fish and shaded by fig and date trees. Lotus flowers (a kind of water lily) often grew in these garden pools. The revered olive tree, described by Homer as a source of liquid gold, has also been cultivated since ancient times along the Mediterranean coast, and today Italy, Spain and Greece produce 75% of the world's olive oil. Green olives are full-grown but unripened when picked, and ripened olives are purplish black and richer in oil.

Vineyards were introduced to Europe by the Greeks from Asia Minor in about 600 BC. The warm, dry Mediterranean climate was so ideal for the proliferation of viticulture that the Roman Emperor Domitian, fearing grain scarcity, had to restrict the spread of vineyards in Italy during the 1st century AD. During the days of the Roman Empire, landscape gardening was highly developed and formal gardens, designed by architects, were often terraced and adorned with stat-

uary and fountains. The emperors in particular enjoyed retreating to their country villas, replete with formal gardens. According to Edward Gibbon, when Diocletian retired permanently to his estate on the Dalmatian coast in the early 4th century, he dismissed with a smile his former co-emperor's urgings to return by remarking that "if he could show Maximian the cabbages he had planted with his own hands at Salona, (Maximian) would no longer be urged to relinquish the enjoyment of happiness for the pursuit of power."

Early gardens were often simple plots for growing herbs and vegetables. In fact, throughout

Ancient olive trees grow in Jerusalem's Garden of Gethsemene (above), where Jesus spent his last hours before his arrest. The courtyard garden at the House of Vetti in Pompeii (below), as it likely looked in the 1st century AD.

antiquity and the Middle Ages, herbs were highly valued for their medicinal and curative properties. Saffron, featured in Mediterranean cooking, was also a source of yellow dye in the ancient world. Thyme was used by

the Greeks as a temple incense, and by the Romans who put it in their bath water to energize themselves. Rosemary, a name derived from Latin and meaning 'dew of the sea', grows along coastal cliff tops where it draws moisture from the sea mists. Rosemary's aromatic leaves are used for seasoning and its small blue flowers are the source of an extract used in perfumes and medicines.

Other flowers native to the eastern Mediterranean include the tulip, hyacinth, crocus and hibiscus. Scrubby woodlands dominate the coastline, where prevalent types of trees include the umbrella pine tree, its nuts used for cakes and sauces. Cork oak is also native to the Mediterranean, which is where most of the world's commercial cork is harvested and processed. The bark of these trees is stripped off every 10 years.

During the Middle Ages, various citrus trees were introduced to the Mediterranean area by the Arabs, including tangerines, oranges, lemons and limes. The Crusades also introduced new plants and gardening techniques to Europe, as did the Moors of Spain and Portugal. During the Italian Renaissance the classical garden was revived, and leading artists of the day were commissioned to design elaborate hillside landscapes of fountains, waterfalls and ponds, mingled with statuary and topiary, often in geometrical designs.

Above: Gardens outside Palma's cathedral, Majorca. Opposite: Egyptian lotus pond.

Italian-designed gardens lie outside the Grand Master's Palace in Rhodes, Greece.

PART II

THE VOYAGE AND THE PORTS

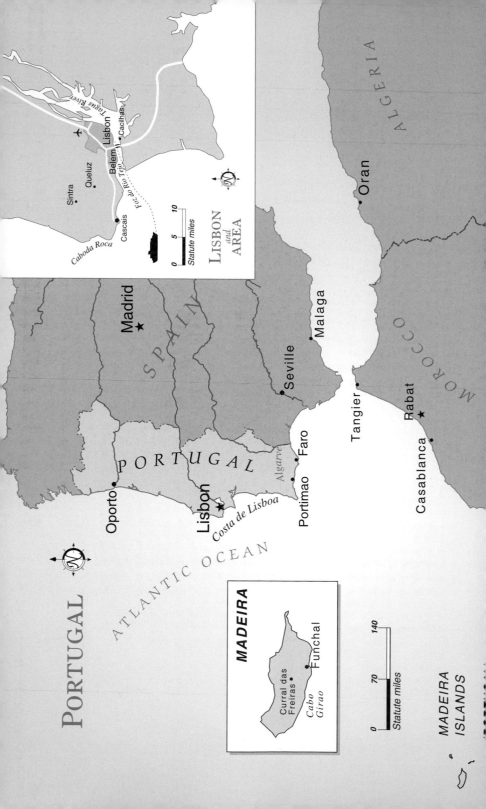

CHAPTER ONE

PORTUGAL

I n Portugal, all school children are taught the words to *The Lusiads* by Luis de Camoes. This epic poem is based on the famous voyage of explorer Vasco da Gama, the first European to journey by sea to India. He left Lisbon in 1497, rounded the Cape of Good Hope and sailed across the Indian Ocean to Calicut, returning home in 1499. The discovery of this sea route gave Portugal access to the riches of the Indies, and marked the beginning of the Portuguese Empire.

Camoes, the greatest figure of Portuguese literature, was well qualified to write his country's epic poem. Born of a poor Lisbon family, he pursued a life of romance and adventure, one that provided inspiration for his fiery love poems and vigorous narratives. In 1546 the poet was banished from the royal circle after falling in love with a lady of the Lisbon court. A few years later he was imprisoned for wounding a court aide in a street fight. To obtain his release from prison, Camoes served military duty in India, after which he was posted as an official to Macao, where he eventually faced charges of maladministration. When the ship carrying him from Macao to Goa in India was wrecked, Camoes managed to save the manuscript he was working on of *The Lusiads*.

The Portuguese people's love of poetry and song is an integral part of their culture, best exemplified by the troubadour-style 'fado', which is a poem or story accompanied by the guitar. Derived from the Latin word for 'fate', the fado can be heard throughout the country where it is performed in village pubs, family restaurants and the sophisticated clubs de fado in Lisbon. Listening to the fado, which speaks through its melody, is an excellent way to get to know Portugal.

PORTUGAL AT A GLANCE

About 11 million people live in Portugal, which includes the Madeira Islands and the Azores in the Atlantic Ocean. The country's last over-seas territory, Macao, reverts to Chinese sovereignty in 1999. Roman Catholicism is Portugal's major religion, and the mother tongue is Portuguese, its vocabulary based on vernacular Latin but also contain-ing words absorbed from Arabic, French and Italian. English and French are the second languages of Portugal.

The country's post-revolution constitution of 1976 established a par-liamentary republic with an elected president and legislative assembly.

The Tower of Belem, built in the 16th century by Manuel I, stands at the entrance to Lisbon's port.

Once the poorest country of Western Europe, Portugal has successfully reformed its economy in recent decades, and the country gained prestige when its government presided over the European Economic Community in 1992. Portugal was also awarded the last world's fair of the 20th century when Lisbon won the bid to host Expo '98, its maritime theme commemorating the role of the oceans in our planet's development.

TRAVEL TIPS

Currency: The unit of currency is the euro. Traveller's cheques and Eurocheques are widely accepted as are most credit cards. ATMs are located throughout the city of Lisbon and are tied to international networks such as Cirrus. Banks are open Monday to Friday, from 8:30 a.m. to 3:00 pm.

Dining: Costa de Lisboa is noted for its seafood, and regional specialties include Caldeirada (fish stew) and clams cooked with garlic and coriander. For dessert, Pasteis de Belem (custard pies) are popular, as are Portugal's fortified wines. Grapes from the Douro district produce the country's famous port wines, which are blended and stored in Oporto. Vintage port, which is wine of an exceptional growing year, is kept in casks for two or three years, then matured in bottles for up to 25 years. Portugal's other classic fortified wine is produced on Madeira Island, a traditional port of call for west-bound sailing ships which would transport this wine to North America. It has been said that the signing of America's Declaration of Independence was celebrated with a sip of Madeira wine.

Opening Hours: Museums and historic attractions generally open from 10 a.m. to 12:30 p.m. and from 2:00 p.m. to 5:00 p.m., with many closed on Mondays.

Shopping: Stores are generally open Monday through Saturday from 9:00 a.m. to 1:00 p.m., reopening, except on Saturdays, from 3:00 p.m. to 7:00 p.m. Shopping centres are open every day, from 10:00 a.m. to midnight. Locally made wares include gold filigree jewellery, azulejos (decorative tiles), ceramics, pottery, basketware and embroideries.

Transportation: Taxis are plentiful and cheap in Portugal. A standard meter fare is charged in the city; outside the city limits, the charge is per kilometre. There is a small surcharge for luggage, and the usual tip is 10%. Buses and trams charge a flat fare, paid to the driver. Special tourist tickets are available in Lisbon.

Telephoning: Crediphones are common throughout Portugal, and phone cards can be bought in post offices and news agents. To phone long distance from Portugal, dial 00 followed by your country code, area/city code, and the local number.

The Madeira Islands were settled by the seafaring Portuguese in the 15th century and became a port of call for ships sailing the Atlantic. Tropical flowers flourish in the mild, maritime climate.

PORTUGUESE HISTORY

Portugal's history began in ancient times. Among its early tribes were a Celtic people called Lusitanians, who came to the area around 1000 BC. The Lusitanians fiercely resisted Roman invasion until their leader, Viratus, was killed in 139 BC. Under Roman domination, the province of Lusitania thrived and Roman ways were adopted, including the Latin language from which Portuguese is derived. The title of Portugal's epic poem by Camoes is *Os Lusiadas* in Portuguese and it means 'sons of Lusus', referring to the Portuguese people.

Lusitania was overrun by Visigoths in the 5th century AD, and they in turn were conquered by the Moors, who invaded the area in 711. But it was the Christian reconquest of the Iberian peninsula that created the country of Portugal, and this process began with the arrival of Henry of Burgundy in 1095. One of a group of French nobles summoned by Alfonso VI of Leon to assist in the fight against the Moors, Henry was assigned a portion of land, a title and a wife named Teresa, who was an illegitimate daughter of Alfonso. Upon his father-in-law's death, Henry engaged in war and intrigues with Alfonso's heirs, and the territory he acquired as Count of Portugal eventually became the independent kingdom of Portugal under his son Alfsono.

Alfonso I was no less a fighter than his father. A small child when Henry died, the boy's mother, Countess Teresa, ruled the county of Portugal with her Spanish lover, Fernando Perez. As a young man, Alfonso allied himself with some discontented nobles and defeated his mother in battle, driving her and Perez into Leon. Alfonso spent the rest of his life embroiled in ceaseless fighting, to increase both his prestige and his territories. In 1139 he defeated the Moors in the Battle of Ourique, and in 1147, with the aid of English, Flemish and German crusaders, he drove the Moors from Lisbon. By this time he had styled himself as King of Portugal and secured Castilian recognition of his title, which was confirmed in 1179 by Pope Alexander III.

The royal court of Portugal remained a tumultuous place for several centuries. It was the scene of family estrangements, shifting alliances, power struggles against the church, and wars with kings of Castile. It was not uncommon for royal sons to turn against their fathers. One of the most tragic father/son feuds involved Alfonso IV who, in 1355, approved the murder of his son's mistress, a beautiful noblewoman named Ines de Castro. Alfonso's heartbroken son promptly led a rebellion, then feigned forgiveness, only to avenge his lover's death when he ascended to the throne as Peter I and had two of her murderers executed by having their hearts drawn out. For this act he became known as Peter the Cruel, and the romantic story of his love affair with de Castro, which produced four children (and possibly a secret marriage), became a favourite theme of Portuguese literature.

The most glorious period of Portuguese history began with the reign of John I, a bastard son of Peter I. Rising to power in 1385, he ushered in an era of maritime exploration and colonial expansion never before seen. His son, Henry the Navigator, developed an interest in Africa during a campaign to conquer Ceuta, a coastal enclave of Morocco, in 1415. Henry established an observatory and a school of navigation and geography at Sagres, in southwest Portugal, and trained navigators would set off from the nearby port at Lagos. They first sailed to Madeira, then to the Azores, before embarking on a painstaking exploration of the African coast, pushing further south with each voyage until they reached the Far East. When Portuguese ships began returning with slaves, gold and other riches, great wealth poured into the royal coffers.

This period of prosperity reached its zenith during the reign of Manuel I (1495-1521), when the Portuguese empire extended across the seas to Africa, Asia and America. Lisbon became the centre of the lucrative European spice trade, and Portuguese mariners would return home with priceless art from other cultures, such as ivory sculptures from Africa and decorated porcelain from China. A distinct style of Portuguese decoration developed, called 'manueline', which reflected the country's maritime expansion. The manueline style embellished Gothic structures with shells, twisted ropes and strange aquatic shapes, mixing these elements with religious or heraldic symbols to create sumptuous ornamentation.

The seafaring trade which brought sudden wealth to Portugal also created corruption among her government officials, who neglected domestic concerns such as agricultural and industrial development. In 1496, Manuel agreed to expel all Jews and Moors from Portugal as a condition for marrying the eldest daughter of Ferdinand and Isabella of Spain, and this drained the country of communities that had contributed to its learning, science and artisanship. Piracy and foreign competition began cutting into Portugal's shipping profits, and the West's centre of trade eventually shifted from Lisbon to Northern Europe.

In 1580, Portugal was seized by Philip II of Spain and remained under Spanish rule until a revolt in 1640 re-established Portugal's royal line. The monarchy endured until 1910, when a revolution established a Portuguese republic. A military coup in 1926 was followed by the right-wing dictatorship of Antonio de Oliveira Salazar from 1932 to 1968. A bloodless coup in 1974 finally brought democracy to Portugal.

LISBON

Lisbon (Lisboa) is situated on seven terraced hills that border the banks of the Tagus River where it broadens to enter the Atlantic. Ships entering this ancient trading port are greeted by the sight of the **Tower of Belem** (1), a 16th-century fortress built at the mouth of the Tagus River. It once marked the starting point for Portuguese caravels setting off on voyages of trade and conquest. Nearby is the **Discoveries Monument** (2), erected in 1960 to mark the 500th anniversary of the death of Henry the Navigator. The cruise ships dock at Gare Maritima de Alcantara, located about two miles from the city centre.

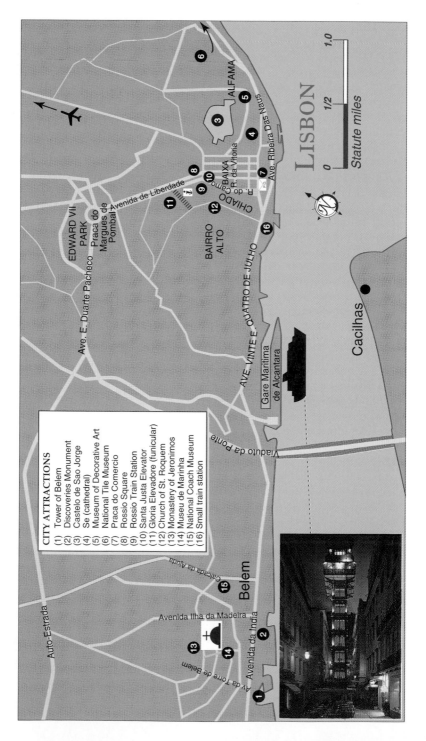

LISBON

Statute miles

0   1/2   1.0

ALFAMA

BAIXA

R. da Vitoria

Ave. Ribeira Das Naus

CHIADO

R. do Carmo

BAIRRO ALTO

AVE. VINTE E QUATRO DE JULHO

Gare Marítima de Alcântara

Viaduto da Ponte

Cacilhas

EDWARD VII PARK

Ave. E. Duarte Pacheco

Praca do Marques de Pombal

Avenida de Liberdade

Auto-Estrada

Calçada da Ajuda

Belem

Avenida Ilha da Madeira

Av da Torre de Belem

Avenida da India

CITY ATTRACTIONS
(1) Tower of Belem
(2) Discoveries Monument
(3) Castelo de Sao Jorge
(4) Se (cathedral)
(5) Museum of Decorative Art
(6) National Tile Museum
(7) Praca do Comercio
(8) Rossio Square
(9) Rossio Train Station
(10) Santa Justa Elevator
(11) Gloria Elevadore (funicular)
(12) Church of St. Roquem
(13) Monastery of Jeronimos
(14) Museu de Marinha
(15) National Coach Museum
(16) Small train station

Praca do Comercio, the main waterfront square in historic Lisbon.

A good starting point for exploring Lisbon is **Castelo de Sao Jorge** (3), a hilltop fort that dominates the city. Possibly built by Romans who occupied the town in 205 BC, the fort stands on the site of an earlier citadel whose inhabitants traded with Phoenician and Carthaginian navigators. The Moors, who conquered Lisbon in 714, were driven out in 1147 by King Alfonso I. In 1260 Alfonso III transferred his court from Coimbra to Lisbon, and it was during his reign (1248-79) that the Algarve was taken from the Moors and the reconquest of Portugal was complete.

At the base of the fort is **Alfama**, a maze of Moorish-built alleys surrounding the 12th-century cathedral, the **Se** (4). Built to withstand attacks from the Moors, the cathedral resembles a fortress, its twin towers supplied with arrow slits for defence. The strength and thickness of its walls saved the cathedral from total destruction during an earthquake that destroyed parts of the city in 1755. Nearby is the Museu de Artes Decorativas (**Museum of Decorative Art**) (5), housed in a handsome four-storey mansion. About a mile to the east is the Museu dos Azulejos (**National Tile Museum**) (6), located in the cloisters of the Madre de Deus Church, where an array of beautiful tile panels are on display. These colourfully painted tiles, called *azulejos*, are seen on buildings throughout Lisbon and are a decorative tradition traced to the Moorish presence in Portugal during the Middle Ages.

Immediately west of Alfama is the new quarter, called **Baixa**, which was rebuilt by the Marques de Pombal following the 1755 earthquake. A monumental square called **Praca do Comercio** (7) faces the Tagus River and is anchored with a massive statue of King Jose I and a triumphal arch which opens onto the Rua Augusta, a wide pedestrian mall running through a bustling area of small shops, sidewalk cafes and flower sellers.

Praca Dom Pedro IV (**Rossio Square**) (8), at the top of Rue Augusta, is faced by the handsome Teatro Nacional (National Theatre) and the **Rossio Train Station** (9), its fanciful facade a mixture of Victorian, Moorish and Gothic architectural styles. Another nearby structure of this era is the **open-work iron elevator** (10) built by a protege of Gustave Eiffel, who designed the Eiffel Tower in Paris.

North of Rossio Square is Avenida da Liberdade, a stately avenue of ornate statues and shady trees that is lined with hotels and shops, and leads to a park named for Britain's King Edward VII. **Gloria Elevadore** (11), a funicular, can be taken up to **Bairro Alto**, another old-quarter neighbourhood of cobbled lanes which survived the earthquake and now bustles with night life at its fashionable bars and restaurants. Amid the art galleries and antique shops is the 16th-century **Church of St. Roquem** (12), its rich interior beautifully decorated with baroque mosaics, precious marbles and gold gilt.

Wedged between Bairro Alto and Baixa is the upscale **Chiado** area, featuring stylish shops and elegant cafes, including Cafe Brasileira - which was a favourite rendezvous for writers in the 1920s. A life-size bronze of Fernando Pessoa, Portugal's most famous 20th-century poet, is seated at one of its outdoor tables.

A few miles west of Biarro Alto is the **Belem** section, where some of Lisbon's most famous landmarks are located, including the modern Discoveries Monument in honour of Henry the Navigator. The 16th-century **Tower of Belem** (1), an example of Manueline architecture, was built by Manuel I to commemorate the discovery of the route to India by Vasco da Gama. The beautiful cloister of the nearby **Monastery of Jeronimos** (13) is another excellent example of Manueline ornamentation. Other attractions in this area are the **Museu de Marinha** (14), one of the finest maritime museums in the world, and the **National Coach Museum** (15) where beautiful gilded coaches are displayed.

OUT-OF-TOWN EXCURSIONS

Trains regularly depart **Rossio station** (9) for the 20-minute ride to **Queluz**, where an 18th-century pink palace with beautiful gardens and Rococo rooms once served as a leisure residence for the Portuguese court. Another 20 minutes further by train is the town of **Sintra**, described by Byron as a 'glorious Eden'. The National Palace stands in the centre of town, while a nearby mountaintop is the setting for romantic Pena Palace, a fairy-tale, Bavarian-style castle which incorporates a variety of architectural styles, including Arab minarets and medieval battlements (photo on page 112).

A half-hour train ride from the **small station** (16) near Praca do Comercio will take you to the seaside town of **Cascais**, which was a fashionable summer resort at the turn of the century. Further west are the windswept beaches of Guincho and the dramatic cliffs of Cabo da Roca - Europe's most westerly point.

MADEIRA ISLANDS

The verdant, mountainous Madeira Islands were originally known to the Romans as the Purple Islands. Rediscovered by the Portuguese in the early 1400s, settlement took place under order of Prince Henry the Navigator. The British temporarily occupied the islands in the early 19th century, but today they are an autonomous region of Portugal. They lie closer to Africa than to Portugal, with the shores of Morocco only 400 miles (640 km) away.

The archipelago's largest island is called **Madeira**, its steep slopes terraced with fields of green and dotted with villages of red-roofed houses. Flowers such as bougainvillea and hibiscus flourish in the balmy climate, and coastal roads cling to mountainsides ribboned with cascading waterfalls. Precipitous viewpoints include the one atop **Cabo Girao**, the world's second-highest sea cliff.

The port of **Funchal** was a favourite winter retreat of Sir Winston Churchill, who came here on painting holidays. Situated on a beautiful harbour at the base of a mountain, Funchal has a bustling local market where fresh flowers, hand-sewn linens and wickerwork are sold. Fine local wines can be enjoyed at one of the bodegas, and afternoon tea is served at the classic Reids Hotel. A popular pastime for visitors is to take a taxi to the nearby 18th-century church in the village of Monte, located uphill from Funchal, and from there embark on a 10-minute ride back down the steep street in a wicker sledge on runners, which is steered by two men dressed in traditional white flannels and straw boaters.

Funchal was founded in 1421 by Joao Goncalves Zarco, whose tomb lies in the local convent church. Other historic attractions are the 15th-century cathedral, the governor's house, and Parque de Santa Catarina, with its harbour views. The main tourist office on Avenida Arriaga hands out a list of scenic island drives and standard taxi fares. For about US$40, a taxi can be hired for the 30-minute drive to **Curral das Freiras** (Shelter of the Nuns), a spectacular valley where nuns would hide in the 16th century whenever pirates pillaged the island.

Visitors to Madeira enjoy their downhill ride in a wicker sledge.

CHAPTER TWO

SPAIN

Sunny Spain, land of fiestas and flamenco dancers, castanets and Moorish castles, is one of the world's most popular tourist destinations. Traversed by mountains and valleys, Spain occupies most of the Iberian peninsula and is separated from the rest of Europe by the peaks of the Pyrenees. The Sierra Nevada is the chief mountain range in southern Spain, where fertile plains are cultivated with citrus groves, olive trees and other crops, including wheat, grapes and cork. The country's fishing fleet nets sardines, cod and anchovies, but tourism is the bread and butter of Spain's economy. The country's natural attractions are readily apparent, its south coast lined with golden beaches and blessed with a mild Mediterranean climate.

Children file past Valencia's 13th-century cathedral during one of the many annual fiestas held throughout Spain.

SPAIN AT A GLANCE

Spain's population, which numbers about 40 million, is predominantly Roman Catholic. Castilian is the standard Spanish language but other languages are spoken in their respective districts, such as Catalan (akin to Provencal), Galacian (akin to Portuguese) and Basque (an independent language). Spain has had a constitutional monarchy since 1975, when King Juan Carlos I became the head of state upon the death of the military dictator Franco.

Spain consists of 17 geographic and historic regions, which generally correspond to the old Christian and Moorish kingdoms. Administratively, the country – which includes the Balearic Islands and Canary Islands – is divided into 50 provinces. This rich regional diversity has at times fomented separatist tendencies, especially among the Basques of Northern Spain and the Catalans, whose historical capital is Barcelona. In 1978 the Spanish Constitution was passed, establishing autonomous communities and granting them their own regional administrations which cooperate with the central administration. Spain's capital is Madrid, and the Spanish enclaves of Ceuta and Melilla in Morocco are remaining remnants of Spain's former empire.

TRAVEL TIPS

Currency: The unit of currency is the euro. Traveller's cheques and Eurocheques are widely accepted as are most credit cards. ATMs are located throughout most cities and are tied to international networks such as Cirrus. Banks are generally open from 9:00 a.m. to 2:00 p.m., Monday thru Friday.

Dining: Spanish cuisine is as varied as the country itself. Catalania is renowned for its casseroles and sauces such as *ali-oli*, which is made with olive oil and garlic. Valencia, famous for its rice dishes, is where *paella* originated, and Andalusia is the place to order *gazpacho* – a spicy vegetable soup served cold. Mayonnaise was originally created in Mahon and other celebrated specialities of the Balearic Isles include *sobrasada*, a sausage-meat spread, and Majorca's *ensaimadas*, exquisitely light pastries. The Canary Islands feature fish, tropical fruits and a hot sauce called *mojo picon* in their dishes. Spain's fine sherry, called Jerez, is a fortified wine unsurpassed in quality and value. Jerez de la Frontera, the centre of Spain's sherry industry, is located in Andalusia between Cadiz and Seville.

Restaurant hours are generally 1:30 to 4:00 p.m. for lunch and 8:30 to 11:30 p.m. for dinner, with extended hours in tourist areas. French-bread sandwiches, called *bocadillos*, are a popular fast food served at cafes and tapas bars. Tapas are bite-sized snacks, often served hot.

Opening Hours: Museums and historic attractions are generally open from 9:30 a.m. to 2:00 p.m. and from 4:00 p.m. to 7:00 p.m., Tuesday through Sunday, with some remaining open all day.

Shopping: Department stores open from 10:00 a.m. to 8:00 p.m. Monday through Saturday, but 'siesta hours' are still common in much

Outdoor tables await at a restaurant in Valldemossa on the island of Majorca.

of Spain, with stores often closing between 1:30 and 4:30 p.m. Spain is known for its finely crafted ceramics, coloured tiles, handmade lace, Andalusian leatherwork and colourful handwoven rugs.

Taxi fares: Taxis are metered, with an extra charge for luggage. A 10% tip is standard. Fares are reasonable, and most taxi drivers will accept US currency.

Telephone Access Codes: Spanish phonecards, purchased at post offices and some shops, can be used in most public telephones. To phone a number outside Spain, dial 07, wait for the international tone, then dial the country code, city code and number of the party you are calling. Personal calling card access codes : AT&T 900-99-0011; MCI 900-99-0014; SPRINT 900-99-0013; CANADA 900-99-0015.

HISTORY

Spain, standing guard over the western entrance to the Mediterranean Sea, has been uniquely influenced by its proximity to Africa. With the coast of Morocco lying only nine miles (14 km) across the Strait of Gibraltar, it's not surprising that Spain was first inhabited by an ancient people from Africa. Called Iberians, they arrived during the Neolithic Period and again at the end of the Bronze Age.

In the 9th century BC, Phoenicians passed through the Strait of Gibraltar and established colonies in Andalusia, notably at Cadiz. In the 3rd century BC, the Carthaginians conquered most of the Iberian Peninsula and founded Cartagena, which became a flourishing port and their chief base in Spain until it fell to the Romans during the Second Punic War from 218-201 BC. Carthage eventually surrendered its Spanish province to the Romans and, except for the Basques of northern Spain, the Iberian population became thoroughly romanized.

Christianity was introduced early, and both pagan and Christian literature flourished. In 409 AD, Spain endured its first wave of Germanic invaders from the north. These included the Vandals, followed by the

The hilltop Alhambra, a splendid Moorish palace, was built in Granada in the 13th century, its open courts adorned with fountains, arches and arabesque ornamentation.

Visigoths, who established their capital at Toledo. The Visigoths were slow to assimilate with the native population of romanized Catholics and in 654 AD the Visigoth king finally imposed a common law on both his Gothic and Roman subjects, who had been living under different codes.

In 710, a nobleman named Roderick succeeded King Witiza, whose thwarted heirs turned to the Moors of North Africa for military help in overthrowing the Visigothic usurper. A Berber army, led by Tarik Ibn Ziyad, crossed the Strait of Gibraltar into Spain where it defeated the Visigothic king. Tarik, however, did not restore the heirs of Witiza but instead sent for African reinforcements. Within a few years, he had conquered most of the Iberian Peninsula, and Moorish domination endured for nearly eight centuries, bestowing on Spain a rich cultural legacy.

The Moors, who were Muslims of Berber and Arab stock, built cities of great wealth and splendour. Their ornate palace complexes, decorated with glazed tiles and alabaster, contained open courts adorned with

Christopher Columbus

Born in Genoa in 1451 to a family of wool weavers, Columbus went to sea as a lad. At the age of 25, while serving as a seaman on a Genoese vessel that was sunk off the south coast of Portugal, Columbus escaped by swimming six miles to shore. He made his way to Lisbon where he joined his younger brother in chart making. By 1478 he was serving as a ship's master and the following year he married a Portuguese woman, whose father was governor of the Madeira Islands. The couple settled at Funchal but, rather than pursuing a career as a professional mariner, Columbus formulated an audacious plan of reaching the Far East by sailing due west. Finding no support in Portugal, England or France, Columbus turned to Spain.

In 1486, he presented his plan to King Ferdinand and Queen Isabella, who were interested but preoccupied with driving the Moors from Spain. For five years Columbus (known in Spain as Cristobal Colon) campaigned the Queen for financial support. Finally, in January 1492, upon the Christians' defeat of the Moors, Columbus secured an agreement in principle. Outfitted with three ships and a crew of northern Spaniards, Columbus set sail from Palos, at the mouth of the Rio Tinto in Andalusia, on August 3, 1492. After stopping at the Canary Islands to make some repairs and take on provisions, the fleet sailed due west on the easterly trade winds, reaching the Bahamas on October 12th.

When Columbus returned to Spain, 33 weeks after his famous departure, he received a hero's welcome. Ferdinand and Isabella summoned him to the Court at Barcelona, where he was received with honours and granted the titles and privileges he had requested, including support for a second voyage. A fleet of 17 vessels set sail from Cadiz in September 1493, carrying men who would colonize the New World for Spain. Columbus, a brilliant navigator, proved to be less competent as a colonial administrator, and his third voyage to the West Indies ended with Columbus brought home in chains, charged with misrule of Spain's colony on Hispaniola. Columbus, still seeking a sea route to the Far East, made one last voyage to the West Indies which ended in shipwreck off the coast of Jamaica. In 1504, the year of Queen Isabella's death, Columbus returned to Spain. Wracked with arthritis and nearing the end of his own life, Columbus was shunned by King Ferdinand. Outraged by the Spanish crown's lack of gratitude, the world's most famous explorer died in neglect, a disappointed man.

*Columbus monument
Barcelona*

a multitude of low arches and marble columns. Moorish craftsmen were famous throughout Europe for their lacy wooden carvings, filigreed jewellery and fine pottery called lustreware. The Moors were also industrious farmers, cultivating the land with extensive irrigation. Amid this material prosperity was a high degree of civilization. The Moors brought Greek learning to Spain, along with advances in science and medicine. Religious tolerance was practised, with Muslims, Christians and Jews – who had settled in Spain in large numbers – living together in relative harmony.

Ruled by various Berber dynasties, the country's flourishing south was a constant temptation to the Christian nobles of the north who had retained a pocket of resistance in Asturias during the Moorish invasion. These nobles slowly regrouped and forged alliances through marriage. In 1137 the House of Aragon united with Barcelona (Catalonia), which had been taken from the Moors by Charlemagne back in 778. In 1212, Alfonso VIII of Castile defeated the Moors and, one by one, their strongholds fell to the Christians. By the time the kingdoms of Aragon and Castile were united under Ferdinand V and Isabella I in 1479, their predecessors had conquered most of Andalusia. Granada, the last refuge of the Moors, finally surrendered to Ferdinand and Isabella in 1492.

Riding a wave of religious zeal and military vigour, the Christian rulers expelled all Jews, who took with them skills, capital and commercial connections. The Muslims (now called Mudejares) were forcibly converted to Christianity. The infamous Spanish Inquisition, established to punish Christian converts who were deemed insincere, became so zealous in its search for heretics that soon no Spaniard was immune from its harsh censorship. Sentencing involved the confiscation of property, torture and execution. (The Muslims were eventually expelled in 1609, and the Spanish Inquisition was finally abolished in 1834.)

The 16th century was Spain's Golden Century, when it became the world's first superpower, with fleets on every sea and an empire that encompassed nearly all of South America and Central America, as well as parts of North America and the Philippines. Year after year Spanish galleons would return from the New World, their holds brimming with gold and silver. Yet, by the end of the 16th century, Spain's gradual decline had already begun. England defeated the Spanish Armada in 1588, marking the rise of Britain and other rival naval powers. Buccaneers preyed on Spain's treasure fleets, and centuries of war and internal strife slowly weakened the once-powerful nation. The last remnants of Spain's vast colonial empire were lost in 1898 during the Spanish-American War, when Cuba, Puerto Rico, Guam and the Philippines all shed the Spanish yoke and entered America's growing sphere of international power.

Following the abdication of Queen Isabella II in 1868, Spain experienced various forms of government – constitutional monarchy, republic, military dictatorship. A second republic was created in 1931 but civil war broke out a few years later. This savage conflict pitted the pro-republican forces (Loyalists) against the Insurgents, who won the civil war in 1939 under the leadership of Spanish general Francisco Franco. A ruthless dictator, Franco declared Spain a kingdom in 1947 with himself regent and, despite civil unrest, Franco retained power until his death in 1975, at which time his successor, Juan Carlos, ushered in a new and enlightened era for Spain.

Juan Carlos was the first Spanish monarch since his grandfather, Alfonso VIII, was deposed in 1931. Although chosen by Franco to be his successor, Juan Carlos surprised the world when, instead of following in Franco's footsteps, he quickly guided Spain down the road to democracy. The country's first free elections since 1936 were held in 1977, and Spain's dramatic evolution from military dictatorship to parliamentary democracy began with the election of Adolfo Suarez as prime minister. Today the future looks bright for Spain. It has thrown open its doors to the rest of the world and now receives more foreign visitors than any other European country, with the exception of France.

BARCELONA

Spain's largest port and second largest city, Barcelona is a fascinating mix of modern and medieval architecture. Four million people live in the metro area of Barcelona, where broad avenues and modern buildings stand in contrast the city's historic heart – called the Gothic Quarter – which contains narrow winding streets and historic landmarks. In 1992 Barcelona successfully hosted the Summer Olympics, an event that revitalized the city and the pride of its citizens.

Placa de Catalunya, in the heart of Barcelona's shopping district.

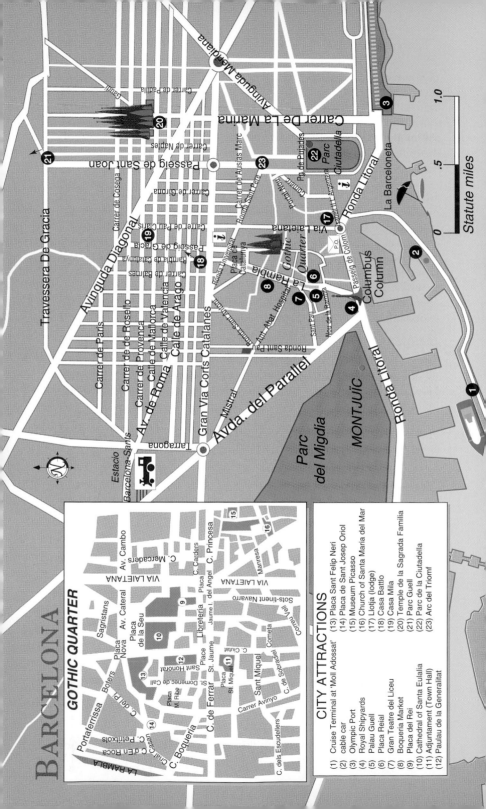

BARCELONA

GOTHIC QUARTER

CITY ATTRACTIONS

(1) Cruise Terminal at 'Moll Adossat'
(2) cable car
(3) Olympic Port
(4) Royal Shipyards
(5) Palau Guell
(6) Plaça Reial
(7) Gran Teatre del Liceu
(8) Boqueria Market
(9) Plaça del Rei
(10) Cathedral of Santa Eulalia
(11) Adjuntament (Town Hall)
(12) Paulau de la Generalitat
(13) Plaça Sant Felip Neri
(14) Plaça de Sant Josep Oriol
(15) Museum Picasso
(16) Church of Santa Maria del Mar
(17) Llotja (lodge)
(18) Casa Batllo
(19) Casa Mila
(20) Temple de la Sagrada Familia
(21) Parc Guell
(22) Parc de la Ciutadella
(23) Arc del Triomf

Statute miles

Founded by Carthaginians, Barcelona is situated on a river plain between mountains and the sea. Its name is said to stem from the great Barca family of Carthage, whose members included the famous general Hannibal. Following the Roman conquest, Barcelona flourished. During the reign of Emperor Augustus (27 BC –14 AD) a fortified village was built on a small hill called Mons Taber, its streets meeting at the forum, which is now the Placa de Sant Jaume. A temple to Augustus stood on the hilltop, and four of its Corinthian columns still stand in the patio of the Catalonian Excursionist Centre.

Barcelona declined during the Visigothic period, then fell to the Moors in the 8th century. The city was taken by Charlemagne in 801 and became an outpost of his empire. Eventually, under the influence of the powerful counts of Barcelona, the city became independent and flourished as a centre for banking, cloth making and maritime trade. At its peak in the late Middle Ages, Barcelona was a Mediterranean seaport rivalling Genoa and Venice.

Since medieval times Barcelona has been a stronghold of Catalan separatism, and from 1932-39 it was the capital of an autonomous government. Today, as the capital of Barcelona province and chief city of Catalonia, Barcelona remains a centre of regional pride and political liberalism. It is also considered the cultural centre of Spain. Modern art thrives in Barcelona, a city where Picasso began his formal art training.

A stroll along La Rambla, Barcelona's famous pedestrian street, is a popular pastime with locals and tourists alike.

His famous Cubist painting *Les Demoiselles d'Avignon* is said to have been inspired by a brothel located in the Gothic Quarter's Carrer d'Avinyo.

The visionary architect Antonio Gaudi has left the most visible impression on this handsome city. Famous in his day for his new and startling style, Gaudi spent most of his life in Barcelona where he was a leading figure of art nouveau. He designed fanciful buildings with undulating lines and facades decorated with sparkling mosaics. His most famous work is the Temple of the Holy Family, a surreal creation of soaring spires and sculpted facades, which is still under construction.

GETTING AROUND

The cruise port – known as the International Passenger Terminal at 'Moll Adossat' (1) – is located about nine miles (14 km) from the airport (US$15 taxi fare). Golondrinas (pleasure boats) provide harbour tours, and a cable car (2) runs between the waterfront and the Montjuic area, where the Olympic stadium and other attractions are located.

One way to explore the city is by purchasing a Bus Turistic ticket which allows you to ride a special bus that runs daily from April through October. You can get on and off at any of its 17 stops, and a Bus Turistic ticket comes with a booklet of discount coupons to the main attractions. Tickets are sold on board the bus and are valid for one day, although the discount coupons are valid for the whole season. Stops include the Columbus Monument and Placa de Catalunya.

ATTRACTIONS

The port of Barcelona is located adjacent to the city centre. A long breakwater protects the harbour area and connects with the city's waterfront at La Barceloneta, a tongue of land formed by accumulated sand after the port was built in the 17th century. Beaches line the east side of La Barceloneta, and beyond lies the **Olympic Port** (3), a lively spot with waterfront restaurants. More bars and restaurants are located west of La Barceloneta along La Fusta wharf, a long promenade connected by a drawbridge to the Espanya wharf, which is where an entertainment complex, including the city's aquarium, is located.

The Columbus Monument, a 200-foot-high statue, stands near the waterfront in the centre of the Placa del Portal de la Pau. An elevator can be taken to the top of this monument for a view the entire city. On the west side of the square is the **Drassanes Reials (Royal Shipyards)** (4), the largest and most complete shipyard to survive from the Middle Ages. Built in 1378, this fine example of Catalonian civil Gothic architecture now houses the Maritime Museum, with reproductions of historical ships.

Barcelona's most famous street, **La Rambla**, stretches for almost a mile, from the Columbus monument to Placa de Catalunya, in the heart of the shopping district. A wide pedestrian promenade flanked by traffic lanes, La Rambla is well suited for strolling, with its outdoor cafes, flower stalls and street entertainers. Points of interest just off La Rambla include **Palau Guell** (5), a mansion designed by Gaudi for his patron Count Eusebi de Guell, and **Placa Reial** (6), a 19th-century arcaded square adorned with Gaudi-designed lampposts. Other attractions along La Rambla include the city's opulent opera house, the **Gran Teatre del Liceu** (7), which was rebuilt following a devastating fire in 1994, and the bustling **Boqueria Market** (8), which is filled with stalls selling fresh produce. The pavement at nearby Pla de la Boqueria was decorated with a design by Joan Miro in 1970.

Until the mid-19th century, when Barcelona expanded, its medieval city was surrounded by walls. Today the central part of the medieval city is known as the Barri Gothic (Gothic Quarter), the heart of which is **Placa del Rei** (9) – the city's oldest square, where Ferdinand and Isabel received Columbus upon his return, in 1493, from his historic voyage to the New World. The buildings facing the square include the Chapel of Santa Agata, the Museu d'Historia de la Ciutat (The City's History Museum) and the Palau Major Reial (Royal Palace). The latter, built from the 11th to the 14th centuries, is a Romanesque building with Gothic additions.

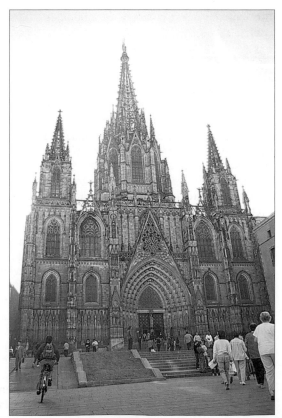

Barcelona's famous Gothic cathedral dates from the 14th century and took 150 years to build.

Barcelona cathedral's soaring interior is a breathtaking example of Gothic architecture.

Overlooking Placa de la Seu, where Barcelona residents gather on weekends to perform a circular folk dance called the sardana, is Barcelona's famous **Cathedral of Santa Eulalia** (10). Begun in 1291, this Gothic cathedral took 150 years to build. Its west front remained unfinished until the late 19th century, when a local industrialist offered to finance the completion of a neogothic facade based on a 15th-century drawing. Treasure-filled chapels line the cathedral's interior, which features a breathtaking display of medieval masonry with ogival ribbed vaults, slender piers, and fine cloisters surrounding a tropical garden. Noteworthy features to look for inside the hall-like cathedral include the carved choir stalls and the alabaster tomb of St. Eulalia, which is an exquisite piece of carving by a disciple of the great Italian sculptor Giovanni Pisano.

The Placa de Sant Jaume is flanked by the **Adjuntament (Town Hall)** (11) and the **Paulau de la Generalita**t (12), the seat of the Catalan government. The 14th century Town Hall features a Gothic facade facing the street of C. Ciutat, and the main neoclassic facade fronts the square. The Generalitat is housed in a Gothic palace with a Renaissance facade.

The **Placa Sant Felip Neri** (13) is a peaceful square located in the old Jewish Quarter (or Call), while the nearby **Placa de Sant Josep**

Oriol (14) and adjacent Placa del Pi are lively squares featuring outdoor cafes, street musicians, and weekly art and antique markets. The church of Santa Maria del Pi features a gigantic rose window, one of the largest in the world. The quaint streets leading off these interlocking squares are fascinating to explore. Carrer de la Palla, which winds its way to the cathedral, is lined with old book and antique shops; Carrer del Pi and Carrer Petritxol both feature shops and restaurants, including granjas – eateries that serve coffee, hot chocolate and bakery items. One of the city's oldest art galleries, the Sala Pares, is located on Carrer de Petritxol.

Separated from the Gothic Quarter by the Via Laietana, but still medieval in origin, is the Ribera Quarter, which became the centre of Barcelona in the 14th century when wealthy merchants built elegant mansions along Carrer Montcada. The popular **Museum Picasso** (15) is housed here in a 15th-century mansion. Picasso, born in Malaga in 1881, was a precocious draftsman who was admitted at the age of 15 to the Royal Academy of Art in Barcelona, and a number of his early sketches are among the works on display in the museum. Nearby is the 14th-century **Church of Santa Maria del Mar** (16), considered the foremost achievement of Catalan Gothic architecture. A few blocks south of the church is the **Llotja (lodge)** (17), a 14th-century structure currently housing the Barcelona Stock Exchange Library and the Academy of Fine Arts. Remodelled in the 18th century, a courtyard and large Gothic hall are among its interesting features.

A facade decorated in the trompe-l'oeil style overlooks a square in Barcelona's Gothic quarter.

In 1860, Barcelona dismantled the city walls and underwent a major expansion. The city's new section, called El Eixample (or 'enlargement'), was laid out in a grid pattern of streets with diamond-shaped intersections. Many of the buildings were designed in the art nouveau style, called Modernismo in Spain, and several famous examples are located on Passeig de Gracia, near Plaza Catalunya. A block named Mancana de la Discordia (which means 'apple of discord') features three buildings of contrasting architecture, all of them built during the first decade of the 20th century. The Casa Lleo Morera presents a modernist floral facade; the Casa Ametller, in the middle, is a neogothic building, its facade decorated with polychrome ceramic; the most famous of the three, **Casa Battlo** (18), stands at the corner of Passeig de Gracia and Carrer d'Arago. Designed by Antonio Gaudi, it features a sparkling mosaic facade and a roof shaped like a dragon's tail.

Another famous Art Nouveau building designed by Gaudi is **Casa Mila** (19), located a few blocks further along Passeig de Gracia. Also known as La Pedrera (The Stone Quarry), this large apartment house of cut stone appears to have been sculpted from play dough and its chimneys squeezed from a pastry tube.

Gaudi's most famous work, and a beloved Barcelona landmark, is the **Temple de la Sagrada Familia** (Expiatory Temple of the Holy Family) (20), begun in 1882 and still under construction. The church's

Casa Battlo, an example of art nouveau architecture, was designed by Antonio Gaudi.

The Church of the Holy Family (Sagrada Familia), designed by Gaudi, is Barcelona's most famous landmark.

west facade – which represents Passion and Death – is being built according to Gaudi's original design. The east facade represents the Nativity, and the Glory is planned on the south. The four towers on each of the three main facades represent the twelve Apostles. A complicated structure of inclined columns and parabolic arches, this unusual church is the ultimate example of Gaudi's artistic audacity and ingenious approach to construction, which allowed him to create his unusual building shapes.

Parc Guell (21), located about a mile northwest of the Church of the Sagrada Familia, is another showpiece of Gaudi's work. The park, named after Gaudi's main patron, is filled with fantastic and dreamlike forms, such as undulating benches and large, multicoloured lizards. The house where Gaudi spent the last 20 years of his life is now a small museum.

The **Parc de la Ciutadella (Citadel Park)** (22) occupies the former site of an 18th-century fortress. Most of the buildings were demolished in 1869, but left standing was the arsenal, a baroque building which is now home to the Catalan parliament and the Museum of Modern Art. The park, a tranquil setting with a small lake and monumental waterfall (featuring rocks designed by Gaudi as a young student), was planned

The tranquil setting of Citadel Park includes fountains and shady areas for relaxing.

for an 1888 exhibition held in Barcelona. The nearby **Arc del Triomf** (23), an exposed-red-brick arch, was erected as a grand entrance to the exhibition.

When Barcelona hosted the 1929 World's Fair, the venue for this event was the hill of **Montjuic**, overlooking the harbour. The site was redeveloped in preparation for the 1992 Summer Olympic Games, and the 1920s stadium was remodelled into the Olympic Stadium. Accessible by funicular from the harbour, the Montjuic's attractions include pavilions, museums, parks, gardens and a huge illuminated fountain. The Poble Espanyol (Spanish Village) is an assortment of buildings from the 1929 world's fair, representing different regions of Spain, and includes several craft workshops.

BALEARIC ISLANDS

Like mainland Spain, the Balearic Islands have been inhabited since prehistoric times. The Iberians, Phoenicians, Greeks, Carthaginians, Romans and Byzantines all laid claim to them at various points in history. In the 11th century they became a Moorish kingdom and a base for powerful pirates, until conquered by James I of Aragon in 1229. When the Spanish civil war broke out in 1936, Majorca and Ibiza were seized by Franco's insurgent forces, but Minorca remained in Loyalists' hands until 1939. Both Catalan dialects and Castilian Spanish are spoken in the Balearic Islands, which has been an autonomous region since 1983.

MAJORCA (MALLORCA)

The largest of the Balearic Islands, Majorca is a beautiful mountainous island, with rolling hills, sandy beaches and stalagmite caves. The island's northwest coast is especially scenic, its terraced cliffsides overlooking rocky headlands and hidden coves. It was here, while staying at an old abandoned monastery in the village of Valldemossa, that

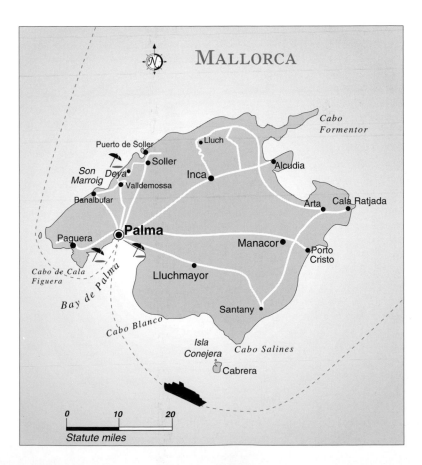

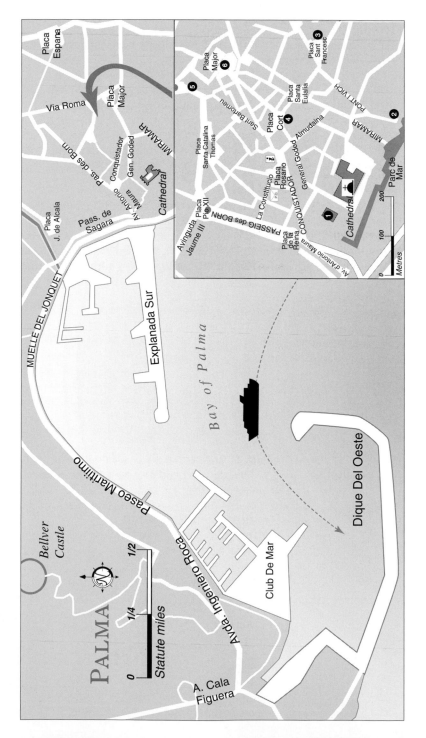

The monastery at Valldemossa where Chopin once spent a winter with George Sand.

Frederic Chopin composed his 24 preludes during the winter of 1838-39. His companion was Mme Dudevant, whose pen name was George Sand. Theirs was a stormy love affair, and she later published a book about her life with Chopin, entitled *A Winter in Majorca.*

The English poet and novelist Robert Graves spent half of his life in the Majorcan village of Deya, not far from Valldemossa. The 1929 success of *Good-bye to All That*, an irreverent book based on his war experiences, allowed Graves to buy land and build a house in Deya, where he wrote, among other works, *I, Claudius*, which was later adapted for television. In 1936, with the Spanish Civil War looming, Graves and his companion Laura Riding left Majorca aboard a British destroyer and returned to England. Ten years later Graves, along with his new wife and family, returned to Majorca where his house, called Canellun, and its garden were just as he had left them.

Another famous artist who called Majorca his home was the Spanish painter Joan Miro. Considered surrealism's greatest exponent, Miro studied in Barcelona, then in Paris, before moving to Majorca in 1941 and establishing a studio in Palma.

Palma, with a quarter of a million residents, is Majorca's chief city and the capital of Baleares province. A popular holiday resort, the city stretches along the Bay of Palma and into the surrounding hills. On a hill overlooking the port is **Bellver Castle**, a former royal palace and a fine example of 14th-century military architecture, with a circular courtyard and sweeping views from its ramparts.

On the far side of the bay – about two miles (3 km) from the cruise dock – is Palma's old town, once encircled by walls, a section of which still stands along the waterfront. Just inside the fortifications is Palma's splendid **Gothic cathedral**, begun in the year 1230, after James I of Aragon seized Palma from the Moors, and finally finished in 1601. Much of the interior was remodelled at the beginning of this century by Antonio Gaudi. The bell tower holds nine bells with the largest, which was cast in 1389, weighing four tons. Opposite the cathedral is **Castillo della Almudaina** (1), originally a Moorish citadel and now a military headquarters.

Other structures of note include the 10th-century **Arab baths** (2), the 13th-century **Church of San Francisco** (3), and the 17th-century **Ajuntament (Town Hall)** (4). The **Forn Teatro (Theatre Bakery)** (5) is well known both for its photogenic facade and its delicious pastries. The nearby **Placa Major** (6) is where a craft market is held several times a week. Pedestrian shopping streets lead north from this square, and fashionable boutiques line Avinguda Jaume III and Passeig des Born, an avenue with a pedestrian promenade down the centre.

In addition to taking a ship-organized shore excursion, renting a car is another good way to explore the island. For about US$60, you can hire a car for the day and enjoy a leisurely drive around part of the island.

The craggy northwest coast is dotted with watchtowers and spectacular viewpoints, including the one at **Son Marroig**, an estate built by Austrian archduke Luis Salvador. The archduke visited Majorca in the

Palma's medieval seawalls.

The spectacular sea views at Deya (above) and Son Marroig (opposite), along Majorca's northwest coast.

mid-1800s and decided to stay. Son Marroig has since been converted into a museum housing his collection of pottery and paintings. The view from the estate's mirador looks down nearly 1,000 feet to a rocky headland from which the waves have carved, over time, a huge sea arch called Sa Foradada (meaning 'perforated').

Nearby are the villages of **Deya**, where Robert Graves lived, and **Valldemossa**, location of La Cartuja, a Carthusian monastery that was converted into lodgings in 1835. The apartments where Chopin and George Sand stayed are furnished in period style and contain a piano used by Chopin. Other picturesque villages along the northwest coast include Puerto Soller, with a natural harbour and fine beaches. Inland, the mountain village of Luch is the location of a monastery set into the side of a cliff.

At the north end of the island is historic **Alcudia**, where a twice-weekly market selling handicrafts and other items is held outside the restored remains of its Moorish city walls. A nearby Roman amphitheatre was excavated in the 1950s.

On the island's east coast, near the fishing port of **Porto Cristo**, are the Caves of Drach, which contain one of the world's largest underground lakes. The pearl factory at nearby Manacor is another popular attraction.

MINORCA (MENORCA)

Today one of the Mediterranean's most desirable holiday islands, Minorca has been inhabited since Neolithic times. Several megalithic monuments of huge undressed stone stand amid the island's gentle ter-

The medieval port of Ciudadela on the island of Minorca.

rain of low hills, patchwork fields and narrow hedge-lined lanes. During the 18th century, England, France and Spain all fought for control of Minorca, but the island was held mostly by the British who gave **Port Mahon** (Mao), the island's chief city, its Georgian-style architecture. Situated at the island's east end, this strategic port was named for the Carthaginian general Mago, and its picturesque harbour is protected by two fortresses. Mahon's tourist information office is at Placa de S'Esplanada, and local highlights include the Ajuntament (City Hall) and Church of Santa Maria (St. Mary's Church). The island was finally awarded to Spain in 1802, but it still retains some British flavour. **Ciutadella** (Ciudadela), at the island's west end, was Minorca's capital before the arrival of the British. A quaint city, its interesting architecture includes medieval churches and splendid palaces. Beautiful beaches line the island's south coast, such as the protected cove at Cala Galdana (see photo page 23) and the sandy beach at Cala 'n Porter which is sheltered from winds by cliffs.

Tarragona: Situated at the mouth of the Francoli River, this Catalonian port was a flourishing commercial centre during Roman times, with Augustus making it the capital of the province of Tarraconensis. Ruins of the town's ancient walls, amphitheatre and aqueduct can be viewed by visitors, as can the 13th century Romanesque-Gothic cathedral which contains one of the finest cloisters in Spain.

VALENCIA

Spain's third largest city, **Valencia** is the capital of Valencia province – the 'garden of Spain' where the famous Valencia oranges are grown. For centuries this province's fertile coastal plain has been cultivated, and the Tribunal de las Aguas, founded in the 10th century, still meets regularly in Valencia to settle disputes over the irrigation of its outlying garden region. Its university was founded in 1501, and the city became a literary and cultural centre, with a famous school of painting. Other major landmarks include a 13th-century cathedral with a Gothic bell tower (called El Miguelete), 14th-century fortified towers (called Torres de Serranos) which were built on Roman foundations, and the 15th-century silk exchange (La Lonja), which is considered one of Spain's finest Gothic buildings.

Situated on the Costa Blanca, the coastal city of **Alicante** is dominated by the great Moorish castle of Santa Barbara. Perched upon a rocky peak, the fortress provides breathtaking views of the city's squares, beaches and palm-lined Explanada de Espana, which runs along the waterfront. A lift, its shaft running deep inside the mountain, transports visitors to the castle. The tourist office is located near the waterfront, in the arcaded Plaza de Ayuntamiento.

Cartagena, a city of great historical importance, was founded by Carthaginians in the 3rd century BC. No traces of the ancient city remain but the ruins of the medieval Castillo de la Concepcion, surrounded by fine gardens, command a splendid view of the city and harbour. The city's museum holds excellent pre-Roman and Roman collections, and outside the city, near the old docks, is the National Museum of Underwater Archaeology.

ANDALUSIA

The southernmost part of Spain, sunny Andalusia is best known for its beach resorts, whitewashed buildings and Moorish castles. **Almeria**, with a sunny, mild climate and a busy seaport, is a popular holiday destination for Northern Europeans. Almeria is also of historical significance with its Gothic cathedral and ruins of a Moorish fort. From the 3rd to 15th centuries, before falling to the Christians in 1489, Almeria was an outlet for the Moorish kingdom of Granada. Today the port city exports the region's celebrated grapes and other fruits, as well as esparto, which is a Spanish grass used for making cordage and paper.

Malaga, a port of access to Granada, is situated on the Costa del Sol where a mild climate, lush vegetation and beautiful beaches attract plenty of tourists. Nearby is the popular resort town Torremolinos. Malaga, the birthplace of Picasso, is a mostly modern city despite its millennia of history. Founded in the 12th century BC by the Phoenicians, the city passed to the Carthaginians, then to the Romans, followed by the Visigoths and, in 711 AD, the Moors. From the 13th to the 15th centuries, Malaga flourished as a seaport of the Moorish kingdom of Granada before falling to Ferdinand and Isabella in 1487. Its

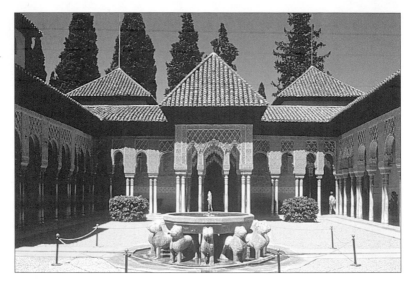

The Court of Lions at the Alhambra palace in Granada.

historic buildings include a 16th-century cathedral, the ruins of a Moorish alcazar, and an imposing citadel called the Gibralfaro.

Granada, which began as a Moorish fortress, is beautifully situated at the foot of the Sierra Nevada, where the Darro and Genil rivers flow together. It became a city of great splendour with construction of its famous palace complex, the Alhambra. A hilltop group of buildings, the Alhambra (which means 'the red' in Arabic) was built between 1230 and 1354. This luxurious royal palace and citadel are considered the finest examples of Moorish architecture in Spain. The halls and chambers surround a series of open courts, including the Court of Lions which contains arcades resting on 124 white marble columns. The palace's sumptuous interior of alabaster and glazed tile is adorned with geometric ornamentation of minute detail and intricacy. When American author and diplomat Washington Irving came to live in the Alhambra in 1829, the palace was crumbling from rot and decay. His book of Spanish sketches, called *Tales of the Alhambra*, helped revive interest in the palace's preservation and, since 1862, an ongoing program of restoration has been in effect.

Sharing the Alhambra's hilltop site are the palace of Emperor Charles V, built in 1526 on the site once occupied by the sultan's private apartments, and the celebrated gardens of the Palacio del Generalife, a summer residence of the Moorish rulers. Granada's 16th-century cathedral was built in the late Gothic and plateresque style. The adjoining royal chapel, a masterpiece of ornate Gothic architecture, contains the marble tombs of Ferdinand and Isabella.

Cadiz, once one of the world's major ports, is an ancient city rich in naval history. Founded by the Phoenicians in about 1000 BC, Cadiz became the wealthiest port in Europe after the discovery of America, when Spanish treasure ships, returning from the New World, unloaded their cargoes here. In 1587 Francis Drake burned a Spanish fleet in Cadiz's harbour, in an operation known as 'the singeing of the King of Spain's beard', and nine years later another English squadron captured and sank most of the ships in this harbour.

Attacks on Cadiz continued but its wealth, based on trade with Spain's colonies, continued to grow, especially after Seville's port – reached by river from Cadiz – became partially blocked by a sandbar. The port of Cadiz was blockaded by the British in 1797, and bombarded by Sir Horatio Nelson in 1800. Five years later, a Franco-Spanish fleet sailed from Cadiz and met its destruction at the Battle of Trafalgar. Today cruise ships pull into Cadiz's natural harbour where disembarking passengers can enjoy the palm-lined promenades of this fine old city. Its 13th-century cathedral was rebuilt in the Renaissance style, and a new cathedral was begun in 1722. In 1980 some Phoenician sarcophagi and a Roman theatre were discovered in Cadiz.

Seville, a busy port connected with the Atlantic by river and canal, has been the chief city of Andalusia since ancient times. The Romans made Seville a judicial centre of Baetica province and built the nearby city of Italica, where the emperors Trajan and Hadrian were born. The city fell to the Moors in 712 AD, and eventually became a flourishing commercial and cultural centre. Two parts of its famous mosque remain, the Court of Oranges and the Giralda tower, which was built between 1163 and 1184.

C E R V A N T E S

Cervantes, the Spanish novelist, dramatist and poet, wrote his masterpiece, *Don Quixote*, while living in Seville in the late 16th century. Prior to that he was a student of Italian literature and philosophy while in the service of a cardinal. He next served in the army, and was wounded and permanently crippled in his left arm during the naval battle of Lepanto, fought between the Christians and Ottomans in 1571 off the coast of Greece. On his way back to Spain, Cervantes was captured by Barbary pirates and sold as a slave. After numerous attempts at escape, he was ransomed by the viceroy of Algiers, the price paid by his family bringing them to financial ruin. While working as a government purchasing agent in Seville from 1588 to 1597, Cervante's unbusinesslike methods resulted in his imprisonment on several occasions, during which he penned parts of *Don Quixote*, a burlesque of the popular romances of chivalry and a huge success when published in 1605 .

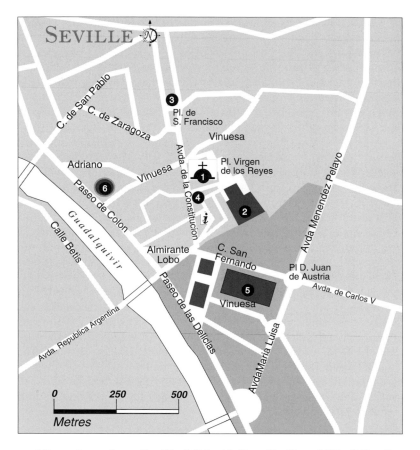

After a long siege, Seville fell in 1248 to Ferdinand III of Castile, and about 300,000 Moors – the majority of the population – left. Following the discovery of the New World in 1492, Seville again prospered as a chief port of trade. A beautiful **Gothic cathedral** (1), one of the world's largest, was completed in 1519 on the site of the main mosque, its square minaret (the Giralda tower) converted to a bell tower in 1568 with the addition of an ornate Renaissance superstructure. Inside the cathedral are invaluable works of art and the tomb of Christopher Columbus. Adjoining the cathedral is the **Alcazar** (2), built by Moorish artisans, its splendid halls and exquisite decorations rivalling the Alhambra in Granada.

In addition to Seville's numerous churches and private castles, other notable buildings include the **16th-century town hall** (3) the **Ionja (former exchange)** (4) containing archives of Spanish America, and the city's **university buildings** (5) which were formerly a large tobacco factory and a setting featured in Bizet's Carmen. Seville is the country's bullfighting capital, and **La Maestranza Bullring** (6), completed in 1763, is the oldest and most beautiful in Spain.

B U L L F I G H T I N G

Bullfighting, an important part of Spanish culture, was introduced by the Moors who fought bulls from horses and killed them with javelins. This Moorish practise evolved into the sport of bullfighting, called *corrida de toros* in Spanish. A controversial spectacle, criticized by some as a form of animal torture, the bullfight is nonetheless popular not only in Spain, but in Southern France, Morocco and several Latin American countries. Held in a large outdoor arena, the modern bullfight unfolds in three ritualistic parts. First, toreros wave capes at the bull and mounted picadors thrust at it with lances. The next stage involves banderillos who, while on the run, poke short barbed sticks into the bull's withers. Finally the matador, holding a small cape and a sword, makes daring passes at the bull who eventually stops charging and succumbs to the matador's dominance. When the bull strikes a stationary stance, with its four feet square on the ground and its head hung low, this is the moment when, according to ritual and law, the matador must shove his sword into the bull's heart. Fighting bulls are specially bred, and successful matadors are highly paid and admired for their skill and courage.

GALACIA

In northwest Spain's Galacia province, the Atlantic ports of La Coruna and Vigo both provide access to **Santiago de Compostela**, one of the chief shrines of Christendom. In the early 9th century, Alfonso II of Asturias had a sanctuary built on the supposed site of the apostle St. James The Greater's tomb. The city, which grew around the shrine, became an important place of pilgrimage during the Middle Ages, second only to Jerusalem and Rome. The Moors destroyed the sanctuary in the 10th century, and a Romanesque cathedral was built on the site between the 11th and 13th centuries, with baroque and plateresque additions made during later restorations. The Hospital Real was built in the early 1500s by Ferdinand and Isabella to accommodate poor pilgrims.

CANARY ISLANDS

These Atlantic isles, lying off the coast of Africa, are volcanic in origin and immensely appealing to pleasure-seeking visitors because of their subtropical climate, clear waters and expansive beaches. Starkly beautiful, the islands are a study in contrasts. Sea cliffs and craggy coves give way to massive sand dunes and vast beaches. Mountain villages with whitewashed houses and red-tiled roofs seem far removed from the resort areas' modern hotels and championship golf courses. Millions of visitors arrive annually by air, while those arriving by cruise ship pull into historic ports of cobblestone streets and Spanish colonial architecture – the same ports that greeted famous sea captains in centuries past.

The islands' original inhabitants were a cave-dwelling people called Guanches, who likely migrated from Africa. The islands were visited by Romans as early as 40 BC, and several classical writers referred to them as the Fortunate Islands. The Middle Ages brought the occasional visit by Arabs and Europeans, but no permanent settlement until 1402, when a Norman named Jean de Bethencourt arrived at Lanzarote. In 1479 a treaty between Portugal and Spain gave the latter sovereignty over the Canaries, and the Spanish conquest of the Guanches was complete by 1496.

The islands became an important base for voyages to the Americas, and they were frequently raided by pirates and privateers. England's Francis Drake attacked Las Palmas in 1595 but was repulsed; the Dutch were more successful four years later, when they ravaged the port. Two centuries later, in 1797, Horatio Nelson tried to capture a Spanish treasure ship at Santa Cruz but was repulsed, losing an arm in the battle.

The Canaries, comprising two provinces, have been an autonomous region of Spain since 1982. Santa Cruz de Tenerife, whose capital is Santa Cruz on the island of Tenerife, encompasses the western islands; Las Palmas,whose capital is Las Palmas on the island of Gran Canaria, encompasses the eastern islands.

Tenerife is the largest of Canary Islands. Its northern valleys are filled with banana and pineapple plantations, and the entire island is dominated by the snowcovered summit of Mt. Teide –Spain's highest point at 12,162 feet (3,707 metres). The visitor centre at Teide National Park provides guided hikes and bus tours, and a cable car carries visitors close to the top of the volcano, where the final ascent is made on foot to the edge of the crater. Tenerife's port city of **Santa Cruz** has several museums and historic structures, including a Moorish bell tower. The 18th-century cannons that held off an attack by Horatio Nelson are still in place, including the one that scored a direct hit on his right arm, which was so badly injured it had to be amputated that evening on board his battleship.

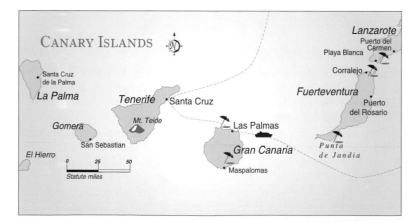

Playa Blanca, Lanzarote

The cliff-edged island of **Gomera** is where Columbus made his last stop, his ships pulling into the port of San Sebastian, before sailing across the Atlantic Ocean in 1492.

La Palma, also called La Isla Bonita ('The Pretty Island'), is a verdant island of volcanic mountains, one of which burst open in 1971. The island's capital of **Santa Cruz de la Palma** is situated on the edge of a crater. A bustling ship-building centre in the 16th century, the port has retained its colonial appearance.

Las Palmas, capital of Las Palmas province, is situated on **Gran Canaria**, an island famous for its enormous beaches and sand dunes, such as those found at Maspalomas. The city of Las Palmas was founded in 1478, and its nearby harbour at Puerto de la Luz is the Canaries' chief port and one of the busiest in Spain. An impressive castle, Castillo de la Luz, protects the harbour, and a Gothic cathedral, dating to the early 1500s, stands in the city's old quarter. It took four centuries to complete the cathedral, hence its 19th-century exterior. The Casa Museo Colon (Columbus Museum) is housed in the palace where Columbus likely stayed in 1492. Not far from Castillo de la Luz, is a fine beach called Las Cantara.

The island of **Lanzarote**, an unusual lunar-like landscape with black and red beaches, features bubbling geysers and grottoes containing emerald-coloured water. The island of **Fuerteventura** offers stunning beaches, including those of powdery sand on the island's south coast.

GIBRALTAR

A British crown colony, Gibraltar is a military fortress perched on a narrow peninsula, called the Rock of Gibraltar, which is connected to the Spanish mainland by a low sandy area of neutral ground. In ancient times, the Rock was regarded as one of the two mythological Pillars of Hercules – the other being Mt. Acha at Ceuta in Africa. These two promontories flank the east entrance to the Strait of Gibraltar and were said to mark the end of the world by the Ancient Greeks.

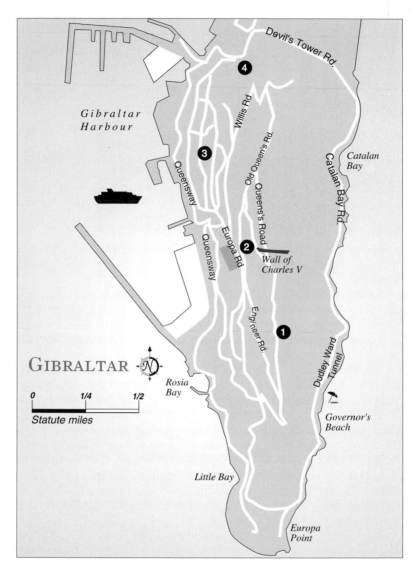

The name Gibraltar is Arabic in origin, derived from Jabal-al-Tarik ('mount of Tarik'). In 711, the Moorish leader Tarik captured the Rock of Gibraltar and built its first fortifications, upon which enlargements and improvements have been made over the centuries. The Moors held Gibraltar until 1462, when the Spanish seized control of the fortress. The British gained possession of 'the Rock' in 1704 and have held it ever since, fending off several sieges by the Spanish and French in the 18th century. During the Spanish civil war (1936-39), a considerable number of refugees fled to Gibraltar. Its fortifications were strengthened during WWII, when most civilians were evacuated.

Gibraltar is only three miles long and less than a mile wide but, as a strategic naval and air base, it has been a source of friction between Great Britain and Spain. Despite Spain's persistent claim to Gibraltar, its residents voted in 1967 to maintain their ties to Britain, and in 1981 Gibraltar's small civilian population, mainly of Spanish, Italian, Portuguese, Maltese and Jewish descent, were granted full British citizenship. In 1985 Spain reopened its border with Gibraltar, after closing it in 1969, and today many of the colony's labourers live in the Spanish border town of La Linea.

The Rock of Gibraltar is made of Jurassic limestone, and is honeycombed with caves, arsenals and a tunnel bisecting the rock from east to west. Valuable archaeological finds have been made in **St. Michael's Cave** (1) where stalagmites and stalactites create a dramatic setting for the daily sound-and-light shows. Tours are available of the tunnels leading off the cave's main chambers. From St. Michael's Cave, it's about a 20-minute walk to the **Apes' Den** (2) where the famous Barbary Apes – a breed of monkey native to Morocco – are fed twice daily. In between feedings, they pass the time snatching purses and cameras from curious tourists.

The view from the Rock's summit is spectacular, looking across the Strait of Gibraltar to Africa. This lookout, as well as the Apes' Den and St. Michael's Cave, can all be reached by cable car from the **town** (3), where a tourist office is located in Cathedral Square. Local attractions include the Governor's Residence, the Law Courts, the Anglican cathedral and the Catholic cathedral. Main Street is lined with shops, pubs and restaurants. At the north end of town is the **Moorish Castle** (4), its Tower of Homage dating from 1333. At the south end of town, just past the harbour, is Rosia Bay. Following the Battle of Trafalgar in 1805, Nelson's flagship *Victory* was brought here and the dead on board were transferred to Trafalgar Cemetery at the south edge of town. Nelson's body was shipped back to England, preserved in a barrel of rum.

The Rock

t's doubtful that Ira Gershwin, when writing the lyrics for the song *Our Love is Here to Stay*, seriously thought that one day the Rockies may crumble or Gibraltar may tumble, but the Rock of Gibraltar is in fact doing both. Heavy rainstorms during the winter of 1997/98 have been blamed for the recent decay of Gibraltar's famous limestone cliffs, huge chunks of which have fallen into Camp Bay on the east side of the peninsula. The rainwater had apparently filled up the natural cracks in the cliffs, causing the limestone rock to split and fall off in various-sized pieces, one of which flattened an empty restaurant.

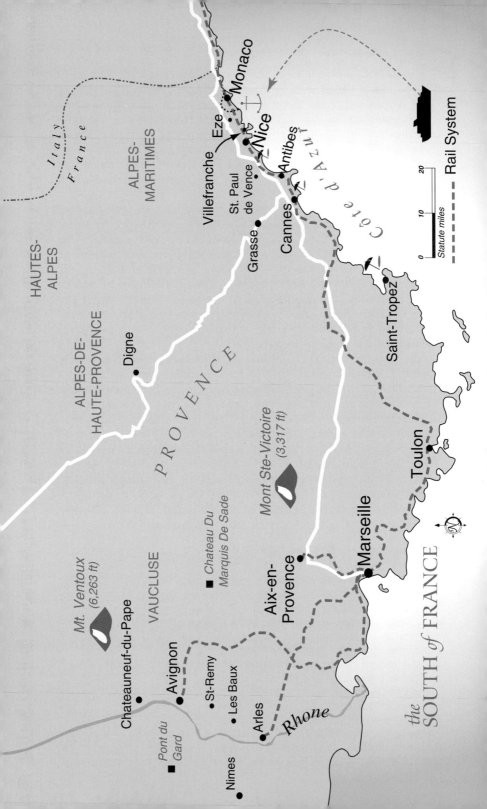

the SOUTH of FRANCE

- - - Rail System

Statute miles
0   10   20

Italy
France

Monaco
Eze
Villefranche
Nice
St. Paul de Vence
Antibes
ALPES-MARITIMES
Côte d'Azur
Grasse
Cannes
HAUTES-ALPES
Saint-Tropez
Digne
ALPES-DE-HAUTE-PROVENCE
P R O V E N C E
Mont Ste-Victoire
(3,317 ft)
Toulon
Mt. Ventoux
(6,263 ft)
VAUCLUSE
Marseille
Chateauneuf-du-Pape
Chateau Du Marquis De Sade
Aix-en-Provence
Avignon
St-Remy
Les Baux
Arles
Rhone
Pont du Gard
Nimes

CHAPTER THREE

FRANCE

French culture has been widely admired since the 13th century, when its poetry, manners and ideal of chivalry were adopted as a model by the other courts of Europe. Today it's the food, the wine and a general *joie de vivre* that many of us admire in the French. In a nation where dining is an art form, and where the arts are for all to enjoy, the many aspects of gracious living fall into fascinating perspective. Politics are important, but so is lunch. And for the average visitor to France, figuring out the lunch menu could well be easier than understanding the many departments, districts, cantons and communes of French government.

France has had a centralized administration since the Revolution of 1789, yet each region has retained its own distinct character. This diversity harks back to the Middle Ages when provinces were ruled by dukes and counts, and feudal power was held by nobles, guilds and the clergy. The country was first settled by Greek and Phoenician traders who landed on the Mediterranean coast in about 600 BC. The Romans began colonizing Provence in the 2nd century BC, followed by Julius Caesar's widespread conquest in 58 BC. For five centuries Gaul, as the Romans called it, was under Rome's rule. Then, in 486 AD, the Franks – a Germanic tribe – routed the last Roman emperor of Gaul and the region soon lay in ruins. The only remnant of Roman civilization was the church, which also faced ruination when Saracens invaded in the 8th century.

The Carolingian dynasty, led by Pepin the Short, rescued the region. His son Charlemagne (Charles the Great) became a legendary figure. Crowned emperor of the West on Christmas Day in the year 800, Charlemagne ushered in an intellectual renaissance. A great leader and administrator, Charlemagne also promoted the rebirth of learning and the arts with the

establishment of his famous palace school, along with numerous schools for children throughout the empire.

A thousand years later Napoleon drew on Charlemagne's example when forging his own empire. One of Napoleon's generals was the father of Victor Hugo, who became a towering figure of 19th-century French literature with such epic novels as *The Hunchback of Notre Dame* and *Les Miserables*. Hugo and other members of the Romantic school revived the legend of Charlemagne, who had been immortalized in medieval poems as the champion of Christendom. The glory days of empire may be over for France, but the country's artistic, literary and culinary culture remains the envy of many a nation.

A FEW WORDS ABOUT FRENCH WINE

France's best wines set the standard for the rest of the world. Alas, these fine vintages are losing their appeal at home, where the younger generation is showing little inclination to learn the complicated labelling system of French wines, one based on regions of origin. These regions, called appellations, vary in size from single small vineyards to large districts. The French tradition of familiarizing oneself with the appellations and, more importantly, the best growers and merchants within each appellation, can be a daunting task for the novice wine drinker who relies on identifying the type of grape when choosing a wine. The French wine industry is currently debating whether or not to modify its labels and display the varietal (variety of grape) along with the appellation.

FRANCE AT A GLANCE

About 57 million people live in France, and Roman Catholicism is the major religion. French, spoken in a variety of regional dialects, is the major language, except in Corsica where an Italian dialect is spoken. The country is governed by a president, who is directly elected for a seven-year term, and who appoints a premier and cabinet that are responsible to the national assembly. France is divided into 22 planning regions, two of which are covered in this chapter, namely Provence-Alpes-Côte d'Azur and Corsica. France is an industrial nation and major economic power, yet more than half of its land area is still used for agriculture. Tourism is also a major industry, with France receiving more international tourists than any other country in the world.

TRAVEL TIPS

Currency: The unit of currency is the euro. Traveller's cheques and Eurocheques are widely accepted as are most credit cards. ATMs are located throughout most cities and are tied to international networks such as Cirrus. Banks are generally open from 9:00 a.m. to 2:00 p.m., Monday thru Friday. Banks are usually open Monday to Friday from 9:00 a.m. to 4:30 p.m.

Dining: Southern France hosts numerous festivals and feasts each year, at which the bounty of land and sea is enjoyed. Fresh herbs, grilled fish, olives, garlic and goat cheese – all are featured in the local cuisine. Famous dishes include bouillabaisse (a fish stew) and salad nicoise, which features tuna, tomato, hard-boiled egg and anchovies. Wines produced in the south of France include the famous white wine of Cassis. The grenache grape is used to make the fruity rosé wines for which Provence has a particularly good reputation.

Opening Hours: Museums and historic attractions generally open from 10:00 a.m. to noon and from 2:00 p.m. to 5:00 or 6:00 p.m.

Shopping: The south of France is famous for its Provencal style of country decor, which is rustic and romantic, featuring cane beds, rush chairs and tapestry throws. Handcrafted items are created in earthy textures, such as wood, pewter and wrought iron, and local specialties include ceramic pots, hand-painted dishes and colourful table linens. Stores are generally open 9:30 a.m. to 7:00 p.m.

Taxi fares: Approximately US$50 per hour, but this is negotiable. A 10% tip is expected. Most drivers will accept US currency.

Telephone Access Codes: Telecartes (telephone calling cards), bought at post offices and tobacconists, can be used for most public telephones. Calling card access codes: AT&T 0800-99-0011; MCI 0800-99-0019; SPRINT 0800-99-0087; CANADA 0800-99-0216.

CÔTE D'AZUR (AZURE COAST)

One by one they were drawn to the shimmering colours and flickering sunlight of the Côte D'Azur. Renoir, Matisse, Picasso – these and other great figures of modern art have lived and worked along the French Riviera, a narrow coastal strip squeezed between the Alps and the Mediterranean. Sheltered from winds and blessed with a mild year-round climate, it was only a matter of time until the entire world discovered the Riviera's famed beauty and fashionable beach resorts.

One of the first 'tourists' to the area was Lord Henry Brougham, a British statesman who served as Lord Chancellor, head of the judiciary, from 1830 to 1834. In December 1834 the British baron was travelling to Italy with his daughter Eleonore for a holiday, when he found the border closed due to an epidemic in Northern Europe. Turning back, the party headed toward Grasse and stopped for the night at a hostel located on what is now known as the Rue du Port in Cannes. Enchanted by the village's seaside setting, Lord Brougham decided to have a residence built there and two years later members of London's high society flocked to the opening of Villa Eleonore.

The small fishing port of Cannes quickly became a gathering place for European aristocracy. Villas and castles were built, and the bare countryside surrounding Cannes was transformed when Lord

Canne's Carlton Hotel. A flower market in Monaco.

Brougham built a canal to supply water to the town and allow the planting of lawns and gardens at the palatial estates. The once-barren countryside, now irrigated, became a paradise of flowers and fruit trees.

A railroad line was built in the 1860s to provide access from Marseille to Cannes, Nice and Monaco. High society of Europe and America journeyed to the Riviera each winter, including Tsar Alexander II and his wife, who arrived in Nice a week after the railroad opened in 1864. Not all visitors were titled, however, for a new class was emerging – the recently rich and powerful of the Industrial Revolution who wanted to celebrate their wealth with opulence and excess. The often flamboyant architecture of the late 19th century is characterized by the Riviera's luxurious villas and grand hotels, such as the Victoria and Negresco in Nice, and the Carlton in Cannes, which opened in 1910, its architect reportedly modelling the palace's two domes after the bosom of a famous courtesan.

When the artist Pierre Renoir left Paris in the late 1800s to live at Cagnes-sur-Mer just east of Antibes, his style of painting had gone beyond impressionism with the sensuous depiction of voluptuous nudes. Henri Matisse, the leader of Fauvism – a style emphasizing the

Fort Carré, built in the 16th century, guards Vieux Port, Antibes.

use of brilliant colours – lived in Nice from 1917 until his death in 1954. And when Pablo Picasso came to the Riviera in 1946 to escape the pressures of Paris, he experienced an artistic rejuvenation while living in a medieval palace at Antibes.

Others have followed in the footsteps of these great artists, seeking solace in the warm sun and azure sea. Where once only footpaths led to fortified towns set high in the hills, panoramic highways now hug this rugged coastline. Back in the 1920s the renowned American writer F. Scott Fitzgerald began touting the Riviera as a summer resort and the idea quickly caught on. Today, in summer, the local population swells with visitors lured by the famous beach resorts and fine art museums of this scenic coast.

GETTING AROUND

The Côte d'Azur's famous resorts lie between Saint Tropez and Monaco, and are connected by roads and regular train service. Cruise passengers arriving at a French Riviera port can visit one or two nearby resorts – either with a ship-organized shore excursion or independently by train, taxi and/or bus. For example, the train ride from Villefranche to Nice is only 15 minutes; Villefranche to Monaco is 20 minutes; and Villefranche to Cannes takes about an hour. There's no train station at Eze but the train does stop at Eze-Sur-Mer, from where it's a two-mile bus or taxi ride up to the village. Buses run regularly between Nice and Saint Paul de Vence (a one-hour ride each way).

Taxis cost upwards of US$50 per hour, depending on your destination. Some approximate fares: Nice – Villefranche (20 minutes) is

Above: Place Rosetti, Old Nice.
Opposite: A street scene in Monaco's La Condamine.

US$25; Villefranche – Monaco (30 minutes) = US$60; Monaco's train station to Monte Carlo's Place du Casino = US$8; Villefranche – Cannes (1 1/2 hours) = US$100. Rental cars are also available, especially in Nice. The cost is approximately US$115 to $155 per day, depending on the size of the vehicle. The coastal highway is especially scenic along the Corniche du Littoral between Nice and Monaco. There are no border restrictions upon entering Monaco.

PORTS OF CALL

The famous resort of Saint-Tropez (pronounced *san-tro-pay*) lies some distance from the Côte d'Azur's other popular ports. Situated about 30 miles (50 km) west of Cannes, this picturesque fishing port of 5,000 inhabitants was made famous by film personalities during the 1960s. The local Musee del'Annonciade, housed in a 17th-century stone church, contains works by Matisse, Dufy and others.

Cannes (pronounced *kon*), home to the famous international film festival, has long been subject to foreign invasions. Throughout the Middle Ages, Cannes experienced repeated raids by the Saracens, and by soldiers passing through on their way to battle. In the 5th century, the holy monk Honorate founded an abbey on the offshore isle that bears his name, and his sister Marguerite founded a convent on the neighbouring Island of St Marguerite where, in 1667, a man whose face was hidden behind a velvet mask was imprisoned. Immortalized by Voltaire and Alexandre Dumas, he became a mysterious figure of literature called 'The Man in the Iron Mask'. His identity has long been open to speculation but he may have been a valet to Louis XIV, jailed for 34 years due to a scandalous secret he knew about the French king.

On March 1st, 1815, Napoleon landed near Cannes when returning from exile on the island of Elba and, with a handful of followers, began his triumphant march northward to Paris. A mere two decades later, Lord Brougham began transforming Cannes into a holiday resort. The town's seaside path, called the 'Chemin de la Petite Croix' after a small cross that marked the gathering spot for pilgrims to the Island of St Honorat, was gradually widened into a road. Today that same path is an upscale esplanade called the 'Promenade de la Croisette', its deluxe hotels and famous blue chairs looking out over a beautiful bay where the fine sand beaches are regularly cleaned by tractor-drawn machines and the water is hydraulically vacuumed.

Cannes held its first film festival in 1939, as an alternative to the Venice Film Festival, which had fallen under the control of the Fascists and Nazis. A 'steamship of stars' arrived that September from America – Gary

Palais des Festivals, inaugurated in 1982.

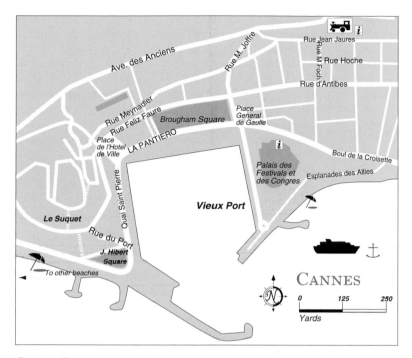

Cooper, Douglas Fairbanks and Mae West were among its passengers. The festival was opened under the presidency of Louis Lumiere, the inventor of cinema, only to be cancelled the next day when Germany invaded Poland. When the war ended, the festival was revived, its principles espoused in the words of writer, visual artist and filmmaker Jean Cocteau, who described the new festival as "a microcosm of what the world would be like if its inhabitants had direct contact with each other and they all spoke the same language".

Roberto Rosellini's *Open City* won the top prize among 44 international films entered in 1946 and the festival quickly became a social event. Financial difficulties, however, forced the Festival's cancellation in 1948 and 1950. In 1951 it was held in May instead of September so as not to conflict with the one held in Venice. In 1953 Brigitte Bardot appeared on the Croisette in a bikini, and in 1954 a starlet named Simone Silva bared her breasts for attentive photographers who wired the picture to newspapers around the world, dramatically increasing the festival's exposure and turning it into a major media event. The following year American actress Grace Kelly was invited to Cannes to help re-establish the artistic merit of the festival. At a press conference she met Prince Rainier of Monaco and a year later they were married at a lavish wedding held during the festival.

The Croisette Palace was eventually replaced with the Palais des Festivals, which was inaugurated in 1982 and is a venue for other festivals, as well as concerts, operas, recitals and ballet performances. The auditorium is named after the composer Claude Debussy (1862-1918) who, as a young boy learning to play the piano, would visit the home of his music teacher at the tip of the Croisette.

The most famous grand hotel on the Croisette is the Carlton, built in 1912. It was joined in 1926 by the Majestic, the favourite rendezvous for Film Festival stars. More recent additions include the contemporary Gray d'Albion and Noga Hilton. Excellent bistros line the Croisette, and prestigious restaurants include La Cote in the Carlton, La Palme d'Or in the Martinez, and La Scala in the Noga Hilton. Shopping streets abound, including the popular Rue Meynadier and the Rue d'Antibes. The historic heart of Cannes is Le Suquet, a hill mounted by winding alleys with marvellous views from the old watchtower. In addition to its restaurants and shops, attractions include the Sarrazine tower, the 17th-century church of Our Lady of Good Hope, a 12th century chapel and the Castre museum.

The highway that leads north of Cannes to Grasse is called the Route Napoleon, for it traces the dirt track Napoleon took after landing near Cannes in 1815. The hilly countryside through which he trekked is now a prime flower-growing region and **Grasse**, founded in Roman times, is the centre of the French perfume industry. In addition to its numerous perfume factories, Grasse attractions include a splendid early Gothic cathedral (12th century), a town hall partially built in the Middle Ages, and a museum containing paintings by Jean-Honore Fragonard who was born in Grasse.

The fortified seaport of **Antibes** (pronounced *an-teeb*), with its school of horticulture, is another centre of this famous flower-growing region. The Grimaldi chateau, built in the 14th century, houses a museum containing numerous works of Picasso, who stayed here for a few months in 1946. Nearby Cap D'Antibes is a fashionable resort.

The walled town of **St. Paul de Vence**, set in the hills above the Bay of Angels, is protected by 16th-century ramparts, and can be explored on foot along its winding cobblestone lanes. Near the town entrance are a park and museum called Fondation Maeght. Built in 1964 by a Paris art dealer, the museum houses an array of modern sculpture and paintings, ceramics and stained-glass.

Shop windows and flower boxes line the winding cobblestone lanes of St. Paul de Vence.

Nice (pronounced *nees*), with a population of 350,000, is the major city of the French Riviera. Founded as a Greek colony (*Nicea* in Latin) in the 5th century BC, the city has endured numerous attacks over the centuries – from pillaging by Saracens in the 9th century to occupation by Mussolini during World War II. At the beginning of the French Revolution in 1789, Nice was a haven for Royalists. Annexed to France to 1793, Nice was restored to Sardinia in 1814, then again ceded to France in 1860 following a plebiscite. Nice became known as the Queen of the Riviera when the British aristocracy began arriving on winter sojourns.

A Tourist Office is annexed to the Nice train station, where detailed walking maps and other brochures are available. Nice is a treasure trove of art museums, including the **Musee Chagall** (1) on Boulevard de Cimiez, which houses a collection of 20th-century religious works by the great Russian painter Marc Chagall. **Musee Matisse** (2) (at the top of Nice's Boulevard Cimiez) houses the personal collection of Henri Matisse in a 17th-century Genoese villa surrounded by gardens and set amid Roman ruins. Nearby is the **Franciscan Monastery and Museum** (3), which illustrates monastic life from the 13th to the 18th century, including a reconstructed chapel and monk's cell.

The four gray marble towers of the **Musee D'Art Moderne** (4), on the north side of the Old Town, contains an outstanding collection of works by avant-

Above: The beautiful buildings of Old Nice. Below: Umbrella tables line the beaches of Nice.

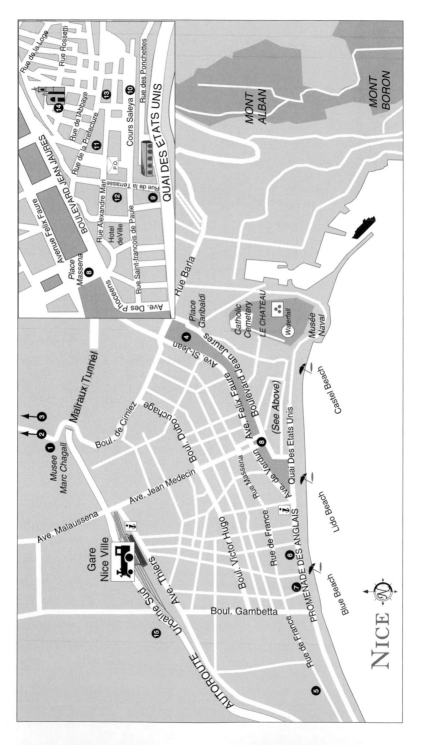

garde artists from the 1960s to present day. West of the Old Town, a few blocks off the Anglais Promenade, is the **Musee Des Beaux-Arts** (5), housed in a late 19th-century mansion built for a Russian princess. Its fine art collection includes paintings by Renoir, Degas and Monet, and ceramics by Picasso. The **Musee D'Art et D'Histoire** (6), with exhibits focusing on the Napoleonic era and the life of locally born general Andre Massena, is housed in the sumptuous Palais Massena, set on grounds overlooking the Anglais Promenade.

The Anglais Promenade follows the curving shoreline of the Baie des Anges (Bay of Angels), past Nice's fine pebble beach. Originally a wide path, this broad boulevard, decked with flower beds and palm trees, was constructed by an Englishman in 1820 and inaugurated in its final form in 1931 by the Duke of Connaught, one of Queen Victoria's sons. Queen Victoria herself also visited Nice, staying at the luxurious Hotel Victoria. The **Negresco** (7), another palatial hotel of that era – sometimes referred to as the Belle Epoque – was built in 1912 by an eccentric Romanian named Henry Negresco.

Avenue Jean Medecin, a busy shopping thoroughfare, leads from the train station to **Place Massena** (8), the city's main square, where gardens lie on either side. From here the waterfront promenade leads past the **Opera House** (9), built in 1885, to the main entrance of Nice's charming Old Town, which is a maze of narrow pedestrian streets, open-air markets, public squares and outdoor cafes. **Cours Saleya** (10) is the scene of Nice's famous flower market – a daily event except on Mondays when a flea market, complete with antique dealers, takes over this bustling strip. Two streets over, on Rue de la Prefecture, is the former **Royal Palace** (11), built in the early 17th century to accommodate the visiting Princes of Savoy. A fine 16th century house is located at No. 18, Rue de la Prefecture.

There are also numerous churches to admire in the Old Town, including the baroque interiors of the 18th-century **Eglise St-Francois-de-Paule** (12) and the 17th-century Eglise St-Giaume (13). **La Cathedrale Sainte-Reparate** (14), built in the 17th century to honour the town's patron saint, overlooks Place Rosetti – the centre of Old Nice, with restaurant terraces and ice-cream parlours.

Rue Rosetti leads from the square up to **Le Chateau** – a hilltop park with an artificial waterfall overlooking Old Nice. A few sections of the ancient castle walls remain, and the road winds past a Catholic cemetery on its way up the hillside. More panoramic views can be enjoyed west of the Old Town, atop **Mont Alban**, with its 16th-century bastions and watchtowers, and from **Mont Boron** where the hillside homes include Chateau de L'Anglais, a pink-coloured Scottish manor. Other unexpected sights in Nice include the onion-shaped cupolas of the **Russian Orthodox Church** (15), located a few blocks west of the train station.

Villefranche, perfectly situated in between Nice and Monaco, is one of the most picturesque ports in the Mediterranean. Ships anchor out-

Villefranche's waterfront promenade leads from the tender dock to the train station, where trains depart regularly for other nearby resorts on the French Riviera.

side its small harbour and tender passengers ashore. A tourist information office is located in the small terminal at the head of the harbour. Beside it is the 14th-century Chapelle St Pierre – restored and redecorated in 1957 by artist, writer and filmmaker Jean Cocteau, a leader of the French avant-garde movement in the 1920s and author of *Les Enfants Terribles*. The nearby Citadel was built by the Duke of Savoy in 1560 and now contains the town

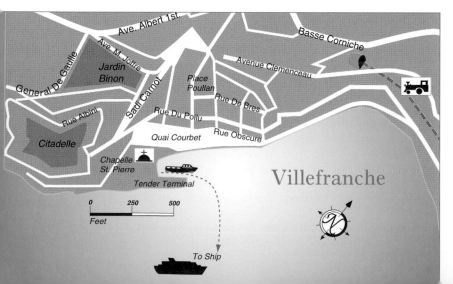

hall, museums and gardens. The train station is a 10-minute walk from the harbour along Quai Courbet and up some stairs.

Monaco, an independent principality and coastal enclave within France, is only 370 acres (150 hectares) in size. This tiny kingdom has been ruled by the Grimaldi dynasty since the 13th century, when a Genoese family first seized control of the fortified medieval town, known today as 'the Rock'. When the family's male line died out, the crown's French successor by marriage assumed the name Grimaldi. In 1861 the principality was returned by Sardinia to France and until 1911 the prince of Monaco was an absolute ruler. A 1918 treaty stipulated that the French government must approve the succession to the throne and, should it become vacant, the principality would become an autonomous state under French protection.

Above: Place du Palais and a palace sentry.
Below: A street scene in Monaco-Ville.

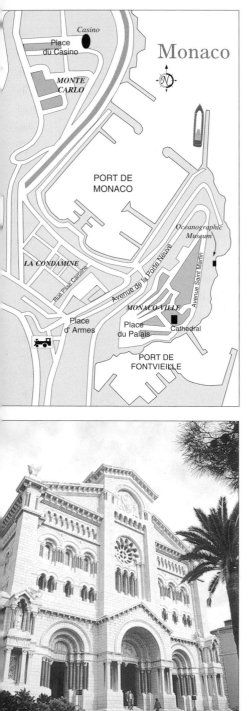

Monaco consists of several sections. The business district, called La Condamine, is where the train station is located. This area is a pleasing mix of open-air markets and residential streets that lead down to the harbour. La Condamine is flanked on its northeast side by Monte Carlo, site of the famous casino, and on its southeast side by Monaco Ville, the capital, which is set upon a rocky promontory. Avenue de la Porte Neuve leads off Place D'Armes up to Place du Palais, where Monaco's reigning prince resides in a grand Italianate palace. Upon his death in 2005, Rainier III was succeeded by his son Albert who, like his father, governs with the assistance of a minister of state (traditionally French), a cabinet and the National Council, which is elected every five years. A changing of the guard takes place at the palace entrance every day at five minutes before noon. One wing of the palace, which contains the Musee Napoleon and royal apartments, is open to visitors.

In 1956 Prince Rainier married the American film star Grace Kelly. She arrived for their fairytale wedding on board the cruise liner *Constitution* and the famous couple were married in Monaco's neo-Romanesque cathedral, built in 1874 to replace the 13th-century

Monaco's neo-Romanesque cathedral was the setting of a royal wedding in 1956, when Grace Kelly married Prince Rainier.

Monte Carlo's famous casino.

Church of St. Nicholas. The cathedral is also the burial place of Princess Grace (*Gratia Patricia* on her tombstone) who died in a tragic automobile accident in 1982.

Avenue St. Martin leads from the Cathedral to the Oceanographic Museum, founded by Prince Albert (Rainier's great-grandfather) in 1910. The underwater explorer and filmmaker Jacques Cousteau was the former head of this important research institute, which employs a staff of scientists. Visitors can view the aquarium, Prince Albert's collection of seashells and Cousteau's diving equipment. Outside the museum a small tourist train called the 'Azur Express' departs on regular circuits of Monaco-Ville and Place du Casino in Monte Carlo.

Monte Carlo's world-famous casino, which opened in 1858, came under the control of Greek shipping magnate Aristotle Onassis in 1954, when he became the principal stockholder of the company controlling the casino. Rainier, however, managed to thwart Onassis's efforts to gain control of Monaco's Societe de Bains de Mer (SBM), which oversees the principality's major hotels and enterprises, including the gambling casino.

By 1962 Monaco had become a tax haven for French citizens and, at the insistence of France, a new constitution was created. Only about 2,500 of Monaco's 30,000 residents are citizens (Monegasques) and they are not admitted to the gambling casino; neither are visitors wearing improper attire, such as shorts, sandals, tennis shoes, jogging suits, jeans or beach attire. The casino opens at noon and charges an entrance fee. All hand bags and cameras must be checked, and a passport is required if you win over 2,000 French francs (approximately US$400). The Casino complex, a dazzling display of gold-leaf and gilt, includes an opera house and private rooms reserved for high rollers.

The entrance to the Casino faces the gardens and fountain of Place du Casino, which is also overlooked by the palatial Hotel de Paris, where Alain Ducasse's Louis XV restaurant enjoys a three-star Michelin rating. On the opposite side of Place du Casino is the historic Cafe de Paris, a lovely spot to have lunch.

The burnished buildings and market-filled squares of Aix-en-Provence (above & opposite). Place Thiars in Marseille (below).

PROVENCE

Inspired by its luminous landscapes and sun-soaked colours, the Dutch painter Vincent Van Gogh called Provence a 'kingdom of light'. This is a land of white limestone cliffs and cobalt blue skies, of yellow sunflowers and ochre earth. The Rhone flows across Provence's western plain, its flat river delta lying in contrast to the rolling hills and mountain ridges which rise in the east and stretch northward from the Mediterranean coast to the French Alps. The countryside

is clothed in vineyards and dotted with medieval villages, their winding streets too narrow for cars, their weathered stone houses adorned with painted shutters and window boxes filled with flowers.

The Romans marched through this landscape and made it a province of Rome in the 2nd century BC. They built roads and bridges, amphitheatres and public baths. By the 4th century AD, the region had become a haven for Christian monasteries. The Middle Ages was a time of invasion – by the Visigoths, the Franks and the Arabs. Then, in 879, the Count of Arles gained control of the region and, from 933 until bequeathed to the French crown in 1481, Provence became part of the Kingdom of Arles. In the 14th century, a series of French-born popes moved the Catholic Church's headquarters from Rome to Avignon, on the banks of the Rhone, where a beautiful Gothic papal palace was built and fine wines were produced at the nearby village of Chateauneuf-du-Pape.

Flowers, fruits and vegetables all flourish in the fertile Rhone valley, and when Van Gogh arrived at Arles from Paris in 1888, he came in search of sensual beauty. Both he and Paul Gauguin had rejected industrial society and were drawn to the pastoral life of Provence. Yet, the two artists found little peace at Van Gogh's house in Arles. Their heated quarrels climaxed with Van Gogh threatening Gauguin with a razor, then cutting off his own ear in a state of deep remorse and temporary insanity.

Gauguin left Provence, but Van Gogh remained in Arles, painting his famous series of sunflowers as well as *The Night Cafe* and *The Public Gardens in Arles*. He was eventually confined in the Arles Hospital, and later in the asylum at Saint-Remy where in 1889 he painted *Starry Night*. Meanwhile, Paul Cezanne was living in near isolation outside Aix-en-Provence, his home town and the historic capital of Provence. Discouraged by ridicule from the critics, he too had fled Paris and the industrial north, returning to his place of birth. Working in seclusion, Cezanne developed his own style while painting vivid scenes of the bright outdoors. He repeatedly painted the craggy peak of Mont Ste-Victoire, showing the surrounding countryside devoid of human presence.

Both Van Gogh and Cezanne were intensely emotional painters, their art a tour de force of colour and movement. Although they often painted scenes of the countryside, the nearby Mediterranean Sea was also a pervasive presence. In Van Gogh's *Wheat Field and Cypress Trees*, the fields resemble a stormy sea and the hills rise like waves into a turbulent sky of swirling clouds.

The sea is what brought the Ancient Greeks to the shores of Provence in 600 BC. Arriving from Asia Minor, they established a colony called Massalia, which the French now call Marseille, and this famous seaport soon dominated the Mediterranean coast for miles in either direction. During the Punic Wars from 264 to 146 BC, Massalia sided with Rome against Carthage, its chief commercial rival.

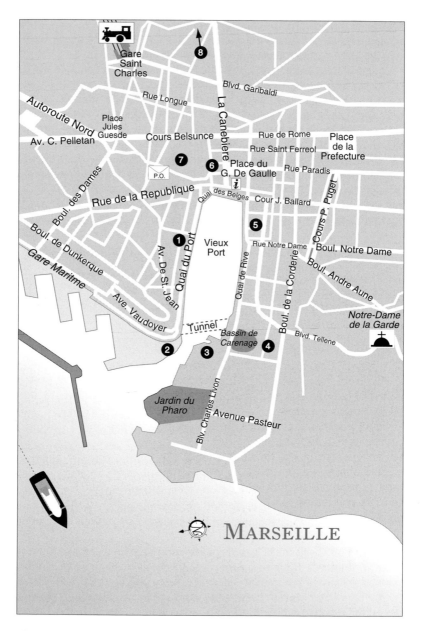

However, after supporting Pompey against Caesar during Rome's civil war of 49 BC, the city lost its territorial holdings. Still, it continued to thrive, especially during the Crusades.

Marseille was incorporated into the Kingdom of France in 1481 and grew steadily until the time of the French Revolution, which began in 1789. The Revolution's battle hymn originated in Marseille, where volunteer fighters marched to the army song *La Marseillaise.* Marseille's maritime commerce eventually suffered during the long Napoleonic wars and the city rejoiced at the downfall of Napoleon at the battle of Waterloo. Prosperity returned with the French conquest of Algeria and the opening of the Suez Canal in 1869.

Today Marseille is one of the world's great seaports, its commerce fed by the rich hinterlands of Provence. The oldest city in France, and the country's second largest with a population surpassing one million, Marseille is connected with Arles and the Rhone Valley by a canal. The southern section of the canal, called the Rove Tunnel, starts near the village of Le Rove and cuts through the Chaine de l'Estaque. At a length of 4.5 miles (7.2 km) and

Notre Dame de la Garde stands on a ridge above Marseille's Old Port.

width of 72 feet (22 m), this tunnel, which opened in 1927, is considered one of the greatest engineering feats since the Panama Canal.

Situated on the Gulf of Lions, Marseille forms a famous sight when approached from the sea, its gleaming white buildings nestled on a semi-circle of barren hills. The bay contains several islands, including a small rocky islet upon which the Chateau d'If was built in 1524 and used as a state prison, made famous by Alexandre Dumas's novel, *The Count of Monte Cristo.* Several forts protect the **Vieux Port** (Old Port), and the church of **Notre-Dame de la Garde** stands on a ridge overlooking the harbour, its steeple surmounted by a gilded statue of the Virgin Mary. Inside are the votive offerings of seamen for the protection Our Lady extends to mariners.

Van Gogh moved to Provence to be "near Africa", and today many of the city's most recent immigrants hail from North Africa. Busy and brash, Marseille is first and foremost a port city, its historical heart residing in the Vieux Port – a harbour filled with fishing boats and sailing yachts. The Tourism Office is located at the head of the harbour and the 17th-century **Hotel de Ville** (City Hall) (1) stands on its north side. Behind it, housed in 16th-century mansion, is the Musee du Vieux Marseille.

Fort Saint-Jean (2) and **Bas Fort Saint-Nicolas** (3) guard the harbour entrance, which can be traversed by an underwater tunnel that sur-

Marseille's city hall overlooks the harbour.

faces on the north side near the city's neo-Byzantine cathedral. On the harbour's south side is the 13th-century Romanesque church of **St. Victor** (4), with 14th-century fortifications. The church's door (circa 1140) is one of the oldest in France, and downstairs the crypts include 5th-century ruins and stela, as well as sculptures dating from the 4th to the 12th century. Also on the harbour's south side is the **Place Thiars** (5) pedestrian zone, an inviting neighbourhood of outdoor cafes.

The city's main avenue, running eastward from the harbour, is Rue Canebiere – named for the old ropewalks that used to operate along its length when ships' lines were made of hemp (called *cannebe* in the Provencal dialect). On Rue Canebiere's north side, housed in the Palais de la Bourse (6), is the city's **maritime museum**, which contains a fine library and a large collection of paintings, drawings and plans. Behind this large white building is the **Jardin des Vestiges** (7), a public park containing excavated ruins of Greek and Roman buildings and a small museum (Musee de L'Histoire de Marseille) featuring a 60-foot Roman boat.

Leading south from Rue Canebiere are Marseille's most fashionable shopping streets – Rue Paradis, Rue Saint Ferreol, Rue de Rome and Boulevard Garibaldi. Boulevard d'Athenes, leading off the north side of Rue Cannebiere, is a direct route to the train station (Gare Saint-Charles). About a half-mile east of the train station, at the top of

Palais de la Bourse now houses Marseille's maritime museum.

Longchamp Boulevard, is the **Palais de Longchamp** (8), built in 1860 by Henri Esperandieu, who also designed Notre-Dame de la Garde. This monumental palace, adorned with fountains and gardens, holds an art gallery and museum.

GETTING AROUND

The cruise ships dock north of the city centre, with most providing a shuttle service into Vieux Port, which is situated a half mile from the train station. Notre-Dame de la Garde can be reached by bus or on foot – it's a half-mile hike up Boulevard Tellene, followed by a steep flight of steps. Passenger ferries run regularly from the head of Vieux Port to Chateau d'If – a 90-minute trip. Taxis are available for hire at the cruise ship pier – standard fares include US$20 to the train station and US$60 for the drive up to the Notre-Dame de la Garde.

Ship-organized excursions are also available, providing city tours and day trips to other parts of Provence, such as **Les Baux**, a medieval town carved out of white limestone atop a huge plateau, its Citadelle providing panoramic views of the valley below. Another interesting stop is **Arles**, a once-flourishing Roman town with ancient remains that include a theatre and an arena built in the 2nd century AD. The arena provided seating for 26,000 spectators and is now used for staging bull-fights.

Trains run regularly from Marseille to these and other Provencal cities and towns, one of the best-preserved being **Aix-en-Provence**, a 40-minute train ride from Marseille. The capital of Provence since the 12th century (except when replaced by Arles), Aix was founded in 123 BC by the Romans near the site of some mineral springs. A popular spa town, its university was founded in 1409, after which Aix became a centre of literature and music, and a sojourn for painters. Students make up nearly a quarter of its population of 160,000, and the town's main attractions are easily explored on foot.

Place d'Albertas,
Aix-en-Provence

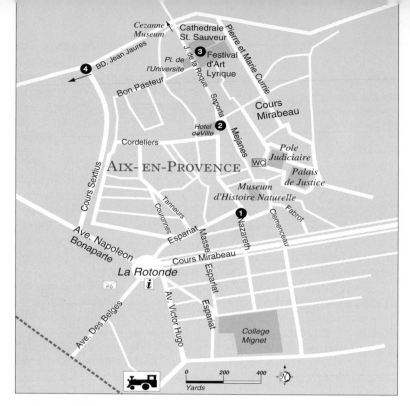

Avenue Victor Hugo leads from the train station to Place Gal De Gaulle, where the local tourist office is located. It overlooks La Rotonde, a huge traffic circle with a fountain in its centre. Leading eastward off La Rotonde is the Cours Mirabeau, the town's main avenue. On its south side are streets lined with 18th-century baroque mansions; on its north side are narrow medieval streets with shops, cafes and various attractions, such as: **Place d'Albertas** (1) where you can admire the sculpted facade of the Hotel d'Albertas (1707), and the nearby Hotel Boyer d'Eguilles (1675), which now houses the Museum d'Histoire Naturelle. City hall and a 16th-century belfry overlook the square at **Place de l'Hotel de Ville** (2) where a bustling flower and produce market is held several mornings each week. Other places of interest include the 13th-century **Cathedral of Saint-Sauveur** (3); and the formal French gardens and 17th-century mansion at **Vendome Pavilion** (4).

While strolling the scenic streets of Aix you will notice bronze studs on the pavement stamped with the letter 'C' – these symbolize the footsteps of Cezanne and mark historic places associated with the great artist (a brochure of this signposted tour is available at the Tourist Office). His studio, located off avenue Pasteur on avenue Paul-Cezanne, has been preserved as the **Musee-Atelier de Paul Cezanne**.

The dramatic coastline east of Marseille features white-stone cliffs, craggy coves and sweeping sea views. The old fishing port of **Cassis** is stunningly situated at the base of Europe's highest cliff – the 1,300-foot Cap Canaille – and is now a summer resort and sojourn for painters.

SETE

The scenic fishing port of Sete, canals crisscrossing its lower town, is situated in the Languedoc region of southern France. The region's name was derived from a medieval French dialect spoken throughout the south of France (*langue d'oc* meaning "language of yes"), back when the counts of Toulouse ruled this former Roman province stretching along the Mediterranean coast, from the foot of the Pyrenees to the Rhone River. The brilliant court at Toulouse was a symbol of tolerance and a centre of literature, attracting troubadours (poet musicians of aristocratic birth).

Sete is a port of access to the nearby medieval cities of Carcassonne and **Montpellier**, the latter's old quarter of winding streets and cafe-lined squares dating to the 8th century. Montpellier's famous university

The Cathedral of Saint-Sauveur in Aix-en-Provence was built in the 13th century.

was founded in the 13th century, its best-known graduate being Francois Rabelais, author of the *Gargantua* novels. Outside the city are country chateaux overlooking estate wineries.

Carcassonne is home to an impressive hill-top fortress, considered one of Europe's architectural marvels. The hill was first fortified by the Romans in the 1st century BC and the towers (still intact) were built in the 6th century by the Visigoths, with fortifications added by the viscounts of Carcassonne in the 12th century. The ramparts had fallen into disrepair when they were restored in the 1800s.

CORSICA

The mountainous island of Corsica, with its many rivers and fragrant flowers, has a pastoral charm which belies its volatile history, including banditry and blood feuds between clans which persisted into modern times. Island industries include the growing of wheat and fruit, the raising of sheep, and the production of wine and cheese. Much of the island is wild, the ground covered with an undergrowth of flowers called Maquis. The fragrance of these wildflowers wafts far out to sea, prompting sailors to call Corsica 'the scented isle'.

The Romans first set sail for Corsica in the 3rd century BC. Their rule ended in the 5th century AD, and throughout the ensuing centuries,

P&O's Oriana lies off Ajaccio, situated on a beautiful bay on the island of Corsica.

the island changed hands numerous times. By the mid-15th century the island was under Genoese control and the port city of Ajaccio was established in 1492. Public unrest, fuelled by the harsh and unpopular Genoese rulers, led to rebellion. In 1736, Corsican rebels convinced the German soldier and diplomat Baron von Theodor Neuhof to become their king. Two years later King Theodore was driven from Corsica by the Genoese with help from the French. His attempts to regain the throne were unsuccessful, and he spent his final years in England where he was once released from debtors prison through the influence of Horace Walpole, author and youngest son of Sir Robert Walpole.

In 1755 Pasquale Paoli led a successful revolt and became president under a republican constitution. By this time Genoa was weary of battling the Corsicans and in 1768 the island was sold to France. In 1769 the French defeated Paoli, who fled to England where his friend James Boswell introduced him into the circle of Samuel Johnson. That same year Napoleon Bonaparte was born of a middle class family in Ajaccio, the island's capital.

The outbreak of the French Revolution brought Paoli back to Corsica, where he was appointed governor in 1791. Accused of counter-revolutionary activities and summoned to Paris in 1793, Paoli drew on British support to expel the French from Corsica. He did not, however, fulfil his ambition to become viceroy of an independent state. Declaring itself a British protectorate, the Corsican national assembly chose a British governor, and bypassed Paoli for another Corsican – Pozzo di Borgo – when choosing a chief of the council of state. Paoli

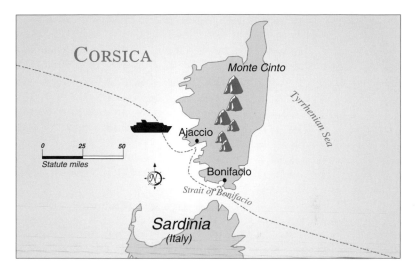

made his final departure for England in 1795 and the following year Corsica was recovered by the French under Napoleon.

World War II brought more invasions, this time by Italian and German troops, who were expelled in 1943. A post-war exodus prompted the French government to stimulate economic development, but the island's separatist sentiment carried on into the 1970s and '80s with occasional bombings and protests.

Attractions in **Ajaccio** include the Maison Bonaparte, where Napoleon was born and raised, the Salon Napoleonien (in the Hotel de Ville), which displays memorabilia of the emperor, and the Musee d'Histoire de la Corse, with exhibits on Corsica's military history. The 16th-century cathedral contains the marble font used for Napoleon's baptism.

Bonifacio, the oldest town of Corsica, is medieval in character. Founded in 828 on the site of a citadel built by Boniface I, Count of Tuscany, the town is situated atop a limestone cliff overlooking the harbour, and is surrounded by a rampart complete with drawbridge. The 12th-century Pisan-style church dates from Pisa's ownership of Corsica before losing the island to Genoa. The coast of Sardinia lies just seven miles (11-1/2 km) across the Strait of Bonifacio.

Grimaldi Coat of Arms

CHAPTER FOUR

NORTHERN ITALY

I taly lies in the heart of the Mediterranean. The north of the country is rooted in Europe while its southern shores stretch, like a bridge, toward the coast of Africa. Many an ancient mariner has landed on Italy's rugged shores, and the eventual rise of Rome turned the Mediterranean into a Roman lake which they called Mare Nostrum ('our sea'). When Rome fell, the northern cities of Genoa, Pisa and Venice emerged as great sea powers and rival city-states. Then came the Italian Renaissance, born in Florence in the early 1400s, and beauty became the byword of Italy. Glorious churches, grand palaces and landscaped gardens were built. Marble fountains and statues soon adorned the squares, and a sense of style became an Italian birthright.

The outpouring of artistry that began with the Renaissance spilled over into all areas of Italian life. Opera flourished in the 19th century, followed by film making and high fashion in the 20th century. Italy is also a leader in cruise ship design and its famous Fincantieri shipyard is one of the busiest in the world, launching ships that are technologically advanced and stylishly appointed.

The country's creative force, fuelled throughout the centuries by political turmoil and military conflicts, has been described by the art historian Bernard Berenson as 'the intensification of life'. Visitors come to Italy to see the ancient ruins and famous works of art, and soon find all of their senses awakened. While pausing to enjoy a glass of Chianti wine or a freshly-brewed cappuccino, they find themselves listening to animated conversations spoken in a language that rolls eloquently off the tongue, and they begin to notice the touches of beauty around them – whether it's a flower box beneath a baroque window or the pleasing arrangement of umbrella tables at an outdoor cafe. This sense of living each moment in a state of beauty, this is the Italian style.

Italy at a Glance

About 58 million people live in Italy and the faith of the majority is Roman Catholic, until recently the state religion. Italian, spoken in regional dialects, is the major language and English is widely understood. The country, proclaimed a republic in 1946, consists of twenty diverse regions which were unified in 1870. Vatican City and San Marino are independent enclaves. The industrial north has always been more prosperous than the agricultural south which, for centuries, languished under French and Spanish rule. Much of Italy is mountainous or hilly and the country's combination of striking scenery, mild climate, artistic treasures and a vibrant culture makes it one of the world's most popular tourist destinations.

Travel Tips

Currency: The unit of currency is the euro. American currency is widely accepted but local currency is needed for trains, buses, casual dining, museums and other tourist attractions. Most shops and formal restaurants will accept credit cards.

Dining: Italian food and wine is highly touted and can be enjoyed in a variety of settings. Bars, open all day, serve alcoholic drinks, rolls, coffee and small sandwiches. There is a service charge for sitting at a table, which is why patrons often stand at the bar. Other casual eateries are: *panineria* (sandwich bar); *tavola calda* (fast-food restaurant); *pizzeria* (specializing in pizza); *rosticceria* (take-out) and *gelateri* (ice-cream parlour). A *trattoria* is an informal restaurant while a *ristorante* offers formal, unhurried dining.

Opening Hours: Museums, galleries and historic sites are often closed on Monday, sometimes Tuesday, but this can vary from region to region, and from museum to museum. Daily hours are generally 9:00 a.m. to 6:00 p.m but can vary considerably.

Shopping: Stores are generally open from 9:00 a.m. to 1:00 p.m. and from 4:00 p.m. to 8:00 p.m. Many stay open late on Saturday evening and are closed Monday morning. Stores catering to tourists often stay open all day and on Sundays. Bartering is not acceptable, except at open-air markets.

Taxi Fares: Rates are approximately US$35 per hour, but you should negotiate the fare before setting off. Some taxi drivers will accept US currency.

Telephone Calls: Most public telephone take local coins and/or telephone cards which can be purchased at the post office or tobacconists.

Card Access Codes: AT&T 172-1011; MCI 172-1022; SPRINT 172-1877; CANADA DIRECT 172-1001.

ITALIAN RIVIERA

The Italian Riviera, extending from La Spezia to the French border, is an international playground of fashionable resorts, hotels and villas. **Genoa** (Genova) lies in the centre, dividing this curve of Ligurian coast into the Riviera di Levante (east) and the Riviera di Ponente (west). Italy's chief seaport, Genoa is one of the busiest in the western Mediterranean with its fine natural harbour and modern port facilities. A seaport since ancient times, Genoa became a free commune in the 10th century and its inhabitants built a powerful navy which drove the Arabs from Corsica and Sardinia, with the aid of Pisa. The two Italian maritime powers then battled one another over control of Sardinia, with Genoa eventually triumphing in the naval battle of Meloria (1284).

Genoa's wealth and power continued to expand until the city, called *La Superba* (The Proud), clashed with the trading interests of Venice. Subsequent wars with Venice, along with internal strife, led to a weakening of Genoa. Then, in the early 1500s, the famous admiral Andrea Doria drove the French occupiers from his city and set up a republican state, framing a constitution for the city and establishing the Doria family as rulers of Genoa. One of Italy's great naval heroes, Doria commanded the Genoese fleet against the Turks and helped capture Tunis in 1535. His family home is located in the lovely

Porta Soprana (above), one of Genoa's medieval gates, and the nearby childhood home of Christopher Columbus (below).

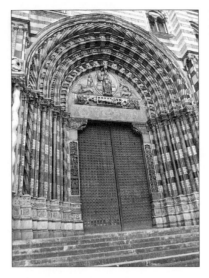

The striped marble facade of Genoa's Gothic cathedral.

Piazza San Matteo (1), in the heart of Genoa's medieval quarter and his tomb is in the church of San Matteo, which dates from the 12th century.

The other famous mariner associated with Genoa is Christopher Columbus. Born Cristoforo Colombo in 1451 to a family of wool weavers, he grew up illiterate and helped his father at the loom before heading to sea as a young lad. He served as a seaman in the Mediterranean but his ambitions would eventually take him far away from his childhood home, located at the base of **Porta Soprana** (2). This medieval gate, built as a defensive rampart in the 12th century, stands at the old entrance to the Roman road that led through Genoa.

Other historic highlights in Genoa's medieval section of steep, narrow alleys (called *caruggi*) are the 12th-century **Cathedral of San Lorenzo** (3), built of black and white marble, and the nearby **Palazzo Ducale (palace of the doges)** (4), built in the 16th century. The Teatro Carlo Felice and Academy of Fine Arts overlook **Piazza De Ferrari** (5).

Churches of note include **San Donato** (6), a 12th-century Romanesque building, and the 16th-century baroque church of the **Santissima Annunziata** (7). **Via Garibaldi** is lined with Renaissance palaces built by Genoese nobility, their frescoed rooms now housing several art galleries, including the collection in **Palazzo Rosso (Red Palace)** (8), which displays works by Titian, Veronese, Rubens and the Flemish painter Van Dyck, who once lived there.

The **Palazzo San Giorgio** (9), overlooking the harbour and now housing the Genoa Port Authority, was built in part with masonry taken

The modern Bigo elevator located on Genoa's waterfront near the aquarium.

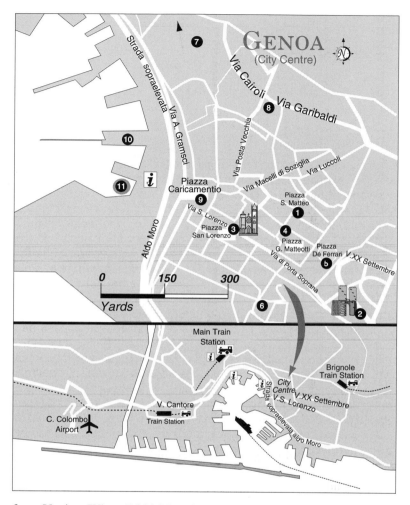

from Venice. When 7,000 Venetians were captured at the naval battle of Curzola in 1298, among them was Marco Polo, who dictated his book *Il Milion* while a prisoner in this palace. A large and modern **aquarium** (10), which opened in 1992, is located on the harbour, along with the **Bigo elevator** – a lift which takes visitors to the top of a mast-like structure (erected during the 1992 Columbus Quincentennial events) for panoramic views of this seafaring city.

Shopping: Via XX Settembre and Via Luccoli, with their range of boutiques, are two of Genoa's most exclusive shopping streets. Via Orefici is lined with goldsmiths, and the market in Piazza Banchi is a good place to buy handicrafts. Local specialties include ceramics, fine lace and delicate ornamental work in silver and gold.

Some of the Riviera's most scenic destinations – Camogli, San Fruttuoso and Portofino – are located near Genoa and can be reached

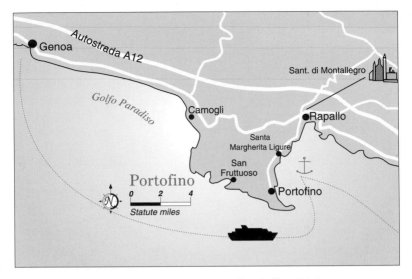

by mini-cruises from the city's harbour. The Italian Riviera was once a secluded coast of craggy coves and tree-clad hillsides where medieval monasteries and tiny fishing ports led a quiet existence. Today these hidden harbours, their colourful houses built by fishermen and lace makers, are among the most picturesque ports of the Riviera.

Best known is **Portofino**, where summer villas, tucked among the umbrella pine and cypress trees, overlook a harbour filled with luxury yachts at the height of the season. The small cruise ships pull right into port, but the larger ships anchor out in the bay and tender their passengers ashore. A haunt of the rich and famous, Portofino is notoriously expensive, but a very pleasant place to stroll and soak up the atmosphere. From the main square overlooking the harbour it's an easy hike up to the **Castello di San Giorgio (Fort of St. George)**, built in the mid-1500s, where you can enjoy excellent views. Just beyond the fort is the church of San Giorgio, said to contain relics of St. George brought back from the Holy Land. Another path leads from the village to the lighthouse at **Punta del Capo**.

A charming way to visit Portofino's neighbouring seaside villages is by boat. In addition to ship-organized boating excursions, a network of local ferry services connects these small ports. They include the resort of **Camogli**, founded by seafarers, and the medieval Benedictine monastery of **San Fruttuoso** which is situated on a secluded cove around the headland from Portofino. In the other direction from Portofino is the resort town of **Santa Margherita Ligure**, with its elegant shops and lively cafes, and nearby **Rapallo**, another charming resort with a beach promenade, boutiques and cafes.

Trains run regularly between Genoa, Camogli, Santa Margherita Ligure and Rapallo. The rail line bypasses Portofino, which is located two miles (3 km) from Santa Margherita (about a 25,000-lire taxi ride).

the ITALIAN RIVIERA

Santa Margherita Ligure (above). Interior of Genoa's Gothic cathedral (opposite). Pretty Portofino (far left).

Scenes from Portofino, a famous Riviera resort.

VENICE (VENEZIA)

Venice, one of world's most beautiful and unique cities, is a living watercolour. Built on 118 alluvial islets within a lagoon in the Gulf of Venice, it began as a small fishing settlement in the 5th century AD, when refugees of the Roman Empire, fleeing the Lombard invaders of Northern Italy, sought safety on these uninhabited islands. The first settlers built huts on the mud banks and dug deep ditches for mooring their boats – the origin of Venice's modern canal system which now includes more than 100 narrow canals crossed by some 400 footbridges. In 697 these fishing communities organized themselves under a doge (derived from the Latin word *dux* = leader) and began to engage in seaborne trade.

The port grew rapidly and by the 9th century it had become the city of Venice, its prosperity making it a target of Dalmatian pirates. This prompted the Venetians to build castellated houses for protection and guard the canal entrances with chains. However, as the pirate attacks increased in frequency, the Venetians responded by arming their ships. The newly born Venetian Navy defeated the Dalmatian pirates in the year 1000, and this important victory was thereafter commemorated with great pomp on Ascension Day, with the doge's gilded galley participating in the 'wedding of the sea' ceremony, which symbolized the marriage of the doges with the Adriatic.

The Crusades brought great wealth to Venice, her fleet transporting Christian armies to the Holy Land, and in 1204 the doge Dandolo led the Fourth Crusade's storming of Constantinople, looting it of treasures. By 1216 the Venetian empire included strategic islands in the Ionian, Aegean and eastern Mediterranean, and the city's native son and world traveller Marco Polo embodied the enterprising spirit of the Venetians. As wealth poured into Venice, its patrician merchants formed an oligarchy that maintained a tight hold on its political power through a secret police and Council of Ten, instituted to punish those who committed crimes against the state.

Venice became the envy of Genoa, a rival republic, and the two maritime powers battled for supremacy with Venice eventually emerging victorious in the late 1300s to become the Christian world's leading maritime state. It controlled all of Venetia on the mainland and, with a mighty shipbuilding arsenal, was known as the 'Queen of the Seas'. Venice's slow decline began in the mid 15th-century when its lucrative eastern trade was threatened, first by the fall of Constantinople to the Turks in 1453, then by the discovery of an all-sea trade route to India and China around the Cape of Good Hope. Much of Venice's seagoing trade fell into the hands of the Portuguese, Dutch and English, but the city remained a force to be reckoned with, and it reached its artistic glory during the Renaissance with large-scale construction of churches and palaces. Venice became a city of colour and light, its buildings designed by famous architects and embellished by artists such as Titian and Tintoretto of the Venetian school of painting.

Venice also shone musically. The Italian composer Monteverdi, the first great figure of opera, was appointed choirmaster of St. Mark's in 1613 and, although he wrote mostly church music, he produced his final operas following the opening of Venice's first public opera house in 1637. Antonio Vivaldi, whose father was a violinist at St. Mark's, also lived in Venice in the early 1700s – teaching, playing the violin and writing music.

The 18th century was a period of economic and political decline for Venice, the city's decadence personified in the Venetian adventurer Casanova who supported himself by writing, gambling and seducing women. Venice's upper class indulged in a social life of nightly theatre-going and gambling at the casino, their sexual dalliances often taking place in private boxes at the opera or inside parked gondolas.

In 1797, Venice fell without a fight to Napoleon's forces and was transferred by treaty to Austrian rule under which the city chafed for several decades. Meanwhile, opera continued to thrive, with Rossini premiering the first of a string of comic operas in Venice in 1810. Italy's foremost composer of opera, Giuseppe Verdi, also premiered a number of his works in Venice amid an atmosphere of tolerance and freedom of expression, and the great German operatic composer Richard Wagner spent his final days in Venice, where he died in 1883. By then Venice had expelled the Austrians and was united with the new kingdom of Italy.

Some Venetians still long for a return to their city's golden era of independence. Calling themselves 'soldiers of the Most Serene Republic of Venice', this fringe political group staged an extraordinary, predawn separatist stunt in May 1997, when eight men stormed the bell tower in St. Mark's Square. A few people were still sipping wine and chatting at one of the square's cafes when a canal ferry docked at the piazzetta and disembarked a ramshackle truck carrying armed men wearing ski masks. They headed straight for the doors of the bell tower, reappearing minutes later on its balcony near the top, where they unfurled the golden pennant with the lion of Saint Mark. The incident ended without a shot being fired when police arrived to recapture the landmark tower.

VENICE

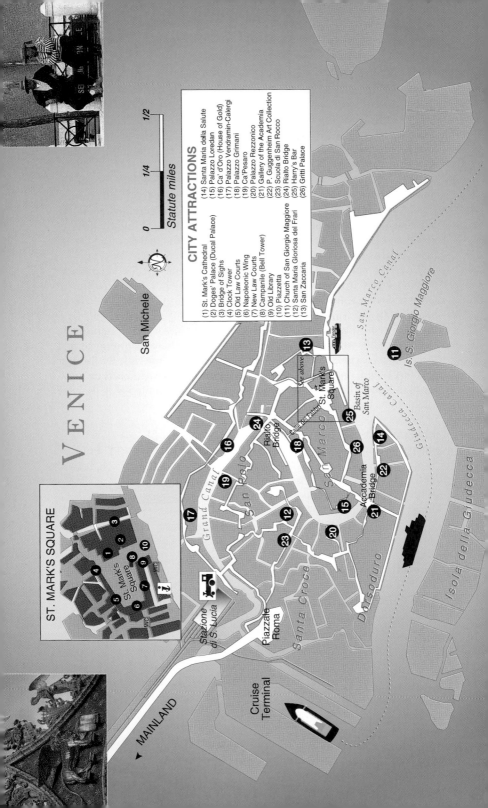

ST. MARK'S SQUARE

St. Mark's Square

- 1
- 2
- 3
- 4
- 5
- 6
- 7
- 8
- 9
- 10

WC
WC
i

CITY ATTRACTIONS

(1) St. Mark's Cathedral
(2) Doges' Palace (Ducal Palace)
(3) Bridge of Sighs
(4) Clock Tower
(5) Old Law Courts
(6) Napoleonic Wing
(7) New Law Courts
(8) Campanile (Bell Tower)
(9) Old Library
(10) Piazzetta
(11) Church of San Giorgio Maggiore
(12) Santa Maria Gloriosa dei Frari
(13) San Zaccaria

(14) Santa Maria della Salute
(15) Palazzo Loredan
(16) Ca' d'Oro (House of Gold)
(17) Palazzo Vendramin-Calergi
(18) Palazzo Grimani
(19) Ca'Pesaro
(20) Palazzo Rezzonico
(21) Gallery of the Academia
(22) P. Guggenheim Art Collection
(23) Scuola di San Rocco
(24) Rialto Bridge
(25) Harry's Bar
(26) Gritti Palace

Statute miles

0   1/4   1/2

N

San Michele

MAINLAND

Stazione
di S. Lucia

Piazzale
Roma

Cruise
Terminal

Santa Croce

Grand Canal

San Polo

Dorsoduro

San Marco Canal

Isola della Giudecca

Giudecca Canal

San Marco Canal

Basin of
San Marco

Isc. S. Giorgio Maggiore

Calle dei Fabbri

See above

Rialto
Bridge

Academia
Bridge

St. Mark's
Square

- 17
- 19
- 16
- 24
- 13
- 12
- 23
- 20
- 18
- 15
- 25
- 26
- 14
- 21
- 22
- 11

Secessionist politics are likely the least of Venetians' concerns. Venice, as everyone knows, is slowly sinking. The city is built on sand, silt and hard clay (which tend to compact over time) and some mainland industries have exacerbated the problem by lowering the area's underground water table, as well as polluting the lagoon. Meanwhile, a shortage of affordable housing has prompted residents to move out of Venice. Thousands of workers commute each day to the city, which is connected to the mainland (2-1/2 miles away) by a rail-and-highway bridge. Many worry that Venice no longer belongs to Venetians, but to tourists and absentee owners who spend little time in their vacation palazzos. Yet, despite the summer tourists and winter floods, this golden city of the seas will no doubt endure, as it has for more than a thousand years.

Narrow, winding canals crisscross the enchanting city of Venice

GETTING AROUND

Venice, compact and free of motor vehicle traffic, is an intimate city and a delight to explore on foot. Narrow lanes (*calles*) lead to hidden squares (*campos*) and across the arched footbridges that span the side canals (*rios*). It's easy to become momentarily lost amid the maze of back streets and winding waterways that lead off the Grand Canal, but the bell tower of St. Mark's Square is usually visible above the surrounding roofs.

By water is an ideal way to see Venice, and there's nothing more romantic than a gondola ride – especially at night when the city's timeless magic is enhanced by the watery reflection of dancing lights

and voices echoing down quiet side canals. Hiring a gondola is fairly expensive; less expensive is a *traghetto*, a two-man gondola that ferries people across the Grand Canal at various, sign-posted places. The most popular and reasonably priced mode of transport is to hop on and off the motorized river boats (called *vaporetti*) that are part of the city's water bus service. They run up and down the Grand Canal, making frequent stops along the way, and it's a short walk from the cruise terminal to Piazzale Roma where a ticket can be purchased at the ACTV booth for a ride along the complete length of the Grand Canal to St. Mark's Square. The cruise ships usually provide their passengers with a shuttle service that runs regularly between the ship and a drop-off point east of St. Mark's Square. Private water taxis can also be hired.

The city's water bus service also provides transport to other islands in the lagoon, such as **San Michele** (the city's cemetery), **Murano** (famous for glass making since the 13th century) and **Burano** (a colourful fishing village and lace-making centre).

Venice's main **shopping** area lies between the Rialto Bridge and Piazza San Marco, where shops and cafes border the square. Fine shops featuring handcrafted carnival masks can be found on Calle dei Fabbri. Other local crafts include glassware and lace.

VENICE ATTRACTIONS:

St. Mark's Square (Piazza of San Marco) is the central meeting place of Venice and one of Italy's most beautiful squares, dominated by the splendour of **St. Mark's Cathedral** (1). Begun in 1063 and modelled after the Church of the Holy Apostles in Constantinople, this 'Golden Basilica' is an outstanding example of Byzantine architecture. It follows the Greek cross plan, with each arm of the cross emphasized by a dome encased with gilt copper sheet and topped with an ornate lantern, making it visible from a distance and serving as a landmark for seafarers. The church's ornate facade consists of clusters of marble pillars and arches containing golden mosaics which glitter in the late afternoon sun. Gold is the dominant decorative element inside the cathedral, its walls completely covered with mosaics from the 12th to 18th centuries. Entrance to the church is free but there is a fee to enter the Sanctuary, which contains the tomb of St. Mark and the gem-encrusted Golden Altarpiece, and the Museum, which houses four gilded bronze horses. These Greek sculptures from the 4th and 3rd centuries BC were brought to Venice from Constantinople in 1204 and were originally displayed on the church's outside gallery, where replicas now stand.

The **Doges' Palace (Ducal Palace)** (2), begun in 814, was destroyed four times by fire and each time rebuilt on a grander scale to become a magnificent example of Italian Gothic architecture. The Palace, as residence of the doge and seat of justice, exudes wealth and power in its majestic halls, famous Golden Staircase and elegant rooms with their frescoed walls and ceilings. The **Bridge of Sighs** (c. 1600) (3) leads from the Doges palace to the former prisons, a hellish place where pris-

The Doges' Palace reflects the wealth and power of Venice when it was a medieval sea power.

oners were held either in humid, above-ground cells that were subject to flooding, or in underground cells lined with strips of lead to make them unbearable in the summer heat. Casanova made his famous escape from the latter in 1756.

Other buildings in St. Mark's Square are the **Clock Tower** (4) (built near the end of the 15th century), the **Old Law Courts** (5) (Procuratie Vecchie) which were begun in the 15th century, and the **Napoleonic Wing** (or New Building) (6), built in 1807, which houses the Correr Museum, its collection of paintings, sculptures and precious objects tracing the history and art of Venice. The **New Law Courts** (Procuratie Nuove) (7) were completed at the beginning of the 18th century. Beneath the portico is the famous Caffe Florian, which was frequented by Casanova, Wagner and Proust.

The **Campanile (Bell Tower)** (8) was built in the 10th century and stands 325 feet (99 metres) high. The Loggetta, at its base, was designed by Renaissance architect Jacopo Sansovino in the early 16th century and is decorated with bronze statues and marble ornaments. The tower collapsed in 1902 and was rebuilt a few years later as an exact replica of the original. Inside, visitors can reach the balcony near the top by climbing the spiral staircase, or by taking the lift.

The **Old Library (Libreria Vecchia)** (9), its construction started in 1537, was designed by Sansovino as a structural counterpoint to the Doges' Palace – the

Prisoners were led across the Bridge of Sighs to their cells.

St. Mark's Square

The golden facade of St. Mark's Cathedral (above). The view of St. Mark's Square as your ship pulls into port (opposite).

The Campanile soars above the other buildings of St. Mark's Square (above & opposite). The Italian Gothic facade of the Doges' Palace (below).

Colourful carnival masks (opposite).
A young Venetian promotes an upcoming classical concert (below).

(Below) The view from the Piazzetta of St. Mark's Basin and the distant church of San Giorgio Maggiore.

P I G E O N S

Pigeons have become a problem for the city of Venice. With an estimated population of 100,000, they now outnumber Venetians and anyone (including tourists) caught feeding the pigeons in St. Mark's Square could face a fine of US$850. This might seem severe, but the pigeons – many of them diseased – have been put on a strict diet of feed laced with anti-fertility drugs in an attempt to reduce their numbers, as well as the 74 tons of droppings they currently produce per year.

former an educational institute, the latter the political centre of power. The Library became the prototype of Venetian classicism, with its double arcade and lavish use of decorative sculptures. It faces the **Piazzetta** (10), which leads from the square to the busy waterfront of St. Mark's Basin. The two columns standing here are from the 12th century – one holding a statue of the Lion of St. Mark, the other a statue of St. Theodore. When standing in the Piazzetta and looking across the water of St. Mark's Basin, you can see an island containing the church of **San Giorgio Maggiore** (11), begun in 1566 and designed by Andrea Palladio, who introduced elements from ancient temples to Venetian church architecture.

Venice contains many splendid churches, including **Santa Maria Gloriosa del Frari** (12) with paintings by Titian, **San Zaccaria** (13) with the *Enthroned Madonna* by Bellini, and the 17th-century **Church of Santa Maria della Salute** (14) which stands on a point of land at the entrance to the Grand Canal.

THE GRAND CANAL

The main thoroughfare of Venice, the Grand Canal is lined with residential palaces (called palazzos), their ornate and rippling patterns reflected on the water. The earliest palaces date to the 12th century and their basic features were carried through the centuries. A ground floor portico (for loading and unloading merchandise) led to a large hall where business was conducted; the family's living quarters were upstairs where a large drawing room overlooked the canal. Each palace was marked by a post, painted with the owner's heraldic colours. Their styles range from early Veneto-Byzantine to Baroque, and Eastern influences are evident in such Oriental touches as delicate lattice work. Because there was little internal strife in Venice, which was ruled by a merchant aristocracy and defended by a navy, the homes of wealthy Venetian families were built not like fortified castles but as lavish palazzos with fairy-tale facades designed for reflection in the waters of the Grand Canal.

One of the earliest palaces is **Palazzo Loredan** (15), now the seat of the City Council, dating from the 13th century and built in the Veneto-Byzantine style. By the early 1500s the Grand Canal was astounding foreigners with its opulent palazzos, such as the late Gothic **Ca' d'Oro (House of Gold)** (16). Now housing the Galleria Franchetti, this splendid structure was built by a leading Venetian family in 1420, its lavish stone-carved ornamentation once coloured with red and blue pigments and glistening gilt.

With the arrival of the Renaissance came modifications to some of the designs such as that of the **Palazzo Vendramin-Calergi** (17), completed in 1509, which introduced classical elements to the traditional Venetian facade. This famous palazzo, now a casino, is where the composer Richard Wagner died in 1883 and it became a motif in Thomas Mann's *Death in Venice*.

Departing the port of Venice, a cruise ship glides past the mouth of the Grand Canal and the Church of Santa Maria della Salute.

Ever more and imposing palaces were built along the Grand Canal, including the 16th-century **Palazzo Grimani** (18), home of today's Appeal Court, and the baroque **Ca'Pesaro** (19), built in 1710 and now housing an art gallery. The **Palazzo Rezzonico** (20) contains beautifully decorated and furnished rooms which are open to visitors as the Museum of the Venetian 18th Century. Plans are underway to open more of the building to the public, including a mezzanine where the poet Robert Browning lived.

Art galleries of note along the Grand Canal include the **Gallery of the Accademia** (21), its 24 rooms containing five centuries of Venetian paintings, with a large number of works by Giovanni Bellini. The **Peggy Guggenheim Art Collection**, housed in the Palazzo Venier Dei Leoni (22), is one of most important collections of contemporary art in the world. The **Scuola di San Rocco** (Great School of San Rocco) (23), on Campo San Rocco, houses a series of painting by Tintoretto.

MOTORBOATS NOT SO SWELL

When the Venice police issue speeding tickets, these go not to heavy-footed motorists but to mariners exceeding the speed limit on the Grand Canal. Supporting a move to tighten local speed limits are the city's gondoliers, skilled oarsmen who find it increasingly difficult to safely manoeuvre their gondolas amid the wash caused by passing motorboats. The graceful gondola has been used by Venetians for nearly a thousand years, but Venice's famed gondoliers are threatening to bring this seafaring tradition to an end by motorizing their fabled craft if the motorboats on the Grand Canal don't slow down and reduce the wash that not only jeopardizes the safe rowing of a gondola but also sends swells slapping against the palazzi lining the canal, which could, over time, contribute to their deterioration.

GRAND CANAL

The Grand Canal is crossed in the centre of the city by the **Rialto Bridge** (Ponte di Rialto) (24), a single marble arch built between 1588 and 1591, to connect Rialto and San Marco islands. The bridge's arcades are lined with shops and nearby open-air cafes are a good place to watch the constant flow of activity in the Grand Canal.

Famous restaurants in Venice include **Harry's Bar** (25), once patronized by Ernest Hemingway, Somerset Maugham and Orson Wells; and the dining terrace of the **Gritti Palace** (26), where former guests have included Queen Elizabeth, Winston Churchill and Greta Garbo.

A gondola wedding party (above). Regata Storica, held each September on the Grand Canal (opposite).

Rialto Bridge (opposite). Palazzos on the Grand Canal (below & bottom). Gondolas are widely available for hire (far right).

ITALY'S INTERIOR

A land tour of northern Italy is an enticing proposition for passengers beginning or ending their cruise at Venice or Genoa. To the north are the majestic Italian Alps, beautiful lakes and Italy's second-largest city, **Milan**. This prosperous city's historic landmarks include the Church of Santa Maria dell Grazie (1465-90), which contains Leonardo da Vinci's famous fresco, *The Last Supper*, and the famous opera house, Teatro alla Scala, which opened in 1778.

The city of **Verona**, a centre of trade since Roman times, reached its apex of power in the late 13th century when ruled by Ghibelline lords of the Della Scala familiy. The ongoing strife between the Ghibellines and the Guelphs eventually weakened Verona, a bloody rivalry that was embodied in Shakespeare's play *Romeo and Juliet*, with Romeo's family belonging to the Guelphs and Juliet's being members of the Ghibellines.

Padua, connected by canal with the Po and other rivers, is home to Italy's second-oldest university (after Bologna's) which was founded in 1222. Galileo taught here, and Dante and Petrarch were students. Other famous landmarks in Padua include the six-domed basilica of St. Anthony, its high altar adorned with bronzes by Donatello.

Bologna has been known as a centre of learning ever since the founding in 425 AD of its Roman law school. The city's famous university was established in about 1088 and, over the years, its faculties were expanded to include medical and theological faculties, and courses in the liberal arts. Bologna's Renaissance architecture includes palazzos, churches and an art gallery featuring works by Bolognese artists.

The canal port of **Ravenna** rose to prominence under the Romans who stationed their North Adriatic fleet at the nearby seaport of Classis. The city's political prominence endured throughout the centuries, and Ravenna also became the Western centre of mosaic art in the 5th and 6th centuries, its masterworks including the decoration of San Vitale, a Byzantine church consecrated in 547.

Nestled in the Appenines near the Adriatic Sea is **San Marino**, the world's smallest republic. A Christian stone-cutter from Dalmatia was said to have taken refuge on Mount Titano in the 4th century, and a community soon formed around the mountain's three peaks. Only 24 square miles in size with a population of approximately 25,000 Italian-speaking inhabitants, San Marino has renewed and expanded several times an initial treaty of friendship and economic cooperation signed with Italy in 1862. The Italian patriot and soldier Garibaldi was granted refuge in San Marino in 1849, and in 1861 Abraham Lincoln accepted an honorary citizenship of the republic.

In **Umbria**, the town of **Orvieto** is famous for its beautiful cathedral, begun in 1290, its black-and-white marble facade decorated with colourful mosaics. **Todi** is another Umbrian town of note, containing Etruscan remains, Roman ruins and Gothic palaces.

TUSCANY

Tuscany is one of Italy's most scenic regions, its gently rolling and verdant hills dotted with stone farmhouses. Vineyards of the Chianti wine region lie between Florence and Siena, and the northwest part of Tuscany is where the famous Carrara marble is quarried. The greatest artists and architects of the Renaissance spent time in Tuscany, which became a centre of art and learning in the late Middle Ages when Dante, born in Florence in 1265, established Tuscan as the literary language of Italy with publication of his masterpiece, the *Divine Comedy*.

Tuscany, called Etruria in ancient times, was home to the Etruscan civilization before it was conquered by the Romans in the mid-4th century BC. The northern Lombards controlled the region next, followed by the Franks who, in the early 12th century, bequeathed Tuscany to the papacy, which set up a longstanding strife between the pro-papal Guelphs and pro-imperial Ghibellines. Amid the political turmoil and bloody battles, the towns of Tuscany prospered as commerce, industry and the arts flourished. Pisa initially emerged as the most powerful city of the region, but Florence eventually gained control and Tuscany became a grand duchy of Florence's ruling Medici family.

The small city of **Siena**, despite frequent wars with Florence, retained its independence and today draws visitors to its rich array of art and architecture. Gracing the fan-shaped main square are the Gothic Palazzo Pubblico and slender Mangia tower, and adorning the city's Italian Gothic cathedral is a striped marble facade by Giovanni Pisano, the adjoining library containing famous frescoes by Pinturicchio.

Throughout the Renaissance, Tuscany was a centre of learning and art. Florence overflowed with famous artists such as Michelangelo and Leonardo da Vinci, both of whom were born in the hill towns surrounding Florence. Other famous Tuscans included Petrarch, Galileo, Machiavelli, Puccini and Carlo Collodi, the 19th-century author of the children's classic Pinocchio.

Livorno, the Tuscan port for Florence, is one of Italy's most important sea ports and home to the Italian naval academy. The port evolved from a fortified castle in the Middle Ages into a flourishing city when developed by Florence's powerful Medici family in the 16th century. Livorno was considered the ideal Renaissance town, until it was bombed during World War II. Parts of its 17th-century city wall still remain and the 16th-century cathedral was restored after the war.

GETTING AROUND

Pisa is about 14 miles (22 km) north of Livorno (40 minutes by car), and Florence is about 62 miles (100 km) distant – an hour-and-a-half drive through the rolling hills of Tuscany. Ship-organized excursions are available to both cities (a half-day tour to Pisa and full-day tours to Florence). Trains run regularly to both cities (Pisa is a stop along the Livorno-Florence route). The Livorno train station is about three miles (5 km) from the cruise ship pier, but some cruise lines offer a shuttle

A stone farmhouse set amid the rolling hills of Tuscany.

service into town with a drop-off about one mile from the train station. The train ride to Florence varies from one to two hours; the train trip to Pisa takes about 15 minutes.

Approximate taxi fares (in US$): Full-day to Florence – $280-$300; half-day to Pisa – $100; cruise ship pier to Livorno train station – $10.

PISA

Pisa was at the height of its power when the tower for which it's now famous first began to lean. This well-known bell tower was meant to complete the city's splendid ensemble of ecclesiastical architecture that was begun in the mid-11th century. Pisa was then a city on the ascent, its growing empire based on both naval and economic power. Over the span of two centuries, Pisa's magnificent cathedral, baptistery and campanile ('Leaning Tower') were built at an open-air site north of the city. Called the 'Field of Miracles', the site proved to be a field of unstable subsoil, for Pisa is situated on the banks of the Arno River, where the ground consists of layers of sandy mud and clay. A former sea port, Pisa now lies six miles inland, its decline as a trading port caused by the silting of the river. Before its decline, Pisa was a powerful maritime republic, rivalling Genoa and Venice. Its navy defeated the Arab forces at Palermo in 1062 and the Pisans built their Romanesque cathedral from Saracen plunder, the facade's elaborate lace-like ornamentation reflecting Islamic influences.

The Baptistery was modelled on the Holy Sepulchre in Jerusalem, and the entire complex of monuments was an attempt by the Pisans to create their own Holy City. All three buildings are clad in white marble, inlaid with horizontal stripes and ornate patterns in dark-green marble. They contain some of Pisa's greatest art treasures – including bronze panels by Bonnanno Pisano and marble pulpits by Nicola Pisano and his son Giovanni. Soon after construction began on the campanile in 1174, it began to lean. By the time it was closed to the public in 1990, the tower was 16 feet (4.9 metres) out of perpendicular alignment. So close was the 13,050-ton tower to toppling, an earthquake or storm could have demolished it. Upon being closed, the tower

Pisa's magnificent medieval cathedral has been eclipsed by its leaning campanile, dubbed the Leaning Tower of Pisa.

was temporarily supported with a steel belt and cables while engineers studied the structure, then began stabilizing it by placing 800 tons of lead weights at the tower's base on the side opposite the tilt. This was followed by the removal of tons of subsoil from beneath the tower in an area away from the incline, prompting the tower to bear down and slightly straighten itself. After 11 years of stabilization work, the bell tower was reopened to the public in late 2001, its lean now back to where it was in 1838. Visitors can once again climb to the top of the structure, but only 30 people are allowed inside at a time.

FLORENCE

The Italians call her *Firenze*, the flowering city, named this by the Romans when this early Etruscan settlement became a town along the Cassian Way. It was a prophetic choice of name because, centuries later, Florence did indeed flower as the birthplace of the Italian Renaissance, which began here in the early 1400s. Lying at the foot of the Apennines, in the broad valley of the Arno River, Florence is a small city. Her beauty is subtle, her colours muted, and just as that famous Florentine, the Mona Lisa, leaves you wondering what's behind her mysterious smile, so too does Florence, with her narrow medieval streets and fortress-like buildings, their austere exteriors offering few clues to the artistic treasures awaiting inside.

The Arno River winds through the centre of Florence.

After Rome fell, Florence was controlled by various invaders until gaining autonomy in the 12th century. Then, in the 13th century, the pro-papal Guelphs and the pro-imperial Ghibellines fought for control of the city. By the end of the century, the Guelphs had captured the city but they then split into warring factions called the Blacks and the Whites. The poet Dante, a White Guelph and member of the losing side, was banished in 1302. Florence also warred against other cities, such as Pisa, and gradually grew as it absorbed neighbouring towns and villages. Bankers and merchants made both themselves and the city wealthy by selling Florentine silks, tapestries and jewellery.

The Black Death of 1348 struck a terrible blow to the city, killing more than half the population. But Florence's most glorious days still lay ahead, her golden age ushered in by the rise to power in 1434 of a man named Cosimo de' Medici. A wealthy and powerfully connected merchant banker, Medici and his descendants would determine the destiny of Florence for the next 300 years. Despised by their enemies and denounced as tyrannical, the Medicis were initially a tolerant and positive force in Florence. Through their passionate patronage of the arts, literature and learning, the early Medicis financed Florence's growing concentration of architectural monuments and artistic masterpieces, the likes of which had not been seen since the Athens of Pericles.

Cosimo de' Medici, a generous supporter of such artists as Brunelleschi and Donatello, and the founder of the Medici Library, was an astute businessman who managed to double his personal fortune while investing in the city and spending lavishly on the arts. His grandson, Lorenzo de' Medici (il Magnifico) became a towering figure of the Italian Renaissance, and was a patron of Michelangelo, Botticelli and others. An astute politician, he held no official title but tactfully wielded power and conducted the affairs of the Florentine state. He was also a scholar and a poet who spent huge sums of his own money to advance the arts and literature of Florence. In 1478 he survived a bloody conspiracy by the rival Pazzi family, in which his brother was stabbed to death during Mass at the cathedral. A wounded Lorenzo managed to escape.

The Florentine republicans also tried to drive the Medicis from power. Each attempt was, ultimately, a failure because the early Medicis enjoyed popular support among the Florentines. There were, however, serious challengers. In 1494, Lorenzo's son and successor, Pietro, was expelled from Florence, and Girolamo Savonarola, a zealous religious reformer and enemy of the Medicis, became the spiritual leader of the city, his impassioned sermons inspiring Florentines to toss their offensive secular artwork into a huge bonfire that was lit in the Piazza della Signoria. However, his incessant preaching and rigid moral demands eventually got on people's nerves, and his attacks on the corrupt Borgia pope resulted in his being excommunicated in 1497. Savonarola was hanged a year later for heresy and the Medicis were eventually restored to power.

The Medici dynasty became affiliated with the royal houses of Europe through marriage, and produced two queens of France and three popes. However, in the process, the Medicis gained a reputation as arbitrary and ruthless rulers. Alessandro, who governed from 1532 to 1537, was so generally hated that his cousin Ippolito was sent by the people of Florence to complain to the Holy Roman Emperor. Alas, Ippolito died en route and many believed he was poisoned by order of Alessandro. Another member of the Medici family finally murdered the despised Alessandro but his successor, Cosmo I, was no better

The Bargello, built in 1255, later became a Renaissance prison.

liked, although he did expand Florence's territory to include most of Tuscany and he became the first grand duke of Tuscany.

The Medicis were no doubt influenced by Niccolo Machiavelli, author of *Il Principe* (The Prince), a famous work describing the amoral, calculating and tyrannical means by which an 'ideal' prince may gain and maintain political power. Machiavelli was born in 1469 to an impoverished branch of a distinguished Florentine family and he rose, in the aftermath of Savonarola's death, from obscure bureaucrat to high-profile republican. His fall came with the return of the Medicis in 1512. Briefly imprisoned and tortured for allegedly plotting against the Medicis, Machiavelli later retired to his country estate to write his chief works.

The decline of the Medici family began in the late 1500s, although the city continued to flower. The Accademia della Crusca was established in 1582, and in 1610 Galileo was appointed court philosopher and mathematician by Cosimo II de' Medici. However, by the late 1600s the Medicis had descended into bigoted and corrupt despotism. The family continued to rule the grand duchy of Tuscany until 1737, when the last male member of the line died. Eventually, Tuscany was annexed by the house of Hapsburg-Lorraine to the kingdom of Sardinia in 1860. When the new kingdom of Italy was formed, Florence was its first capital from 1865 to 1871.

Few of Florence's famous art treasures were damaged in World War II, but Ponte Vecchio – built in the 14th century – was the only bridge to survive. A major disaster struck in November 1966 when the River Arno flooded its banks. Art experts from around the world came to help repair the buildings and statues damaged by water and mud, and beauty was restored to the city in which the Renaissance first flowered.

FLORENCE ATTRACTIONS:

Most of Florence's monuments are located within walking distance of one another but be prepared for a wait when visiting some of the popular galleries and museums. Their opening hours vary; many are closed by 2:00 p.m. (especially on Sundays) and remain closed on Mondays.

No tour buses are allowed into the town centre and passengers (including those on ship-organized excursions) are dropped off a few blocks east of the **National Library** (1) in the vicinity of Piazza Piave. The train station is located on the other side of the town centre, next to the **Church of Santa Maria Novella** (2), built by Dominicans in the late Middle Ages (1278-1350). Its patterned marble facade was remodelled in the 15th century by Leon Battista Alberti, which is why the lower part reflects the Gothic style while the entablature is of Renaissance design. The church's Italian Gothic interior contains numerous art treasures, including a famous wooden crucifix carved in 1410 by Filippo Brunelleschi – the first great architect of the Italian Renaissance.

Brunelleschi began his career as a sculptor and goldsmith but, after failing to win a commission to design the bronze doors of the Florence baptistery, he switched to architecture. He went to Rome to study classical buildings and, upon returning to Florence, he launched a new style of architecture based on the systematic use of perspective and a mastery of construction. His elegant designs can be seen all over Florence. Construction of the **Ospedale degli Innocenti** (Foundling Hospital) (3) began in 1419 and its motif – a series of round arches supported by columns – became a prototype of Renaissance architecture. The perfect proportions of the hospital arcade were repeated by Brunelleschi in the **Church of San Lorenzo** (4) which he designed in 1421 for the Medicis, who were so impressed with his plans for a burial chapel they were adding to the existing Romanesque church that they asked him to newly design the entire church.

The cloister of the Church of San Lorenzo, its series of round arches a typical feature of Renaissance architecture.

Florence's massive cathedral (the Duomo) is the focal point of the city, its dome a symbol of the Italian Renaissance.

The structure for which Brunelleschi is best known, however, is the soaring dome of the city's Gothic cathedral of **Santa Maria del Fiore (the Duomo)** (5). Of revolutionary design, Brunelleschi's dome is one of the most celebrated and original in architectural history. Constructed from 1420 to 1434, this massive dome is the focal point of the city. Its daring structural technique consisted of building the dome in two separate shells, the stronger inner shell supporting the lighter outer shell. An ingenious interlinking of the bricks helped make the counter-balanced dome self-supporting, which allowed Brunelleschi to dispense with the expense and delay of wooden scaffolding and centering.

Brunelleschi also designed the lantern atop the dome. The cathedral itself, the fourth largest in the world, was built between 1296 and 1375. The original unfinished facade was torn down in 1587 and not until

The marble facade of Florence's famous Duomo and, in the foreground, part of the Baptistery.

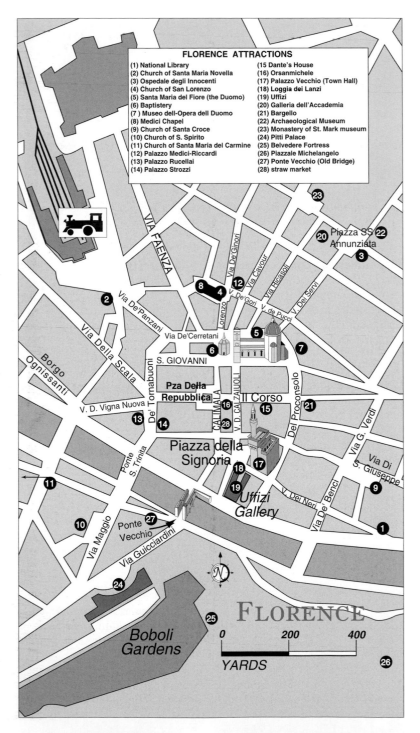

FLORENCE ATTRACTIONS

(1) National Library
(2) Church of Santa Maria Novella
(3) Ospedale degli Innocenti
(4) Church of San Lorenzo
(5) Santa Maria del Fiore (the Duomo)
(6) Baptistery
(7) Museo dell'Opera dell Duomo
(8) Medici Chapel
(9) Church of Santa Croce
(10) Church of S. Spirito
(11) Church of Santa Maria del Carmine
(12) Palazzo Medici-Riccardi
(13) Palazzo Rucellai
(14) Palazzo Strozzi
(15) Dante's House
(16) Orsanmichele
(17) Palazzo Vecchio (Town Hall)
(18) Loggia dei Lanzi
(19) Uffizi
(20) Galleria dell'Accademia
(21) Bargello
(22) Archaeological Museum
(23) Monastery of St. Mark museum
(24) Pitti Palace
(25) Belvedere Fortress
(26) Piazzale Michelangelo
(27) Ponte Vecchio (Old Bridge)
(28) straw market

Piazza SS Annunziata

Via Faenza
Via De'Panzani
Via Della Scala
Borgo Ognissanti
V. D. Vigna Nuova
Via De'Gori
Via De'Ginori
Via Cavour
Via l'Ricasoli
Via De Servi
V. de Pucci
Via De'Cerretani
S. GIOVANNI
Pza Della Repubblica
Il Corso
Del Proconsolo
CALIMALA
V. D. CALZAIUOLI
Piazza della Signoria
Ponte S. Trinita
De Tornabuoni
Uffizi Gallery
V. Dei Neri
Via De' Benci
Via G. Verdi
Via Di S. Giuseppe
Ponte Vecchio
Via Guicciardini
Via Maggio

FLORENCE

Boboli Gardens

0   200   400

YARDS

1871 was a design by Emilio de Fabris approved for the new facade. White, green and pink marble – consistent with the rest of the building – was used. The slim campanile (known as 'Giotto's Tower') was designed by the great Florentine artist Giotto di Bondone and begun in 1334. It stands 269 feet (82 metres) high.

The octagonal **Baptistery** (6), originally built in the 4th and 5th centuries when Florence was a Roman town, was considered a classical temple by medieval Florentines. Its current appearance dates from the 11th to 13th centuries, and the panels of its famous bronze doors were designed by two sculptors: Andrea Pisano, whose stories of John the Baptist embellish the South Door (1330-1336), and Lorenzo Ghiberti whose submissions won him commissions to design the North Door (1404-1424) and the East Door (1425-1452). The stunningly beautiful East Door became known as the 'The Gates of Paradise' when thus described by Michelangelo.

The nave (above) and dome (opposite) of the Duomo.

A copy of the Gates of Paradise now hangs in the east portal, the original being restored for exhibition in the **Museo dell-Opera del Duomo** (7) which houses works of art removed from the Duomo, the Campanile and the Baptistery. Works on display include Donatello's *Mary Magdalen* and an unfinished *Pieta* (1550-53) by Michelangelo that was intended for his tomb.

Michelangelo lived with the Medicis from 1490 to 1492, and the family employed him both in Florence and in Rome under the Medici popes Leo X and Clement VII. In between his painting commissions at the Sistine Chapel in Rome, Michelangelo was summoned back to Florence to design a chapel and library, attached to the family's parish Church of San Lorenzo (4). The **Laurentian Library** was built to house the Medici family's huge collection of books and manuscripts. Michelangelo strived to challenge classical ideals and create new architectural forms, and an example of his daring is reflected in his design of the library's vestibule, which contains what has been described as a

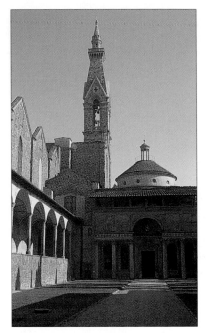

The Pazzi Chapel, annexed to the Church of Santa Croce, was designed by Brunelleschi.

'nightmarish' stairway appearing to flow downwards and outwards, defying anyone to mount the steps.

The Church of San Lorenzo's **New Sacristy (Medici Chapel)** (8),was conceived as an architectural-sculptural ensemble and is Michelangelo's only work in which his statues are in the setting specifically designed for them. The plans were changed while work was underway, with Michelangelo completing only two of the four planned tombs, before returning to Rome in 1534. One tomb was for Lorenzo de' Medici, who died at 27, and his statue atop the tomb depicts the young man in a pensive attitude, flanked by the statues *Dawn* and *Dusk*. The opposite tomb of Giuliano de' Medici is watched over by the statues *Night* and *Day*. The meaning of these allegorical figures is described in some notes found on one of the artist's drawings: "Day and Night speak, and say: We with our swift course have brought the Duke Giuliano to death." The statue of Giuliano, set in a niche, bore no resemblance to the deceased but Michelangelo was said to have remarked, 'A thousand years from now, nobody will know what he looked like.'

Michelangelo's own tomb is in the **Church of Santa Croce** (9), positioned immediately to the right as you enter. He reportedly chose this spot so that on Judgment Day, when the dead are raised, the first thing he would see through the opened doors of Santa Croce would be

The Church of Santa Croce holds the tomb of Michelangelo and others. (Opposite page) Piazza della Repubblica.

Brunelleschi's dome. The tomb of Galileo is situated on the left side of the church, opposite Michelangelo's. Machiavelli's tomb is halfway down the nave on the left, and the composer Rossini's tomb is at the end of the nave. The interior of this Gothic church (with a 19th-century facade) also contains early 14th-century frescoes by Giotto, who departed from the Byzantine style of depicting religious symbols to create, instead, dramatic biblical scenes. Works here by Donatello include his *Annunciation* and *Crucifix*. Donatello, an innovative sculptor who freed sculptures of their architectural setting, was interested in ancient monuments and he travelled to Rome in 1430 with Brunelleschi. The **Pazzi Chapel**, annexed to Santa Croce, is a Brunelleschi design and was begun about 1430. He also designed the **Church of S. Spirito** (10), begun in 1434, about the same time he was designing the **Church of Santa Maria del Carmine** (11) – a domed, central-plan church and the first of its kind for the Renaissance.

The **Palazzo Medici-Riccardi** (12) built from 1444 to 1459, became the model for other private Florentine palaces, such as **Palazzo Rucellai** (13) and **Palazzo Strozzi** (14). The Medicis rejected Brunelleschi's model for their new palace, considering it too grandiose, and went instead with a design by Michelozzi, one that did not outwardly flaunt their wealth and power. Its austere Tuscan Gothic exterior of rusticated masonry contrasts sharply with the interior's elaborately decorated salons and the central courtyard's classical arcades, which imitate Brunelleschi's Foundling Hospital. Other buildings of note include **Dante's House** (15) and the **Orsanmichele** (16), a granary that was transformed into a church in 1336. The nearby **Piazza della Repubblica**, a 19th-century square dedicated to Vittorio Emanuele II (first king of a united Italy), is situated on the site of the Roman town's ancient forum.

Florence's main square is **Piazza della Signoria**, overlooked by the fortress-like **Palazzo Vecchio (Town Hall)** (17) where elected members of the Signoria would temporarily live while serving their term of

A replica of Michelangelo's David (detail below) stands outside the Town Hall (above).

office. Begun in 1298 and built to withstand armed assault in an era when political turmoil and social tensions often led to bloodshed, the building's tall tower was both a symbol of civic pride and a watch tower, with the two marble statues flanking the doorway designed for holding chains. Under the arches of the gallery are the coats of arms of the Tuscan communes ruled by Florence. Inside the palace the grand Salone dei Cinquecento (Room of the Five Hundred) is richly decorated with frescoes by Vasari and sculptures by Michelangelo.

The statues standing in front of the Palazzo include a copy of Michelangelo's *David* (1501-1504), one of his greatest sculptural achievements. When commissioned, the statue was supposed to depict a biblical shepherd boy and occupy a pier buttress of the Duomo, but Michelangelo's interpretation of David produced instead a heroic Renaissance man whose masculine nudity made the statue unsuitable for an ecclesiastical site. A committee decided to erect it in front of the Palazzo Vecchio, and it took five days to move the colossal statue (which stands over four metres) to this site. The statue was stoned by citizens offended by its nudity, and David's private parts were covered with gilded leaves until 1545. In 1873 the statue was removed to the Academy, with a copy placed on its original site.

The statue to *David*'s left is *Hercules and Cacus* (1525-1534) by Baccio Bandinelli, whose sculptural talents were widely ridiculed by his contemporaries. When the marble block for this statue fell off the transport into the River Arno,

*Fountain of Neptune in Piazza della Signoria (above). The Uffizi
Gallery (below) contains a vast collection of Renaissance paintings.*

the joke was that the stone had thrown itself into the river rather than
endure mutilation by Bandinelli. The *Fountain of Neptune* (1560-1575)
to *David*'s right was the work of Bartolomeo Ammanati who, soon
after its completion, experienced a religious crisis prompted by the
counter-Reformation and disowned his works because of their nudity.
The Florentines call this sculpture the 'White Giant' because of the
enormous size of the white sea
god standing in the centre of the
fountain. Statues on display in the
Loggia dei Lanzi (18) include
Perseus (1533), a masterpiece in
bronze by Benvenuto Cellini, and
the *Rape of the Sabines* (1581-
1583) by Giambologna.

The famous **Uffizi Gallery**
(19) is housed in a Renaissance
palace that was built to house the
administrative offices (*uffizi*) of
the Medicis. This U-shaped building was designed by Giorgio
Vasari, a favourite portrait artist
of the Medici family. When the
family installed their art collections here, it became Europe's
first modern museum. The
gallery, located on the second
floor, consists of 45 rooms divid-

Ponte Vecchio, Florence's oldest bridge (above). A perfect morning for fishing along the banks of the Arno River in Florence (below).

ed into sections. The famous artists represented in this vast collection of paintings include Leonardo da Vinci, Michelangelo, Raphael and Giotto, with numerous works by Sandro Botticelli.

Other art museums of note are the **Galleria dell'Accademia (Academy)** (20), which houses the original *David* by Michelangelo, as well as his unfinished *Slaves*. The **Museo Nazionale** in the 13th-century **Bargello** (21), a former Renaissance prison, contains an outstanding collection of Renaissance sculpture with works by Donatello, Michelangelo and Cellini, and the bronze panels submitted by Brunelleschi and Ghiberti in 1402 when they competed for the commission to decorate the north doors of the Baptistery. The **Archaeological Museum** (22) houses Etruscan and Graeco-Roman art, and the **Monastery of St. Mark Museum** (23) contains some of the best works of Fra Angelico, a Dominican monk.

The **Pitti Palace** (24), originally built for the Pitti family in the 15th century, was expanded after it was bought by the rival Medici family. Works by Titian and Raphael are displayed in the Palatine Gallery, which is housed in the Royal Apartments on the right-hand side of the courtyard. Behind the Pitti Palace, which served as the Royal Palace of a united Italy from 1865 to 1870, lie the terraced Boboli Gardens (1550). A back entrance leads to the **Belvedere Fortress** (25), its grounds a popular picnic site for Florentines, with views overlooking the city's medieval maze of churches, squares and red-tiled roofs. The **Piazzale Michelangelo** (26), (farther up the hill) is where the tour buses stop to give their passengers an overview of Florence, the River Arno and its many bridges.

Florence's heritage continues to inspire new generations of artists.

Ponte Vecchio (Old Bridge) (27) was built in 1345 and was the only bridge not blown up by the retreating Germans during World War II. It is lined with jewellers and goldsmiths' shops and is topped with a corridor designed by Vasari for Cosimo I de' Medici (1537-1569). Used by successive Medici grand dukes when crossing the bridge, the Vasari Corridor is lined with paintings and, although not open to the general public, the corridor is accessible as part of a recently introduced city tour called the Prince's Route. The elegant **Ponte Santa Trinita**, the next bridge downriver and the pride of Florence, was designed by Bartolemeo Ammannati in 1567 and was painstakingly rebuilt after World War II.

Shopping: Florentines are renowned for their skilled craftsmanship, especially in leather work, glassware, ceramics, art reproductions and high fashion. Boutiques selling fine leather goods and designer clothing are found on Via de'Tornabuoni and Via della Vigna Nuova. More leather shops are found near Santa Croce. For antiques, including paintings, ceramics and sculptures, try Borgo Ognissanti or cross the river to Via Maggio (one block west of the Pitti Palace). The Ponte Vecchio is a good place to shop for jewellery. Souvenir shoppers might try the straw market located in an open-air loggia (28) on Via Calimala.

ELBA – Lying off the coast of Tuscany, the island of Elba is well known as Napoleon's place of exile from 1814 to 1815. Its principal north coast port of Portoferraio, strongly fortified by Florence's Medici family from the 16th to 18th centuries, is today a seaside resort. Napoleon's house, the Villa dei Mulini, where he resided as sovereign of the island, is now a museum.

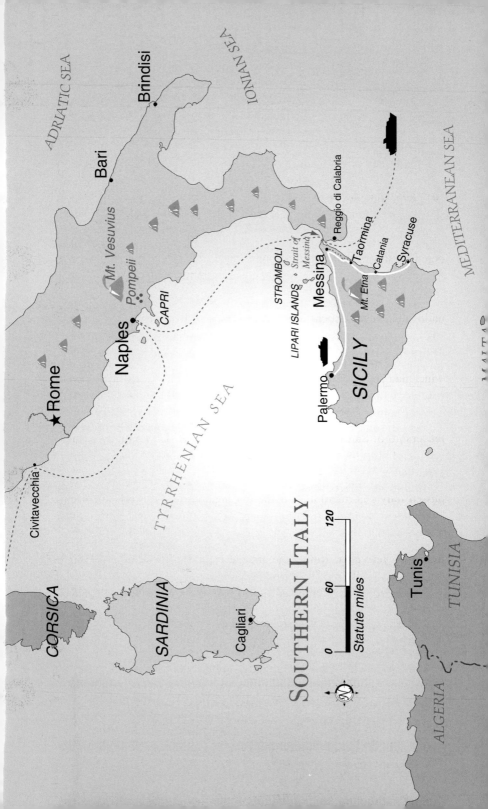

SOUTHERN ITALY

Statute miles

0   60   120

ADRIATIC SEA

IONIAN SEA

MEDITERRANEAN SEA

TYRRHENIAN SEA

Brindisi

Bari

Mt. Vesuvius

Pompeii

CAPRI

Naples

★Rome

Civitavecchia

CORSICA

SARDINIA

Cagliari

Reggio di Calabria

Taormina

Catania

Syracuse

STROMBOLI

Strait of Messina

Messina

LIPARI ISLANDS

Mt. Etna

SICILY

Palermo

MALTA

Tunis

TUNISIA

ALGERIA

CHAPTER FIVE

SOUTHERN ITALY

I taly's southern states, while rich in natural beauty, have long been the poor cousin to the country's industrialized north and central regions. Centuries of exploitation by European dynasties and powerful feudal lords had kept the south in a state of backwardness, hindered by superstition and ignorance, when Italy – which hadn't been a unified political entity since the fall of the Western Roman Empire back in the 5th century – began its long struggle toward reunification.

Called Risorgimento (Italian for *resurgence*), this period of cultural nationalism and political activism was inspired by several 18th-century writers and it gained momentum in the early 1800s when the southern states, long dominated by foreign rulers, began to revolt against their repressive regimes. In 1820 there were uprisings in Naples and Sicily, which had been politically joined as the Two Sicilies in 1816, followed by insurrections in Sardinia in 1821. Despite severe reprisals, the uprisings continued, led by different factions.

One of these revolutionary groups, favouring a united Italy under the leadership of Sardinia's King Victor Emmanuel II, eventually gained control of the movement. Its cause was supported by the military hero Giuseppe Garibaldi, and in 1861 the kingdom of Italy was proclaimed with Victor Emmanuel as king. The newly declared kingdom encompassed Italy's northern and southern states, but Rome, situated in central Italy, remained part of the independent Papal States, which were protected by the troops of Napoleon III. The reunification of Italy was finally completed in 1870 when the Papal States were seized by Italian troops. A year later, Rome, the ancient capital of the Roman Empire, was once again the capital of a united Italy.

For general information and travel tips on Italy, please see pages 187 to 189.

Victor Emmanuel Monument, Piazza Venezia, Rome.

St. Peter's Square (above). Motor scooters are a popular mode of transport in Rome (opposite).

ROME (ROMA) – The Eternal City

One of the world's most exciting cities, Rome is the intellectual, cultural and religious centre of Italy. The three million residents of the city contend with a contrast of busy streets and squares brimming with works of art, beautiful fountains and monuments to history. In ancient times, Rome was the centre of one of the world's most successful empires. Long believed to have originated as a pastoral settlement on seven hills bordering the banks of the River Tiber, Rome likely began as a river port founded by salt merchants. Salt, indispensable for rearing livestock, was brought there from the nearest seaport which lay downriver, and a local labour force soon gathered to unload, warehouse and trade this valuable commodity. Several tribes lived in the area – the Sabines to the north, the Etruscans to the north and west, and the Latins to the south and east.

Palatine, a fortified hill of Rome, was taken in the 8th century BC by the Etruscans and, although the founding of Rome is shrouded in myth, historians traditionally set the date at 753 BC. The Etruscans, skilled engineers, built a defensive wall around the seven hills and transformed the existing group of villages into a city, draining the swampy plain of the Forum and building a temple on Capitoline Hill. According to legend, Romulus, son of Mars, was the city's founder. He and his brother, abandoned at birth in a royal plot, were suckled by a she-wolf and raised by a shepherd couple. Romulus eventually killed his brother and populated his new city with fugitives. These early Romans, in search of wives, seized women from the neighbouring Sabine tribe.

Savouring the sweet life in the squares of Rome. (Above) The Spanish Steps. (Opposite) Piazza Della Rotonda.

In about 500 BC, the Romans overthrew their Etruscan rulers and established a republic that lasted four centuries. As the city grew, so too did its political structure. The ruling patrician class slowly ceded legislative power to the assemblies, and they in turn were eventually controlled by the senate which, as supreme power of the state, led Rome in her quest for empire and world supremacy. This expansion began with the conquest of central and southern Italy, then the defeat of Carthage to gain control of Sicily, Sardinia, Corsica, Spain and the northern shores of Africa. Macedonia was next, followed by Greece and Egypt.

However, as the empire grew, so too did turmoil back in Rome, where corruption, class dissension and barbarism threatened the republic's survival. Pompey emerged as master of Rome and, upon his return from a victorious foreign conquest, he allied himself with Julius Caesar, a popular democratic leader of patrician ancestry. Their allegiance, always tentative, dissolved with the death of Caesar's daughter Julia, who was married to Pompey. The two leaders led their mutual armies into battle against each other and Caesar, a military genius, emerged victorious – the new master of Rome.

Under the leadership of Caesar, a brilliant orator and patron of the arts, Roman culture thrived and was permeated by Greek thought, literature and language. Caesar's assassination in 44 BC marked the end of the Republic and the beginning of the Empire. Initially there was anarchy, until Octavian, Caesar's nephew and protege, emerged as leader. He defeated Antony and Cleopatra and became the first emperor of

The Forum was the centre of republican Rome and the scene of Julius Caesar's assassination.

Rome, receiving from the senate the title 'Augustus'. Peace reigned for the next two centuries and imperial Rome grew into a city of over two million inhabitants. The city boasted a police force, fire brigades and a postal system. Aqueducts supplied water to public baths, and the wealthy had running water piped right into their villas. Efficient transportation was provided by an extensive system of roads and bridges. Indeed, at the height of Roman imperialism, all roads did lead to Rome for it was the centre of the western world.

Rome's decline came quickly as the West sank into anarchy and Italy was ravaged by invaders. Rome was sacked twice and finally fell in 476, its last emperor deposed by the Goths. However, amid the political disintegration of Rome there rose a new power – that of Roman Catholicism. The grandeur that once epitomized imperial Rome would eventually return with the splendour of the Italian Renaissance, patronized by the powerful papacy which ruled a swath of central Italy – from Rome to Ravenna – for more than 11 centuries. The Papal States were defeated in 1870 by patriot forces determined to create an Italian nation, but not until the Lateran Treaty of 1929 – which made the pope sovereign within Vatican City – did the papacy recognize the secular state of modern Italy.

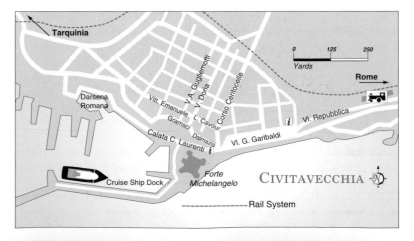

GETTING AROUND

Civitavecchia, its harbour favoured by the Emperor Trajan in the early 2nd century AD, is still the chief port of Rome. Civitavecchia is a 1 1/4 hour drive from Rome and, in addition to full-day coach tours offered by the cruise companies, independent travellers can hire a taxi (a full day in Rome costs about US$250 to $300) or take the train. The Civitavecchia train station is a 20-minute walk or US$10 taxi ride from the cruise ship dock and it's about an hour long train ride to Termini station in downtown Rome. If you're touring Rome on your own, plan your itinerary ahead of time and don't try to see too many attractions. Taxis are plentiful, especially at Piazza Venezia and St. Peter's Square, and there are plenty of outdoor cafes and other casual eateries where you can pause for a quick snack or refreshment while sightseeing and shopping.

ROME ATTRACTIONS:

The **Colosseum** (1), completed in 80 AD during the reign of Titus, is a huge concrete amphitheatre containing miles of stairways, and tier upon tier of marble seats which accommodated more than 50,000 spectators. A masterpiece of engineering, the stadium's efficient flow of people in and out of the building was achieved by utilizing 80 ground-floor entrances, each numbered to direct people to the staircases leading to their seats. Entertainment was provided by hundreds of rigorously trained gladiators (Latin for *swordsmen*), who were slaves or prisoners forced to perform exhibition combats in which they were paired off and would fight to the death – unless the crowd indicated to the victor that he spare the life of the defeated gladiator.

Gladiators were also forced to fight wild beasts, and those who revolted against this barbaric treatment were brutally killed by their

The Colosseum's interior, missing its arena floor (right), and a night-time view of its exterior (below).

Arch of Constantine, raised in 312 AD.

Roman masters. The famous slave Spartacus, who died a century before the Colosseum was built, escaped from a gladiators' school at Capua (near modern Naples) and fled into the mountains, where he organized an army of fugitives who defeated several Roman forces before they were finally crushed. Spartacus was killed in battle and 6,000 of his followers were crucified even though 3,000 Roman prisoners had been found, unharmed, in his camp.

Southwest of the Colosseum stands the **Arch of Constantine**, a triple-arcaded triumphal arch raised in 312 AD to celebrate Constantine I's victory over Maxentius at the Milvian Bridge near Rome, making him the unchallenged ruler of the West. The road heading south from the Arch led to the Circus Maximus where chariot races were held. The race-track was overlooked by the **Palatine** (2), one of Rome's seven hills and the site of the city's original 8th century BC settlement. During the city's republican period, notable citizens built homes atop the Palatine, and various emperors built palaces there during the imperial period.

Lying along the Palatine Hill, in a shallow valley between the Colosseum and Capitoline Hill, is the **Roman Forum** – the centre of republican Rome where the senate met, citizens strolled the basilicas and famous speeches were delivered by such famous orators as Caesar and Cicero. Victorious generals would ride in triumphant procession along the Sacred Way, the most famous street in ancient Rome, which runs the length of the Forum.

The restored **Arch of Titus** (commemorating his conquest of Jerusalem in 70 AD) stands at one end of the Sacred Way, not far from the Colosseum, and the **Arch of Septimius Severus**, raised in 203 AD, stands at the other end. Beside it are the ruins of the rostrum (raised platform) where Mark Antony delivered the funeral address in Caesar's

honour. On the other side of the Arch of Septimius Severus is the **Curia** (3), a large brick senate hall dating from the 3rd century AD. Other important monuments in this large complex of ruins include: **The Temple of Antonius and Faustin**, (4), erected in 141 AD to commemorate the emperor and his wife; and the **Basilica of Maxentius** (5), completed by Constantine in 312.

As the empire grew, the Roman Forum could not accommodate additional structures, so certain emperors – following Julius Caesar's example – built along its outskirts. The remains of these imperial forums can still be seen along Via dei Fori Imperiali, a busy main street which leads to

(Above) The Temple of Antonius and Faustin is one of several buildings still standing in the Roman Forum (top).

Piazza Venezia, the hub of central Rome. In the northwest corner of the square is the Palazzo Venezia, an early renaissance palace from which Mussolini, standing in the balcony over the main portal, would deliver speeches to the crowd-filled piazza below. Dominating Piazza Venezia is the **Victor Emmanuel Monument** (6), the huge marble 'wedding cake' commemorating the first king of a united Italy. Begun in 1885, it took forty years to complete. The ceremonial staircase leads to the Altar of the Nation which contains the Tomb of the Unknown Soldier, guarded by two sentinels. Above the shrine stands a statue of Romas flanked on both sides by celebratory reliefs. In the centre of the monument is a colossal equestrian statue of Victor Emmanuel.

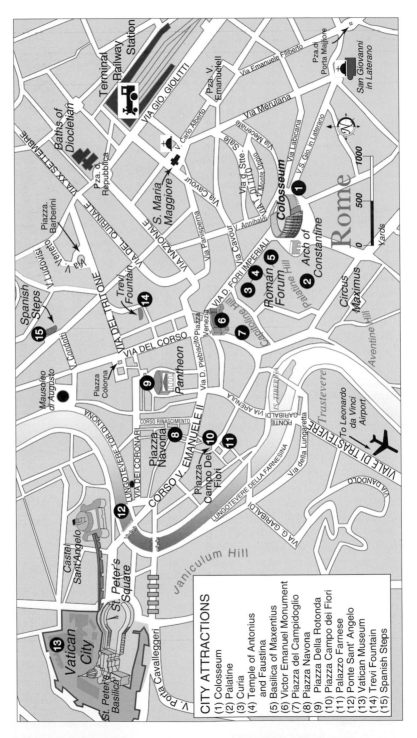

CITY ATTRACTIONS
(1) Colosseum
(2) Palatine
(3) Curia
(4) Temple of Antonius and Faustina
(5) Basilica of Maxentius
(6) Victor Emanuel Monument
(7) Piazza del Campidoglio
(8) Piazza Navona
(9) Piazza Della Rotonda
(10) Piazza Campo dei Fiori
(11) Palazzo Farnese
(12) Ponte Sant' Angelo
(13) Vatican Museum
(14) Trevi Fountain
(15) Spanish Steps

Behind the Victor Emmanuel Monument, on **Capitoline Hill**, is the **Church of Santa Maria d'Aracoeli**. One of the oldest Christian churches in Rome, officiated by the Franciscan Friars Minor since 1250, its unadorned brick facade is reached from street level by a long stairway that was built in 1348. Another broad stairway right beside it leads to the **Piazza del Campidoglio** (7), an architectural complex designed by Michelangelo in the 1530s, at the request of Pope Paul III, and completed long after the artist's death. This complex occupies the most famous of Rome's seven hills – the Capitoline – which was the focal point of Rome's religious life in ancient times. Michelangelo's artistic genius is reflected in the harmonious composition of this piazza, its trapezoidal shape created by its three buildings having been placed not at right angles to one other but at an angle of 80 degrees.

Upon ascending the staircase, visitors face the **Palazzo Senatorio** (Senators' Palace), now the Town Hall, which dominates the piazza. To the right is the **Palazzo dei Conservatori** (Conservators' Palace) which displays works of art, including the famous Capitoline Wolf – a 5th century bronze statue of the she-wolf (symbol of Rome) suckling the infant Romolus (founder of Rome) and his brother Remus, figures added by a 15th-century artist. To the left is the Palazzo Nuovo, which houses the **Capitoline Museum**, its works of art including a 2nd century equestrian statue of the emperor Marcus Aurelius, the only bronze equestrian statue to survive from imperial Rome. It had stood in the centre of the piazza atop a pedestal until it was removed in 1981; an exact replica was mounted in its place in the spring of 1997.

The main thoroughfare of Corso Vittoria Emanuele II runs through the centre of Old Rome, where narrow, winding streets lead to such famous attractions as the cafe-lined **Piazza Navona** (8), considered one of Rome's most beautiful squares with its baroque fountains and churches, and the **Piazza Della Rotonda** (9) which is dominated by the Pantheon, a domed temple from the early 2nd century AD, its impressive interior the best preserved of imperial Rome's surviving structures. **Piazza Campo dei Fiori** (Field of Flowers) (10) is the scene of a colourful outdoor market each weekday morning, and the nearby **Palazzo Farnese** (11) is a beautiful Renaissance palace now housing the French Embassy.

Ponte Sant'Angelo

Piazza Navona (above) and the interior of the Pantheon (opposite).

The elegant **Ponte Sant' Angelo** (12) leads across the River Tiber to Castel Sant'Angelo. Three of the bridge's arches are original – built by Hadrian's successor – and in 1688 the bridge was extended and embellished with ten angels designed by Bernini. **Castel Sant'Angelo**, built in 139 AD as a mausoleum for the emperor Hadrian, was eventually used as a fortress for

FOUNTAIN FROLICKS

Completed in 1762, the **Trevi Fountain** (14) is one of Rome's most popular attractions. Its centrepiece is a statue of the god Oceanus riding in a sea chariot drawn by two Tritons, and the fountain was used for a scene in Fellini's famous film *La Dolce Vita*, in which characters played by Marcello Mastroianni and Anita Ekberg go wading in it. Such behaviour is, in real life, frowned upon because of the risk of vandalism, both deliberate and accidental, and the city of Rome imposes a stiff fine on anyone caught bathing in a public fountain. The fine was increased in the summer of 1997 after a 43-year-old Roman and his two companions went for a dip in the Bernini-designed *Fountain of the Four Rivers* in Piazza Navona. When the Roman climbed onto the marble tail of a water creature, a piece broke off and fell into six pieces. Most Romans were understandably indignant, with film director Franco Zeffirelli even suggesting corporal punishment, but the vandal himself was unrepentant, not only refusing to apologize but also threatening to sue the city for damages because he hurt his foot in the incident.

Trevi Fountain

popes seeking refuge in times of peril. It later served as a prison, and is now a museum containing beautifully decorated papal apartments and prison cells.

Vatican City, a tiny sovereign state in the heart of Rome, contains some of the world's most famous buildings and works of art. **St. Peter's Basilica**, the world's largest church, stands on the site of an early shrine to St. Peter. In the 4th century, Emperor Constantine built a church over the grave of St. Peter, and it was in this wood-roofed basilica that Charlemagne and other emperors and popes were crowned. In 1506, Pope Julius II decided a new church should be built to replace the dilapidated original, and Bramante was commissioned to design it. A succession of architects worked on St. Peter's, including Michelangelo who took over in 1547 and added the gigantic dome. The church was finally completed in 1626 and its sublime interior of creamy marble and glittering gilt is filled with masterpieces, including Michelangelo's famous sculpture, *La Pieta*, in one of the side chapels. Bernini's baldachino – a bronze canopy – stands above the high altar from which only the pope may read mass.

Piazza San Pietro (**St. Peter's Square**) was designed by Bernini in the 1650s at the request of Pope Alexander VII. He called for a grand approach to St. Peter's that wouldn't obstruct the view of the faithful who gather in the square when the pope makes an address from the church's central balcony or from a window of the adjacent

Bernini's baldachino (above) and the nave (below) of St. Peter's Basilica.

St. Peter's giant dome was designed by Michelangelo.

Vatican Palace. Bernini met this criteria with a sweeping colonnade that curves along both sides of the square. The Egyptian obelisk in the centre of the square was brought to Rome in imperial times by the Emperor Caligula, and the monumental avenue leading to the piazza was added by Mussolini.

The **Vatican Museum** (13), next door to the Vatican Palace, is a complex of eight museums and five galleries containing one of the world's most extensive art collections, including ancient Egyptian artifacts, Roman statues and paintings by Raphael. The ceiling and altar wall of the **Sistine Chapel**, where the cardinals meet to elect a new pope, were painted by Michelangelo. Considered works of unsurpassed grandeur, the ceiling frescoes depict biblical scenes and the altar wall was selected for Michelangelo's painting of the *Last Judgment*. A major restoration of these works was undertaken from 1980 to 1992, which entailed cleaning away a layer of dirt to reveal the original vibrant colours of the frescoes. Amid the spectrum of colours used by Michelangelo, the two that stand out are green and violet – the liturgical colours of the Mass.

Rome's main shopping area lies between the Via del Corso and the **Spanish Steps** (15) – the city's most fashionable gathering place. At

THE VATICAN SWISS GUARDS

Since the 15th century, Swiss mercenaries have fought in various European armies. Called Swiss Guards, these mercenaries were put at the disposal of foreign powers in return for money payments. In 1874 the Swiss constitution forbade all recruitment of Swiss soldiers by foreign powers, with the exception of Vatican City. Founded in 1505 as the personal guard of the pope, the Swiss Guard in the Vatican carry on a centuries-old tradition of swearing to serve the pope. Recruited from Switzerland's Catholic cantons, the guardsmen on sentry duty are garbed in colourful costume of Renaissance design and wear ceremonial armour. A 100-member force, its members live in Vatican City and must observe strict rules, including a midnight curfew.

the foot of the Steps, named for a palace that housed the Spanish Embassy, is a boat-shaped fountain designed by Bernini. Famous **shopping streets** lead off the piazza, namely Via Condotti and Via Borgognona, both lined with sophisticated boutiques. Less expensive shops are found on Via Frattina. The Steps themselves were designed in the early 18th century and built by the French to connect the Spanish Quarter at the bottom to the French Quarter at the top. A 16th-century church, built on behalf of French King Louis XII, stands at the top of the Steps. Artists and writers have long been attracted to this part of Rome, including Keats, who lived and died in a house next to the Steps. His residence is now a museum, called the Keats and Shelley Memorial House, and is dedicated to these two Romantic poets.

Tarquinia's museum features Etruscan artifacts housed in a 15th-century castle.

Not far from the Spanish Steps are some of Rome's most luxurious hotels, including the famous Hotel Excelsior on legendary **Via Veneto**, where movie stars and deposed royalty held court at sidewalk cafes in the late 1950s, their antics captured in candid photos by a new breed of photographers called paparazzi. The elegant Hotel Eden on Via Ludovisi, with sweeping views from its rooftop bar and restaurant, was the favourite haunt of Hemingway, Fellini and Ingrid Bergman.

TARQUINIA

While most passengers arriving in Civitavecchia usually head straight to Rome for a full day of sightseeing, some choose the optional excursion to Tarquinia. In 449 BC the Etruscans, whose kings had founded and ruled Rome for about a century, established the ancient city of Tarquinni. These people (possibly from Asia Minor) had first settled in the Tuscany area of Italy in the 8th century BC, about the same time the Greeks began to settle along the southern shores of Italy. The Etruscans, their commercial empire rivalling those of Greece and Phoenicia, didn't form a unified nation, but rather a network of city-states, each of which succumbed, one by one, to the Romans in the 5th and 4th centuries BC. Such was the fate of Tarquinni, but its large necropolis of tombs remained intact and today visitors can gaze at their unique murals, inspired perhaps by Egyptian wall art and painted

The remains of the forum and its buildings in Pompeii.

around 500 BC. The Etruscan National Museum, housed in a 15th-century castle in the nearby town of Tarquinia, contains an extensive collection of Etruscan artifacts.

NAPLES (NAPOLI)

The beautiful Bay of Naples had lured many a visitor to its scenic shores when British admiral Horatio Nelson pulled into port during the summer of 1798. Nelson joined a long list of illustrious guests, including Goethe, who were graciously entertained by Sir William Hamilton, the British ambassador to Naples from 1764 to 1800. Sir Hamilton, after years of scholarly pursuits, had embraced the Neapolitans' carefree attitude to life and thrown himself with gusto into the pursuit of pleasure. His beautiful young wife and former mistress, Lady Emma Hamilton, was a confidante of the Queen of Naples – whose court was a centre of scandal and intrigue – and it was through this friendship that the British fleet, under the command of Nelson, was allowed access to the Spanish-controlled ports of Naples and Syracuse to take on water and provisions when all other Mediterranean ports had been shut off by the French. Nelson went on to destroy the French fleet off the mouth of the Nile River and, upon his return to Naples, he was given a hero's welcome and was bestowed with a British peerage. He also fell deeply in love with Lady Hamilton, and so began their notorious love affair.

Such is life in southern Italy, a land of sunshine and song, idyllic islands and fragrant breezes. In ancient times, wealthy Romans built themselves country villas at Herculaneum and Pompeii, situated at the base of Mount Vesuvius, and the tiny island paradise of Capri, in the Bay of Naples, became a holiday retreat for the early emperors Augustus and Tiberius. The cataclysmic eruption of Mount Vesuvius in 79 AD brought a thunderous end to the good life when Herculaneum and Pompeii were buried under cinders, ashes and mud, then long forgotten until they were rediscovered in the 18th century.

A wedding couple crosses the busy street in Piazza Trieste e Trento.

When the Englishman Thomas Cook, the world's first tour operator, brought a group of British tourists to Italy in 1864, the excavated site of ancient Pompeii was perceived as a somewhat shocking, pleasure-seeking city brimming with bars, brothels and priapic statuary. Some Victorians believed the eruption of Vesuvius was a fire sent from heaven to punish Pompeii for its wickedness, a belief that only added to its attraction. The Romans did like their wine strong, but the presence of lead in the water pipes had deadened their taste. As for the Priapus figure displayed at the entrance to their homes, this Roman god of male generative power was meant to ward off evil influences. And, although the Romans' favourite form of entertainment was the circus-like spectacle of gladitorial contests, there was also a refined side to Pompeii, preserved in the luxurious and lavishly decorated villas of the wealthy.

A trip to the top of Mount Vesuvius to peer into the smouldering volcano's crater was part of a 19th-century Cook's Italian Tour, and the company eventually bought the Italian-built funicular which carried visitors up the final ascent of the cone. A further section was added to connect the funicular with the main line, and those who rode the Vesuvius railway included Edward VII and Ulysses S. Grant. The line was completely destroyed in 1944 when the volcano erupted for the third time this century. The volcano's smouldering presence has made Neapolitans somewhat superstitious, and twice a year they gather by the hundreds with their archbishop at the Cathedral of San Gennaro to pray to a 4th-century saint and witness a 'mir-

Maritime Station was built during Mussolini's dictatorship.

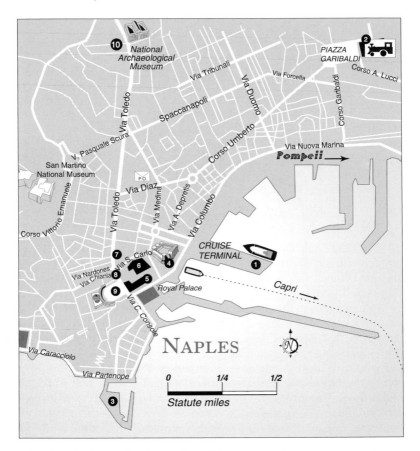

acle' in which his blood, kept in gold vials, liquefies – a sign that disaster will not strike the city. Scientists have confirmed that the substance is blood, but they have yet to explain why it regularly liquefies.

When Antonio Bassolino was elected mayor in 1993, Naples had become over-populated and run down, and was best known for giving the world pizza and the actress Sophia Loren, who grew up in its slums. The new mayor decided to revitalize his city's cultural heritage by cleaning up the historic piazzas and restoring neglected churches, museums and palaces. In the process, he rekindled Neapolitans' pride in a city that had been founded as Neapolis (New City) by the Ancient Greeks and was, centuries later, the glittering capital of the Kingdom of Naples.

Getting Around: Naples is not a pedestrian-friendly city. Simply crossing some of the busy streets is challenging, for no one seems to take any notice of whether a traffic light is red or green. Fortunately, many historic buildings are located a short distance from the **Maritime Station** (Stazione Marittima) (1) where the cruise ships dock. Further afield is the Archaeological Museum, about a US$10 taxi ride away.

The **train station** (2) is on Corso Garibaldi, about one mile from the cruise dock – a US$10 taxi ride. The bus costs about US$1 and tickets are sold at newsstands. The Circumvescuviana train runs every 30 minutes to Herculaneum, Pompeii and Sorrento, and tickets are sold in euros. The train ride from Naples to Pompeii is a 40-minute trip (disembark at the Pompeii Excavation site); from Naples to Sorrento is one hour and 20 minutes.

Several companies operate jet boats, hydrofoils and ferries from Naples to Capri and Sorrento. Fastest and most expensive are the jet foils; slowest and cheapest are the ferries. A terminal is located beside the Maritime Station, with numerous departures by hydrofoil to Capri (approx. $25 round trip, 40 minutes each way), and to Sorrento (approx.$20 round trip, 45 minutes each way). Boats also run between Sorrento and Capri.

The west entrance to Castel Nuovo (above) and detail of the arch (opposite).

Shopping: Naples-area artisans are known for their fine craftsmanship in cameos (carved from shells), ceramics, wood inlay and embroidered goods. In Naples, the Galleria Umberto I and Via Chiaia both offer upscale shopping.

NAPLES ATTRACTIONS

The city's medieval past is evidenced by several Neapolitan castles overlooking the harbour, including the 12th-century **Castel dell'Ovo** (3) which stands on a rocky islet, and **Castel Nuovo** (4), a symbol of power and the scene of fierce battles between the French and Spanish. Surrounded by a moat, the castle was originally built in 1279 by Charles I of Anjou, then rebuilt by Spanish and Tuscan craftsmen following the bloody wars of the 15th century. Naples became a centre of sculpture under the rule of Alfonso of Aragon, who captured Naples in 1442. His admiration of classical antiquity is reflected in the triumphal arch he had built between the two towers that flank the castle's west entrance. Dozens of Renaissance sculptors worked on its complex design from 1451 until its completion 30 years later.

(Above) Galleria Umberto I.
(Opposite) The gates to the Royal Palace.
(Below) Piazza Plebiscito.

The Palazzo Reale (**Royal Palace**) (5), built in the early 1600s, has been damaged, restored and remodelled over the centuries. The past home to various Neapolitan royal families, including the Spanish Bourbons, its sumptuous interior of frescoed walls and grand staircases is filled with baroque furniture, period mirrors and chandeliers, Chinese porcelain vases, gilt bronzes, and paintings by celebrated artists.

Naples is famous for its music, both classical and popular, some well-known Neapolitan songs being *Funiculi Funicula* and *O Sole Mio*. The great tenor Caruso was a Naples native, and numerous works –

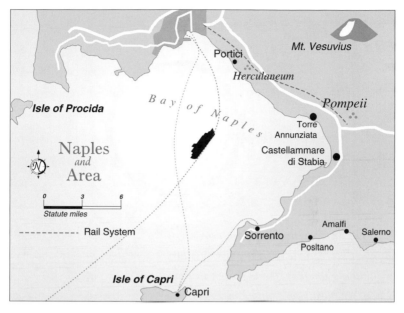

including *La Sonnambula* by Bellini – have premiered at the Teatro di S. Carlo (**San Carlo Opera House**) (6), second in Italy only to La Scala in Milan. It first opened in 1737, then was reconstructed following a fire in 1816. The red and gold interior, which seats 3,000 and provides perfect acoustics, is also a visual feast, with its seven levels of private boxes, each row adorned with gilt balustrades.

Galleria Umberto I (7), named for King Umberto I, is an iron- and glass-roofed gallery constructed in the late 1800s, which today is filled with elegant shops and cafes. More fine shops are located on Via Chiaia, off **Piazza Trieste e Trento** (8), a lovely square with a fountain in its centre that connects with **Piazza Plebiscito** (9), which opens to the sweeping facade of the Chiesa di S. Francesco di Paola (Church of St. Francis). Completed in 1847, the church was modelled on the Pantheon in Rome, while the curving colonnade arcade is reminiscent of the one in St. Peter's Square. A large and majestic square, it is a popular photo shoot for Neapolitan wedding parties.

The highly acclaimed **National Archaeological Museum** (10), housed in a 16th-century building, contains one of the world's largest collections of classical antiquities, including the historic riches recovered from Herculaneum, Pompeii and other sites. Paintings, mosaics, statues, busts, vases and domestic implements are among the discoveries on display.

POMPEII & HERCULANEUM

Nestled at the foot of Mount Vesuvius, the Roman centres of Pompeii, a prosperous walled city, and Herculaneum, a seaside resort town, were both recovering from the earthquake of 63 AD when disaster struck on

(Above) The basilica and antiquarium of Pompeii. (Opposite & next page) Visitors walk along ancient streets frozen in time when Mt. Vesuvius erupted in 79 AD.

an August day in 79 AD. The day began like any other, the residents of Pompeii going about their business as bakers, merchants, artisans, prostitutes and slaves who were in service to the wealthy owners of fine villas. The public baths were busy, as usual, and the city's shops and streets were filled with people, many pausing to read or add to the graffiti written on public walls. Chariots and carts rolled by, following the worn ruts in roads.

Then, suddenly, the ground began to shake. Instantly everyone knew they were in the grip of another devastating quake, but there was little time to react before catastrophe struck. A thunderous cloud of ash and

The cast of a Pompeii resident caught in his final moment of life.

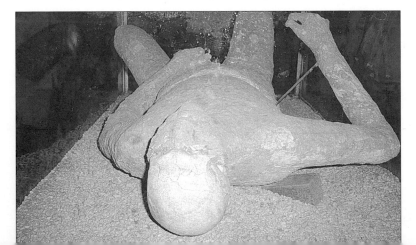

lava exploded from the summit of Mount Vesuvius, erupting with such force that it blew away part of the mountain. As people ran for their lives, they were suffocated by gaseous fumes, while those still inside their homes were buried beneath a torrential downpour of cinder and ash. The residents of Herculaneum made a desperate rush for the town exit but there was no escaping the darkness that descended on them. When it was all over, in a space of a few hours, Pompeii lay buried under 20 feet (7 metres) of ash and Herculaneum was sealed under a 40- to 100-foot layer of rock that formed when the ash was hardened by falling rain.

Entombed for centuries, the ancient townsite of Herculaneum was first discovered in 1706, when a well was being dug, and systematic excavations began in 1738. The larger site of Pompeii was discovered in 1748, providing the world with a detailed look at everyday Roman life as it existed in 79 AD. Archaeologists discovered hundreds of personal items in the city's private residences, including furniture, ornaments and beautifully preserved wall paintings in the villas of the

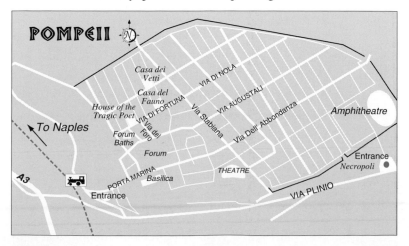

town's patrician class. By pouring liquid plaster into hollows left by disintegrated bodies, they were able to make hauntingly life-like casts, called 'impressions', of the people caught in their final moments – embracing, fleeing, retrieving valuable objects from their homes.

Today's visitors to Pompeii enter through the main gate (Porta Marina) near the forum, or through a back gate near the amphitheatre. A restaurant and shop carrying books and maps is located just north of the forum on Via del Foro (Forum Street). Areas of interest include the remains of the civic forum's public buildings, such as the Temple of Apollo and the Basilica, and the forum baths with a hot-water boiler and cold-water pool.

Just wandering the streets of Pompeii is a fascinating experience. The raised sidewalks and stepping stones were designed to keep pedestrians' feet dry when rainwater collected in the streets, and cat's eyes – small white marble stones – were set in the streets (and villa floors) to illuminate them at night. The villas and other private homes have been given descriptive names, and at the entrance to the House of the Tragic Poet is a 'Beware of Dog' sign, written in Latin with an accompanying mosaic of a guard dog. The best preserved villa is Casa Dei Vetti, where visitors can admire the home's atrium, frescoed walls and garden courtyard.

Mount Vesuvius, its sides scarred by lava flow, is visible from Naples, but reaching its crater takes some effort since a chair lift is no longer in operation. The mountain's fertile lower slopes are cultivated with vineyards which produce the famous Lachryma Christi (Tears of Christ) wine. The base of the volcanic mountain is encircled by a railroad and a trail can be hiked to the crater's rim.

CLASSIC CUISINE

The Italian Standards Institute recently released a criteria for 'genuine pizza', a Neapolitan dish that many people – including the president of the Italian Pizza Academy – consider to be classic cuisine. To meet the certification standards, which are based on the pizzas made primarily in Naples, a restaurant must dice the tomato a certain size (8 mm), use mozzarella cheese made from buffalo milk and bake the pizza at 390 to 453 degrees Fahrenheit. In Naples, where chefs have been making pizza for more than two centuries, the thick-crust style is used, but some chefs in Rome are insisting they will stick to their thin-crust style.

Meanwhile, some of Pompeii's archaeologists are working with a nearby winery to recreate the wine that was drunk by Romans when the eruption of Vesuvius in 79 AD brought all imbibing to a halt. A small vineyard has been planted in a plot that was used by a wine merchant of Pompeii, and the grapes will be cultivated and the wine fermented according to instructions contained in the Latin works of ancient authors.

CAPRI

The tiny island paradise of Capri, with its lush vegetation and delightful climate, has been an exclusive retreat since the days of the Roman Empire, when Emperor Tiberius owned 12 villas on the craggy island. Twentieth-century residents have included Gracie Fields, Rudolph Nureyev and the Swedish physician and writer Axel Munthe, who built Villa San Michele, now a museum, at Anacapri, one of two towns on the island. The main town of Capri, set atop limestone cliffs where herds of *capra* (goats) once roamed, overlooks Marina Grande where the passenger ferries dock and a visitor information office is located. Capri, a charming town of narrow lanes and tiny squares, can be reached by funicular, bus or taxi. The island's footpaths provide spectacular views of a cliff-edged sea, where coastal attractions include the Blue Grotto (a sea cave bathed in iridescent blue light) which can be reached by boat from Marina Grande.

AMALFI COAST

The Amalfi coast, from Sorrento to Salerno, is one of the most scenic in the Mediterranean, with its cliff-clinging roads and spectacular views. One seaside resort after another lies along this enchanting stretch of coast, including **Sorrento**, home of the legendary sirens who tried to lure Odysseus onto the rocks, and **Positano**, where John Steinbeck, in 1953, lived in one of its multi-coloured houses connected by hillside stairs above a crescent bay.

Amalfi, a small fishing port and picturesque resort overlooking the Gulf of Sorrento, was founded by Romans. It became, in the 9th century AD, an Italian maritime republic rivalling Pisa, Venice and Genoa in wealth and power. In the 12th century Amalfi was captured by Normans and sacked by Pisans, then hit by a destructive storm in 1343. Its Sicilian-Arab cathedral, built in the 11th century with later additions, reflects the influence of Arab invaders who had seized Sicily in 917 and raided the mainland, until they were driven out by the Normans.

Salerno flourished during the Middle Ages, establishing a medical school in the 9th century and erecting a Sicilian-Norman cathedral in the 11th century. During World War II, allied forces landed on the beaches near Salerno, where fierce fighting forced the Germans to retreat toward Naples.

SICILY (SICILIA)

The largest of the Mediterranean islands, Sicily is covered with hills and mountains which include Mt. Etna, an active volcano and the island's highest point at 10,700 feet (3,261 metres). The island was a granary of the ancient world with its fertile soil and a long, hot growing season, and agriculture remains the major industry with wheat, barley and maize as well as olives, citrus fruits, almonds and wine grapes all grown here. The per-capita income is low and unemployment is high on this densely populated island of over five million people. Hindering

Sicily's mountainous and fertile landscape.

this densely populated island of over five million people. Hindering government reforms is the Mafia, which originated in feudal times when lords hired brigands to guard their estates in exchange for protection from royal authority.

Sicily's first inhabitants were tribes named Sicani and Siculi. They were followed by the Phoenicians, who settled on the west coast, around modern Palermo, between the 8th and 6th centuries BC. Carthaginians settled nearby, at modern Trapani. The island's east coast was colonized by the Greeks who founded Syracuse, Catania and Zancle (now Messina). Syracuse emerged as the leader of these flourishing Greek colonies, which eventually rivalled the city-states of Greece itself. By 400 BC Sicily was a battleground between the rival empires of Carthaginia and Greece, a situation that would be repeated time and again as foreign powers fought for control of Sicilian soil. During the Punic Wars, Rome and Carthaginia battled for possession of Sicily, and when the Romans eventually seized control of the island, it became the 'Breadbasket of Rome'. Sicilian culture was enriched with Hellenization, but the Romans also exploited the island and established large estates that would eventually hinder its economic development.

After the fall of Rome, the island eventually passed to the Byzantines in 535 AD. The Arabs raided the island for two centuries before it finally fell in the 9th century. Next came the Norman conquest of Sicily in 1060, led by Roger I, whose son Roger II became the first king of Sicily, his brilliant court introducing Arab learning to western Europe. The Kingdom of Sicily came under Spanish rule in 1282, after it rebelled against Charles I of Naples, a brother of the French king. This would be the first of many times Sicily would struggle for independence from foreign rule, including revolts in 1820 and in 1848/49 when the bombardments of Messina and Palermo by Ferdinand II prompted Sicilians to call him 'King Bomba'.

Sicily finally voted to join the kingdom of Sardinia after being conquered in 1860 by Giuseppe Garibaldi, a popular Italian patriot and leading figure in the Risorgimento. Sicily's most recent invasion came during World War II when, in July 1943, Allied forces staged a large-scale amphibious landing from North African bases and, following a month of heavy fighting, Sicily was once again conquered. After centuries of exploitation by outsiders, Sicilians today are trying to rid their island of the Mafia – a name that came into being during the 19th century when it was applied to organized groups of brigands who disregarded legal authority, preferring to obtain justice directly, as in the vendetta. Despite this ongoing battle against organized crime and corruption, the Sicilians' independent spirit remains undefeated.

The Messina lighthouse guides passenger ferries from the Italian mainland into port.

PALERMO

The capital and largest city of Sicily, Palermo began as an ancient Phoenician seaport and was a Carthaginian military base when it was conquered by the Romans in 253 BC. However, it was during the Arab occupation of 831 to 1072 AD that the city prospered, rivalling Cairo with the Oriental splendour of its palaces, mosques and minarets. An important trading port between East and West, the city continued to flourish under the Normans – most notably during the reign of Roger II, whose court was a centre for the arts, letters and sciences.

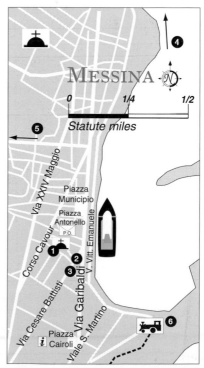

Messina's Norman-Romanesque cathedral was rebuilt following the 1908 earthquake. The bell tower's rare clock mechanism sets the statues in motion at mid-day.

Today's Palermo, plagued by poverty and heavy traffic, contains some unique and resplendent works of art which are located within walking distance of one another. Most notable is the Cappella Palatina (**Palatine Chapel**), located inside the **Norman Royal Palace**, which is the seat of the Sicilian parliament. This Arab-Norman chapel, built in 1132 by Roger II, is an artistic treasure containing glittering mosaics and a honeycombed ceiling. The pink-domed San Giovanni degli Eremiti (**Church of St. John of the Hermits**) was built in 1132 on the site of an old mosque, and its lovely cloister is filled with palm and citrus trees. Other historic buildings are the 12th-century cathedral; the National Gallery of Sicily, housed in the 15th-century Palazzo Abbatellis; and the Gothic Palazzo Chiaramonte, built in 1307. Shoppers in search of Sicilian handicrafts should visit the flea market on Via Papireto, behind the cathedral.

MESSINA

Situated on the Strait of Messina across from the Italian mainland, Messina is a busy seaport and the gateway to Sicily, with passenger ferries regularly pulling in and out of the harbour. Messina is a modern city that was rebuilt following a devastating earthquake in December 1908 which claimed 80,000 lives and destroyed 90 per cent of the buildings, including fine churches and palaces. The main attraction for pas-

The Sanctuary of Christo Re, a fortress possibly built by Richard the Lionheart en route to the Holy Land.

passengers arriving by ship at Messina is the nearby medieval town of Taormina with its Graeco-Roman theatre, but there are several interesting sights right in port, within walking distance of the pier. The main **shopping** area is along Via Garibaldi, Piazza Cairoli and Viale San Martino.

The **Norman-Romanesque cathedral** (1), was originally built by the Norman king Roger II in 1197. Modified over time, it was damaged by earthquakes in 1638 and 1783, then almost entirely destroyed by the 1908 earthquake. It has been reconstructed to its original Norman appearance, including most of the mosaics and works of art. The bell tower houses an astronomical clock, one of the largest and most complex of its kind, which was brought from Strasbourg in 1933, and which springs into mechanized action at mid-day.

The church of the Annunziata dei Catalani (**The Most Holy Annunciation of the Catalans**) (2) was founded in the 12th century on the ruins of an ancient temple of Neptune. Reflecting both Byzantine and Arab influences, the church today stands several metres below street level because of the city's progressive raising, due to earthquakes and reconstructions. Two of the original Quattro Fontane (**Four Fountains**) (3) still stand at the former cross-roads of via Austria and via Cardines. Baroque in design, two of them are now kept in the **Regional Museum** (4) which is about 1-1/2 miles from the cruise pier along the waterfront,

An original baroque fountain can be viewed down the street from the Catalans.

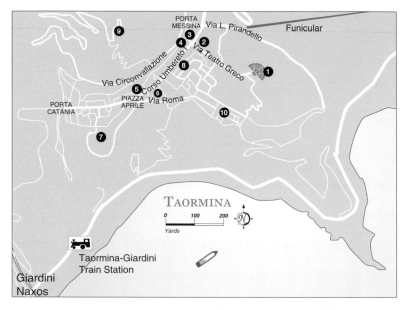

and which houses among its works of art a collection of Renaissance paintings, including one by native-born Antonello da Messina.

The **Sanctuary of Christo Re** (King Christ) (5) enjoys a prominent position on a hill overlooking the city and harbour. Originally a Norman castle, it may have been constructed by Richard the Lionheart. Serving as a royal residence, then a prison in the 19th century, it was rebuilt after the 1908 earthquake and is now a crypt containing the Messinese who died in World War II.

Taormina is located 27 miles (43 km) south of Messina, and can be reached by ship-organized shore tour, by train or by taxi. A return taxi ride from Messina to Taormina, with a two-hour wait at Taormina, costs about US$150. The Messina **train station** (6) is about half a mile from the cruise pier, and the train ride to Taormina takes about 45 minutes. The Taormina- Gardini station is situated below Taormina at the base of a hill and from there you can embark on a steep hike up to the town or hire a taxi (about US$20). A cable car, based about one mile from the train station, costs approximately US$2 each way.

TAORMINA

A medieval town and fashionable resort of undisputed charm, Taormina stands perched above the Ionian Sea, its steep stairways and twisting paths providing views of verdant hillsides covered with palms and pines. On clear days the active volcano of Mt. Etna dominates the southwest horizon, its massive peak rising to nearly 11,000 feet. Taormina's famous **Graeco-Roman amphitheatre** (1), built by the Greeks in the 3rd century BC, is beautifully situated to embrace this magnificent coastal setting of sea, sky and snowcapped mountain.

Taormina's Graeco-Roman amphitheatre (opposite). Churches and sea views await at Piazza Aprile (below).

Enlarged and rebuilt by the Romans in the 2nd century AD, the theatre today hosts an annual summer arts festival.

Just inside the town's north gate (Porta Messina) is the **Piazza Vittorio Emanuele** (2), site of the town's ancient Greek agora and later a Roman forum. The **Palazzo Corvala** (3), now housing a tourist information centre, was restored in 1945 and its features, spanning three historic periods of construction, include an Arab tower. The **Santa Caterina Church** (4) was built in the 17th century on the site of the Roman odeum, the remains of which are visible inside the church. The town's main street of Corso Umberto I, called 'Valeria' in ancient times, leads to Piazza Aprile – a large square overlooking the sea and site of the 17th-century **Chiesa di San Giuseppe** (5) and **Chiesa di Sant-Agostino** (6), built in 1448 and now the town library.

Farther along Corso Umberto I is the town's cathedral – **San Nicola** (Mother Church) (7) – which is similar in plan and from the same period as the Messina cathedral. A slight detour leads to the **Convent of San Domenico** (8), begun in 1374. Other sights include the **Naumachie** (a Roman wall that protected a large cistern) (9), and the ruins of **Castello Saraceno** (10), which sits on the site of the ancient acropolis and is reached by a long stairway. A stroll through the **public gardens** (11) is also recommended. **Shops** selling local handicrafts line the Via Teatro Greco (leading to the amphitheatre) and Corso Umberto I.

South of Taormina are the coastal cities of Catania and Syracuse. **Catania**, like Messina, is a port of access to Taormina. The city was heavily damaged in World War II, and in past centuries has been struck by earthquakes and volcanic eruptions, including one in 1663 when a mile-wide stream of lava flowed over the city. The 19th-century composer Vincenzo Bellini was born in Catania and his former home is now a museum. The cathedral (originally built in the 11th century) contains Bellini's remains, as well as the chapel of St. Agatha, the city's patron saint.

Syracuse (Siracusa) is best known for its Archaeological Park which contains a 5th century BC amphitheatre – one of the most complete Greek theatres to survive from antiquity – as well as the ruins of a Roman amphitheatre. Near the entrance to the park is Latomia del Paradiso, a garden area where a series of quarries served as prisons for the defeated Athenians who attacked Syracuse in 413 after it had become a rival city.

SARDINIA

The large and mostly mountainous island of Sardinia is as much renowned for its beautiful beaches and blue-green seas as its historical landmarks. This pastoral island does not lack, however, a fascinating past. A centre of trade in prehistoric times, Sardinia was mentioned in Egyptian texts as early as the 13th century BC, and remnants of those distant days lie scattered across the island in the form of conical stone towers (called *nuraghi*). The island became a source of grain and salt for the Romans. Then, with the fall of Rome, it was invaded by various forces. From the 11th to 14th centuries, Sardinia passed back and forth between Genoa and Pisa as they fought for supremacy over the island. The House of Savoy, a dynasty of western Europe, was eventually awarded Sardinia in 1720 in exchange for Sicily (which went to the Holy Roman Emperor) and Duke Victor Amadeus II became the first king of Sardinia, its kingdom including Savoy, Piedmont and Nice.

Italy's famous revolutionary hero Giuseppe Garibaldi, born at Nice in 1807, served as a youth in the Sardinian navy. He was a man of action and when revolution swept across Europe in 1848, Garibaldi fought for Sardinia against Austria. In 1851 he bought part of the small island of **Caprera**, which lies off Sardinia's **Costa Smerald**a (Emerald Coast) of low cliffs and idyllic coves. He had, by then, abandoned the republican cause to throw his support behind Victor Emmanuel II, king of Sardinia, and in 1860 Garibaldi led the victorious conquest of Sicily before crossing to the mainland to conquer Naples. After relinquishing his conquests to Sardinia, he retired to his island property and shortly thereafter Victor Emmanuel II was proclaimed king of a united Italy.

When the Aga Khan, cruising the Mediterranean by yacht, sought shelter from a storm along the Costa Smeralda in 1965, he was smitten with the scenic beauty that had attracted the seafaring Garibaldi a century earlier. He built the upscale resort village of **Porto Cervo** and thus began the Costa Smeralda's incarnation as a chic enclave for wealthy vacationers, many of whom arrive by luxury yacht. Less-developed (and less expensive) beach resorts lie west of Porto Cervo along the island's northern tip of beach-fringed bays.

Ports of call on Sardinia include **Porto Torres** and **Alghero** – a 14th-century walled town and popular resort with sandy beaches and limestone cliffs where the Grotto of Neptune, a huge cavern, has been carved by the pounding sea. Six miles north of Alghero, on the road to Porto Torres, is a concentration of prehistoric tombs carved into the hillside, their chambers connected by corridors. Bronze statuettes depicting people, gods and animals have been retrieved from the tombs and nuraghi of Sardinia's earliest inhabitants. These are on display at the Archaeological Museum in **Cagliari**, the island's capital. Cagliari was a Pisan stronghold during the wars with Genoa from the 11th to 14th century, and its Romanesque-Gothic cathedral, extensively rebuilt, reflects this Pisan influence, as does the massive Tower of St. Pancreas, built by Pisans in 1304. The city also has a Roman amphitheatre.

Cruise passengers watch the sun set behind the volcanic Lipari Islands lying north of Sicily.

CHAPTER SIX

MAINLAND GREECE

G reece is a mystical land of impassable mountain ridges and fertile plains filled with olive trees and orange groves. Monasteries dot pine-forested slopes and isolated valleys run down to the sea. Strabo, a Greek geographer from the 1st century BC, wrote that 'the sea presses in upon the country with a thousand arms', for no point in Greece is further than 65 miles from the coast. With limited natural resources, the Greeks have always looked to the sea for their livelihoods through fishing, shipping and trade. Today the country's merchant marine is one of the largest per capita in the world, and an extensive ferry system connects Greece's mainland ports and widely scattered islands.

This seafaring tradition harks back to ancient times when the first stirrings of Western civilization began on the shores of mainland Greece, then spread outward, across the Mediterranean Sea, to far-flung islands and distant coastlines. The well-travelled Herodotus, known as the Father of History, wrote a long and engaging narrative of antiquity's major events, a classic work that was being used as a reference in 2003 by a team of marine archaeologists searching for artifacts when a fisherman's net snagged two ancient helmets in the waters off Mount Athos. This was the site, pinpointed by Herodotus, where an invading Persian fleet sank during a storm in 492 BC, marking the decline of Persia's military might and the ascent of classical Greece.

Many of our modern institutions, such as democracy, are based on concepts that originated in classical Greece and formed the foundations of modern law, science, engineering, architecture and philosophy. The early Greeks' pursuit of knowledge is reflected in the myriad of words they have given the English language, from arithmetic to zodiac. The Greek gods and heroes are part of our everyday vocabulary, their names associated with everything from spacecraft to jogging shoes, as in Apollo (the god of light) and Nike (the winged goddess of victory). And when satellites beam us televised coverage of the Olympic Games, the torch-bearing runner who lights the eternal flame is reenacting yet another time-honoured ritual rooted in ancient Greece.

When Athens hosted the summer games in 2004, the Olympics returned to their country of origin for the first time since the modern games began there in 1896. The Marathon was raced on its ancient course, starting at the town of Marathonas and finishing in Athens at the Panathinaiko Stadium, its horseshoe-shaped marble-clad seating built for the 1896 Olympiad as a replica of the ancient stadium that had stood on the same site. While the world watched, the athletes and spectators recaptured a moment from the past that was once the glory of Greece.

GREECE AT A GLANCE

The term Greek derives from *Groeci*, the Latin name for a small Hellenic tribe of ancient Greece, and the Greeks refer to their country as Hellas. About 10 million people currently live in Greece and the faith of the majority is Eastern Orthodox. Greek, with a variety of local dialects, is the dominant language, and the well educated speak a more 'classical' version of the language than the masses. English is widely spoken. The Greek alphabet has fewer letters than the English, and when a Greek word or name is translated into English there are often several variations in the spelling.

The scenery of Greece is diverse, ranging from pine-forested mountain slopes to sandy beaches. Although only 25% of the land is arable, farming is a major industry. Goats and sheep are raised in the arid mountain pastures and the crops grown in the valleys below include corn, wheat, citrus fruits, olives and grapes. Greece's large urban areas are the capital of Athens (including the port of Pireaus) and Thessaloniki in Macedonia. Since 1973, Greece's form of government has been a presidential republic.

TRAVEL TIPS

Currency: The unit of currency is the euro. Most banks are open from 8:00 a.m. to 1:00 p.m., Monday through Friday. The currency exchange dispenser at the National Bank of Greece on Syntagma Square in Athens is open 24 hours a day.

Dining: The Greeks usually have lunch at 2:00 p.m. and dinner after 8:30 p.m., but restaurants often open earlier in tourist-oriented centres. A typical Greek meal begins with a plate of mezedes (hors d'oeuvres) such as salami, fish, dolmades (stuffed vine leaves) and tiropites (cheese pies). Main dishes include kalamaraki (squid fried in olive oil) and moussaka (a baked casserole of mincement, eggplant, onions and other ingredients). Olive oil is used extensively in Greek cooking and salads, along with fresh herbs and cheeses such as feta. For dessert, try a baklava – layered pastry with nuts, which is often served warm. Ouzo is Greece's national aperitif. A strong spirit, it is served either neat or watered down, which turns the clear beverage milky.

Shopping: Stores generally are open from 9:30 a.m. to 8:00 p.m., with some closing for a few hours in the early afternoon. Bartering is acceptable in Greece. The country's excellent handicrafts include ceramics, wood carvings, handwoven carpets and embroidered tablecloths. Wool sweaters, leather goods and gold or silver jewellery are often good buys. Fishermen's caps and natural sponges are popular souvenir items.

Outdoor tables at a restaurant in Navplion (above). Greece's rugged mainland coastline (below).

Getting Around: Many transportation improvements were made in and around Athens in preparation for the 2004 Olympics. The new international airport for Athens is located at Spata, about 18 miles east of the city centre, and is connected by a six-lane highway and a rapid transit rail line, the latter providing 20-minute connections.

Connections between Athens and the port of Pireaus (a distance of six miles) can be made by taxi or by a new subway system, with stations located at Syntagma Square, Monastiraki Square and Omonia Square in downtown Athens. If you're returning to the ship after a day in port, be sure to allow at least an hour to travel between downtown Athens and Pireaus by taxi, for the streets in between are often heavily congested and traffic can move very slowly.

Telephone Access Codes: AT&T 00-800-1311; MCI 00-800-1211; SPRINT 00-800-1411; CANADA DIRECT 00-800-1611.

ATHENS

Athens, the capital and largest city of Greece, is situated on a plain dotted with low hills, the most famous of which is the Acropolis – 'high point of the city'. This is where the Parthenon, a masterpiece of classical Greek architecture, has stood for more than 2,000 years. Constructed of white marble in the 5th century BC, when Athens was at its height as a military power and of intellectual life, the Parthenon has survived

The Parthenon (opposite) stands atop the Acropolis. The changing of the guard in Syntagma Square (below).

centuries of wars, sieges, sackings and pilferings. Dedicated to the virgin goddess Athena, this ancient temple rises above the congested streets of downtown Athens as testament to the city's glorious past.

At the foot of the Acropolis lies the ancient marketplace, the Agora, where democracy originated and the seeds of Western culture were sown. The proud and patriotic citizens of ancient Athens supported the statesman Pericles, whose reforms included payment for jury duty, enabling even the poorest citizens to serve. Pericles, a patron of the arts, commissioned the city's best architects and sculptors to design and oversee the completion of the Parthenon and other great buildings, including a theatre for staging the plays of Euripides and Sophocles. It was during this 'Golden Age' of Athens that Socrates strolled barefoot in the streets, engaging people in dialectic conversation and rational debate.

Years later, as the 5th century BC drew to a close, Athens faced ruination at the hands of its rival city-state Sparta. After succumbing to Sparta in the Peloponnesian War, Athens attempted to regain its past glory, rebuilding both its navy and the fortified walls that protected the city and connected it to the port of Pireaus. But the city-state had lost its imperial status and Athens declined into a provincial city. Its great contributions to civilization endured, however, as Hellenistic culture spread Athenian achievements throughout the world.

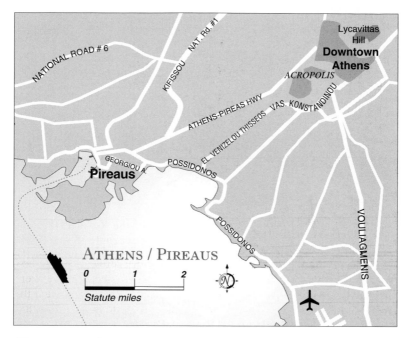

EXPLORING ATHENS

Athens, located six miles inland from the port of Pireaus, is a sprawling metropolis of four million people – about a third of Greece's population. One of Europe's most affordable cities, its major historic sites are situated right in the downtown core, within walking distance or a short taxi ride of one another. The heart of Athens is pedestrian-friendly, with traffic restricted inside the commercial centre. The main travel information bureau is located on **Syntagma (Constitution) Square** (1), a centre of activity with hotels, banks, coffee shops, bars and night clubs surrounding the square. Overlooking the Square's east side is the **House of Parliament**, originally constructed (1836-1842) as a palace for King Otto, Greece's first monarch, and Queen Amalia. The Tomb of the Unknown Soldier (1929) stands in front where it is guarded day and night by two soldiers. A changing of the guard takes places every hour.

Just south of the Parliament Building is the **National Garden**

Temple of Olympian Zeus

The quiet streets of Plaka lead up to the Acropolis.

(2), designed for the Royal Palace and first planted between 1838 and 1860. Further south, along Amalias, is the **Arch of Hadrian** (3), built of Pentelic marble. (Penteli is one of the mountains surrounding the basin of Athens.) On the northwest corner of the site is the **Temple of Olympian Zeus** (4), completed in 131 AD by the Roman emperor Hadrian.

To the west of Amalias lies the lovely neighbourhood of Plaka, where narrow stone-paved streets wind past neoclassical homes and sidewalk cafes. On foot is the best way to approach the Acropolis, and a morning ascent along the quiet roads of Plaka will reward you with enchanting, ever-changing vistas. On the upper slopes is **Anafiotika** (5), a village of small white houses erected in the 1830s by master builders from the Aegean island of Anafi, who were hired by the first King of Greece to build his palace. To stave off homesickness while living in Athens, they recreated their island village along the edge of the Acropolis. One of Plaka's most famous structures is the **Monument of Lysicrates** (6), a round structure built in about 334 BC. Its engaged columns are the oldest known example of exterior Corinthian capitals. Along the northern edge of the Plaka area is **Cathedral**

Famous monuments atop the Acropolis (above) include the Propylaea (below) and the Caryatids of the Erechtheum (bottom).

Square (7) where the city's Great Metropole Cathedral, built in the mid-1800s, overshadows the much smaller Little Metropole, built during the 12th and 13th centuries.

The **Acropolis** was regained by Greece in 1833 when the Turkish guard departed. The sacred rock, which had been used as a fortress for 1,500 years, was then declared a national monument. Archaeological work began almost immediately to excavate and restore the site, and what we see today is the result of extensive reconstruction. A mosque built inside the Parthenon during Turkish occupation was torn down, as were ramparts, walls and a Frankish tower. Restoration work is ongoing and has taken place within the Parthenon since 1983, preventing public admission.

Entrance to the Acropolis is made along a processional way that passes through the colonnaded buildings of the **Propylaea** (8), its interconnected stone structures including the Temple of Athena Nike. This imposing entrance prepares you for the sight of the **Parthenon** (9), the great temple of

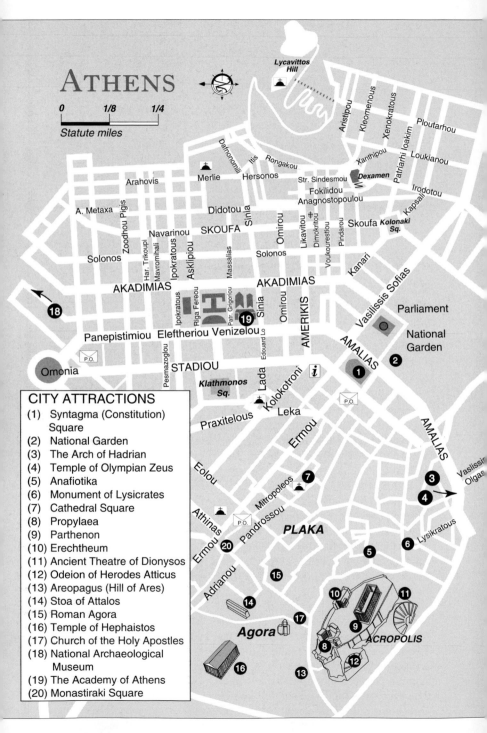

ATHENS

0   1/8   1/4

Statute miles

CITY ATTRACTIONS

(1) Syntagma (Constitution) Square
(2) National Garden
(3) The Arch of Hadrian
(4) Temple of Olympian Zeus
(5) Anafiotika
(6) Monument of Lysicrates
(7) Cathedral Square
(8) Propylaea
(9) Parthenon
(10) Erechtheum
(11) Ancient Theatre of Dionysos
(12) Odeion of Herodes Atticus
(13) Areopagus (Hill of Ares)
(14) Stoa of Attalos
(15) Roman Agora
(16) Temple of Hephaistos
(17) Church of the Holy Apostles
(18) National Archaeological Museum
(19) The Academy of Athens
(20) Monastiraki Square

Odeion of Herodes Atticus (above). Ancient Theatre of Dionysos (opposite).

Athena. Designed by the architect Ictinus and built using white, fine-grained marble, the columned Parthenon is a masterpiece of refinement and restraint. Originally it housed a colossal statue of the goddess Athena, which was created by the famous sculptor Phidias, her skin made of ivory and her draperies of beaten gold. Other temples on the Acropolis include the **Erechtheum** (10), the roof of its south porch supported by the figures of six maidens, called the Caryatids. These famous figures are all copies of the originals, four of which are housed inside the Acropolis Museum. The fifth is being restored, and the sixth was removed by Lord Elgin in 1806; it is now on display in the British Museum.

Situated on the southern slope of the Acropolis are the **Ancient Theatre of Dionysos** (11), originally built of wood then reconstructed with marble during the 4th century BC, and the **Odeion of Herodes Atticus** (the Herodeion) (12), which was built in 161 AD by a wealthy Athenian and is still used today for summer concerts. West of the Acropolis is the **Areopagus (Hill of Ares)** (13) on which the city's supreme court of law once stood. This outcrop of slippery stone is also the spot from which St. Paul delivered his first sermon to the Athenians in 51 AD.

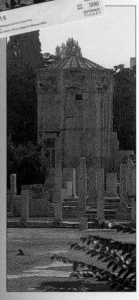

The road below the Areopagus connects the Acropolis with the **Agora**, the 'gathering place' of ancient Athens. Political meetings, religious festivals, dramatic contests and athletic competitions took place in this civic and commercial centre, where temples and altars stood alongside law courts and libraries. Philosophers such as Socrates strolled the open squares and shady colonnades, while chariots wheeled along a broad street called the Panathenaic Way, which was the annual scene of a grand procession that ascended the Acropolis during the festival of the goddess Athena. The town's craftsmen and merchants lived on the southern edge of the Agora, in modest homes with inner courtyards. On the nearby hill of Pnyx, in full view of the Acropolis, Athenians would gather to hear famous orators – such as Pericles – deliver their speeches.

Temple of Hephaistos (top). Tower of the Winds (above). Stoa of Attolas (opposite).

The **Stoa of Attalos** (14), rebuilt in the 1950s according to its original design, is a classic example of Greek civic architecture. Originally a shopping arcade with 21 shops on each of its two floors, the Stoa now houses the **Agora Museum** and contains excavated items of everyday use in the ancient Agora, including bronze ballots from the law courts and terracotta animals from a child's grave. Behind the Stoa of Attalos is the **Roman Agora** (15), a marketplace completed in 10 BC, its marble-paved pedestrian mall once lined with colonnades, shops and shrines built with financial assistance from Julius Caesar and the Emperor Augustus. Still standing is the **Tower of the Winds**, an octagonal structure which served as a water-clock, compass and weather-vane.

Academy of Athens (above).

The **Temple of Hephaistos** (16) was dedicated to the goddesses Hephaistos and Athena, both patron divinities of the arts and crafts. Built in 449 BC, the Temple housed statues of the two goddesses and is today one of the best preserved Greek temples of ancient times. A fountain house, its water supplied by an underground terracotta pipeline, once stood beside the site now occupied by the **Byzantine Church of the Holy Apostles** (17), built in 1000 AD and restored in the 1950s.

A shopping street near the Agora (above right). Grecian busts and statuettes (opposite) are popular souvenirs.

The **National Archaeological Museum** (18) houses an impressive collection of antiquities extending from Neolithic to Roman times. The **Academy of Athens** (19), completed in 1887 and flanked by columns topped with statues of Athena and Apollo, is a fine example of neo-classical architecture. The summit of **Lycavittos Hill** can be reached by funicular, footpath or road, and provides panoramic views of the city and surrounding area – a spectacular sight when the sun is setting.

Shopping: Some of the best streets for souvenir hunting are in the vicinity of Monastiraki Square. The market on Pandrossou Streets sells a selection of handicrafts, and the pedestrian mall that runs along the north side of the Agora is lined with stalls selling leather goods, silver jewellery and an array of ceramics, including Grecian urns, busts and statuettes. Other popular shopping streets are found in the vicinity of Syntagma Square and Kolonaki Square, the latter being where high-fashion boutiques and specialty shops selling quality gifts are located.

PELOPONNESUS

Until a canal was built in the late 1800s, a narrow neck of land connected the Peloponnese peninsula with central Greece. In ancient times this isthmus served as a land bridge for tribes migrating into the area from the north but it eventually posed a barrier to trading ships travelling between the Adriatic and Aegean seas. The citizens of Corinth, with harbours on both sides of the isthmus, solved the problem and grew wealthy in the process by building a connecting road across which they hauled ships on rollers. Attempts at constructing a canal began in 67 AD under the Roman emperor Nero, but it wasn't until completion of the Corinth Canal in 1893 that a 4-mile-long waterway was finally cut through the thick rock.

The Peloponnese peninsula was first inhabited as early as 4000 BC by a primitive people. Their Neolithic culture was gradually displaced by the Greek-speaking Mycenaeans, who brought with them advanced

A small cruise ship is pulled through the narrow Corinth Canal.

techniques in pottery, metallurgy and architecture. This Mycenaean civilization (also referred to as Helladic) had mercantile contact with the island of Crete, which was the centre of Minoan culture. From 1600 to 1400 BC these two rival civilizations competed for maritime control of the Mediterranean, with the Mycenaeans finally triumphing after several devastating earthquakes struck Crete.

In the 14th and 13th centuries BC, war-like Achaean tribes from the north invaded the Peloponnese. As these migrating Achaeans swept southward, the Ionic tribe assimilated with the Mycenaeans and the centre of Greek culture became Mycenae. This era is now called the Heroic Age, thus named for the incredible feats of Hercules and the events described in Homer's *Iliad* and *Odyssey*, including the Trojan War (c. 1200 BC). The Mycenaeans' mythological gods and heroes are reflected in Peloponnese place names, starting with Pelops who won his wife in a chariot race by bribing, then murdering, the opposing charioteer, thus bringing a curse upon his descendants.

When a new wave of invaders called Dorians arrived in about 1100 BC, their arrival marked a cultural decline. Many of the displaced Achaeans left and migrated across the Aegean Sea to Asia Minor. The conquering Dorians built huge stone buildings, and Argos, Corinth and Sparta became powerful city-states. Corinth, strategically situated on on the Isthmus of Corinth and protected by a citadel, became a wealthy maritime power and rival of Athens in the 7th century BC. Sparta was Corinth's traditional ally and, by the 6th century BC, was Greece's strongest city. Located in a mountain-walled valley, Sparta became an armed camp, its culture dominated by war. Sickly boy babies were abandoned in the mountains, while those fit for military service were taken from their mothers at the age of seven to begin training. State business was conducted in secrecy while serfs, closely monitored for fear of insurrection, farmed the land.

All of Greece's city-states participated in the Isthmian games, held at Corinth every two years in spring, and the Olympic games, held in summer every four years at Olympia. The warring city-states were as proud of a victory at the Olympic games as they were of winning a battle, and this nationalistic spirit fuelled a competitiveness among the participants. Home-coming champions were hailed as heroes and showered with gifts and privileges. The Games began in 776 BC, possibly earlier, and running was initially the only event. Over time, new events were added, including the pentathlon, chariot racing and a foot race with armour. Greek women held their own games called Heraea. The Olympic games were eventually discontinued in the 4th century AD by the Romans, who had conquered the Peloponnesus in 146 BC.

The once-powerful Peloponnesian League of city-states, led by Sparta, had allowed prolonged power struggles with Athens, and each other, to weaken them all and open the door to foreign invasions – a situation that would prevail until an 1821 rebellion in the Peloponnesus launched the Greek War of Independence.

Olympia, located about 15 miles (24 km) from the port of Katakolo, was an important centre of worship and the venue for the Panhellenic Olympic Games. Situated in the beautiful valley of Alpheios, the site contains ruins of the great temple of Zeus which housed a statue by Phidias, the famous sculptor whose works adorned the Parthenon. Counted among the Seven Wonders of the World, this colossal ivory and gold statue of Zeus sitting on an ornamented throne was later removed to Constantinople where it was destroyed by fire in 475 AD. Other sculptures from the Temple of Zeus are on display in a nearby museum, along with the outstanding statue of *Hermes with the Young Dionysos* by Praxiteles (c. 340 BC). Ruins associated with the Olympic games include the remains of the Gymnasium and the Stadium. The sacred flame of the modern Olympic games begins its journey here with a torch-lighting ceremony held in front of the Temple of Hera, the oldest Doric temple in Greece.

The hill-top town of **Mistra (Mystras)**, about 30 miles from the port of Githio, is the most representative example in existence of a Byzantine city from the 14th and 15th centuries. The medieval castle overlooking the town was built in 1249 by Frankish crusader Guillaume de Villehardouin. He and his knights were defeated 10 years later by the Byzantines, who built a palace for the emperor as well as numerous churches and monasteries decorated with beautiful frescoes. The town, its wealth generated by a lucrative silk industry, grew down the hillside, with the upper and lower sections connected by two gates. The lower town contains most of the monasteries and churches, while the upper town contains the Palace of the Despot (a rare example of civic Byzantine architecture), an adjacent church and the Frankish castle, which is reached after a 30-minute ascent. The magnificent view from the castle includes a bird's eye look at the gullies of Mt. Taygettus – where the Spartans are said to have tossed sickly babies. Nearby mod-

A cruise ship anchors off Navplion on the Peloponnese peninsula.

ern Sparta bears little resemblance to the ancient city-state that once dominated the central Peloponnese peninsula. Relying on their military power for protection, the Spartans didn't bother building walls, so only a few temple ruins remain.

The fortified island village of **Malvasia (Monemvasia)**, a unique and intact medieval town, is joined by a causeway to the Peloponnese mainland where a modern tourist resort, with fine beaches, lies in contrast to the Byzantine churches and Venetian mansions contained within the walls of Malvasia. A fortress in the Middle Ages, Malvasia was also a commercial port which exported malmsey wine.

Navplion (Nafplio) is not only a fascinating port of call, it provides access to the famous sites of Mycenae, Epidaurus and ancient Corinth. Navplion's name derives from Nauplius who, according to Greek mythology, was the son of Poseidon and father of Palamedes, a hero of the Trojan War. The old quarter, situated on a peninsula, is medieval in character. It was originally built by the Venetians when Venice was a dominant sea power in the Mediterranean. The **Bourtzi** (1), an island fortress at the harbour entrance, was built by the Venetians in 1473.

Looming high above the red-roofed buildings is another Venetian fortress, the **Palamidi** (2). It was successfully stormed by the Ottoman Turks in 1715, when they captured the town. The view from the Palamidi is breathtaking and can be gained either by ascending the stone steps that lead to its 700-foot summit (a fairly strenuous climb best made in the coolness of early morning) or by taking a taxi or ship-organized excursion.

At the foot of the Palamidi, beside the Cultural Centre of Navplion, is the Tourist Information

The Bourtzi fortress (opposite).

An elegant square on V. Konstantinou Street (below).

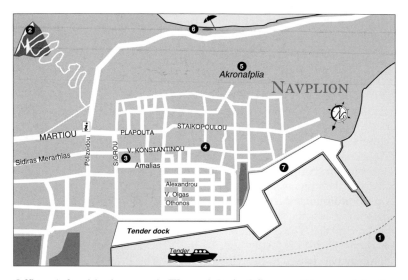

Office. A few blocks away is **Three Admiral Square** (3), named for the English, French and Russian admirals who defeated an Egyptian fleet that was bringing reinforcements to the Turks during the Greek War of Independence. Elegant neoclassical townhouses overlook this square on V. Konstantinou Street, which leads west to **Syntagma (Constitution) Square** (4) where, on its west side, the Archaeological Museum is situated, housing a collection of Mycenaean artifacts.

Greek insurgents took Navplion from the Turks in 1822 and the town was, from 1830 to 1834, the first capital of independent Greece, its first National Assembly convening next to the museum in a Turkish mosque on Staikopoulou Street. Both Konstantinou and Staikopoulou are picturesque pedestrian streets lined with restaurants and shops. Side streets with stone steps lead off Staikopoulou, up the hillside toward **Akronafplia** (5), a barren hilltop fortified over the centuries by various occupants and now the site of two hotels which can be reached by a lift or by a road that runs past **Arvanitia** (6), a fully serviced beach. The town's **promenade** (7) is pleasant for strolling with its waterfront cafes and views across the harbour.

Ship-organized shore excursions from Navplion generally

The view from atop the Palamidi fortress in Navplion.

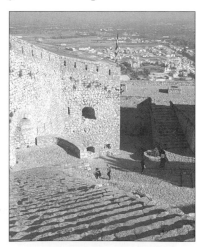

include a half-day coach trip through the scenic countryside to Mycenae, Epidaurus or Corinth, often with a stop at the top of Palamidi on the way back to the ship. One option for passengers interested in viewing a Mycenaean ruin is to visit nearby **Tiryns**, 3 miles (5 km) away (US$25 return fare by taxi). Although not as extensive as Mycenae, this ancient citadel was the mythological birthplace of Hercules. Its impressive entrance ramp evokes a sense of past power, when the palace was protected by two massive walls with an outer and inner gate designed to trap attackers between the walls.

Massive walls remain at the entrance to the citadel at Tiryns.

Mycenae, 13 miles (21 km) north of Navplion, is one of Greece's most famous archaeological sites. The centre of the far-reaching Mycenaean civilization, these ancient ruins are shrouded in a dark history of murder and betrayal. Agamemnon, the great king of Mycenae, is a tragic figure of Greek mythology. He belonged to the deadliest of dysfunctional families, a curse having been brought upon it by his grandfather Pelops. Agamemnon's father didn't help matters by murdering his brother's children and serving them for dinner. When Agamemnon left for the Trojan war, he sacrificed his eldest child to guarantee good winds for his sailing ships. This deed incurred the hatred of his wife Clytemnestra, who murdered Agamemnon upon his return. To avenge their father's death, Orestes and Electra murdered their mother.

Several hundred years later, the poet Homer wrote about Mycenae and his writings were used by the 19th-century archaeologist Heinrich Schliemann to provide clues as to where to dig at this ancient site. Spurred by Homer's references to gold, Schliemann's dramatic discoveries included royal tombs filled with gold treasures. The site's heavy fortifications and massive masonry include the Lion Gate, Europe's oldest monumental sculpture, which in ancient times was closed by a double wooden door sheathed in bronze and secured with a wooden bar. The largest of the beehive tombs, located outside the walls of the city, is the Treasury of Atreus (also called Agamemnon's Tomb).

Epidaurus, situated 15 miles (24 km) east of Navplion (US$60 return taxi fare), is an ancient sanctuary and the site of Greece's best-preserved amphitheatre. Greek drama lives on at the 14,000-seat theatre of Epidaurus, which was considered beautiful and harmonious when

Orange groves and other crops grow in the verdant Peloponnese countryside near Navplion.

built in the 4th century BC and is still acclaimed for its excellent acoustics. Since the theatre's restoration in the 1950s, theatrical events have been staged here each summer, including the late Maria Callas performing the title role of Bellini's opera, *Norma*. To commemorate, in September 1997, the 20th anniversary of the famous diva's death, friends from the world of opera gathered for a seaboard ceremony off Epidaurus. As a recording of her voice resounded across the water, olive wreaths were tossed into the Aegean Sea, where her ashes had been scattered two decades earlier.

Old Corinth, 40 miles (65 km) from Navplion, was occupied throughout history by the Romans, who razed the town, then rebuilt it, and by Goths, Crusaders, Ottoman Turks and Venetians. Corinth was finally returned to Greece when captured by Greek insurgents in 1822, only to be destroyed by an earthquake in the 1850s. A new city was founded nearby, and the ancient ruins remaining at Old Corinth include the Temple of Apollo, a Roman amphitheatre and a hilltop fortress. A short distance away is the four-mile-long (6.4 km) Canal of Corinth, built between 1881 and 1893, which cuts across the Isthmus of Corinth. Its sheer rock walls rise 285 feet (87 metres) above the water on both sides, accentuating the narrowness of the canal, which can be transited only by smaller ships.

CENTRAL & NORTHERN GREECE

On the northern shores of the Gulf of Corinth, the port of Itea accesses the ancient site of **Delphi**, where the great temple to Apollo was first built in the 6th century BC. Apollo, one of the most important Olympian gods, was associated with prophecy, and Delphi was the seat of ancient Greece's most famous and powerful oracle. Pilgrims seeking help brought gifts which lined the Sacred Way leading to the temple, where a priestess sat on a tripod inhaling divine vapours and uttering oracular messages. It has long been speculated that the 'divine vapours'

Pythia inhaled were volcanic gases, and geologists now surmise that a major fault zone below the temple provided pathways for seeping gases, including ethylene and methane – known to have narcotic effects. Delphi played a unique role amid the warring city-states, for its splendid setting on the lower slopes of Mt. Parnassus was a meeting place for the important Amphictyonic League, as well as the site of the Pythian Games, held every four years.

Meteora, about 75 miles (120 km) from the port of Volos, is a surrealistic sight of barren rock formations rising from a flat, fertile plain. Their geological origins still a mystery, these pinnacles of rock became a place of refuge for monks during the Middle Ages. What began as small cells evolved into great monasteries holding rich murals and religious treasures, and they form a surreal sight perched atop columns and crags of black rock. Ropes and pulleys are still used for transporting provisions, but visitors can now walk up steps cut into the precipitous slopes. These who make the strenuous climb are rewarded with sweeping views of the plain of Thessaly – ringed by mountains, including Mount Olympus, which separate Thessaly from the plains of Macedonia.

Macedonia's port of **Thessaloniki (Salonika)** is Greece's second-largest city and was named the 1997 Cultural Capital of Europe. Its world-renowned museum houses treasures of Philip of Macedon, father of Alexander the Great, and in 1997 it hosted a special exhibit of priceless icons, manuscripts and other objects never before seen outside the monasteries of Mount Athos. Consisting of 20 monasteries of the Eastern Orthodox Church, this theocratic community is perched high above the water on the southernmost tip of the Khalkidhik peninsula. Since the first monastery was founded around 953 AD, this community of monks has been allowed to govern itself by committee and its strictly enforced rules include the banning of all females and dogs. When US ambassador Thomas Niles visited Mount Athos in 1994, he chose to sleep outside one of the monasteries on a cot, as did the rest of his large retinue, rather than be separated from his beloved dog, Mr. Wheat.

Monastery of Saint Nicholas
Anapafsas, Meteora.

the **GREEK ISLES**

Statute miles
0   50   100

CHAPTER SEVEN

THE GREEK ISLES

T he only way to see the Greek isles is slowly, by boat. At least that's what Cary Grant told Doris Day in the 1962 comedy, *That Touch of Mink*, when he likened these islands to fine paintings. "You mustn't rush up to them," he said. Anyone who has stood at a ship's rail and watched the sun rise above a Greek isle will know exactly what he meant. A seaborne arrival, as the morning sun warms the terraced hillsides and whitewashed houses of a sleepy fishing port, is a travel experience of unsurpassed romance.

Greece has more than 2,000 islands, comprising about one-fifth of the country's total land area, yet only some 200 are inhabited. When the Greek government announced a plan in 1995 to resettle some of its uninhabited islands, the response – both domestic and foreign – was overwhelming. Thousands of people from all walks of life sought to move to one of the many islands left abandoned after World War II when their inhabitants emigrated in droves to the cities. Whether or not Greece's repopulation plan is successful, it's obvious the allure of the Greek isles is as strong as ever.

For general information and travel tips on Greece, please turn to pages 256 and 257.

A ship's tender heads ashore at the Greek Island of Patmos.

THE CYCLADES

The Cyclades, comprising about 220 islands in total, stretch across 1,000 square miles (2,600 sq. km) of the Aegean Sea. Serving as stepping stones for migrating tribes in ancient times, these scattered islands were inhabited before 4000 BC by a primitive people who, as they progressed from Stone Age to Bronze Age civilization, developed a culture called Cycladic, which is a Greek term for circular. Delos was the centre of this culture, with other islands forming a rough circle around it.

Today the island group's administrative centre is located on Syros, but its historical heart remains on Delos – the mythical birthplace of Apollo. According to Greek legend, Apollo's mother Leto was a lover of Zeus, and she was cursed by his jealous wife. A pregnant Leto wandered the earth until the god Poseidon took pity on her and gave her a place to rest by anchoring the floating island of Delos with four diamond columns. There she gave birth to Zeus's children – a girl named Artemis and a boy named Apollo, who became the most important of the Greek gods.

The Cyclades are quintessential Greek islands, with their charming fishing harbours and cozy seaside villages. Box-shaped houses climb the hillsides and dome-roofed chapels cling to cliffsides, their dazzling whiteness appearing in stark contrast against the deep blues of the sky above and the sea below. The most popular of the Cyclades are the tourist-oriented islands of Santorini and Mykonos, which lies close to uninhabited Delos.

MYKONOS (MIKONOS)

This arid island, 35 square miles (90 sq. km) in size, is the most cosmopolitan of the Cyclades. Although extremely popular with tourists, Mykonos has retained a Cycladic charm with its whitewashed houses and hilltop windmills. Shops, cafes and tavernas line the town's water-

Mykonos Harbour is a popular port of call in the Greek Islands.

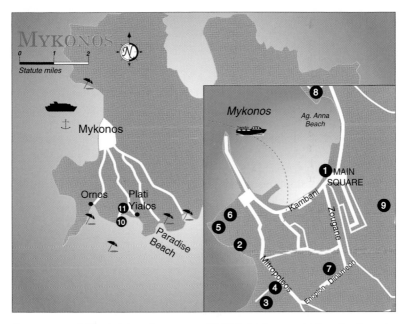

front area while serious shoppers will delight in wandering the town's winding backstreets. Originally designed to disorient marauding pirates, these twisting alleyways are now lined with boutiques frequented by the rich and famous. Jacqueline Onassis, Ingrid Bergman and Elizabeth Taylor are some of the famous women who have shopped at Galatis on the town's **main square (Platia Manto)** (1), also referred to as 'taxi square'.

Little Venice (2), a neighbour-hood located south of the main harbour, is where you'll find local artwork and handicrafts. The waterfront buildings in this section are a reminder of the island's Venetian period, as is the **Roman Catholic Cathedral** (3), its entrance hall bearing the coat of arms of the Ghisi family who took over Mykonos in 1207. Next door is the **Greek Orthodox Cathedral** (4) and nearby, on a promontory overlooking the sea, is the **Church of Paraportiani** (5), its cluster of whitewashed chapels a much-photographed sight. A short distance away is the **Folklore Museum** (6), housed in the 300-year-old house of

a former sea captain. Other local museums are the **Aegean Maritime Museum** (7), the **Archaeological Museum** (8) and a **working windmill** (9) on the east side of town. More windmills stand on a headland south of Mykonos town.

The island's south coast boasts a string of beautiful beaches, all a short taxi or bus ride from the town. **Psarou** (10), one of the finest (and busiest) features restaurants and a variety of watersports. **Plati Yialos** (11) also has restaurants and is popular with families. The beaches lying to the east – Paranga, Paradise, Super Paradise and Elia – are designated nude beaches, and can be reached by boat from Plati Yialos or by road from Mykonos town.

Cruise ships stopping at Mykonos usually offer excursions to the neighbouring island of Delos. Several local operators also provide excursions to Delos, selling tickets at the boat dock.

DELOS

The smallest of the Cyclades, this tiny island was of great commercial and political importance in ancient times, when its temple of Apollo held the treasury of the Delian League, a confederation of Greek maritime states led by Athens. Council members of this league, which was formed in 478 BC to finance a war against Persia, would meet on the politically neutral island of Delos and contribute funds, troops and ships to the league. Its treasury was moved from Delos to the Athenian Acropolis in 454 BC but the island continued to prosper, becoming the site of a thriving slave market in the 2nd century BC. Sacked by Mithridates VI of Pontus (modern Turkey) in 88 BC, Delos never recovered and was abandoned near the end of the 1st century BC.

Excavation of its temples, theatres, commercial buildings and private houses began in the 1870s and today the uninhabited island is visited by day trippers arriving solely to see its ancient ruins, which include the small sanctuary of Dionysos dating to 300 BC, a restored temple to the goddess Isis, and the famous Terrace of the Lions, carved from marble in the 7th century BC.

Fira town is perched high above the harbour on Santorini.

SANTORINI (THIRA)

Myth and modern science meet on the island of Santorini, believed by many to be the lost kingdom of Atlantis which was destroyed by a volcanic explosion in about 1500 BC. This popular belief endures despite claims by Greek philosopher Aristotle that his teacher Plato invented this fabled city as an allegory for his fellow Athenians, using Atlantis to illustrate a Utopian state.

The stunning setting of crescent-shaped Santorini does little to dispel the island's legendary past. Set on the exposed rim of a submerged volcano, Santorini's harbour is a flooded crater. Cruise ships anchor in this watery caldera and tender passengers ashore to the base of an idyllic clifftop town where a switchback staircase ascends the crater wall. The town of Fira can be reached on foot, by donkey or by cablecar. Whatever your chosen mode of ascent, the view from above is spectacular. Across the bay from Fira lies the quiet island of Thirasia, a fragment of the caldera's rim that was once joined to the main island until an eruption in 236 BC. Dotting the bay are the smaller Burnt Islands which rose from the caldera in subsequent eruptions. Palia Kameni emerged in 196 BC, and Nea Kameni was formed and enlarged by a series of eruptions, the first occurring in 1711, the

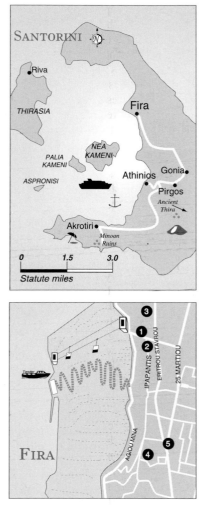

second in 1866, and the most recent in 1925. In the past, a reliable warning of an imminent eruption occurred when the surrounding sea turned a milky colour due to an increase in underwater sulphur emissions.

Before the catastrophic eruption of c. 1500 BC, Santorini was colonized by Minoans from Crete. Archaeological digs indicate these people heeded the warning earthquakes and abandoned the island before the massive explosion. The island was next settled by Phoenicians, a seagoing people from modern Lebanon who, by 1250 BC, had displaced the Aegeans as navigators and traders of the Mediterranean. The island was later colonized by Laconians from the Peloponnese peninsula, under their leader Thira, which is the official name of the island. A new centre was established on the island's east coast, its archaeological

Cruise ships anchor below the spectacular cliff-top town of Fira on the island of Santorini.

remains dating mainly from late Hellenistic and Roman times. From the Middle Ages onwards, the island was called Santorini after St. Irene, protector of the island. The Greek god of fertility and wine, Dionysus, is also associated with Santorini – appropriately so because excellent grapes for wine making thrive in the volcanic soil.

Santorini is now a fashionable resort, its terraced streets of white-washed buildings lined with chic shops and restaurants, but the numerous domed churches are still prominent amid the tourist attractions. Near the **cable car ticket office** (1) are the town's two museums – the **Archaeological Museum** (2) containing artifacts from ancient Thira (major frescoes from the Minoan site were removed to the National Archaeological Museum in Athens) and a private cultural museum housed in a restored mansion near the **Roman Catholic Cathedral** (3). More churches, including the **Greek Orthodox Cathedral** (4), are situated a few blocks south of here, as is **Platia Theotokopoulou** (5), the town's main square where tourist services are located.

At the south end of the island, near Akrotiri, is the ancient **Minoan site**. Still under excavation, it was discovered in the late 1960s by Professor Spyros Marinatos, who was trying to prove that the Santorini blast had created a tsunami wave that wiped out the Minoan civilization on Crete. This theory has been largely discredited, but what Marinatos did discover was an extensive ancient city preserved for 35 centuries beneath tons of volcanic ash. Streets of multi-storeyed warehouses and homes, their walls decorated with vivid wall paintings, were revealed as the ash was cleared away, but the absence of skeletons indicated there had been a mass evacuation prior to the explosion. Geological evidence indicates the island was racked beforehand by earthquakes, ample warning for the island's residents. Most of the beaches on Santorini are black, due to the fallen volcanic ash.

CRETE

In ancient times, during the 2nd millennium BC, one of the world's earliest civilizations thrived on the island of Crete. Called Minoan for the legendary King Minos, its great palaces were adorned with colourful murals and enormous clay pottery. The most famous palace ruins are found at Knossos, near the port of Iraklion, on Crete's north coast. Built on a hillside, the original palace was destroyed by an earthquake around 1700 BC, then rebuilt on an even grander scale. Although it was damaged by another earthquake around 1450 BC, recent excavations of the 'new' palace have revealed a labyrinth of rooms and passages, porticoes and staircases, richly decorated with lyrical wall paintings and once serviced by a complex drainage and water-supply system.

Iraklion's Old Harbour with its 13th-century fortifications.

Minoan habitation of Crete began about 3000 BC. The island's forests supplied wood for boat building, and the residents of Crete engaged in seagoing trade. Their island lay only 400 miles from the northern shores of Egypt, where an advanced civilization influenced the cultural development of Crete. Neolithic village life evolved into an urban society centred around great palaces, such as the one at Gournia, near the modern port of Aghios Nikolaos, and at Phaestus, on the island's south coast. The Minoans even developed a system of writing but they built no military fortifications or religious temples. The swirling, free-flowing motifs of Minoan art were often inspired by nature, their gambolling dolphins or leaping mountain goats portrayed with a joyful fluidity of movement.

When Dorian Greeks settled on the island several centuries after the collapse of the Minoan civilization, they established dozens of city-states, Knossos emerging as one of the most powerful. The island remained a centre of trade, and was a pirate haven from the 3rd century BC until it was conquered by the Romans in 68 BC. The Byzantines were next to rule Crete, starting in 395 AD, followed briefly by the Arabs in 824, before the island was reconquered by the Byzantines in 961. Next to rule the island, from 1204, were the Venetians, who built a wall around Iraklion (then called Candia) to defend this important trading port from pirates. When the Ottoman Turks over-ran the island in the 1648, the garrison at Iraklion fought off the invaders for 21 years before surrendering in 1669.

A mountainous island of deep gorges and farm-filled valleys, Crete's long history of invasion and resistance has resulted in an independent people who are proudly Greek. Famous Cretans include the 16th-century painter El Greco, the Nobel Laureate Odysseus Elytis, and Nikos Kazantzakis, author of *Zorba the Greek*. The indomitable spirit of the Cretans was personified in the great statesman Eleutherios Venizelos, born in Crete and educated in Athens, who returned in 1896 to play a prominent role in the island's insurrection against Turkish rule. Turkey, at the intervention of European powers, was eventually forced to evacuate, and in 1908 Crete proclaimed its union with Greece.

Crete would come under invasion once again, during World War II, when British and Greek forces on the island were overwhelmed by a German airborne invasion. The German troops occupying the island eventually surrendered to the British navy in late 1944.

The singer Nana Mouskouri was born in Chania, on Crete's north coast, shortly before the Second World War, and her childhood recollections include the excitement of the olive harvest when she dipped

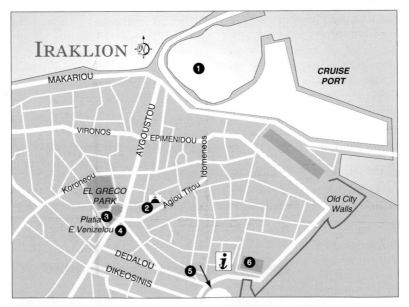

her mother's freshly baked bread into newly pressed extra virgin olive oil. Nutritionists would approve, because the good health enjoyed by the citizens of Crete has been attributed to their steady diet of extra virgin olive oil, made from the first pressing and flavoured with fresh herbs grown in the mountains.

Iraklion (Heraklion), capital and major cruise port of Crete, was founded by Muslim Saracens in the 9th century, before falling under Byzantine rule in 961. The walls that still ring the city were built by the Venetians after they took possession of Crete in the 13th century. The largest of the six bastions is Martinengo Bastion, where a stone slab marks the burial place of the famous Greek writer Kazantzakis, who died in 1957.

GETTING AROUND

Passengers can either book a ship-organized tour to nearby Knossos or go independently by taxi (the fare is approximately US$30 return). Your ship-organized excursions may also include a half-day coach tour to the Minoan ruins at Phaestos. These ruins, set on a plateau, are not as extensive as those at Knossos, but the drive across the island offers an opportunity to see some of Crete's mountainous landscape, including a stunning view from Phaestos of the mountain-bounded plain of Mesara.

A taxi into town costs about US$5, but it's a fairly pleasant and easy walk from the cruise dock. Follow the waterfront to the **Old Harbour** (1) for a look at its Venetian fortifications, then proceed up Avgoustou toward the town's central platia (square), named for the great statesman Eleftherio Venizelou. Along the way you'll pass some beautiful neo-classical buildings and the Byzantine church **Agios Tito**s (2), named for Crete's patron saint, who is credited with converting the islanders to Christianity.

There are several outdoor cafes at **Platia Venizelou** (3) and, standing in the centre of the square, is a marble Renaissance fountain called The Lions. Across the street is the **Agios Markos** (St. Mark) (4), built by the Venetians in the 13th century and now housing an exhibition

Agios Titos, a Byzantine church, was named for Crete's patron saint.

centre. The maze of back streets lying east of the square contains more outdoor cafes and a selection of shops, including the boutiques on Daedolou Street, which leads to **Platia Eleftherias** (5). Here, on the square's north side, are the **Visitor Information Office** and the **Archaeological Museum** (6). Built between 1937 and 1940, the museum stands on the former site of a Catholic monastery from the Venetian period, which was destroyed by an earthquake in 1856.

A quiet square near Agio Titos (above). Minoan vase dating from 1700 BC in Archaeological Museum (opposite).

The grounds of the museum hold gardens, benches and a coffee shop. Inside the museum is an extensive collection of Minoan artifacts, including original wall paintings from the palace at Knossos. A pamphlet showing the floor plan and a description of each room's exhibits is provided when you purchase your admission ticket. A wooden model, helpful for envisioning what an ancient Minoan palace complex looked like, is located upstairs.

KNOSSOS

About three miles (5 km) from Iraklion is the site of the ancient palace at **Knossos**. Many legends are associated with this great palace, including the myth of the Minotaur – a monster with the head of a bull and the body of a man – who was confined within a labyrinth beneath the palace, where he devoured sacrificial youth sent as tribute from Athens.

Ruins of the palace of Knossos (bottom of previous page). Minoan wall art at Knossos (opposite).

The palace was built around a central courtyard and boasts excellent masonry construction. The columns were originally made of wood – those we see today are reproductions. English archaeologist Sir Arthur Evans spent years uncovering the ruins (between 1898 and 1935) and reconstructing the buildings. Some archaeologists have criticized these reconstructions, but they do offer the lay person a good idea of what the palace looked like in Minoan times. Highlights of the site include the Queen's Megaron, approached by the Grand Staircase, which is decorated with the Dolphin Fresco. Adjacent is the Queen's Bath, containing a terracotta bathtub.

THE DODECANESE

Pronounced *doh dek en ees* and meaning 'twelve islands', this island group in the eastern Aegean Sea is situated much closer to the shores of Turkey than those of Greece. However, the Greek culture that has endured on these islands, despite centuries of foreign occupation, began in antiquity. Initially influenced by the Minoan civilization of Crete, the Dodecanese were eventually settled by the Dorians, who had established the Greek city-states of Sparta and Corinth before migrating across the Aegean Sea. Those who landed on Rhodes discovered a fertile island blessed with a subtropical climate.

When the Greek cartographer Eratosthenes compiled a map of the known world in the 3rd century BC, the central point on his chart was

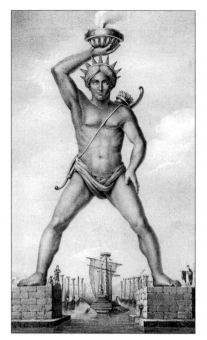

The Colossus of Rhodes (above).
Street of the Knights (below).

the island of Rhodes. Situated only 12 miles from the shores of Asia Minor (modern Turkey), the busy port of Rhodes was a trade link between East and West. Built in 408 BC as a planned 'modern' city with a grid system of streets and a water/sewage system, it was protected by a fortified wall. These were prosperous times for Rhodes and, after withstanding a siege in 305/4 BC, the city commissioned three local sculptors to create a colossal bronze statue of Helios, the sun god, which was erected at the harbour entrance but later destroyed by an earthquake. Rhodes was one of the most beautiful and best organized cities of the Hellenistic world. The arts and sciences flourished, and Rhodes became a centre of learning, its 800-seat theatre used for teaching philosophy and oration, with Julius Caesar among those who studied there.

Rhodes, however, had begun to decline economically and it descended into a period of obscurity that lasted until the Knights of St. John landed on its shores in 1306. A religious-military order founded in Jerusalem in the middle of the 11th century, the Knights of St. John had been driven from the Middle East by Arab forces and were stationed on Cyprus when their Grand Master negotiated a deal to purchase Rhodes from the Genoese who were then administering the Dodecanese Islands.

The Knights of Rhodes, as they called themselves during their 213-year rule of the island, were supported financially by the feudal lords of Europe, for they were regarded as spearheads of Western expansionism and defenders of Christianity against the Arab 'infidels'. The order was a hierarchical organization of knights (noblemen), chaplains and sergeants (sons of freemen), who hailed from seven European nations – Provence, Auvernge, France, Italy, Aragon, England and Germany. Each national group was called a 'tongue', had its own 'inn' or meeting place within the fortified city, and was responsible for defending a specific section, or 'curtain', of the wall.

Prosperity returned to Rhodes under the Knights. Their imposing Palace of the Grand Master stood on the town's highest ground, while the winding streets below teemed with merchants, both local and foreign, as well as bankers, artists and tradesmen. Goods arrived and departed by ship, including perfumes, saffron, pepper, caviar and wax. Wheat was imported from Cyprus and Sicily, wine from Crete and Italy. Hostilities between the Knights and the Turks were set aside in favour of trade – silks and carpets from Asia Minor were exchanged for woollens and other commodities from Western Europe. Local labourers produced textiles, soap and sugar, and major building projects undertaken by the Knights kept the masons employed. The sounds of feasting and carousing spilled into the streets while the wealthy nobility strolled the town's beautiful gardens in their elegant clothes.

All of this prosperity came to an end when Turkish forces laid siege to mighty Rhodes in 1480. With a fleet of 170 ships carrying 100,000 soldiers, the Turks mounted attack after attack, finally taking the Tower of Italy and penetrating the city walls. Knights raced from other parts of the city to fight the invaders, who finally retreated after a bloody battle and soon sailed away. An earthquake struck Rhodes the following year, completing the devastation wreaked by the Turkish siege, but the Knights rebuilt the town and helped the struggling populace by providing tax exemptions and wheat distribution.

More than 40 years passed before the Turks attacked again, bombarding the town's landward fortifications while a huge fleet blockaded the harbour. Led by Sulayman I, thousands of Turks were killed but they relentlessly continued their attack until the townspeople, running out of food and the will to resist, convinced the Knights to surrender. On January 1st, 1523, the Knights and about 5,000 Rhodians boarded ships and set sail for Crete, leaving Rhodes to the Ottoman Turks. The Turks held the Dodecanese for the next 400 years, until they were occupied by Italian forces in 1912. Captured by the Allies during World War II, the islands were returned to Greece in 1947.

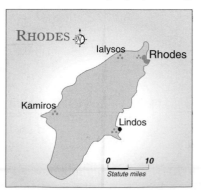

Sea Gate is one of several fortified entrances to the walled town of Rhodes.

RHODES ATTRACTIONS

The cruise ships dock in the city's commercial harbour, opposite the medieval fortress of Old Rhodes. It's a short distance to the walled town where you could easily spend an entire day wandering the cobble-stone streets of this medieval fortress. The town was badly damaged by earthquakes in the mid-1800s, and many of the buildings and fortifications were repaired during the Italian occupation. Further damage was caused by incendiary bombs during World War II. The Greek Archaeological Service is now in charge of restoration and conservation of this World Heritage Site.

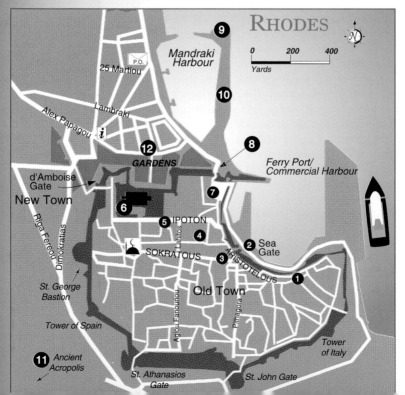

The harbour and walled town of Rhodes (above). Courtyard in the Grand Master's Palace (opposite).

The **Gate of the Virgin** (1) and the much-photographed **Sea Gate** (2) both provide access into the walled town from the harbour front. Not far from the Sea Gate is busy **Platia Ippokratous** (3), its outdoor cafes, shops and fountains overlooked by the Kastellania (Courthouse) of the Knights. Nearby, off Mousio (Museum) Square, is the **Archaeological Museum** (4), housed in the New Hospital of the Knights, which is one of the most handsome and best preserved buildings from the time of the Knights. Here the sick were cared for by physicians under the supervision of eight 'brothers' – one from each 'tongue' (nationality) of the Order.

D'Amboise Gate (below), was named for a French Grand Master.

The Hospital's north side runs along **Ippoton (Street of the Knights)** (5), which was the most important thoroughfare in the medieval town. It ran through the middle of the Collachium, a section of town once separated from the

A Hellenistic statue from Kos in courtyard of the Grand Master's Palace (above). Bronze deer at harbour entrance (below).

rest by an inner wall. The knights lived inside the Collachium, spending their days engaged in military exercises and prayer. Each 'tongue' had an 'inn' along the Street of Knights at which its members could gather to dine and discuss matters. At the top of the Street of the Knights stands the **Grand Master's Palace** (6). Built on the site of a Byzantine citadel, the Palace became the town's administrative centre and was the last refuge for its citizens during times of attack.

Left to crumble by the Turks and damaged by earthquakes, the final blow to the Palace occurred in 1856 when some gunpowder stored in the vaults of the nearby Church of St. John blew up, leaving only the palace's ground floor standing. The Italians restored and modified the palace between the two world wars, when it became a residence and headquarters for Fascist Minister C.M. de Vecchi.

Interior highlights of the Palace include a grand staircase, made of marble, which leads to the upper storey. There a series of vaulted halls contain carved furniture, Chinese vases and marble sculptures from the Hellenistic period, including a copy of *Laocoön* that was created in the 1st century BC by three Rhodian sculptors. The expansive floors of these chambers are covered with Hellenistic and Roman tile mosaics brought by the Italians from buildings on the island of Kos.

North of the Street of the Knights is the Platia **Argirokastrou** (7) where the ancient ruins of the Temple of

Venus (Aphrodite) are situated opposite the **Freedom Gate** (8). Beyond this gate is Mandraki Harbour, the ancient port that was guarded by the Colossus of Rhodes. Today a bronze deer stands on either side of the harbour entrance. During the reign of the Knights, the **Fort of St. Nicholas** (9), which stands at the end of the stone pier, was an important fortress protecting the harbour from Turkish assaults; the tower now houses a lighthouse. The three windmills still standing on the **Mole of St. Nicholas** (10) were used by the Knights for grinding wheat. West of the medieval town is the **ancient acropolis** (11) where the ruins include the Temple of Apollo, the Odeum and the Stadium.

Before the town of Rhodes was established in 408 BC, the island's three important cities were Ialysos, Kamiros and Lindos on the southeast coast. **Lindos**, overlooking the shipping lane to the east, was a major naval and trading centre between the 8th and 6th centuries BC. The town's acropolis – a promontory rock overlooking the sea – was both a fortress and sanctuary housing a temple of Athena. In the year 51 AD, the Apostle St. Paul landed by small boat in the bay and introduced Christianity to the island. The ancient acropolis was further fortified during the Byzantine period, then by the Knights.

A hike up the stairway leading to the fortress rewards visitors with a panoramic view of two crescent-shaped beaches and the hillside village of Lindos, its narrow streets and whitewashed

Windmill on the Mole of St. Nicholas (above). A typical street of Old Rhodes (below).

The ringing of church bells and fragrance of flowers fill the air on the peaceful island of Patmos.

buildings containing mansions from the 17th century. The Byzantine church of the Panayia was built in the 15th century, and later decorated with wall paintings. A coach tour to Lindos is often offered as a half-day shore excursion from Rhodes; the return taxi fare from Rhodes is about 25,000 drachmas. Buses run regularly between Rhodes and Lindos; the **bus station** (12) is located north of the Old Town's north wall.

PATMOS

The serene and scenic island of Patmos has been a place of pilgrimage ever since St. John the Evangelist landed on its shores in 95 AD. One of the three apostles closest to Jesus and author of the fourth Gospel, an elderly John was banished by the Roman Emperor Domitian to the tiny island of Patmos, where he sought shelter in a cave. Now called the **Holy Grotto of the Apocalypse** (1), it was in this cave that God revealed to John a magnificent yet terrifying vision, described in the Book of Revelation, which John spent the next 18 months dictating to his disciple Prochorus.

Ten centuries later, a Byzantine monk named Hosios Christodoulos, who had built a monastery on the island of Kos, travelled to Constantinople to request permission to found the **Monastery of Saint John the**

A fresco in the Monastery of St. John the Divine.

Skala's waterfont (above). A shady street in Skala (below). Natural sponges (bottom) have been harvested in the Med ever since the ancient Greeks began using them for bathing and scrubbing.

Divine (2) on Patmos. His request was granted, in exchange for his holdings on Kos, and construction of the monastery commenced in 1088, its thick walls and battlements built to protect the main church, several chapels and a treasury of icons and gold-embroidered vestments. Its forecourt is decorated with frescoes illustrating the life of St. John, and its library contains priceless books and manuscripts, including one from the 6th century containing portions of St. Mark's gospel. The fortress-like monastery stands on a hill above the whitewashed village of **Chora (Hora)** (3), which is a labyrinth of interlocking lanes, houses and bell-topped chapels.

Getting Around: Patmos is an ideal island to tour independently because it is small and the roads are fairly quiet. The large cruise ships anchor outside the small port of **Skala** and tender their passengers ashore. A taxi stand with a dis-

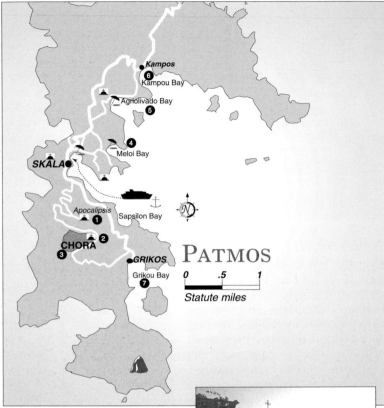

PATMOS

Kampos
Kampou Bay

Agriolivado Bay

Meloi Bay

SKALA

Apocalipsis
Sapsilon Bay

CHORA

GRIKOS
Grikou Bay

0   .5   1
Statute miles

patcher is located near the cruise
ship quay and tender dock. Taxi
drivers will transport visitors up
the hill to the monastery, then
return at an appointed time to
bring them back down, for a fare
of about US$20. Buses also run
between Skala and Chora. It
takes about half an hour to walk
the path up to the cave, then on
to the monastery. Scooters can
be hired in town – US$10 for
two hours.

Beaches on the island can be
reached by hired boat or by road.
Just north of Skala and within
walking distance (about 20 minutes) is the sand and gravel
beach at **Melloi** (4). Further

A tiny square in Chora.

along is the sandy beach at **Agriolivado** (5). One of the island's best beaches is **Kampos** (6), a ten-minute taxi ride or 20-minute boat ride north of Skala. **Grikou Bay** (7), below Chora, has a sandy beach.

SAMOS

The mountainous and fertile island of Samos has been inhabited since the Bronze Age. In the 11th century BC, Samos was colonized by Ionic Greeks, becoming over time a centre of culture, commerce and maritime power. The many poets, sculptors and scholars who were born or lived on Samos included the early philosopher Pythagorean who founded the Pythagorean school, its teachings in mathematics, geometry, medicine and astronomy leading to numerous discoveries, including the belief that the earth was a spherical planet revolving about a fixed point. According to the Greek historian Herodotus, the legendary fabulist Aesop also lived on Samos in the 6th century BC. Initially a slave, he eventually gained his freedom and wrote the famous Aesop's fables.

NORTHEAST AEGEAN ISLANDS

Lying off the coast of Turkey, these remote and widespread islands include rugged **Limnos (Lemnos)**, which was volcanic in origin and sacred to the Olympian god Hephaestus (originally an Asian fire god). Fruit trees and wheat are grown in the island's fertile lava soil, which has also produced since ancient times a medicinal earth used for treating open wounds and snake bites. The island was a colony of Athens in c. 500 BC, and excavations at Hephaestia have revealed a theatre of the Hellenistic period, which was repaired in Roman times. With the decline of the Byzantine Empire, Limnos was captured first by the Genoese in 1204, then by the Venetians in 1464, who held the island for just 15 years before it was seized by the Ottoman Turks. A Genoese-Turkish fortress overlooks the small fishing harbour of Myrina, the island's capital and primary port.

Lesbos (Lesvos), a centre of Bronze Age civilization, became a cultural centre of Greece in the 7th century BC. The female poet Sappho, who wrote love lyrics to other women, was born here in the early 6th century BC and the term 'lesbian' is derived from the name of her island home. Other famous figures associated with Lesbos include the statesman Pittacus, who ruled the island for ten years, and the philosophers Aristotle, Theophrastus and Epicurus, who taught at the Philosophical Academy. After revolting against Athens in 428 BC, Lesbos later passed to Macedonia, Rome, and the Byzantine Empire. It was captured by Ottoman Turks in 1462 and, along with Limnos, was returned in 1913 to Greece.

Olive groves and citrus fruits flourish on the island's fertile hillsides. Mitilini is the chief town, its harbour overlooked by Gattelusi Castle, which was originally constructed by the Byzantine emperor Justinian. The Theatre of Mytilene, built in Hellenistic times on the slope of a hill, is where Pompey reportedly sat on a luxurious throne and watched performances lauding his military successes.

IONIAN ISLANDS

This chain of lush, mountainous islands lying off the west coast of Greece is shrouded in myth – both ancient and modern. The island of Ithaca was, according to Homer's legends, the home of Odysseus who, in the course of his 10-year odyssey, struggled with angry gods and insistent sea nymphs before returning home to his waiting wife and son.

A modern Greek tale unfolded on another Ionian island – the tiny isle of Skorpios – when its owner, the shipping tycoon Aristotle Onassis, married one of the world's most famous women, Jacqueline Kennedy, in October 1968. Born in Turkey, Onassis was 16 when he left his homeland in 1922 to revive the family tobacco business in Argentina. Receiving Greek citizenship in 1925, Onassis bought his first ship in the early 1930s and, upon marrying the daughter of an influential Greek ship owner in 1946, Onassis, his father-in-law and a brother-in-law formed the most powerful shipping clan in the world. Onassis, founder of Olympic Airways, was no stranger to controversy when he set his sights on the widely-admired widow of President Kennedy. Mrs. Kennedy had been placed on a pedestal following her husband's assassination and, like a fallen Greek goddess, she stunned the world with her marriage to a man who was much older, shorter and wealthier than she, with a fortune estimated between $500 million and $1 billion.

Shipping has long been big business in the Ionian islands. Corfu (Kerkira) was settled in 730 BC by Corinthian colonists, who then competed with Corinth for the shipping trade in the Adriatic. An early naval battle was waged between these two maritime rivals in 665 BC, and this was just the beginning of numerous wars and invasions that would, over the centuries, leave their mark on each of the Ionian Islands. During the 14th and 15th centuries the maritime power of Venice seized all the islands from the Byzantine Empire, and they remained part of the Venetian Republic until it fell in 1797. The islands were then transferred by treaty to France, only to be seized two years

The lovely Ionian Islands are known for their dramatic scenery and sugary white beaches.

Corfu town (above) and a local restaurant (opposite).

later by a Russo-Turkish fleet. In 1807 Russia returned
them to France, but they were soon occupied by the
British navy and remained under Britain's protection
until they were at last ceded to Greece in 1864.

CORFU (KERKIRA)

Corfu has long been considered one of Greece's loveliest islands.
Homer wrote glowingly about Phaeacia – a luxurious and joyful island
whose seafaring people welcomed sailors – and it's quite likely Corfu
was this island, upon which Odysseus was shipwrecked. Other poets
and writers since Homer have been smitten with the beauty of Corfu,
including Goethe, Oscar Wilde and Lawrence Durrell, who believed
that Shakespeare, in *The Tempest*, modelled Prospero's island on
Corfu.

The Turks also coveted Corfu, but the island's inhabitants resisted
Turkish invasion, including two famous sieges in 1537 and 1716. Corfu
is a fertile island, and its major industries are farming, fishing and
tourism. Corfu town, one of Greece's largest medieval towns, is beautifully preserved with cobblestone alleyways which wind past churches,
fountains and statues. To the east, on a promontory once guarded by a
moat and bridge, are the remains of the **Old Fortress** (1) built by the
Venetians in 1546. To the west stands the Venetian-built **New Fortress**
(2). Originally constructed in 1577, its maze of tunnels and moats was
later modified by the French and British, whose citadel stands at its
heart.

The town's main square – the **Esplanade** (3) – contains a cricket
pitch and Victorian bandstand, and is bordered on its west side by
Georgian and Venetian townhouses, their overhanging balconies decorated with wrought-iron railings. The Liston – an arcaded sidewalk of
cafes and restaurants – was built by the French under Napoleon. This

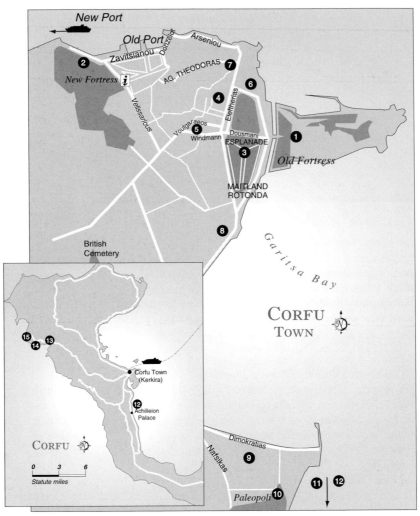

beguiling blend of architecture is repeated throughout the historic quarter – the 16th-century red-domed **Church of St. Spyridon** (4), the 17th-century Venetian lodge now housing the **Town Hall** (5), and the 19th-century colonnaded **Palace of St. Michael and St. George** (6), built as a residence for the British Lord High Commissioner. Another beautiful building houses the **Corfu Literary Society** (7), the oldest in Greece.

It's a pleasant walk along Garitsa Bay to the **Archaeological Museum** (8), with its fine collection of excavated artifacts. At the south end of the bay is the **Church of Saints Jason and Sosipater** (9), a 12th-century Byzantine church decorated with beautiful icons. Just south of the bay, near the public beach, is the **Palace of Mon Repos** (10). Set amid gardens, this mansion was built in 1831 as a summer residence for Britain's Lord High Commissioners. It became a royal residence and was the birthplace of Prince Philip, Duke of Edinburgh, who is a grandson of George I, the Danish prince who reigned as Greece's king from 1863-1913. Greece abolished its monarchy in 1973, when the country became a presidential republic, and in 1990 the Palace was expropriated by the Greek government.

About a mile past the Palace of Mon Repos is **Kanoni** (11) with its captivating view across a mountain-bounded inlet dotted with two idyllic islets: one joined to shore by a narrow causeway and containing the monastery of Vlacherna; the other covered with green foliage which all but hides its 13th-century chapel. (Buses travel regularly between Kanoni and the Esplanade.) South of Kanoni is the gaudily grand **Achilleion Palace** (12), which was used as a springtime retreat by Germany's Kaiser Wilhelm II in the early 1900s.

The cliff-edged coves of **Palaeokastritsa (Old Castle)** (13), on the island's west coast, are also exceptionally beautiful. Buses run regularly between Corfu town and Palaeokastritsa, its beautiful beaches and turquoise waters considered by some archaeologists to be the ancient site of Homer's city of the Phaeacians. The sea caves here can be explored by peddle boat. For panoramic views of the coves, follow the road west of Lacone to the **Byzantine monastery** (14), perched atop a cliff, or carry on further to **Bella Vista** (15) – a natural terrace overlooking the sea near the ruins of Angelokastro, a 13th-century fortress.

CEPHALONIA (KEFALONIA)

The largest of the Ionian islands, Cephalonia is a pastoral place of lush valleys and a rugged coastline indented with beach-lined bays. Mt. Ainos rises over 5,000 feet and was in ancient times crowned with a temple to Zeus. In 1953, the island was devastated by earthquakes of such force Mt. Ainos was split and Argostoli, the island's main town, was demolished. Today, fishing and sheep farming are major industries on the island, and local products include honey and white wine.

Fiscardo, a traditional fishing port at the island's northern tip, swells with visiting yachts in summer and attracts celebrities such as Tom Hanks and Bruce Springsteen. The movie *Captain Corelli's Mandolin*, staring Nicholas Cage and Penelope Cruz, was filmed here in 2000, its story based on the occupation of the island by Italian troops during World War II and their subsequent massacre by invading Germans after the fall of Mussolini.

The cruise ships pull into **Sami**, on the island's northeast coast, from which island roads lead to local attractions. At the south end of the island stands the Monastery of Agios Andreas and, looming above it, a Venetian castle built in 1504, which affords splendid views of a valley and villages spread out below. At the island's southeastern tip, in the hamlets of Katelios and Sama, are two outstanding beaches and the ruins of a 3rd century BC building from the Roman era, possibly the home of a wealthy businessman, containing well-preserved mosaics.

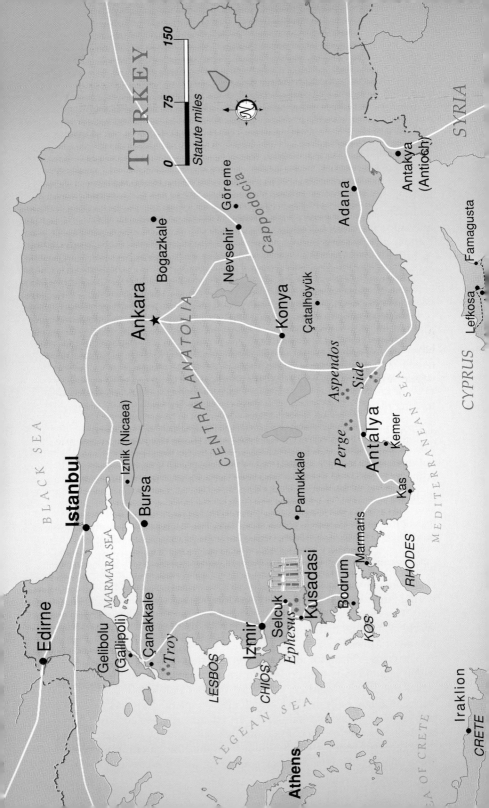

CHAPTER EIGHT

TURKEY
AND THE BLACK SEA

F or centuries, visitors have recorded their first impressions of Turkey as being exotic and mysterious. Part Europe, part Asia, Turkey remains a unique Mediterranean destination with a complex history and a diversity of natural beauty. Arching gold beaches and lush stands of palm and cypress trees are juxtaposed with ruins and artifacts – some of which date back to the Bronze Age.

Recent evidence suggests Turkey's history dates back even farther than the Bronze Age. If ever there was a Garden of Eden, it may well have been situated in a narrow valley of southeastern Turkey where researchers have found DNA traces of the founder crop of einkorn wheat. A number of experts believe this area, on the edge of the ancient Fertile Crescent of Iraq, is where agriculture and the beginning of collective society was invented 10,000 years ago.

Yet, despite its ancient past, Turkey is very much a modern nation. A democratic republic, Turkey has embraced westernization while retaining its exotic eastern culture.

Ferries and fishermen gather near the cruise ship dock at Karaköy in Istanbul.

Turkey is a fascinating study in contrasts between its long history of Muslim traditions and those of the modern world.

Turkey at a Glance

Turkey's population, about 63 million, is almost exclusively Sunni Muslim. The official language is Turkish – not Arabic – and English, French and German are widely understood. With a parliamentary system, the Turkish Republic is a democracy with a Council of Ministers, headed by the Prime Minister, who governs the nation along with an elected Grand National Assembly.

Larger than France, Turkey covers an area over 300,000 square miles with more than 5,000 miles of coastline. European Turkey is largely rolling agricultural land while the Asian side of the country is bordered by the Black Sea Mountain Chain to the north and the Taurus Mountains to the south. This part of Turkey is dominated by the vast semi-arid plateau of Anatolia, although many parts of the lower interior are lush and fertile, with numerous rivers and lakes.

Travel Tips

Currency: The unit of currency is the Turkish lira (TL) and bank notes start at 50,000 TL. At the time of writing, the annual inflation rate was around 100 per cent. US currency is accepted everywhere and ATM machines issuing Turkish lira at competitive exchange rates are located at most ports.

Visa: Depending on your citizenship, a Turkish visa may be required. Citizens of the United Kingdom, Ireland and the United States need a visa, which can be purchased at a kiosk adjacent to the immigration booths at Ataturk International Airport for approximately US$20. Passengers arriving by ship should obtain a visa before leaving home. Canadians and Australians do not require a visa.

Health Concerns: Inoculations for cruise passengers planning to stay a few days in Istanbul or along the Aegean coast are not normally necessary. However, if you intend to travel further inland before or after your cruise, you should consult your physician.

The excellent Metro transit system can be boarded near the Eminönü area with stops throughout "Old Stamboul."

Getting Around: If arriving at Ataturk International Airport, taxis are available to downtown Istanbul with fares about US$25. However, it is a good idea to agree on a price to your destination with the driver first by showing the written name of your hotel or producing a map. If a driver won't quote you a rate, move on to the next taxi.

A more economic and relaxing to reach your hotel from the airport is via the government-owned **HAVAS** buses. These green and yellow buses have plenty of cargo area for luggage and the cost per person equals about US$3. These buses take you right to the Taksim area of Istanbul – one of the main hotel areas. The buses are stationed outside the exit area of the arrivals level and will let you off at one of three stops: Aksarray in the old part of Istanbul; Sishane just over the Ataturk Bridge; and Taksim, the hub of the Beyoglu area. If, however, you are travelling from the city to the airport you will have to get the bus at Taksim as it makes no other stops on its way to the airport.

In Istanbul, and other Turkish cities, once you are in town, taxis are a good way get about and are reasonably priced. The fare, for example, from Taksim to the Fatih or Sultanahmet mosques is about US$4 to $5. Another efficient way to get around is by the ubiquitous dolmus (meaning 'stuffed' – which they often are at rush hour). These small buses are usually beige or tan coloured, with their destinations displayed on the windscreen. Payment, in local currency, is made as you get off. Istanbul's Metro, a sort of art-deco street car, is also good – and cheap.

Dining: Turkish cuisine is renowned for its excellence and variety. Popular dishes include *kebap* which is grilled or roasted meat, and fish which are still plentiful in Turkish seas. Restaurant dinner hour normally begins at about 7:00 p.m. A popular alcoholic beverage is raki – the grandfather of absinthe-type drinks – which goes well with hors d'oeuvres and is traditionally enjoyed prior to the main meal of the day. Turkey produces some good wines from the Thrace, Anatolia and Aegean regions. *Buzbag*, a popular red from Eastern Anatolia, is often touted as Turkey's most original wine. Most city water in Turkey is chlorinated, though bottled water is recommended for drinking.

Istanbul viewed from the Sea of Marmara. On the left is the Sultanahmet (Blue Mosque), in the centre is Hagia Sophia, and the tower to the right is the Topkapi Palace. (Opposite) Entrance to the Grand Bazaar. (Bottom) Inside the Grand Bazaar.

Although Turkish coffee is very good, tea is more popular with the Turks. The favourite tea (cay) is deep red and known as 'rabbit's blood'. Served piping hot with sugar in small, tulip-shaped glasses, it is often offered as a traditional expression of hospitality.

Opening Hours: Most stores open by 10:00 a.m. and many business hum along well after 6:00 p.m. The covered bazaar in Istanbul is open from 8:00 a.m. to 7:00 p.m. but it is closed on Sunday. Bank hours seem to vary but generally the doors open at 8:30 a.m., closing at noon for lunch and re-opening from 1:30 until 5:00 p.m. Museums are open between 10:00 a.m. and 4:00 p.m. every day except Mondays. An exception is Topkapi Palace, which closes on Tuesdays.

Shopping: Turkey is renowned for its carpets and kilims (fine carpets for walls), tiles and porcelain, and silks. Turkey is also an excellent place to buy jewellery, Meerschaum pipes, brass work and leather products. Handmade ceramic tiles, bowls, plates and other pottery are also widely available, their colourful designs often replicated from 17th and 18th century works.

Most cities and towns in Turkey have a central bazaar where merchants display their products. Turkish merchants are well known to enjoy pre-sale banter and haggling is part of the process. It is very common for a merchant to offer you tea and ask you to sit down while he tells you about his wares. If you are seriously looking to buy something, this is an aspect of Turkish culture to be enjoyed. The art of bargaining starts with a figure about half the asking price and settles at between 60 and 80 per cent of the merchant's initial price.

Telephone Access Codes: AT&T (0080012277), Sprint (0080014477) MCI (0080011177). To make collect calls, contact the operator in the destination country: US: (0080012277), UK: (00800441177), Canada: (00800331177).

TURKEY'S HISTORY

The world's first settlement is thought to date back over 8,000 years to a Neolithic centre at Çatalhöyük, about 120 miles northeast of the coastal resort city of Antalya. The entire Anatolian plateau harboured numerous tribes, but it wasn't until the Hittites, who were of Indo-European extraction, moved west into the Capadocian area around 1800 BC that Turkey's history began. With their capital at Bogazkoy (70 miles east of Ankara), the Hittites were the chief power and cultural force in western Asia from 1400 to 1200 BC, successfully smelting iron and posing a threat to Babylonia, Syria and Egypt.

By 1000 BC, the Hittite empire had been subdued by invaders and it was also around this time that Ionians, fleeing Dorian invaders on mainland Greece, began settling along the coastline of Aegean Turkey. The region's fertile land and excellent harbours provided prosperity for these Greek pioneers and various cities thrived, particularly Ephesus.

Well before the Romans arrived in Turkey, one of the world's greatest cities was being settled by the Greeks on a small promontory on the Sea of Marmara. Legend has it that a Greek soldier named Byzas received direction by the Delphic oracle, who advised him to settle "opposite the land of the blind". When Byzas stood at the first hill of Istanbul (where Topkapi Palace now stands), he saw opposite the Greek town of Chalcedon and concluded the oracle meant the Chalcedonians were blind not to have settled where he stood. If legends have any truth, he was right. Standing at Topkapi's Mecidiye Kösk viewing the Bosphorus and Golden Horn flowing together into the Sea of Marmara, is a view of great beauty. Byzas established his colony on the acropolis of the city in 667 BC, making Istanbul now over 2,600 years old.

The view from Topkapi Palace across the Bosphorus to Chalcedon, the 'Land of the Blind', or as it is now known, Kadiköy.

Politically, the city's position held great importance. Ancient Byzantium was ideally situated to control shipping to and from the Black Sea and, straddling Europe and Asia, it was a critical trade portal between the Orient and Europe. Surrounded on three sides by water and with substantial land walls, it was virtually impregnable to attack.

For almost 1,000 years, Byzantium was little different from other Greek cities of Asia Minor, with first the Persians, then the Spartans and the Athenians gaining control of the city. Eventually, Byzantium, like most other cities of the Mediterranean, fell under Rome's rule, becoming an important port and garrison for the Empire. So things remained until the 4th century, when an event unparalleled in the history of the Roman Empire occurred: the voluntary retirement of Emperor Diocletian. This caused an eruption in the Empire as armies aligned with three competing Caesars, one of whom became known as Constantine the Great. His shrewd tactics and vision resulted in a string of victories and eventual capitulation of his rival Licinius at Nicomedia.

Some historians point to Constantine as the single most influential ruler in western civilization, and no one more deserved the title of 'Great' than did Byzantine's first emperor. Constantine moved the Roman capital to Byzantium and on the 11th of May in 330 he formally dedicated the city, now called Constantinople, to the God of the Christians. Today, the most visible remains of Constantine's great building effort is his column near the entrance to the Covered Bazaar.

The Byzantine Empire reached its apex during the reign of Justinian I, from 527 to 565 AD, when its borders stretched from Spain to Iraq. Many edifices and magnificent churches were built across the Empire and a great revival of Hellenism took place in art, architecture and literature. The most magnificent church, and most closely associated with Justinian, is the Hagia Sophia, built near the acropolis of the city.

Although the Byzantine Empire remained relatively intact for another 500 years, the ebb was apparent by the 11th century with the permanent loss of most of Asia Minor to the Turks, which greatly diminished Constantinople's ability to defend its European possessions.

The Byzantine Empire's fortunes darkened irrevocably during a chaotic period following a power struggle for the throne early in the 13th century. The Venetians were enlisted by the usurper Alexius IV and in 1204, under the guise of the Fourth Crusade, they attacked Constantinople and for the first time in almost a thousand years the city fell. Pillaging of the city stripped it of most of its splendour and wealth and many of these treasures were taken to Venice. This sacking of the Greek Orthodox capital of Constantinople by Latin Roman Catholics made permanent the schism between the two great Christian religions.

The Latins were finally pushed out of Constantinople in 1261 by the Byzantine emperor Michael Palaeologus. His son, Andronicus enjoyed a long reign of over 40 years, during which time the Empire declined. However, through his patronage of the arts, Byzantium flowered culturally, producing a renaissance which included such works as the Deesis

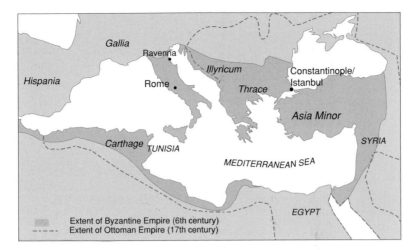

Extent of Byzantine Empire (6th century)
Extent of Ottoman Empire (17th century)

panel in Hagia Sophia and the splendid mosaics in the St. Saviour in Chora church. But the end for the great Byzantine Empire was quickly approaching. The Ottoman Turks, successors to the Seljuk dominance of Asia Minor, conquered Bursa in 1326 and Nicaea in 1331. With the sudden death of Andronicus III in 1341, the Empire convulsed in a bitter civil war, followed by the Black Plague. Militarily and financially spent, Byzantium had few allies and was forced into an appeasement policy with the ever-encroaching Ottoman Turks.

Finally, in 1453 the Turks succeeded in surrounding the 'Queen of Cities' and on May 29th, using a specially made cannon (the largest the world had known), they blasted a hole in the Theodosian Walls and took the city. Their leader, Mehmet II, was 21 when he made his triumphal entry into the city. To the Greek and Armenian citizens he granted privileges they were to enjoy, with few exceptions, throughout Ottoman rule, including the freedom to practise their religion. Mehmet, called Fatih (the Conqueror) by his followers, made Constantinople his capital and restored the city's greatness with a massive rebuilding program and by bringing in populations from other conquered towns.

Mehmet the Conqueror.

The Ottoman Empire enjoyed another 100 years of expansion which culminated with Süleyman the Magnificent's capture of Belgrade, Budapest and very nearly Vienna. However, the reign of his son Selim II, know as 'The Sot', marked the slow decline of Ottoman influence. Corrupted from within by palace intrigues and by the violent resistance of the Janissaries – an elite

A 17-century map of Istanbul.

corp of the Ottoman army – to any reforms, the Empire's steady decline followed. While Europe embraced new battle tactics and technology, Ottoman Turkey continued using methods from the 15th century.

In the early 19th century the sultan Mahmut II ushered in an era of reform but suffered political and military setbacks, such as the loss of Greece in 1830. Mahmut eliminated the Janissary Corps, created a new, more modern army and supported the improvement of education, thus laying the foundation for secularization throughout Ottoman society. He also banned turbans, which were replaced with the Moroccan fez.

Throughout the 19th century, succeeding sultans continued to spend extravagantly, building huge palaces along the Bosphorus. Serious conflicts, such as the Crimean War, debilitated the Empire's finances, and by 1881 the Empire was on the brink of bankruptcy. The government was forced into taking loans at high interest rates and into making political and trade concessions with the European powers.

The unravelling Ottoman Empire collapsed when Turkey blundered into the First World War on the side of Germany. Despite winning the tactical battle of Gallipoli, Turkey's fate was tied to that of Germany and with its surrender in 1918, the party was over for the Ottoman dynasty. Plans were made to alter Turkey's borders, with Greece the main benefactor. However, the European allies, which helped land Greek troops at Izmir in May of 1919, underestimated the determination of the Turkish people to hang onto their country. The Turks rallied around the hero of the Battle of Gallipoli, Mustafa Kemal (known later as Ataturk – see sidebar page 324), who hastily organized an army and routed the Greek invaders in a counterattack which began in late August 1922. Within a few weeks, the Turkish mainland was completely liberated, an armistice signed and the Ottoman dynasty abolished.

In July 1923, the Turkish government signed the Lausanne Treaty with European powers. Ankara became the capital of the new Turkish State and the Republic was proclaimed, with Mustafa Kemal elected president. The new Turkey's ideology was, and remains, 'Atatürkism'. Its basic principles stress the republican form of government, representing the power of the electorate. A secular administration, it supports nationalism, modernization and a mixed economy with state participation in many of the vital sectors. Although the country's democracy is underpinned by a military determined to keep Turkey secular, the process of participatory democracy continues to work for the country.

ISTANBUL

The Queen of Cities, as Istanbul has been called over the centuries, is one of the most fascinating ports in the world. If Istanbul is the home port for your cruise, you should try to add at least two days for touring the city. Although no longer the capital of Turkey (which moved to Ankara in 1923), an aura of power remains in Istanbul, for it is still the country's financial and business centre, and home to most of its head offices. Called Constantinople for over 1,500 years, its name was formally changed to Istanbul (meaning 'to the city' in Turkish) in 1930.

Now a museum, Hagia Sophia remains magnificent.

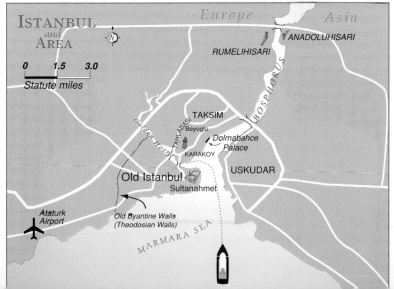

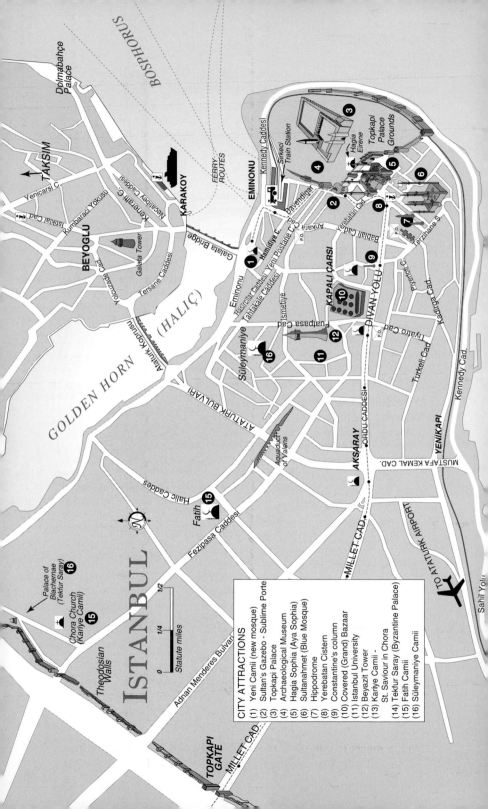

ISTANBUL

CITY ATTRACTIONS
(1) Yeni Camii (new mosque)
(2) Sultan's Gazebo - Sublime Porte
(3) Topkapi Palace
(4) Archaeological Museum
(5) Hagia Sophia (Aya Sophia)
(6) Sultanahmet (Blue Mosque)
(7) Hippodrome
(8) Yerebatan Cistern
(9) Constantine's column
(10) Covered (Grand) Bazaar
(11) Istanbul University
(12) Beyazit Tower
(13) Kariye Camii -
        St. Saviour in Chora
(14) Tektur Saray (Byzantine Palace)
(15) Fatih Camii
(16) Süleymaniye Camii

BOSPHORUS

Dolmabahçe Palace

TAKSIM

BEYOGLU

KARAKOY

EMINONU

Sirkeci Train Station

Hagia Eirene

Topkapi Palace Grounds

GOLDEN HORN (HALIÇ)

Galata Bridge

KAPALI CARSI

DIVAN-YOLU

SÜLEYMANIYE

ATATÜRK BULVARI

Aquaduct of Valens

Fatih

AKSARAY

YENIKAPI

MUSTAFA KEMAL CAD.

MILLET-CAD.

Palace of Blachernae (Tektur Saray)

Chora Church (Kariye Camii)

Theodosian Walls

TOPKAPI GATE

MILLET CAD.

TO ATATURK AIRPORT

Sahil Yolu

Kennedy Cad.

Statute miles
0   1/4   1/2

The best place to start touring this magnificent city is the Galata Bridge, near the cruise ship dock at Karaköy. The view is expansive and beautiful, taking in the Bosphorus, the Golden Horn, the Sea of Marmara and the old city of Istanbul. A thousand years of architecture, from the Theodosian walls (completed in 447 AD) to the Topkapi Palace (built in 1465), can be seen in a glance, while below, on the river, ferries jockey for position at the docks.

Galata Bridge joins Karaköy with the Eminönü dock area. Near the bridge is one of the old city's important mosques, the **Yeni Cami** (1), meaning the 'New Mosque', for

The view from Galata Bridge to Karaköy

it was the last of the great classical Ottoman mosques built. It was first commissioned in 1597 by Safiye, mother of Sultan Mehmet III. Unfortunately for her, both the architect and her son died during construction and it took more than a century before it was completed.

About halfway along the Eminönü dock area will be your first opportunity to hitch a ride on Istanbul's excellent **Metro**, which winds through the city. You can also catch the Metro just outside of the **Sirkeci Train Station** a few hundred paces further along. However, there is still much to see on foot, as you walk up old Constantinople's first hill, beginning with the Sirkeci Train Station – termination of the famous Orient Express which made its first run to Istanbul in 1888. Further along, are the palace walls and **Alay köskü (sultan's gazebo)** (2) where the sultan observed the comings and goings of his Grand Vizier across the street. The entrance to the Vizier's palace and offices was known as the **Sublime Porte**, the diplomatic reference to Turkey for hundreds of years. Nearby is the first entrance to the grounds of Topkapi Sarayi, the Great Palace of the Ottomans.

Topkapi Palace (3) – Built by Mehmet the Conqueror in 1467, Topkapi Palace was, for 400 years, the residence of sultans and the centre of imperial administration. The palace is the most extensive structure of Ottoman architecture, covering an area almost half the size of Monaco. It took its name from the Cannon Gate of the Byzantine seawalls, which translated into *Topkapi* in Turkish. It was not until the reign of Süleyman the Magnificent (1520-1566), under the urgings of his Russian wife Roxelana, that accommodations for wives and concubines were included at the palace.

Now a museum complex, the Topkapi Palace contains unrivalled collections of porcelains, armour, jewels and other objects of art for-

merly belonging to the Sultans. Visitors can wander freely throughout the grounds' public areas. There are two entrances into the first court, with the northern one (near the Alay köskü) taking you to the **Archaeological Museum** (4), the Museum of the Ancient Orient and the famous Tiled Pavilion. The southern gate, known as the Bab-i Hümayun or Imperial Gate, is the main entrance. This gate also takes you by the old Byzantine church of **Hagia Eirene**, built during Justinian's reign at about the same time as Hagia Sophia.

The **Museum of the Ancient Orient's** collection isn't large but is of great importance with its pre-Islamic Arab artifacts, as well as Babylonian and Assyrian exhibits. These include the beautiful panels of lions and monsters, which once decorated the processional way to the Isthar Gate at Babylon. Also displayed are clay tablets of the famous 1286 BC treaty between Egypt and the Hittites (the oldest known example of a written international treaty). The **Archaeological Museum** was the first systematic attempt by the Ottoman Empire to preserve the nation's antiquities and it contains the superb Alexander Sarcophagus, discovered at Sidon (modern Sayda in Lebanon) in 1887. This sarcophagus is not that of Alexander the Great but derives its name from carved sculptures depicting Alexander hunting. In a nearby room is the haunting and beautiful statue of the Ephebos Youth, for which the room is named.

Leaving the grounds of the first court, you pass through the impressive Bab-üs Selam (Gate of Salutation). Built into the wall to the right of the gate is the Executioner's Fountain, where he

Gate of Salutation or main entrance to Topkapi Palace (top). The famous Topkapi dagger (centre). Pavilion of the Holy Mantle (bottom).

THE SULTAN'S HAREM

For the sultans, home was the harem. These private apartments housed, in addition to the sultan's four main wives (the maximum number under Islamic law), his concubines and numerous relatives (including confined princes), eunuchs, guards and servants. At the height of its use, the Topkapi Palace population numbered over 3,000. Numerous staircases, corridors and courtyards are linked by narrow passageways, exuding the claustrophobic world of palace intrigue where, for generations, the women behind the sultan – often his mother – controlled the reins of power.

On half a dozen levels, hundreds of attractive girls and women lived their existence almost exclusively within the walls of the harem. They usually came from non-Muslim parts of the empire (Islamic law forbidding enslavement of Muslim women) and were almost always captured in war or bought on the slave market. The sultans were especially partial to Caucasian girls, who fetched a high price in the slave market. Because life for these women was so privileged, some parents would voluntarily send their daughters to Istanbul, even after slave trading was banned in the 19th century.

Girls came to the harem as young as five years of age and were called *acemi* (beginner). After training for domestic duties, they became a *cariye*, a concubine of the lowest rank. They could then begin to assume greater importance, for each was the potential *valide sultan* (mother of the sultan). The sultan normally had about a dozen favourite concubines, and if one became pregnant she was called *kadin efendi*. If she successfully brought a child into the world, she acquired the title *haseki sultan* and was given her own apartment.

If the child was a male and the mother was a favourite of the sultan, she could become one of his four official wives. Depending on the woman's power and skill, she would do her utmost to manoeuvre her son as heir to the throne. Roxelana, a kadin of Suleyman, went so far as to convince the sultan to kill his first son so that her alcoholic son, Selim II, would assume the throne.

would wash his hands and sword after performing a decapitation out-side the gate. The inner palace grounds contain many important exhibits and attractions. For Muslims, the most significant is the **Pavilion of the Holy Mantle**, displaying the sacred relics of the Prophet Muhammad, including his sword and robe (the Holy Mantle).

The Treasury of the Topkapi Palace is considered one of the richest in the world. Among its priceless artifacts, which were made for the sultans, is the famous Topkapi Dagger. The centrepiece of the 1960s film *Topkapi*, the dagger's sheath is pierced with diamonds and its gold hand is set with huge emeralds.

Hagia Sophia (Church of the Divine Wisdom) (5) – On first enter-ing this venerable building, one senses the volume of history it has withstood. First a church, then a mosque, and now a museum, Haghia Sophia has been in existence for nearly 1,500 years. Considered one of the most beautiful buildings ever constructed, it was the largest church in Christendom until the construction of St. Peter's Basilica in Rome.

Standing just outside the Imperial Gate of the Topkapi Palace, the Hagia Sophia is the third edifice of the same name to rest on the site. The first church, dedicated in 360 AD, was destroyed by fire during a mob riot, as was the second church during the Nika Revolt in early 532, during the early years of Emperor Justinian's reign. Successfully putting down the riot with the help of his general Basilierus and the considerable backbone of his wife Theodora, Justinian resolved to build the grandest church ever, regardless of expense. He appointed Anthemius as head architect, whose assistant Isidorus, as a director of the ancient Academy in Athens, became a link between the worlds of ancient Greece and medieval Byzantium.

The venerable Hagia Sophia, or Aya Sophia, anchors the old part of Istanbul. Hagia Eirene is seen at left, behind the Topkapi walls.

View of the upper south gallery where the Deesis is located.

The architects, given carte blanche and 10,000 workers, began the project just five weeks after the riots. Provincial governors were ordered to send to the capital any surviving classical remains that might be suitable for incorporation in the new edifice. In response, eight porphyry columns of the pagan Sun Temple of Rome were sent, as were eight green marble columns from Ephesus.

The church was completed in 537 and according to Procopius, the historian of the day, it greatly impressed the Christian world. With a huge dome over 100 feet in diameter, 160 feet high and pierced with 40 windows, it appeared "suspended from heaven by a golden chain". To most observers, the church seemed nothing less than a miracle. When Justinian first walked into the church, he stood silent for a long time before uttering, "Solomon, I have surpassed thee."

What makes Hagia Sophia such an architectural marvel is not the height nor breadth of the dome, but the two semi-domes at either end. In addition to lengthening the nave, the semi-domes give the observer, on first entering the church, an unobstructed view to the top of the church. Decorative aspects of note include the beautiful marble casings throughout the interior, such as the butterfly marble over the main entrance. The unique capitals of the columns, with their surface decoration of acanthus (symbolizing heaven) and deeply undercut palm foliage, produce an effect of both lightness and strength, and resemble white lace on a dark background. The monograms on the capitals are those of Justinian and Theodora.

The mosaics of Hagia Sophia are one of the most fascinating aspects of this church. Although various figures adorned the church in the 6th through 8th centuries, these were removed during the iconoclastic years which ended in 846 with the unveiling of mosaics in the apse showing the Madonna with the Christ-Child on her knees. Other mosaics include those at the east end of the south gallery, next to the apse, depicting the Empress Zoe and her third husband, Constantine IX, on either side of

(Above) 19th-century view of Hagia Sophia. (Above right) Empress Zoe and Constantine IX with Christ. (Right) South aisle. (Bottom) The Deesis.

Christ. Just to the right of this mosaic is an imperial portrait showing John II Comnenus and Empress Eirene with the Mother of Jesus holding an infant Christ. A side panel shows the heir, Prince Alexius, who ascended to the throne at 17 but died shortly after.

The most significant of the Byzantine mosaics in Hagia Sophia is the sad and beautiful Deesis, located in the east wall of the buttress in the south gallery. Likely produced in the early 14th century, this work is an example of Constantinople's cultural renaissance after the restoration of the city from the dark years of Latin control. Although most of the mosaic is lost, the facial features of its three subjects remain intact and show Christ, with an expression of grief, flanked by the young Virgin on one side and a pleading St. John the Baptist on the other.

Sultan Ahmet Camii (The Blue Mosque) (6) – Built by the young Sultan Ahmet I between 1609 to 1616, the Blue Mosque is widely considered the city's most splendid. The domes and semi-domes cascade gracefully from the summit within a stand of six slender minarets

(Right and below) Interior and exterior of Blue Mosque. (Bottom) Hippodrome.

which represented that Ahmet was the sixth Sultan. Ahmet was an enthusiast about his mosque and often pitched in to speed up construction. He didn't have long to enjoy it for he died of typhus, at the age of 28, within a year of its completion. His tomb is at the northwest side of the mosque.

When walking the short distance from Hagia Sophia to the Blue Mosque, visitors enter a square which was the heart of ancient Byzantium. Law courts, a large public library and a book market all stood where gardens now flourish. Just to the east of the large fountain are the Baths of Roxelana, wife of Süleyman. The main entrance to the Blue Mosque is at the eastern side of the courtyard and, as with all mosques (camii in Turkish) you'll be asked to remove your shoes before entering.

The Blue Mosque's reputation as a must-see attraction is deserved, for the interior is stunning. Four fluted piers, pushing towards the centre, resemble trunks of huge trees as they disappear into the arching canopy of the dome and four semi-domes. Sunlight, filtered and diffused by coloured glass, pours in from 260 windows. Along the lower part of the walls, especially in the galleries, is a profusion of beautiful blue and green Iznik tiles, for which the edifice is named.

Just to the west of the Blue Mosque is the ancient **Hippodrome** (7) where chariot races and other events entertained the citizens of Constantinople. An immense structure, it could seat 100,000 spectators.

The central line of the race course is still visible today and was marked by obelisks and columns, three of which remain.

The Egyptian Obelisk, from the 15th century BC, is about 65 feet in height and is actually the top third of the original obelisk. The sculpted reliefs around the base depict Emperor Theodosius sitting in his box at the Hippodrome, holding a head wreath to honour the winner of a race.

The middle column, called the Serpent Column, is the oldest Greek monument in the city. Erected in 479 BC in the Temple of Apollo at Delphi, it was brought to the city by Constantine the Great. The third column, erected by Emperor Constantine VII Porphyrogenitus in 940, is over 100 feet high and was once plated in bronze gilt, which was removed during the Latin conquest of the city in 1204. A favourite pastime in early Ottoman years was to climb this column as a daring feat.

It's about a 25-minute walk from Sultanahmet to the Covered Bazaar and you may want to take this opportunity to board the Metro at the station just west of the Hippodrome on the Divan Yolu. Just a few steps from this station is the fabled **underground cistern** (8) known as the **Yerebatan Saratu** (underground palace). This giant reservoir, built in the 6th century, was supplied with water from the Belgrade Forest 12 miles west. Supported by 336 columns, the cistern was the main water source for the city and was specifically built to survive periods of siege.

The **Divan Yolu** has been the main road of this city for over 2000 years. The Milion (first mile) started at an archway just beyond Haghia Sophia and from this point all distances in the Byzantine Empire were measured. The first Metro stop along Diva Yolu is called Çemberlitas which refers to the nearby **Column of Constantine** (9), sometimes referred to as the Burnt or Hooped Column. This column was erected in 330 to mark the city's dedication and a number of relics, including bits of the True Cross, are reportedly sealed beneath the foundation.

Turning north from the Hooped Column, you soon encounter the walls of the Nuruosmaniye Mosque and the entrance, through a shady courtyard, to the Bazaar. Beggars and peddlers often line the walkways leading to the Bazaar and occasionally a musician can be heard.

Kapali Çarsi (Covered Bazaar) (10) – Also known as the Grand Bazaar, this is a huge labyrinth of shops, banks, cafes, restaurants, mosques and a post office crammed into a grid of narrow streets and protected from the elements by a multitude of domed and vaulted roofs. Mehmet the Conqueror built the first covered market on this site in 1461; it has been rebuilt several times following fires and earthquakes.

Come prepared to spend. It is the world's largest covered bazaar and, with 4,000 shops, the place to buy Turkish souvenirs. Whether you are interested or not in a carpet, you'll be approached by numerous young men wanting to show you their selection. If you are interested in a carpet or kilim, this is a good place to shop – the selection is excellent and the competition for business is intense.

Located northwest of the Grand Bazaar is the **Istanbul University** (11) and the **Beyazit Tower** (12) – built as a fire lookout in 1828. The

University dates from just after the Conquest in 1453. With the establishment of the Turkish Republic, the university was completely reformed and modernized with the construction of its present buildings.

West of the Bazaar along Millet Caddesi, are the beautiful **Theodosian Walls**, first built in the fifth century by Theodosias and fortified many times right up to last Byzantine emperor, Constantine XI. The Topkapi Gate is where the Turks first blasted through on May 29th, 1453. These walls inspired Lord Byron to write to his mother, "I have seen the ruins of Athens, of Ephesus, and Delphi. I have traversed a great part of Turkey, and some of Asia; but I never beheld a work of nature or art which yielded an impression like the prospect on each side from the Seven Towers to the end of the Golden Horn."

Although crumbling, the walls testify to the survival of this great city for over 1,000 years. Extending more than four miles from the Sea of Marmara to the Golden Horn, the walls were actually a system of three defences with an outer moat (where the highway now is), an outer wall and the main inner wall studded with 96 towers. Although the first phase of the walls was completed in 413 under Theodosius II, a violent earthquake in 447 destroyed much of what had been built. This occurred at a critical moment when Attila the Hun was advancing on the city. Reconstruction began immediately and within two months the walls were rebuilt and were far stronger – successfully repelling Attila.

From the Edirnekapi gate, it's a short walk to the beautiful **Church of St. Saviour in Chora (Kariye Camii)** (13) and the haunting ruins of **Tekfur Saray** (14), an annex to the nearby Byzantine Palace of Blachernae. The palace facade is decorated with geometrical designs in red brick and white marble, typifying the later period of Byzantine architecture of the 13th and 14th century.

The remains of the last Byzantine palace of Constantinople stand near the Theodosian Walls. Shown below is Tekfur Saray.

The Lowdown on Carpets

The creation and use of carpets in Turkey dates back to at least 2500 BC, with depictions on rock tombs showing men with implements used for rug weaving. The cool, mountainous region stretching from Turkey to Persia, where sheep fleece and camel and goat hair grow long and fine, is where the art of carpet-weaving reached its peak in the 16th century. Lying east and southeast of Ankarra, this famous region of carpet production is among the few places in the world where carpets are still hand-made.

Towns such as Kayseri, Konya and Hereke produce wool and silk carpets which have been in demand for centuries. Marco Polo claimed the best and most beautiful carpets in the world came from Konya.

The most common material used in Turkish carpets and kilims is sheep's wool, and weavers still use the time-honoured double knot, or Gordes knot. A well-made woollen carpet can take one or two weavers up to a month to make, and prices range from US$50 for small throw rugs to several hundred dollars for larger carpets. Silk carpets can be priced in the thousands of dollars.

The quality of a carpet depends on the quality and type of wool, and the number of knots per square inch of surface which can vary from 40 to 1,000 knots. Traditional woollen Turkish carpets are more vibrant and brighter than Persian carpets and often contain patterns dating back many centuries. Kilims, flat woven rugs without any pile, are very popular because of their traditional Turkish design and deep colours.

Patterns found in Turkish carpets not only indicate the vintage of the design, but also the region where the carpet was most likely produced. Motifs from nature include birds, camels and flowers. Other patterns utilize symbols, such arrows for courage, and colours, such as blue to represent the infinite. Prayer mats are distinguished by the pointed shape of their central panel.

Istanbul's Covered Bazaar.

Admirers of Ottoman architecture point to the Süleymaniye as the most important mosque in Istanbul.

For many visitors to Istanbul, visiting the Chora church is a priority. The phrase 'in Chora' means 'in the country' and the original church (of which nothing now remains) stood outside the walls built by Constantine. The present building dates from the late 11th century, with elaborate remodelling carried out in the 12th and 14th centuries. The mosaics and frescoes of this church are regarded as the most important series of Byzantine artwork in the world, exquisite in detail and anticipating the great Renaissance which soon took hold in Europe.

A visit to the mosques of **Fatih** (15) and **Süleymaniye** (16) as well as **Valens Aqueduct**, which spans the valley between the two mosques, is well worth the effort. The Fatih Mosque, largest mosque in Istanbul, named after Mehmet the Conqueror, is more sombre in appearance than the Blue Mosque, but is nonetheless impressive, if only for its sheer size. It is said that when Mehmet the Conqueror discovered his mosque was not quite as high as Hagia Sophia he ordered the architect's hands cut off. In any event, both the architect and Mehmet are buried behind the mosque, and visitors can view the tomb of the great conqueror.

The Süleymaniye Mosque, the second largest in the city, is one of Turkey's finest imperial Ottoman mosques and is representative of the 'Golden Age' of the Empire. Designed by the great architect Sinan, the Mosque was completed in 1557 and stands just below Istanbul's third hill, on a slope down to the Golden Horn. A structural masterpiece, it assured Sinan's place as a genius of architecture. At the entrance is a grand porticoed courtyard with columns of rich marble and granite. At the corners of the courtyard rise four minarets, representing Süleyman as being the fourth sultan to reign in Istanbul. Cleverly disguising buttresses and eschewing aisles and numerous columns, Sinan created a vast interior enlivened by light filtered through beautiful stained glass windows. Süleyman's majestic tomb is located behind the mosque and his catafalque is capped by the huge white turban he once wore.

The **Valens Aqueduct** was built about 375 AD to bring water from the Belgrade Forest into the centre of the city. Although damaged by earthquakes, it was kept in good repair by the Byzantine emperors and the Ottoman sultans, and was used until the late 19th century when it was replaced by a modern water distribution system.

Dolmabahçe Palace – Many Turks in the late 19th century saw in this palace all that was wrong with the Ottoman Empire. Excessive, expensive and out of touch with the rest of the country, the Dolmabahçe Palace's construction helped bring the empire to the point of bankruptcy. An inlet was filled in to form the palace site (Dolmabahçe means 'filled-in garden') and a royal park was created with a series of kiosks and pavilions built close to the Bosphorus. The sultan Abdul Mecit decided to build a much larger and more luxurious palace, designed in a neo-baroque style and completed in 1854. The opulent furnishings of the palace included the largest chandelier in the world, weighing four-and-a-half tons and hanging in the State Room.

The palace was home to the last sultan, Mehmet VI, whose ignominious departure entailed being smuggled aboard a British frigate. The palace was also the principal residence of Mustafa Ataturk, who died here in November 1938.

KARADOY AND BEYOGLU

The districts of Karaköy and Beyoglu, on the north side of the Golden Horn, are almost as old as the main city and were for centuries home to 'foreign' merchants and dignitaries. Karaköy is the Turkish name for the old Galata area, which was once the Genoese stronghold. A walled mini-city, Galata had a reputation for debauchery.

Beyoglu is the Turkish name for the old Pera district, and was actually an upper-middle class suburb of Galata. During the 18th and 19th centuries, along a road which became known as the Grand Rue de Pera, palatial mansions and embassies were built. You can take the 19th-century tram part way along Grand Rue de Pera – now called Istiklâl Caddesi – or explore on foot. Just off Galatasaray Square, halfway along Istiklâl Caddesi, is an avenue

which leads to Tepebasi and the site of some renowned grand hotels. The best known of these is Pera Palas, which was built in 1876 as the terminal hotel for the Orient Express.

At the south end of Istiklâl Caddesi, where the avenue forks to the right, is the entrance to the underground funicular railway known as the Tünel, built in 1875 and dubbed 'The Mouse's Hole' by locals. It takes just over a minute to descend to the bottom of the hill near the Galata Bridge. A more preferable route is to turn left and continue down the steep street of Galip Dede Caddesi to see the famous Galata Tower. Built in 1348 as the apex of Genoese fortifications, it has been restored and houses a restaurant on its upper levels with magnificent views.

THE TURKISH COAST

The **Dardanelles**, known in ancient times as the Hellespont, is a famous strait and the site of many legendary events. Leander swam across this strait nightly, from Asia to Europe, to meet his beloved Hero, a Greek priestess. This romantic gesture was repeated by the poet Lord Byron, to prove it could be done. Armies have crossed this strait, including that of Alexander the Great when he crossed into Asia.

One the most tragic battles of the first world war, resulting in the death or injury of over 500,000 soldiers, also took place at the Dardanelles, and is known as the Battle of Gallipoli after the nearby town. The plan was set in motion by a young Winston Churchill, then First Lord of the Admiralty, who saw a chance to seize Constantinople and secure a route to Russia, England's ally. However, Churchill prematurely sent a British fleet into easy gun range of the hills overlooking the strait and, after a number of ships went down, the navy retreated to wait for land troops. By the time the Allied army was ready, two months later, the Turks had fortified their position. The landing of allied forces at Suvla on the west coast of the peninsula resulted in severe casualties of British, Australian and New Zealand troops, as well as for the Turks. The man most directly responsible for the Turkish victory was the future president of Turkey, Mustafa Kemal Ataturk.

About 20 miles (32 km) south of Çanakkale lies the ancient Hellenic city of Troy, site of the legendary Trojan war described by the Greek poet Homer in his work the *Iliad*. Long dismissed as fiction, the city was only discovered in the latter part of the 19th century by the German archaeologist Heinrich Schliemann. Uncovering the ruins in a series of mounds, Schliemann proved, by Homer's description, that there was indeed a great city just west of the Dardanelles.

The Galata Tower (opposite) provides a sweeping view of old Istanbul. The replica of the wooden horse at Troy (right).

A T A T U R K

Mustafa Kemal Ataturk, founder of the Turkish Republic and its first president, stands among the great leaders of the 20th century for his military prowess, political acumen and vision for his country. His statue and name appear everywhere in Turkey and, although he was an autocrat, there is little doubt Ataturk (a name he adopted in 1934 meaning "father of the Turks") remains a loved and respected figure.

Born in 1881 in Thessalonica, he was first enrolled in a traditional religious school. In 1893, he entered a military high school where his mathematics teacher gave him the name Kemal (meaning perfection) in recognition of his superior achievement. He graduated from the War Academy in Istanbul with the rank of Staff Captain and moved quickly up the ranks while remaining politically active.

Ataturk was respected by his fellow officers and his superiors for his great strategic talents. He anticipated his adversaries' moves and acted quickly, as demonstrated at Gallipoli when the Allies faltered in the first stage of that battle. Although briefly married, Ataturk was most attached to his country and his goal of creating a secular state.

An account of Ataturk's 15-year presidency is a saga of dramatic modernization. He created a new political and legal system, granted equal rights to women, substituted the Latin alphabet for Arabic script, and banned the fez. He improved education, social services, the arts and sciences, agriculture and industry, and protected numerous Byzantine ruins and other sites throughout the country.

Ataturk remained in office until his final illness in 1938. He spent the summer of that year at the Dolmabahçe Palace, living in a few rooms in one of the wings. One evening he left the palace and took a taxi up the Bosphorus to Arnavutköy, where his alarmed staff found him later that night partying with local fishermen in a taverna. This was Ataturk's last foray, for he was diagnosed as having advanced cirrhosis of the liver and was confined to bed. On November 10, 1938, the father of modern Turkey died. He was interned in Ankara and eventually placed in a huge mausoleum built to honour Turkey's greatest hero.

In 1981, to commemorate the centennial of his birth, the United Nations and UNESCO honoured Ataturk as a statesman who abhorred war, repeating one his famous quotes:

"Unless the life of the nation faces peril, war is a crime."

Although the ruins of Troy are not impressive, the fortifications are well preserved and certainly convey the scene to those familiar with the famous story of Paris, Helen, Achilles and Odysseus. At the entrance to the archaeological site stands a replica of the famous wooden horse.

EPHESUS

One of the most important archaeological sites in the Mediterranean is undoubtedly the ancient city of Ephesus. Of great importance for over a thousand years, Ephesus at one time rivalled Rome for opulence and beauty. The ruins are extensive and well preserved and one can easily visualize this bustling port city of over 200,000 citizens.

Located near the mouth of the river Cayster (now Kuçuk Menderes), Ephesus (Efes in Turkish – which is also the name a fine local beer) was an important port. Over the centuries, however, the river silted up and the coastline is now about five miles to the west of the city.

Ionian Greeks first settled in Ephesus around 1100 BC. The site was a place of wor-ship for a native nature goddess associated with the Greek goddess Artemis, and around 550 BC a large temple was built in her honour.

Artemis, goddess of nature.

Over the next few centuries the city changed hands, from the Lydians under King Croesus to the Persian Empire and back to the Greeks by Alexander the Great in 334. The city continued to thrive as a Greek sea-port until 133 BC, when it was taken by the Romans and maintained as the leading city of their Asian province. Its great Temple of Artemis, renamed the Temple of Diana by the Romans, was considered one of the Seven Wonders of the Ancient World, although little remains today.

As the termination of the famous Silk Route and the world capital of the slave trade, Ephesus was wealthy and secure for over three hundred years, until it was sacked by Goths in 262 AD. Later, during Byzantine control, it became an important see and a church council was held here in 431 with Emperor Theodosius II in attendance.

By this point, however, Ephesus was already in decline and with a harbour rapidly filling with silt, the city lost its value as a port. By the 6th century Ephesus was reduced to little more than a village and, with the advent of the Ottoman Empire, it was completely abandoned. The site was re-discovered by a British archaeologist in 1869, after six years of searching. Most of the ruins visible today date from the Roman peri-od of the 1st century BC to the 2nd century AD.

One of the most beautiful pieces of architecture remaining is the Library of Celsus, built in the early 2nd century by a Roman consul as a

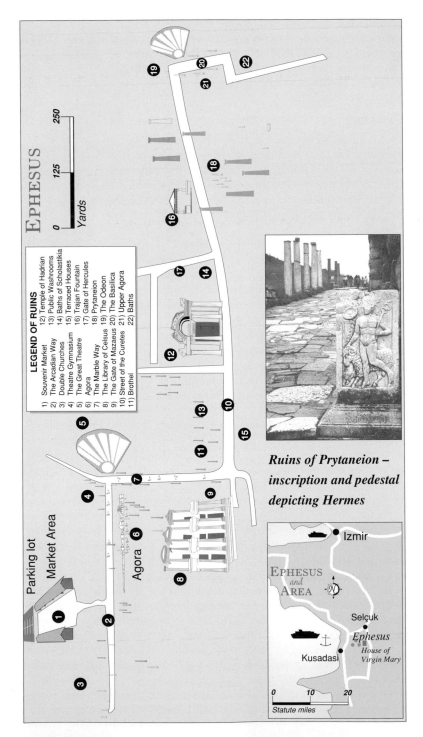

EPHESUS

LEGEND OF RUINS

1) Souvenir Market
2) The Arcadian Way
3) Double Churches
4) Theatre Gymnasium
5) The Great Theatre
6) Agora
7) The Marble Way
8) The Library of Celsus
9) The Gate of Mazaeus
10) Street of the Curetes
11) Brothel
12) Temple of Hadrian
13) Public Washrooms
14) Baths of Scholastikia
15) Terraced Houses
16) Trajan Fountain
17) Gate of Hercules
18) Prytaneion
19) The Odeon
20) The Basilica
21) Upper Agora
22) Baths

Yards 0 125 250

Parking lot

Market Area

Agora

*Ruins of Prytaneion –
inscription and pedestal
depicting Hermes*

EPHESUS *and* AREA

Izmir

Selçuk

Ephesus
House of
Virgin Mary

Kusadasi

0   10   20
Statute miles

memorial to his father. The library once contained over 10,000 scrolls and books. Statues of the four virtues (wisdom, thought, knowledge and valour) adorn the niches between the columns.

From the entrance of the site at the souvenir market you walk along the **Arcadian Way** for a few hundred yards before coming to the Great Theatre. From here you can enjoy an excellent view over the city's old colonnaded main street, once lined with statues and lit by oil lamps at night. Just beyond the present car park is where the Church of Councils was held, and was the spot where Pope Paul VI led prayers when he visited Ephesus in 1967.

Library of Celsus.

The Apostle Paul's connection with Ephesus (described in Acts 17-19) occurred during his second and third missionary journeys into Anatolia between 53 and 57 AD. For two years, with Ephesus as his base, Paul wrote letters and preached to the locals, urging them to put aside their idols of Artemis. This outraged the local silversmiths, who enjoyed a lively trade making Artemis statues, and they provoked a riot that resulted in Paul's incarceration. Forced to leave Ephesus upon his release, Paul journeyed to Jerusalem where he was arrested, sent to Rome and executed during the persecutions of Emperor Nero.

House of the Virgin Mary – According to legend (which began with a German nun who discovered the site in the 19th century) St. John the Apostle brought Mary to Ephesus around 38 AD, and she retired to a cottage which can be visited at Meryemana near Selcuk.

The Apostle Paul spent two years in Ephesus, which was a productive time for his writing.

*The impor-
tant naval
port of
Izmir also
has one of
the best
bazaars in
Turkey.*

**The Clock Tower and the miniature
Hisar Mosque are two landmarks
of Izmir.**

Kusadasi, a popular port of access to Ephesus, has become a frenetic resort town serving ruins-bound travellers. Although there are some decent beaches to the south of the town, they are generally busy. However a walk across an extended causeway links the town to pretty Pigeon Island, with a 13th-century Byzantine castle surrounded by gardens and restaurants. The town bazaar is a good place to shop.

Turkey's third largest city and second largest port, **Izmir** is also an important military base and a NATO command centre of southeast Europe. Of the original Hellenistic city-states situated along the Turkish Aegean coast, only Izmir, known until this century as Smryna, survived. It was possibly the birthplace of Homer, and was the largest and most prosperous city of Asia Minor. Unfortunately, the modern city bears little evidence of its ancient past, yet it's an interesting city to stroll with several sites situated close to the downtown. These include the **Roman Agora**, just a few blocks from the main centre of town, the **main bazaar**, the **Clock Tower** and the 16th-century **Hisar Mosque**.

South of Izmir and Kusadasi is the resort town of **Bodrum** which occupies the site of ancient Halicarnassus. Bodrum offers many attractions, including a fascinating Museum of Underwater Archaeology which features Byzantine ships and is housed in the magnificent crusader castle overlooking the harbour. The Castle of St. Peter was built in the 15th century by the Knights of St. John using stone quarried from the ruins of the Mausoleum of Halicarnassus (one of the Seven Wonders of the Ancient World). The castle fell to the Ottomans in 1523 during the reign of Süleyman the Magnificent. In the castle's English Tower, the banquet hall has been restored and here visitors can enjoy a glass of wine while reading graffiti that was carved into window niches by homesick knights. A boat trip can be taken from the harbour to one of the nearby coves hidden along the coast to the west, and a dolmus can be taken to the pretty fishing villages of Turgutreis or Gümüslük.

(Above) Beaches and sunshine prevail at Antalya. (Below) The well preserved gate of Hadrian.

ANTALYA

This beautiful city is situated far enough south to enjoy good weather during the shoulder seasons and is often referred to as Turkey's Riviera with miles of golden sand stretching north to Kemer. The old port is situated on a small cove surrounded by ancient fortifications. The steep hillside was first settled in the 2nd century BC and fell under Roman control soon thereafter. The Emperor Hadrian visited the city in 130 AD, an event commemorated by a triumphal gate which is still in excellent condition. During the Middle Ages, Antalya was a Byzantine stronghold and

an important staging point for shipping troops and supplies to the Holy Land during the Crusades. Captured by Seljuk Turks in the 12th century, it became the most important port on the Mediterranean coast and fell under Ottoman rule in the 15th century.

Antalya Archaeology Museum, located northeast of beautiful Mermerli Beach, contains important artifacts from the Paleolithic Age to Ottoman times. A hall lined with marble statues and sarcophagi includes numerous items recovered from the nearby site of Perge.

Sites within the town's historic Kaleiçi District include a clock tower, which stands beside the ancient city walls, and the Truncated Minaret Mosque, a former church which has seen Roman, Byzantine, Seljuk and Ottoman modifications. The elegant fluted minaret, built in the 13th century and known as the Grooved Minaret, has become a visual symbol of Antalya.

Mermerli Beach is situated about one and a-half miles from the Kaleiçi District. In between, Ataturk Park provides cool shade and good views of the Mediterranean Sea and Taurus Mountains.

Perge (10 miles – 16 km from Antayla), was settled by the Hittites as early as 1500 BC and St. Paul stopped here on one of his journeys when Perge was an important city of the area.

Aspendos (25 miles – 40 km east of Antalya) is the site of a well-preserved theatre of antiquity with seating for over 15,000. A beautiful old Seljuk bridge crosses the Lopru river on the road to Aspendos.

Side (42 miles – 70 km east of Antalya), is one of the best-known classical sites in Turkey, built on a harbour whose name meant 'pomegranate'. Today this pretty resort town is popular for its comprehensive ruins which include the Apollo Temple and a magnificent theatre built on colonnaded arches.

THE BLACK SEA

When the Latin poet Ovid, famous throughout the Roman Empire during the time of Augustus, was inexplicably exiled to a Black Sea out-

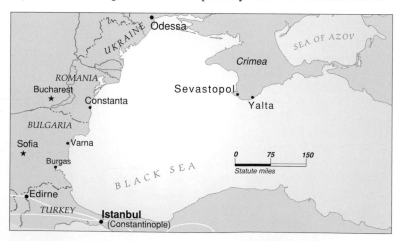

post in 8 AD, he poured his despair into a five-volume work called *Tristia* (sorrows). By the late 19th century, the Black Sea region was no longer regarded as a place of exile but rather as a fashionable retreat for members of the Russian nobility. Count Leo Tolstoy spent his last summers at cottage overlooking the Black Sea, and Anton Chekhov wrote *The Three Sisters* while staying at a Crimean resort.

The 1917 Bolshevik Revolution replaced the privileged classes of czarist Russia with Communist party leaders and Kremlin military brass, yet they too followed the aristocratic tradition of retreating to a Black Sea dacha (country cottage) each summer. Former Soviet president Mikhail Gorbachev was vacationing at his villa in the Crimea in August 1991 when he was placed under house arrest during an unsuccessful coup d'état in Moscow.

The lands bordering the Black Sea have changed hands many times over the centuries. Navigated since prehistoric times, the Black Sea contains mud that is rich in hydrogen sulphide, which causes the water to look black. Sheltered from the north by mountains, the Black Sea's waters remain warm year-round and its coastline was colonized as long ago as the 8th century BC by the ancient Greeks. Eventually the Greek colonies fell under Roman rule, and the founding of Constantinople increased the strategic importance of the Black Sea. Its southern shores remained mostly under Byzantine control following the decline of the Roman Empire, but its northern shoreline was invaded by Asian nomads, called Tatars (or Tartars), and the area became part of the Mongol empire. In the 13th century, the Genoese ventured into the Black Sea where they established prosperous coastal commercial settlements. The Turks followed in the 15th century, and their expanding Ottoman Empire soon controlled all of the Black Sea coast.

In the 18th century, Russia, under Catherine the Great, began to flex its military muscle by annexing the Crimea. This region had become independent of the Ottoman Empire and was blocking Russia's access to the Black Sea. Russia, in addition to its ongoing disputes with the Ottoman Emprie over control of the Bosperous and Dardanelles, was eager to expand into the Balkans in pursuit of warm-water ports accessible to the Mediterranean. These imperial ambitions were thwarted by the Crimean War of 1853 to 1856, in which the allied powers of Turkey, England, France and Sardinia defeated Russia when, after a long and bloody siege, its naval base of Sevastopol in the Crimea fell.

Military alliances had changed dramatically by the time a World War II meeting took place at nearby Yalta in 1945, attended by British Prime Minister Churchill, American President F.D. Roosevelt and Soviet Premier Stalin. Cloaked in secrecy, the agreements reached by the 'Big Three' included territorial concessions to the Soviet Union, with Roosevelt later accused of delivering Eastern Europe to Communist domination. The Soviet Union has since collapsed, and the Crimea, once called the 'Soviet Riviera' because of its subtropical climate and numerous resorts, has returned to quieter times.

Ports of Call

Yalta is the largest resort in the Ukraine-administered Crimean peninsula. Many of its hotels, sanatariums and guest houses were built as villas by the Russian nobility, and the nearby town of Livadiya became a summer residence of the Russian czars in 1861. The Livadiya palace, built in 1910, was the meeting place of the Yalta Conference in 1945 and is now a sanatarium.

The Ukrainian port of **Odessa** was the leading Soviet Black Sea port before the dissolution of the Soviet Union, and its cosmopolitan population consists of Ukrainians, Russians, Jews and Greeks. Originally an ancient Greek colony called Odessos, the port became a Tatar fortress and trade centre in the 14th century. Odessa's cultural attractions date mainly from the 19th century and include a university, a historical museum, an astronomical observatory, a ballet theatre, an opera house and a picture gallery. The French statesman Armand Emmanuel du Plessis duc de Richelieu served Russia as governor of both Odessa in 1803 and the Crimea in 1805, and a monument to Richelieu stands at the top of a magnificent flight of granite steps leading to the harbour.

These steps were the scene of a famous workers' riot in 1905 when the mutinous crew of the *Potemkin*, a Russian battleship of the Black Sea Fleet, arrived in port. The mutiny was ostensibly caused by the crew's refusal to eat bad meat, an action tantamount to mutiny in the eyes of the ship's commander. In accordance with Russian naval custom, he ordered the random selection and execution of a number of sailors, whose comrades in turn killed the commander and several officers. When the ship docked in Odessa, the commander's body was exhibited to the crowd ashore, and the ensuing riot was crushed by mounted Cossacks charging down the Richelieu Steps, leaving some 6,000 people dead. The *Potemkin* meandered around the Black Sea in search of support, her crew eventually scuttling her in shallow water off Constanta, where the mutinous sailors disembarked and scattered.

Constanta, Romania's main seaport and a popular seaside resort, began as a Greek colony called Tomi, and became Ovid's place of exile in the 1st century AD. Ovid, whose erotic and mythological poems later became a primary source of inspiration for the artists of the Renaissance, wrote his final works at Tomi, including the *Epistulae ex Ponto* (letters from the Black Sea). In the 4th century, Constantine the Great changed the city's name to Constantiana. Captured by the Turks in 1413, the port city became part of Romania in 1878. Local sights include an Orthodox cathedral, several museums and extensive Roman and Byzantine remains.

An excursion into **Bucharest**, Romania's largest city, takes visitors into the heart of Walachia. The 'bread basket' of Romania, the principality of Walachia was founded in the late 13th century when the Mongol wave receded and local inhabitants descended from their mountain refuges. Vlad IV, who ruled Walachia in the mid-15th century, maintained order by sentencing 20,000 people to death in the space

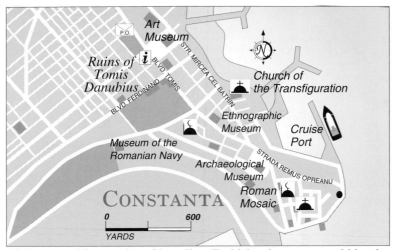

The map shows Constanta with the following labels: Art Museum, P.O., STR. MIRCEA CEL BATRIN, BLVD. TOMIS, Ruins of, Tomis, Danubius, BLVD. FERDINAND, Church of the Transfiguration, Ethnographic Museum, Cruise Port, Museum of the Romanian Navy, STRADA REMUS OPREANU, Archaeological Museum, CONSTANTA, Roman Mosaic, 0 600 YARDS.

of six years. His practise of impaling Turkish prisoners earned him the name Prince Vlad the Impaler and, as the son of Prince Vlad Dracul (Vlad the Devil), he also became known as Dracula or son of the Devil. Bucharest was the residence of the Walachian princes and became the capital of Romania in 1861. Much of the Old City was demolished by President Nicolae Ceaucescu during the 1980s to make room for a model socialist-planned city. Historic landmarks include several churches from the 17th and 18th centuries; the Museum of Romanian History was built during Ceaucescu's dictatorship.

Like many a Black Sea port, **Varna** began as a Greek colony, then passed to the Roman Empire in the 1st century AD. Under subsequent Byzantine rule, the city's 5th-century basilica and 6th-century fortress were built. Then, in 679, the Byzantine emperor Constantine IV was defeated by the Bulgarians, a Turkic-speaking people called Bulgars, who had merged with earlier Slavic settlers and adopted their language. The first Bulgarian empire was established in 681 but was eventually subjugated by the Byzantines in 1018. The second Bulgarian empire rose in 1186 but was absorbed by the Ottoman Empire two centuries later. Varna was captured by the Turks in 1391 and the 1444 Battle of Varna was the last major attempt by Europe's Christian Crusader forces to stem the Ottoman tide. Not until 1878 was Varna and the rest of Bulgaria liberated from Turkish rule.

Sofia, the capital of Bulgaria, has undergone several name changes. The city flourished under the Roman emperor Trajan as Sardica. Following its destruction by the Huns in 447, the city was rebuilt by the Byzantine emperor Justinian I and renamed Triaditsa. The Bulgars renamed the city Sofia or Sophya in 1376. Soon after, Sofia passed to the Ottomans and became the residence of Turkish governors overseeing the Ottoman Empire's Balkan possessions. Situated on a high plain surrounded by the Balkan Mountains, Sofia is filled with historic churches, mosques and synagogues. City landmarks include the parliament building, the state opera house, the former royal palace, the 4th-century Church of St. George and the 6th-century Church of St. Sofia.

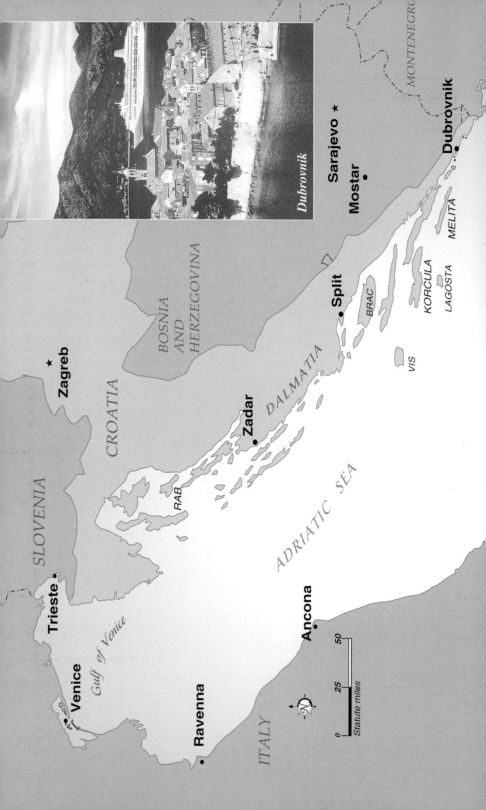

Dubrovnik

SLOVENIA

Trieste

Venice

Gulf of Venice

Zagreb

CROATIA

RAB

BOSNIA
AND
HERZEGOVINA

Zadar

DALMATIA

Split

BRAC

VIS

KORCULA

LAGOSTA

MELITA

Sarajevo ★

Mostar

Dubrovnik

MONTENEGRO

ADRIATIC SEA

ITALY

Ravenna

Ancona

Statute miles

0   25   50

Chapter Nine

CROATIA

C roatia's island-dotted Dalmatian coast, famous for its scenic beauty, has been coveted over the centuries by Roman emperors, Venetian doges, Turkish sultans and Hungarian kings. The mainland shore is dominated by the Dinaric Alps, their steep slopes forming a dramatic backdrop for the convoluted coastline's many harbours and headlands. Immediately offshore lies a string of islands, large and small, said to number 1,200 in total, where pine-scented coves and secluded beaches are lapped by the clear blue waters of the Adriatic Sea.

In the 19th century, Dalmatia was swapped between Austria and France, with Napoleon at one point incorporating this territory into the Illyrian provinces, thus reviving a name from ancient times. Subduing the Illyrians had never been easy. The Ancient Greeks, although attracted to mines located inland from the coast, had largely left the region's warlike tribes alone. The rugged terrain and unnavigable rivers made overland incursions difficult, and the Illyrians, who mingled with the Celts and whose tribes included the Dalmatians, practiced piracy.

The Roman province of Illyria was established in the 3rd century BC and Dalmatia was finally subdued and incorporated into Illyria under Augustus (35-33 BC). Two centuries later the future emperor Diocletian was born near the Dalmatian port of Salona (modern Split). He rose from humble beginnings to high military command in the Roman army, which proclaimed him emperor in 284 AD.

Diocletian, who reigned for over two decades, appointed three co-emperors to protect the Roman Empire from invasion. This dividing of the empire into four political sections was initially successful, but would eventually fail due to quarreling among Diocletian's successors. As for Diocletian, he abdicated in 305 and retired to his castle at Salona, refusing to return and help restore stability to the empire, despite the urgings of his former co-emperor Maximiam who had abdicated at the same time. Gardening had become one of Diocletian's favourite pastimes and a source of happiness. Dalmatia's climate and soil are ideal for growing olives, grapes and oranges, as well as herbs such as sage and rosemary, but Diocletian was especially proud of his cabbages, and no longer interested in pursuing power.

The eventual fall of Rome brought chaos to Europe and in the 7th century the city of Dubrovnik was founded by Roman refugees fleeing Slav invaders, who in turn settled in Dubrovnik. The city became a link between the Latin and Slavic civilizations, as well as a powerful merchant republic. Over time, massive stone walls and forts were constructed to protect the medieval seaport from enemy attack.

In 1000 AD, the rising sea power of Venice sent its newly formed navy to the Dalmatian coast to defeat the pirates who hid out among the many islands, from where they staged repeated raids on Venice. When the Venetian doge Pietro Orsielo II captured the town of Korcula, his victory marked the final defeat of the Dalmatian pirates. Venice soon controlled the Adriatic, with the exception of Dubrovnik, which maintained its autonomy even while under various protectorates, including the Byzantine Empire, Venice (1205 to 1358), Hungary and Turkey. Not until 1808, when its government was abolished by Napoleon, did Dubrovnik relinquish independence.

Following World War I, Italy finally regained a foothold in Dalmatia when it received Zadar and several islands under the terms of the Treaty of Rapallo. Croatia, which had been part of the Austro-Hungarian Empire prior to World War I, was incorporated into the new Kingdom of the Serbs, Croats and Slovenes, its name changed in 1929 to Yugoslavia – a federation of six republics, namely Serbia, Croatia, Bosnia and Hercegovina, Macedonia, Slovenia, and Montenegro.

The German army invaded Yugoslavia during World War II and Dalmatia was placed under Italian military control. Yugoslavia's occupation by Axis Powers was met with organized resistance by guerrilla warriors fighting from mountain strongholds, and leading this resistance was Josip Broz, who had adopted the name Tito.

Born in a Croatian village, the son of a blacksmith, Tito began his march to power as a soldier, then as a union organizer and political agitator. By 1945, Tito was the virtual dictator of Yugoslavia. Upon his death in 1980, ethnic tensions amongst the federation's member republics resulted in a violent breakup. Croatia was the second largest Yugoslav republic when it seceded on June 25, 1991. A six-month battle with federal troops (mostly Serbian) ensued and Croatia's independence was recognized by the European Community on January 15, 1992.

CROATIA AT A GLANCE

About 5 million people live in Croatia, the majority of which are Roman Catholic Croats who use the Roman alphabet of western Europe. A minority (12%) of the population consists of Eastern Orthodox Serbs who use the Cyrillic alphabet of eastern Europe. Some Italians live in and around the city of Zadar (Ital. *Zara*), the historic capital of Dalmatia.

The country is nearly 22,000 square miles in size (about the size of Vermont) and encompasses Dalmatia, most of Istria, Slavonia, and Croatia proper, where the capital of Zagreb is located. A river plain lies in the east, where farming is a major industry, while the Adriatic coastline to the west is mostly mountainous, its many bays and harbours sheltered by a chain of islands. Tourism, fishing and farming thrives along the scenic Dalmatian coast, its climate similar to coastal California.

DUBROVNIK

An important seaport and tourist resort, Dubrovnik has emerged in recent years as a popular port of call for cruise travellers. Of primary interest is the city's historic section – a medieval fortress built on a promontory. Stone walls up to twenty feet thick encircle the old town, which has retained and restored much of its medieval architecture, earning it UNESCO recognition as one of the world's heritage treasures. An earthquake and fire in 1667 destroyed much of the city and in 1991-92 Dubrovnik withstood damage while under siege by the Yugoslav army.

Getting Around: The ships dock in Gruz Harbour, about 1 1/2 miles northwest of the old town. A regular shuttle bus runs between the cruise port and a stop just outside Pile Gate, one of the entrances into the walled town, which is open to pedestrian

Dubrovnik's medieval walled town is a world heritage treasure.

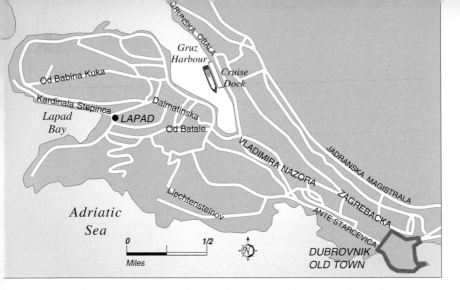

traffic only. The cruise harbour is a pleasant place for water-front strolls, and the shuttle bus winds through an attractive residential area that lies between the port and the walled town. Taxis are also available at the pier.

Currency: Several money exchange offices are located in or near the cruise terminal. The unit of currency is the Kuna (HRK), which consists of 100 lipas. Major credit cards are accepted at most shops and restaurants.

Telephones: Public phones are located at the cruise terminal and these accept personal calling cards. Access codes: AT&T 0800-22 0111; MCI 0800-22-0112; Sprint 0800-220-113. Phone cards can be purchased at the post office in the port building, open Monday through Saturday from 8:00 a.m. to 8:00 p.m.

Shopping: Croatian handicrafts include embroidery and fine lace, woolen and leather items, woodcarvings, ceramics and filigree jewellery. Shops remain open throughout the day, possibly closing for an hour or two over lunch.

Dining: Seafood such as calamari, cuttlefish, shrimp, lobster and oysters are featured in Dalmatian dishes, often cooked in olive oil and seasoned with garlic and local herbs. The Italian influence is enjoyed in a prevalence of pasta, pizza and risotto (rice cooked in meat sauce and seasoned with saffron).

Local Attractions: Pile Gate (1), which dates from 1537, marks the starting point of a walking tour through the Old Town's cobbled streets and marble-paved squares. Set in a niche over the gate's Renaissance arch is a statue of Saint Blaise, the city's patron saint.

After passing through Pile Gate, visitors come upon **Onofrio Fountain** (2), one of Dubrovnik's best known landmarks and a popular gathering place for locals. Built in 1438 as a water supply system, the fountain was damaged in the 1667 earthquake but 16 of the original sculptures still adorn it.

Nearby, on Cvijete Zuzoric Street, is the **Dubrovnik Tourist Board** (*i*), open daily from 8:00 a.m. to 8:00 p.m.

Also in the immediate vicinity is the 14th-century **Franciscan Monastery** (3) which houses one of Europe's oldest pharmacies, founded in 1317 and still functioning. Medical books and laboratory equipment are on display in the monastery's museum. The monastery, its Gothic porch and ornamented cloister having survived the 1667 earthquake, also displays a painting that depicts the city as it looked before the great earthquake.

Placa (also call the Stradun) is the Old Town's main street and is lined with shops and restaurants. Numerous narrow lanes lead off Placa and are interesting to explore. **Europe's second-oldest synagogue** (4) is located in the block between Boskoviceva and Zudioska.

At the eastern end of the Plaça, overlooking the harbour, is the Old Town's main square, dominated by the **Clock Tower** (5), first built in 1444 and most recently restored in 1929, its two bronze figures regularly ringing out the hours.

Several historic buildings are located around the square, including **St. Blaise's Church** (6), constructed in the baroque style in the early 1700s. It occupies the site of a 14th-century church from which were recovered two stone statues and a gilded silver statue of Saint Blaise (Dubrovnik's patron saint), now displayed in the existing church's main altar.

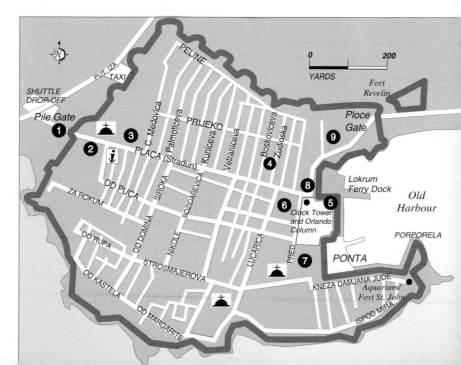

Modern yachts now fill the berths in Dubrovnik's Old Harbour.

The 15th-century **Rector's Palace** (7), reflecting late Gothic and early Renaissance styles, was built to house the offices and private chambers of Dubrovnik's governing rector. The building, today used for concerts during the Summer Festival, is now a museum with furnished rooms depicting how the aristocracy once lived. The 16th-century **Sponza Palace** (8) originally served as the town's mint and customs house, and now houses the State Archives, which includes a priceless collection of manuscripts.

The **Dominican Monastery** (9), built between the 14th and 16th centuries, contains a collection of Renaissance paintings by local and Italian masters.

A tour of the fortifications encircling the Old Town, built between the 8th and 16th centuries, affords panoramic views of the city and surrounding sea. Numerous forts (shown on the map) were built within and without the massive stone walls, which are still used for salt panning.

Some of the outlying areas of Dubrovnik can be visited by ship-organized shore excursions, including the seaside resort of Cavtat and the walled town of Ston, considered a smaller version of Dubrovnik.

KORCULA

The beautiful island of Korcula (Ital. *Curzola*), lying off the Pelijesac Peninsula, is covered in pine forests, pastures and vineyards. Colonized by Greeks in the 4th century BC, Korcula became a medieval stronghold for pirates conducting raids on Venice. According to some sources, the famous Venetian traveller Marco Polo was born on Korcula. The island's chief town, also called Korcula, has retained its medieval cathedral and fortifications.

SPLIT

The Roman emperor Diocletian put the seaport of Split on the map when he built his magnificent palace here for his retirement in 305 AD. Situated on the outskirts of Salona, an ancient city founded by the Romans, the palace was transformed into the city of Spalato (now Split) when the people of Salona fled here in the 7th century to flee invaders. Split eventually became an archiepiscopal of the Roman Catholic Church and a flourishing port of medieval Dalmatia.

Today Split (population approximately 200,000) is a major commercial centre, where shipbuilding and other industries thrive. Yet, its scenic location and historic monuments have made this seaside resort an important tourist destination. Diocletian's palace is the most impressive of the city's Roman ruins, but other ancient structures include the cathedral and baptistery (both originally Roman temples), the town hall and parts of the walls and gates.

RAB

The pastoral island of Rab (Ital. *Arbe*) was under Venetian rule from the 10th century until 1797. Today a popular seaside resort, the island, 40 square miles in size, has retained its ancient walls and ruins of the palace of the Venetian governors. Also of interest are the 12th-century cathedral and medieval palace where the archbishop resided.

Korcula

MEDITERRANEAN SEA

CYPRUS ★ Nicosia

ETE

0   100   200
Statute miles

N

Ashdod
Gaza

Alexandria   Port Said

El 'Alamein   Lower Egypt   ISRAEL

Sinai

Giza ⛰ ★ **Cairo**

Memphis

Suez Canal

Mt. Sinai

EGYPT   Eastern
Desert

Sharm el
Sheik

Western
Desert

Nile River

RED SEA

Hurghada

Upper Egypt

Dendera
Valley of the Kings ● **Luxor**
Esna   **(Thebes)**
Edfu
Kom Ombo

Philae ● **Aswan**
High Dam

*Lake
Nasser*

Abu Simbel

SUDAN
Nubian Desert

Great Sphinx at Giza

Chapter Ten

EGYPT

E gypt is a country of epic proportions, both historical and geographical. Its ancient civilization is measured not in centuries but in millennia, and its vast desert, covering 95% of the country's nearly 400,000 square miles, is bisected by the longest river on earth – the Nile.

The story of Egypt is the story of the Nile. Indeed, Egypt owes its existence to this river which flows its length. The river's fertile valley and fan-shaped delta cover only 4% of the country's total area but provide almost all of its arable and habitable land. The Nile has been the country's lifeblood for some 7,000 years, beginning with hunters and shepherds who roamed the river valley in pre-dynastic times. Eventually they learned to control the river's annual inundation by digging irrigation canals, and farming of the fertile floodplain began.

Supported by an agricultural society, a long line of pharaohs became almighty rulers of Egypt. They were divine kings, descended from the gods, and they oversaw the construction of colossal stone structures along the banks of the Nile. Built to preserve life beyond death, these awe-inspiring temples and tombs still stand, their imperious facades exerting a sense of power and mystery on the mere mortals gazing up at them. Huge temple gates, massive columns, giant statues and of course pyramids – all were built to last for eternity and many of them have, preserved for thousands of years by an arid climate and a dry soil of sand and silt.

Egypt at a Glance

The Arab Republic of Egypt, with a population exceeding 60 million, is governed by a 1971 constitution. The president, elected every six years, holds executive power and the government must approve the formation of any political parties. Islamic groups are illegal, although the Muslim Brotherhood (created in 1929) is tolerated. Most Egyptians are of complex racial origin, being descended from ancient Egyptians, Berbers, black Africans, Arabs, Greeks and Turks. More than 90% of the people are Sunni Muslims, while a sizeable minority are Coptic Christians. Arabic is the official language; English and French are also spoken by the well educated. Nearly one third of Egypt's workers are engaged in agriculture and the principal crop is cotton, which is one of the country's principal exports along with petroleum and metals. The Suez Canal and tourism are important sources of foreign exchange.

TRAVEL TIPS

Currency: The Egyptian pound (LE) is equal to 100 piastres. British and American currency is widely accepted.

Documentation: In addition to a valid passport, visitors to Egypt need a visa, which must be purchased ahead of time if you are arriving by ship at Alexandria or Port Said.

Shopping: Always barter – it's expected – except in department stores. Gold cartouches are unique and popular Egyptian souvenirs, but be careful when buying gold jewellery. If you're interested in a piece, ask to see its stamp indicating the number of karats. Egyptian cotton is among the finest in the world and attractive cotton clothes, including the traditional galibeya, are widely sold. Handcrafted items in brass, copper and Egyptian alabaster are also popular.

Shore Excursions: Visitors arriving by cruise ship at Alexandria or Port Said are strongly advised to take a ship-organized excursion into Cairo, a sprawling city of more than 13 million residents, due to the distances involved and the heavy traffic in Cairo.

LAND OF THE PHARAOHS

Ancient Egypt – its fields, towns, temples and tombs lining both banks of the Nile – was buffered from invasion by the river's natural borders. Desert plains lay to the east and west, the Mediterranean Sea to the north, and a series of cataracts south of Aswan in Upper Egypt. The shepherds then living in the Nile valley were descendants of the Hamitic branch of the Caucasian race, and their villages evolved over time into towns which became the centres of principalities later called *nomes* by the ancient Greeks. Grouped by region, these nomes collectively became the kingdoms of Lower and Upper Egypt. In about 3100 BC, these two kingdoms were unified by Menes, who was believed by ancient Egyptians to be a descendant of the sun god Ra. During his long reign, the city of Memphis was founded in Lower Egypt on the Nile delta, 14 miles (24 km) south of modern Cairo.

Egypt's famous Old Kingdom (2682-2181 BC) emerged during the rule of Djoser (Zoser). Memphis had become the seat of the royal government and, under Djoser's reign, Egypt's territory expanded into the Sinai Peninsula. Amid a flourishing era of arts and sciences, the pharaoh's vizier Imhotep designed the Step Pyramid – the first great stone structure ever

(Above) The famous Pyramids of Giza. (Opposite) Tutankhamun's gold mask is displayed in the Egyptian Museum in Cairo.

built. Located at the necropolis of Saqqara, it consisted of six massive tiers climbing to a height of 60 metres, its pyramid shape clearly visible from Memphis.

Stone construction continued to evolve and, during the reign of Sneferu, the first smooth-sided pyramid was constructed at Saqqara. This is known as the 'bent pyramid' for its sudden change of angle partway up. Sneferu ordered another one built nearby, which was an architectural success called the 'red pyramid' because of the iron oxide in its stone. However, it was during the reign of Khufu, Sneferu's son, that the largest surviving pyramid was built at Giza, a plateau situated on the southwestern outskirts of modern Cairo.

Rising 481 feet (146 metres) above the ground, the **Great Pyramid of Khufu** (Cheops) was built using an estimated 3.2 million blocks of limestone, each weighing an average of 2.5 tons. Khufu's son Khafra built a somewhat smaller pyramid at Giza, although it appears larger than Khufu's because it stands on a slight rise. The Great Sphinx, a representation of Khafra carved from a knoll of rock, is located next to the causeway leading from the pharaoh's granite-lined temple to his pyramid. A third pyramid, covering less than a quarter of the area of the Great Pyramid, was built by Menkaura, a son of Khafra.

It took approximately 20 years to build the Great Pyramid and hundreds of thousands of workers were employed each flood season to labour on this project. After the building site was carefully levelled, the cardinal points were determined through astronomical observations, providing for a precise alignment of the pyramid's sides. The entrance is north-facing, allowing the pharaoh's mummified body to face the north star from within the burial chamber, which is located deep within the pyramid's core and reached by cramped passages. Two air shafts, straight narrow tunnels, lead from the chamber to the outside and are aligned with various stars. The apex was crowned with gold sheet, symbolizing the pyramid's association with the sun god Ra.

Much of the building stone was quarried nearby, and granite, for lining the burial chambers, was transported from Aswan. Work was carried out during the Nile's inundation, when floodwaters would have allowed boats carrying massive granite columns and heavy blocks of limestone to navigate close to the pyramids. The inundation season, when farmers were idle, was an ideal time for the pharaoh to employ them as labourers, helping to raise the blocks – each weighing about 2 1/2 tons – into place. The method used is still open to speculation. They likely used cranes, levers and rockers, along with ramps built along the terraced sides of the pyramid. It is believed that as the outer casing of limestone was applied from top to bottom, the ramps were removed.

Egypt's second great era was the Middle Kingdom (2055-1650 BC). This period lasted nearly 400 years, during which the centre of political power shifted from Memphis in Lower Egypt to Thebes (modern Luxor) in Upper Egypt. Then, in 1550 BC, the Theban ruler Ahmose I ushered in a new era of greatness for the pharaohs of ancient Egypt. Called the New Kingdom (1550-1069 BC), these were glory days for the ancient city of Thebes. Columned temples and avenues of sphinxes were built on such a massive scale that the sprawling ruins prompted Napoleon's troops, when approaching this great centre of antiquity in 1798, to pause and lay down their arms at its majestic sight.

Across the river from Thebes, where the sun sets on the west bank of the Nile, lies the traditional burial ground of the New Kingdom pharaohs and their families. Cut into barren cliffsides, the tunnel entrances of these treasure-filled tombs were concealed with rocks and sand in an attempt to foil grave robbers. The Valley of the Kings would eventually contain more than 60 royal tombs, including that of the boy-king Tutankhamun, which was discovered intact by Howard Carter in 1922. Priceless treasures found in Tutankhamun's tomb, including the solid gold sarcophagus that held his mummified remains, are on display in the Egyptian Museum in **Cairo**.

Cairo's famous suburb of **Giza**, on the city's southwestern outskirts, is where the Great Pyramids and the mysterious Sphinx loom above the desert horizon. The ancient city of **Memphis** once stood a short distance south of modern Giza and its surviving necropolis (called Dahshur, the nucleus of which was Saqqara) contains the first pyramid ever built, the 'bent pyramid', and the first true pyramid, the 'red pyramid'.

ALEXANDRIA

Situated on a narrow peninsula, Egypt's leading port of more than three million people is built over the ruins of an ancient city once known throughout the Mediterranean as a centre of learning and culture. The names associated with Alexandria are legendary, starting with

Alexander the Great, king of Macedon, who founded the city in 332 BC. The city then was considered more Greek than Egyptian, with its gridded street plan and large population of Hellenistic Greeks. Its famous library and museum, no longer standing, attracted scholars such as Aristarchus of Samothrace, who collated the Homeric texts, the mathematician Euclid, and the anatomist Herophilus, who founded the university's medical school.

But it is Cleopatra, co-regent of Ptolemaic Egypt from 51 to 30 BC, who is most often associated with ancient Alexandria. Famous for her intelligence and political astuteness (her beauty was more myth than reality), Cleopatra conducted her famous love affair with Marc Antony in a palace overlooking the East Harbour. Later submerged underwater when earthquakes altered the city's coastline, the ruins of Cleopatra's ancient court remained hidden beneath the sea until they were discovered in 1996 by a team of French marine archaeologists.

Another famous landmark was the lighthouse on the island of **Pharos,** joined to the mainland by a causeway. This celebrated lighthouse, one of the Seven Wonders of the World, was built during the city's Roman occupation in about 280 BC. It was destroyed by an earthquake in the 14th century and the fortress of Qait Bey now stands on its site. The greatest of Rome's provincial capitals, Alexandria received antiquities from all over Egypt to decorate its new temples. Under Augustus, Cleopatra's Needle (now standing on the Thames embankment in London) and New York's Central Park obelisk, were brought as a pair to Alexandria from a New Kingdom temple at Heliopolis near modern Cairo.

Although much of ancient Alexandria lies underwater or is covered by modern buildings, there are some accessible monuments, such as **Pompey's Pillar** – a granite column erected in c. 297 AD near the temple of Serapeum – and the **Konel-Shugafa catacombs** – a labyrinth of rock-cut tombs constructed in the first two centuries AD. Excavations near the Mosque of Nebi Daniel have uncovered remains of the central city during its Roman period, including an amphitheatre, baths and a gymnasium complex. Alexandria's Graeco-Roman Museum houses a large collection of Greek, Roman and Coptic art.

Port Said: Located at the entrance to the Suez Canal, this port was founded in 1859 by the builders of the canal. Named for Said Pasha, then leader of Egypt, the city today is a fuelling point for ships using the canal. Sardine fishing, once a thriving industry, disappeared when the Aswan High Dam was constructed in the 1960s and essential nutrients no longer flowed from the delta into the Mediterranean Sea. Salt is still produced here, and the city, a principal port for steamer service on the Nile, is connected by rail with other major cities. Port Said is also a cruise ship port, providing access by modern highway to Cairo.

The **Suez Canal**, level throughout with no locks, connects the Mediterranean Sea with the **Red Sea** – a remarkably warm body of water supporting a brilliant abundance of marine life.

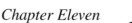

Chapter Eleven

MALTA, TUNISIA & MOROCCO

Malta has no rivers or lakes, no natural resources and few trees, but its strategic location in the centre of the Mediterranean has made it the jewel in many a crown. Sir Winston Churchill called this former British colony a "tiny rock of history and romance". For centuries its natural harbour – one of the finest in the world and situated at the crossroads of Mediterranean shipping – brought war and conquest to its doorstep. Following a siege by the Turks in 1565, the Knights Hospitalers fortified the port of Valletta so extensively it became one of the greatest strongholds in the Mediterranean.

Malta contains some of the world's oldest stone monuments, these pre-dating Stonehenge in England, and had already been inhabited for some four thousand years when the Phoenicians arrived on the island's rocky shores in about 1000 BC. The Greeks followed, occupying the island in 736 BC and naming their colony Melita, "the island of honey", for the golden-coloured limestone found here. Malta later passed to the Carthagians, then to the Romans. Saint Paul brought Christianity to Malta when he was shipwrecked on the north coast in 60 AD.

When the Roman Empire was divided in 395 AD, Malta and its smaller neighbouring islands of Gozo and Comino became part of the Eastern Roman (Byzantine) Empire. An Arab conquest in 870 was fol-

(Left) Valletta's natural harbour is one of the finest and most defensible in the world. (Below) A cruise ship enters Grand Harbour.

lowed by a Norman invasion in 1090. Malta was a feudal fief of the kingdom of Sicily when Emperor Charles V of the Holy Roman Empire granted the island in 1530 to the Knights of St. John of Jerusalem, who had been driven out of Rhodes by the Ottoman Turks.

The Knights ruled Malta until 1798, when Napoleon invaded and occupied the islands during his Egyptian campaign. The Maltese appealed to Great Britain and 1799 Lord Horatio Nelson besieged Valletta, compelling the French to withdraw. For the next century and a half, Valletta was the headquarters of the British Mediterranean Fleet, its harbour further fortified and an extensive naval dockyard built in

THE KNIGHTS OF MALTA

Knights of Saint John of Jerusalem

The Knights Hospitalers were a military and religious order, founded around 1100 in Jerusalem where the Hospital of Saint John provided medical care to Christian pilgrims. Brothers of the order, which was controlled by a grand master, were sworn to poverty, obedience, chastity and to assistance in defence of Jerusalem. Members of the order hailed from eight European nations, these respective groups called 'tongues' or 'langues' to avoid patriotic conflicts. When the Knights were driven from the Holy Land in 1291, they moved their headquarters to Cyprus, then to Rhodes in 1309, and finally to Malta in 1530. The order, now devoted to hospital service, has offices in various European cities and its dress is a black gown with a white cross. (See pages 286-87 for more on the Knights.)

The Maltese Falcon

According to legend, the annual tribute paid by the Knights of Malta to Spain's Charles V was the gift of a falcon, the basis of the famous 1941 John Huston film. Falconry, the sport of hunting birds or small animals with falcons, had spread from Asia to Europe during medieval times and was, until the 17th century, a popular sport of royalty and the nobility. Peregrine falcons were taken from their nests when young and trained to sit quietly, when hooded, on the falconer's wrist. When released, a trained falcon would attack its prey – usually killing it cleanly by breaking its back – then leave it untouched.

Grand Harbour. During World War II, Malta withstood almost daily German and Italian air raids, and in 1942 King George VI awarded the British colony the George Cross for heroism. Malta became independent in 1964 and a few years later Britain handed the naval dockyards over to Malta. A haven for NATO warships until 1979, Malta's former naval base has since been devoted to shipbuilding and dry dock repairs.

Upon joining the European Union in 2004, Malta became the smallest member nation and, as such, negotiated certain concessions regarding the potential influx of labourers (which could quickly swamp such a small country) and speculation in property ownership by non-residents. The Maltese have always been a pragmatic and resourceful people, and their small but diversified economy, which includes financial services, electronics, manufacturing and tourism, qualified the country for EU membership. Other industries include tourism and, despite the poor soil, agriculture. Nearly everything in Malta is built of golden limestone, and fresh water is produced at its seawater reverse osmosis plant, one of the world's largest, with the rest provided by wells.

MALTA AT A GLANCE

Malta has been a republic since 1974, when the first Maltese president took office. The two official languages are English and Maltese, which is of Semitic origin and similar to Arabic but with an alphabet and grammatical structure derived from Latin. Italian is also widely spoken, with Malta lying just 58 miles south of Sicily. British colonial influences include driving on the left and an enthusiam for marching brass bands, which are an integral part of the local festivals. Malta remains a bastion of Roman Catholicism and has retained strong economic ties to Europe. With a population of 400,000, Malta's three inhabited islands cover an area of 122 square miles.

Aerial view of Valletta.

(Above) Malta's golden-coloured lime-stone prompted ancient Greeks to name the island Melita, 'the island of honey'. (Left) A colourful Maltese fishing boat, the eyes of Osiris bringing good luck.

Shopping & Currency: Malta is famous for its handmade lace, silk cloth and filigree ornaments in gold and silver. Other items to look for include pottery and blown glass. The main shopping area in Valletta is Republic Street. Other shopping venues are the harbourfront promenade in Sliema, and the Ta' Qali Crafts Village near Mdina. Shops are generally open from 9:00 am to 1:00 pm, and from 4:00 pm to 7:00 pm (or later) except on Sundays and holidays. The Maltese lira has been replaced by the euro as the unit of currency.

VALLETTA

Named for French Grandmaster Jean de La Vallette, who oversaw construction of the town's fortifications and defended Malta from a Turkish siege in 1565, Valletta is today the capital of Malta, its parliament housed in the Palace of the Grandmasters in the very core of the fortified town. Built on a rocky promontory between two deep harbours, Valletta was described by Sir Walter Scott as "the most superb place I have ever visited."

The **Tourist Information Office** *(i)* is at Freedom Square, just inside City Gate. Lining the cobbled streets, which are laid in a gridwork pattern, are the churches and inns (auberges) built by each nationality (langue) of the Knights. Republic Street, now a pedestrian shopping mall, leads from Freedom Square to three adjoining squares in the town's centre where several landmark buildings are located.

St. John's Co-Cathedral (1) ('co' because there's another cathedral in Mdina, the former capital) was built by the Knights between 1573

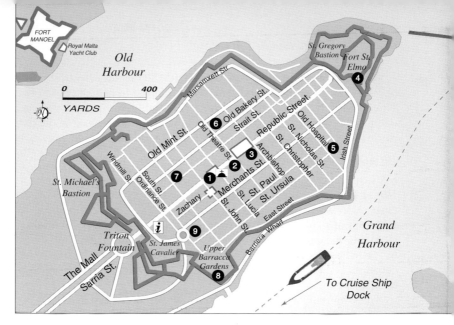

and 1577, and contains the crypt of Jean de La Vallette. The magnificent interior of gold and marble contains a succession of chapels, each representing one of the Order's langues.

Overlooking Republic Square is the **National Library** (2), and in adjacent Palace Square stands the **Palace of the Grandmasters** (3), a masterpiece of military architecture completed in 1574. Its marble halls are graced with priceless paintings and its ground floor armory features weapons and armour from different periods.

The **National War Museum** (4) in Fort St. Elmo commemorates Malta's heroic role in WWII when the island refused to capitulate to relentless bombing by the Italians and Germans.

The **Mediterranean Conference Centre** (5) is housed in the original hospital (Sacra Infermeria) of the Order of St. John. Built in 1574, the former hospital was restored and converted to a conference centre in 1976. The hospital's Great Ward became the Exhibition Hall, one of the longest in Europe. Hospital artifacts, including silver plates upon which patients were served their food, are on display in the Fine Arts Museum, along with paintings by Carpaccio, Tintoretto and other Renaissance artists. Regular performances are held in the **Manoel Theatre** (6), built in 1731 and featuring an opulent interior.

The **National Museum of Archaeology** (7) is housed in the Auberge de Provence. On display are pottery, sculptures and other objects found at various prehistoric sites on the islands. These megalithic stone structures were built between 3800 and 2000 BC, and were dedicated to a fertility goddess. They are among the world's earliest freestanding structures.

Lovely views of Grand Harbour can be enjoyed from **Upper Barracca Gardens** (8), originally the private gardens of the Italian Knights. Nearby **Auberge de Castille** (9) is one of the grandest inns built by the Knights.

Across Grand Harbour, south of Valletta, lie the three historic towns of **Vittoriosa, Cospicua and Senglea** – referred to as Cottonera (The Three Cities). Local attractions include the Folklore Museum (housed in the Inquisitor's Palace) and the Maritime Museum, housed in the former bakery of the Royal Navy and featuring model ships and galleys.

ISLAND ATTRACTIONS

Sites of interest outside Valletta include the ancient stone temples at **Hagar Qim** and **Mnajdra**, and the nearby **Blue Grotto,** a stunning sea cave. Also worth visiting is the medieval walled town of **Mdina**, its labyrinth of narrow winding streets containing palaces and churches, including the cathedral dedicated to Saint Peter and Saint Paul. Close by, in the town of **Rabat**, are early Christian catacombs (underground cemeteries) and the Museum of Roman Antiquities with fine mosaics on display.

These outlying places can be visited by ship-organized excursions or by taking the local transit buses, painted orange and yellow, which can be boarded at the main terminus just outside the Valletta city gates. Buses 38 and 138 go to Hagar Qim and Mnajdra; Bus 65 goes to Mdina and Rabat. Check with your ship's shore excursion office or the tourism information office in Valletta (see map) for more detail regarding bus schedules and fares.

TUNISIA & MOROCCO

The coastal lands of North Africa, from western Libya to Morocco, were once referred to as the Barbary States. Lying between the vast Sahara desert and the Mediterranean Sea, this region was initially inhabited by Berber tribes who farmed the coastal plains and lived in mountain villages. The origins of the Berbers are uncertain – they may have come from Phoenicia (modern Lebanon) or from the Basque region of northern Spain – but their culture dates to ancient times, as evidenced by Egyptian tomb paintings from 2400 BC.

NORTH AFRICA'S MOVIE ROLES

Many films have been shot in the red mountains, desert plains and old walled towns (medinas) of North Africa. Desert scenes in *The English Patient* were shot near Tozeur, a Tunisian oasis town which was once a staging point for camel caravans travelling from the Sahara to the Mediterranean. Scenes from *Raiders of the Lost Ark* were also shot in Tunisia, as was footage for the original *Star Wars* movie and *The Phantom Menace* where scenes set on the desert planet of Tatooine were shot near the southern city of Tatouine.

Morocco, meanwhile, has served as a movie backdrop for decades. Alfred Hitchcock filmed scenes for his 1956 thriller *The Man Who Knew Too Much* at the Hotel La Mamounia in Marrakesh, and David Lean shot *Lawrence of Arabia* at locales in and around Ouarzazate, in the heart of the Atlas Mountains with scenes featuring the sun-baked kasbah (mud fortress) of Ait Benhaddou. A permanent film studio was founded at Ouarzazate in 1984, when *The Jewel of the Nile* was shot there. As for *Casablanca*, the 1940s film classic, a small part of the movie was shot in Tangier, but the majority of scenes unfolded in a Hollywood back lot.

In the 9th century BC, the ancient city of Carthage was founded on the Bay of Tunis by Phoenicians from Tyre. Carthage grew to become a powerful city-state, her seafaring explorers venturing great distances in pursuit of trade, and the Carthaginian empire expanded to include Malta, Sardinia, the Balearic Islands and most of the Iberian Peninsula. However, an ongoing rivalry between two blocs of leading families eventually weakened Carthage from within, while expansion into Sicily ultimately led to a series of wars with the growing Roman Empire. Called the Punic Wars, these conflicts were fought in three distinct stages between 264 and 146 BC.

The **Second Punic War**, from 218 to 201 BC, is sometimes called the Hannibalic War, after the famous Carthaginian general. A member of the great Barca family, Hannibal is considered one of the greatest military geniuses of all time for his march into Italy. Setting out from Spain with a small force of hand-picked troops, Hannibal followed a little-known overland route, crossing the Pyrenees and then the Alps with elephants and a full baggage train.

(Above/Below) Amphitheatre at El Djem is second in size only to Rome's Colosseum .

A just and merciful leader, Hannibal defeated the main Roman army but could not assail Rome's strong walls due to a lack of support from Carthage. The tide slowly turned in favour of Rome and the Second Punic War ended with Carthage surrendering its Spanish province and its war fleet to Rome. During the Third Punic War, the Romans blockaded the once-great city of Carthage and razed it.

The Berber States fell under Roman rule, and Carthage became an important centre of Roman administration under Augustus.

When Christianity spread throughout the Roman Empire, most Berbers became Christian, with a sizeable minority embracing Judaism. Invasions by various barbarian peoples followed the decline of Rome, until the region was conquered by Arab Muslims in the 7th century. The Berbers were converted to Islam and they formed the backbone of the Arab armies that conquered Spain in the early 8th century. Berber-Arab conflicts were common, however, and repeated uprisings fragmented the region until two Berber dynasties – the Almoravids and Almohads – imposed order on the warring tribes. Eventually the Berbers were absorbed by the Arabs, with the exception of those living in the mountains, who retained their warlike traditions and fiercely resisted French and Spanish occupation of North Africa.

In the 13th century, the Christians of Spain and Portugal began expelling the Moors from the Iberian Peninsula, driving them back across the Strait of Gibraltar into North Africa. By the early 15th century, the Portuguese and Spanish were attacking the Moroccan coast and the chief ports all fell to the invading Christians. Galvanized by the Christian threat, the Muslims eventually recaptured most of the European-held strongholds in Morocco. Meanwhile, the Ottoman Turks had swept westward across North Africa, conquering Cairo in 1517 and Algiers in 1518.

This Turkish conquest, led by the corsair Barbarossa, prevented the region from falling to Spain, and the last drive by Holy Roman Emperor Charles V to expel the Turks failed in 1541. Tunisia became an autonomous province of the Ottoman Empire, governed by Turkish beys, and for the next three centuries the Barbary States were a base for Muslim pirates, who profited from the booty, ransom and slaves gained from attacks on Mediterranean shipping and from raids on coastal towns. The European naval powers attacked these corsairs and repeatedly bombarded and blockaded the pirate strongholds, but they generally found it was easier to simply pay the demanded tributes for immunity. By the 19th century, however, opposition had strengthened and when the pasha of Tripoli demanded more tribute than previously agreed upon from an American naval officer, the United States refused payment and blocked Tripoli. This, however, did not daunt the pirates and, with negotiations failing to resolve the issue, the war continued, with Tunis drawn into the struggle. A settlement was finally reached in 1805 and, following the capture of Algiers by the French in 1830, the rulers of the Barbary States were pressured into giving up piracy.

Seeking repayment of heavy debts incurred by the beys of Tunisia, the European powers of France, Great Britain and Italy intervened in Tunisia's finances in 1869. Tunisian attacks on Algeria, a French possession, prompted France to invade Tunisia and make it a French protectorate in 1881, despite Italy's opposition.

Major battles of World War II were fought on Tunisian soil after British General Montgomery defeated the German forces in Egypt and forced them to retreat all the way to Tunisia, where they became trapped by American and British troops occupying territories to the west, including Casablanca, which was the scene of a major Allied landing in November 1942. A year later, American president Franklin D. Roosevelt and British prime minister Winston Churchill met in Casablanca, where they issued a joint declaration pledging the war would end only with the unconditional surrender of the Axis powers.

Following the war, nationalist movements intensified in Morocco and Tunisia. Full independence for Tunisia was negotiated with France in 1956 and the following year the bey was deposed and Habib Bourguiba, a Sorbonne-educated lawyer, became the first president of the new republic of Tunisia. Meanwhile, most of Morocco had become a French protectorate in 1912, with full independence gained in 1956. The Moroccan sultan became King Muhammad V, and he was succeeded by his son Hassan II in 1961 who ruled for 38 years until his death at age 70 in 1999. King Hassan, who was succeeded by his son Crown Prince Sisi Mohammed, was a staunch supporter of the West and a friend of Israel who worked secretly for Middle East peace.

Today, both Tunisia and Morocco are moderate Arab states, their populations largely Berber and Arab. Islam is their state religion and Arabic is the official language, with French widely spoken. Mineral production and agriculture are major industries, with citrus fruits, olives and other crops grown on the coastal plains. In Morocco, water for irrigation is drawn from artesian wells, while Tunisia is more dependent on rainfall. Desert oases, found in both countries, form in places where the water table reaches the surface, often as springs. They range in size, from a pond surrounded by date palms to cities surrounded by cultivated fields. In Morocco's oasis city of Marrakesh, an 11th century sultan built a network of underground canals, still in use today, for irrigating the imperial city's extensive gardens.

Casablanca's Hassan II Mosque, with its soaring minaret and intricate ornamentation, is a showpiece of modern Islamic architecture.

Travel Tips:

Currency: Tunisia's unit of currency is the dinar (TD) which is divided into 1000 millimes. Morocco's unit of currency is the dirham (DH), which is divided into 100 centimes.

Opening Hours: Shops in the medinas (old walled towns with narrow winding lanes) are generally open for business from 8:00 a.m. to 9:00 p.m. daily, with a Friday break for prayers. Museum hours vary and most take a mid-day break.

Shopping: Bartering is done at the souks (markets) where rows of stalls sell a variety of handcrafted items in copper, brass and wrought-iron. Silk caftans, painted ceramics, inlaid wooden boxes and Berber carpets are all popular items, as of course are the country's leather goods. They are made of a special goatskin leather, called 'morocco', that is dyed on the grain side and boarded or embossed to show the characteristic grain. Often crushed and glazed, morocco is hard but pliable, and valued for bookbindings and purses.

Tunisia:

Tunis, popular with northern European tourists seeking a sunny getaway, is the capital of Tunisia. The cruise ships dock at La Goulette, a port suburb lying east of the city centre. The winding streets of the medina, the historic heart of the city, are worth exploring for their colourful souks, the Great Mosque and a Turkish palace housing the Dar Ben Abdallah Museum. West of the medina, in the ville nouvelle built by the French during the city's colonial era, is the grand Hotel Majestic. It stands at the northern end of Avenue de Paris, and its impressive facade is a fine example of French colonial architecture.

The famous **Bardo** museum, housing one of world's finest collections of Roman mosaics, is located about four miles (6.5 km) northwest of the city centre. The site of the ancient Phoenician city of **Carthage** lies 10 miles (16 km) east of the city core. Its seaside ruins are mostly of Roman origin and include baths, villas and a museum. About two miles (3 km) past Carthage, along the coast, is the whitewashed, clifftop village of **Sidi Bou Said**, which is popular with tourists who enjoy strolling the cobble streets of this quiet residential area. Further afield, about 100 miles (160 km) south of Tunis, past the port of Sousse, is the ancient Roman amphitheatre at **El Djem**. This is the second-largest amphitheatre after the Colosseum in Rome, and its thick walls are of staggering proportions.

Morocco:

Casablanca is called Dar-al-Baida in Arabic, but the city's Spanish name is embedded in the minds of many as the exotic setting for the 1940s film classic starring Humphrey Bogart and Ingrid Bergman. The real city bears little resemblance to its Hollywood counterpart but, with a population exceeding two million, Casablanca is the country's largest city and principal port. Dominating the modern city's skyline is the

Hassan II Mosque, the world's third largest mosque, after those at Mecca and Medina. It was built between 1986 and 1993 by thousands of labourers and craftsmen, and is decorated with ceramic mosaics, carved Moroccan cedar, filigree-patterned gypsum and marble pillars. Its minaret is the world's tallest at 660 feet (200 metres), and the roof over the main prayer hall is retractable. (See photo on page 357).

The former imperial city of **Marrakesh**, founded in 1062, is stunningly situated at the base of the snowcapped Atlas Mountains. The city's ruling sultans and grand viziers built rambling palaces and walled gardens, where reflecting pools and palm trees stand amid a fragrant profusion of flowers, such as jasmine and bougainvillaea. Rising high above the winding streets of the medieval medina is the **Koutoubia** minaret, built by the Almohad dynasty of Berber rulers in the late 12th century. It is the oldest of their three famous minarets – the other two being the Tour Hassan in Rabat, Morroco's capital, and the Giralda in Seville, Spain. Other historical sites include the ornately refurbished **Ali ben Youssef Medersa**, a religious school founded in the 14th century, which contains an arcaded central courtyard and upstairs study rooms.

The focal point of Marrakesh's medina is the **Djemaa el-Fna**, a huge square of non-stop activity where snake charmers and fortune tellers jostle for space with acrobats and magicians. Leading off the square is a maze of alleys filled with souks selling spices and slippers, kaftans and carpets. In contrast to the cacophony of customers bartering for wares in the crowded souks, is the nearby tranquillity of the luxurious **Hotel La Mamounia**, set in an enclosed park which was originally established as a sultan's wedding gift to his son. This legendary hotel, with its pillared lobby and red-carpeted corridors, opened in 1922 and its former guests include the Aga Khan, Richard Nixon, Orson Welles, General de Gaulle and Jimi Hendrix. Sir Winston Churchill was a frequent guest during the '40s and '50s, and the Churchill Suite is one of the hotel's most popular rooms, decorated with photos of the former British prime minister, along with a replica of his hat and cane and his last unfinished painting of the gardens.

CEUTA:

A Spanish enclave in Morocco, Ceuta has been a Spanish possession since 1580 when it passed to Spain from Portugal. Strategically situated on the Strait of Gibraltar, this peninsula's promontory formed one of the Pillars of Hercules back in ancient times (see Gibraltar, page 157). Originally a Phoenician colony, then a city held in turn by Carthaginians, Romans, Vandals, Byzantines and Arabs, this seven-square-mile headland is today a free port, European in appearance, with a large harbour able to accommodate the cruise ships that visit as part of a growing tourism industry.

Carnival Liberty, 2005
110,000 tons

Galaxy, 1996
77,000 tons

CostaVictoria, 1996
75,000 tons

Crystal Symphony, 1995
50,000 tons

CARNIVAL CRUISE LINES: Owned by the world's largest cruise corporation, Carnival is known for its affordably priced 'Fun Ships'. A newcomer to the Med, Carnival is offering 12-day, round-trip cruises from Rome on board the new *Carnival Liberty*, which carries 2,974 passengers. Ports of call include Dubrovnik, Venice, Naples and Cannes. www.carnival.com

CELEBRITY CRUISES: Founded in 1990 by the Greek cruise line Chandris Inc, Celebrity Cruises is now owned by Royal Caribbean Cruises Ltd. and is a premium brand offering gourmet cuisine, sophisticated service and finely appointed ships. *Millennium* (1,950 passengers) cruises the Med on 12-night itineraries between Barcelona and Venice. *Galaxy* (1,750 passengers) offers 11-night round-trip itineraries from Rome, featuring eastern ports such as Istanbul, Athens and the Greek islands. Celebrity cruisetours include land tours of Italy and Spain. Officers are Greek and service staff are international. www.celebritycruises.com

COSTA CRUISES: The Costa family of Genoa, Italy, has been in shipping since the 1800s. They introduced their first passenger ship in 1948, and today the growing Costa fleet is Europe's most popular cruise line. The Costa style is upbeat, with an international ambiance, authentic Italian and Continental cuisine, and contemporary decor on its new ships. North Americans comprise 10 to 25% of the passengers on Med sailings. Genoa and Savona are Costa's base ports, and itineraries range from 5 to 12 nights, covering the entire Mediterranean. Officers and service staff are international. www.costacruises.com

CRYSTAL CRUISES: This luxury cruise line offers a variety of 7- and 12-night itineraries on *Crystal Symphony* and *Crystal Serenity* (1,080 passengers). Base ports include Barcelona, Monte Carlo,

Rome, Venice and Athens. Crystal ships are spacious and have all outside staterooms, most with a balcony. Officers are Scandinavian and service staff are international. www.crystalcruises.com

CUNARD: This prestigious British line began operations in 1840 when Sir Samuel Cunard, a Canadian pioneer of regular transatlantic navigation, formed a fleet of four ships to deliver mail between Liverpool, Halifax and Boston. Cunard, now owned by Carnival Corporation, currently operates the new ocean liner *Queen Mary 2* (2620 passengers) as well as the venerable *QE2* (1780 passengers), both offering traditional elegance and British ambiance. Southampton is a base port for both ships, which offer 10- to 18-night Med itineraries. Officers are Norwegian and British, and service staff are international. www.cunard.com

Queen Mary 2, 2004
150,000 tons

HOLLAND AMERICA LINE: This premium cruise line commands a loyal following, its finely appointed ships offering such traditional features as wraparound teak decks. In business since 1873, HAL operated transatlantic service between Rotterdam and New York for decades before turning to cruises in the late 1960s. Now based in Seattle, HAL's Dutch officers and service staff of Indonesians and Filipinos have built a solid reputation for running immaculate ships with a high level of service. HAL's flagship *Rotterdam,* carrying 1,668 passengers, offers 10- and 12-day itineraries between Lisbon and Athens. In 2006 the new *Noordam* offers 10-day itineraries out of Rome. *Prinsendam*, a luxury ship carrying 800 passengers, offers 12- to 16-day itineraries. HAL cruisetours are offered for Portugal, Spain and Italy. www.hollandamerica.com

Rotterdam, 1997
60,000 tons

Noordam, 2006
85,000 tons

MSC ITALIAN CRUISES: This Italian line is owned by Mediterranean Shipping Company, one of the world's largest freight container companies, and offers 7-

to 12-night cruises out of Genoa and Venice. The company's mid-sized ships, which include the *Lirica* (christened by Sophia Loren in 2003), appeal to experienced travellers who prefer traditional cruise liners, and the mix of passengers is international. Officers and service staff are mostly Italian. www.msccruises.com

NORWEGIAN CRUISE LINE: One of the first lines to invent modern cruising in the mid-1960s, NCL remains innovative with its unstructured dining, casual atmosphere and good youth facilities. *Norwegian Jewel*, launched in 2005 and carrying 2,400 passengers, offers 7-day return cruises from Barcelona and 12-day eastern itineraries using Barcelona, Athens and Istanbul as base ports. Officers are Norwegian, service staff are international. www.ncl.com

Norwegian Jewel, 2005
92,000 tons

OCEANIA CRUISES, INC:
This luxury line's mid-sized ships carry 684 passengers in style, offering gourmet cuisine and attentive service in a country-club casual atmosphere. The *Regatta* and *Insignia* (former Renaissance ships) offer 10- to 14-day itineraries that begin or end in Lisbon, Barcelona, Rome, Athens and Istanbul. Officers and service staff are international. www.oceaniacruises.com

Regatta, 1998
30,000 tons

ORIENT LINES: This premium line has developed a reputation for interesting itineraries around the world which appeal to the seasoned traveller. The mid-sized *Marco Polo* offers 10- to 23-day Med itineraries that feature Greece, Italy and the Riviera, with base ports being Athens, Venice, Rome and Barcelona. Land tours of Italy are also available. Officers are European and service staff are Filipino. www.orientlines.com

Marco Polo, 1966
20,000 tons

PRINCESS CRUISES: This premium cruise line, owned by Carnival Corporation and based in Los Angeles, has many years experience in the Med. A variety of 12-night itineraries are offered on *Grand Princess* and *Golden Princess*, sisterships carrying 2,600 passengers and featuring an abundance of outside staterooms with private balcony. Barcelona, Rome and Venice are the base ports, with land tour packages of Italy also available. *Sea Princess*, carrying 1,950 passengers, offers 14-night return cruises from Southampton, England. Officers are European and crew are international. www.princess.com

Golden Princess, 2001
109,000 tons

RADISSON SEVEN SEAS: This award-winning luxury line has two ships currently working the Mediterranean on a variety of 7-day one-way itineraries between such base ports as Monte Carlo, Rome, Venice, Athens and Istanbul. Offering small-ship intimacy and gourmet cuisine, Radisson's *Seven Seas Navigator* carries 490 guests in outside suites (most with balcony) and *Seven Seas Voyager* (launched in 2003) carries 700 passengers in outside suites with balcony. Officers are Scandinavian and service staff are European. www.rssc.com

Seven Seas Navigator,
1999 – 30,000 tons

ROYAL CARIBBEAN INT'L: Miami-based RCI operates popular round-trip cruises out of Barcelona, which can be combined with land tours of Spain. RCI's alternating 12-night itineraries, currently serviced by *Brilliance of the Seas,* feature the French Riviera and several Italian ports before rounding the "boot" and either proceeding into the Adriatic to call at Venice, Dubrovnik and Corfu, or into the Aegean for stops at Ephesus, Athens and the Greek isles. Alternating 7-night cruises of the Western Med can be taken on *Voyager of the Seas.* RCI's handsome megaships carry 2,000 to 3,000 passengers and offer a relaxed, upbeat atmosphere and excellent children facilities. The funnel of each ship features a rock-climbing wall on its aft side with a relaxing lounge and bar at its forward side and has become the company's trademark. Officers are Scandinavian and crew are international. www.royalcaribbean.com

Brilliance of the Seas,
2002 – 90,000 tons

Voyager of the Seas,
1999 – 137,000 tons

Seabourn Spirit, 1989
10,000 tons

Wind Spirit, 1988
6,000 tons

SEABOURN: This luxury line offers fine dining, spacious and elegant accommodations, and white-glove service. The fleet's mega-yachts, carrying 200 passengers in outside suites, feature a fold-out marina at the stern. Itineraries include calls at less-visited islands and ports, and customized shore excursions. Officers and service staff are Norwegian, European and American. www.seabourn.com

SEA DREAM YACHT CLUB: Founded in 2001 by Norwegian industrialist Atle Brynestad (founder of Seabourn) this innovative company's twin yachts each carry 55 couples in relaxed and casual elegance, providing the private-yacht experience on 7-day cruises of the French Riviera, Croatian coast and Greek isles. Base ports include Nice, Rome, Venice and Istanbul. Officers and service staff are international. www.seadreamyachtclub.com

SILVERSEA: Consistently rated the Number One Small Ship Cruise Line by Conde Nast Traveler, this luxury line offers interesting Med itineraries ranging from six to 14 days. Officers are Italian and service staff are European. www.silversea.com

WINDSTAR: This is a premium line of high-tech sailing ships, each accommodating about 150 passengers (except *Wind Surf* which carries 312 passengers). Noted for their fine cuisine and attentive service, Windstar ships appeal to clients seeking both relaxed luxury and a bit of sailing adventure. The line offers 7-night Med itineraries that include some of the smaller ports along the French Riviera and Greek Isles. Officers are British and service staff are international. www.windstarcruises.com

INDEX

**PHOTO AND ILLUS-
TRATION CREDITS:**

Costa Cruise Lines 13;
Michael DeFreitas 7, 24
(bottom); 26 (all images),
27 (top), 77, 78 (bottom),
100, 109 (top), 110, 111,
116 (top), 131, 135, 147,
148, 149, 164 (top & bot-
tom), 166, 168, 189, 190,
199, 201 (top & bottom),
204 (middle & bottom),
209, 213 (top), 215, 216
(bottom), 221, 223, 224,
225 (top), 227, 229, 229
(top), 232 (top right & bottom), 233 (top), 235, 348,
352 (bottom); Fosart 316
(top left); Martin Gerretsen
6, 24, 337; Greek National
Tourism Organization 48,
70 (bottom) Gr. Grigoriou,
264 (inset, top left), 273 G.
Kavallierakis, 286; Holland
America Line 261 (top),
276, 317 (middle); Italian
Ministry of Culture 4 (bottom); R.H. Judd Archives
50, 51, 60, 65, 74, 327;
Frank Kelly 344; Malta
National Tourist Office 351,
352 (top); Alan Nakano 18,
19, 21 (both), 162; New
York Public Library 49;
Raymond Norris-Jones 258
(bottom), 277; Orient Lines
Inc. 8; Gordon Persson 26,
258 (top), 259, 263 (bot-
tom), 340, 341; P&O
Cruises 184, 335;
Portuguese Trade &
Tourism Commission 17, 20
(top), 112, 120, 121, 124,
125, 127; Princess Cruises
12, 39, 203, 280; Royal
Caribbean International 10
(inset), 35, 40; Royal
Olympic Cruises 357;
Seabourn Cruise Line 29,
266, 278 (Harvey Lloyd),
297; Norma Stone 355;
Thomas Cook Archives 83,
87; Richard E. Thomson
45; Tourist Office of Spain
20 (bottom), 21 (top & middle), 106, 129, 132, 151,
152, 157; Topkapi Sarayi
Museum, Istanbul, 307
(bottom); Turkish Ministry
of Tourism 103 (top)304
(bottom) 312 (middle), 314,
320 (carpet), 321, 323,
324, 325: Wood River
Gallery (Circa Art) San
Rafael,USA 3, 38, 46-47,
54, 62, 92, 93 (bottom), 99
(top left), 107 (bottom), 108
(all images) 109 (middle &
bottom), 117 (inset), 296
(top), 308.
All other photos by Anne
Vipond.